The One Year Devotions for Boys 2

TYNDALE HOUSE PUBLISHERS, INC.
CAROL STREAM, ILLINOIS

THE ONE YEAR® DEVOTIONS FOR Boys 2

Damion A. Swift
   If found call (307)-54x
750 9, or (307)-898-8950.
or return at 1310 Shu. Road (Shannon
                              Road).

Visit Tyndale's exciting Web site at www.tyndale.com.

TYNDALE and Tyndale's quill logo are registered trademarks of Tyndale House Publishers, Inc.

The One Year is a registered trademark of Tyndale House Publishers, Inc.

The One Year Devotions for Boys 2

Copyright © 2002 by Children's Bible Hour. All rights reserved.

Edited by Linda Piepenbrink and Deb Bible

Designed by Jacqueline L. Nuñez

Stories written by Andy Duffy, Anna E. Baumeister, Agnes G. Livezey, Alicia H. Guevara, A. J. Schut, Agnes Kempton, Annette S. Bury, Brenda Decker, Bob Hostetler, B. J. Bassett, Beverly J. Porter, Barbara J. Westberg, Beverly Kenniston, Beverly McClain, Bernard Palmer, Barbara Riegier, Beth Terpstra, Carol Albrecht, Carolyn E. Yost, Cindy Huff, Cathy L. Garnaat, Charissa S. Schalk, Charles VanderMeer, Cameron Wroblewski, Doris Bantjes, Donna Bennett, Darlene Griffin, Doris J. Schurchard, Dean Kelley, Donna K. Lappert, Deana L. Rogers, Doris L. Seger, Donna M. Grimes, Diana M. Martin, Deborah Stanton, Diane Strawbridge, Dawn Yrene, Eunice C. Matchett, Gwen D. Foust, Gayle J. Thorn, Harriett A. Durrell, Harry C. Trover, Hope L. Aderman, Hazel M. Percy, Heather M. Tekavec, Hazel W. Marett, Jorlyn A. Grasser, Jessica C. Principe, Jennifer Dorsey, Jackie Krutke, Jan L. Hansen, Janice M. Jones, Jonnye R. Griffin, Joyce R. Lee, Joanne Wilson, Janet Weaver, Katherine Chapman, Katherine E. Swarts, Kathy J. Hoffner, Kathy Lahey, Kelly M. Schaefer, Katherine R. Adams, Karen R. Locklear, LeAnn F. Campbell, Linda A. Prince, Lois A. Witmer, Linda C. Avallone, Lucinda J. Rollings, Letitia L. Zook, Linda M. Weddle, Mary Ellen Cowling, Mary F. Watkins, Mark L. Redmond, Mary Mosher, Melissa Bamburg, Melissa Montgomery, Melinda M. Torgerson, Michael R. Chapman, Mary Rose Pearson, M. Tanya Ferdinandusz, Nancy G. Hill, Nancy I. Merical, Nancy K. Potter, Nathan Runyon, Nani T. Bell, Peggy Gibson, Phyllis I. Klomparens, Phyllis M. Robinson, Ruth Andrews, Rhonda Brunea, Robert Byers, Rosemary C. Wilson, Raelene E. Phillips, Rose Goble, Ruth I. Jay, Rita Lackey, Rose R. Zediker, Richard S. Maffeo, Robert Truesdale, Rita Valladares, Susan Dillon, Sandy K. Vaughn, Sherry L. Kuyt, Suzanne M. Lima, Sharyl Noelle, Steven R. Smith, Taire A. Street, Teresa B. Chiano, Teddie M. Bryant, Violet E. Nesdoly, V. Louise Cunningham, Vera M. Hutchcroft, William A. Walker. (The writer's initials appear at the end of each story.)

AU indicates author unknown.

All stories are taken from issues of *Keys for Kids*, published bimonthly by the Children's Bible Hour, P.O. Box 1, Grand Rapids, Michigan 49501.

Unless otherwise indicated, all Scripture quotations are taken from the *Holy Bible*, New Living Translation, copyright © 1996. Used by permission of Tyndale House Publishers, Inc., Carol Stream, Illinois 60188. All rights reserved.

Scripture quotations marked NIV are taken from the Holy Bible, *New International Version,*® *NIV.*® Copyright © 1973, 1978, 1984 by Biblica, Inc.™ Used by permission of Zondervan. All rights reserved worldwide. www.zondervan.com.

Scripture quotations marked NKJV are taken from the New King James Version.® Copyright © 1982 by Thomas Nelson, Inc. Used by permission. All rights reserved. *NKJV* is a trademark of Thomas Nelson, Inc.

Scripture quotations marked NASB are taken from the New American Standard Bible,® copyright © 1960, 1962, 1963, 1968, 1971, 1972, 1973, 1975, 1977, 1995 by The Lockman Foundation. Used by permission.

Scripture quotations marked KJV are taken from the *Holy Bible,* King James Version.

For manufacturing information regarding this product, please call 1-800-323-9400.

Library of Congress Cataloging-in-Publication Data

One year book of devotions for boys.
    p. cm.
    Includes index.
    Summary: Presents stories for meditation, memory verses from Scripture, and questions to internalize the messages for each day of the year.
    ISBN 978-0-8423-3620-8
    ISBN 978-0-8423-6014-2 Vol. 2
    1. Boys—Religious life—Juvenile literature.   2. Devotional calendars—Juvenile literature. [1. Devotional calendars.   2. Christian life.]   I.Title: Devotions for boys.   II. Tyndale House Publishers.
BV4541.2 .054 2000
242'.62—dc21
                                                      00-028667

Printed in the United States of America

16   15   14   13   12   11   10
12   11   10   9   8   7   6

Table of Contents

INDEX OF TOPICS

INDEX OF SCRIPTURE READINGS

INDEX OF MEMORY VERSES

HEAVEN

Read: 1 Corinthians 15:35-44

"Mom, I wish I could explain to little Lindsey about colors," said Maxwell with a sigh. "This afternoon I mentioned that the sky was so blue, but she couldn't understand what that meant."

"I know. Lindsey doesn't see color because she's blind," said Mom. "But her other senses seem to be more keen than ours. For one thing, she recognizes people by their footsteps or voice. We couldn't do that with very many people!"

Just then Brian burst into the kitchen. "Can I have a cookie, please?" he begged, opening the cookie jar.

"Yes, but just one," agreed Mom. "What did you learn at Bible club today, Brian?"

"About heaven," replied Brian, after swallowing a mouthful of cookie. "But I don't understand it very well."

"I don't understand it, either," said Maxwell. "I can't quite picture what we'll be doing there all the time."

Mom thought hard. "Maxwell," she said slowly, "remember how difficult—even impossible—it is for Lindsey to understand what colors are? In the same way, it's impossible for us to understand exactly what heaven is like. It's a completely different world, and we can't totally know what it will be like."

"What if we don't like it?" asked Brian, only half joking.

Mom smiled. "Do you think Lindsey would hesitate if she had the chance to see?"

"Of course not," said Maxwell and Brian at the same time.

"But she doesn't understand what it's like to be able to see," Mom told them.

"No, but she knows that sight is something wonderful," said Maxwell, "even though she doesn't quite understand it. She knows it's great because of what we tell her about it."

"And we know that heaven is going to be wonderful because of the things *God* tells us about it," replied Mom. "All our comparisons and descriptions fall far short of the glorious reality of heaven." *MTF*

HOW ABOUT YOU?

Do you ever wonder and question and argue—and even worry—about heaven and how life there will be different from your life here on earth? Although heaven will certainly be different, be assured that it will be wonderful and far better than life on earth.

MEMORIZE:

"Now we see but a poor reflection as in a mirror; then we shall see face to face. Now I know in part; then I shall know fully, even as I am fully known."
1 Corinthians 13:12,

HEAVEN WILL BE WONDERFUL

OPEN WIDE

Read: Joshua 24:14-16

"Want me to feed Celina today?" Miguel asked his mother.

"Sure, thanks," replied Mom, as she handed Miguel a baby spoon and jar of mashed peas.

"Open wide," Miguel said, dipping the spoon into the baby food jar and putting a spoonful of the peas into Celina's mouth. Celina spit the green peas back out. "Hey! You're supposed to eat them!" scolded Miguel. He tried to put another spoonful of peas into her mouth, but she clamped her lips shut and turned her head away.

Mom chuckled. "You can keep offering them to her, but if she won't accept them, I'm afraid you can't make her eat them." She took a jar from the cupboard and handed it to Miguel. "Here, try some carrots instead."

Miguel held out some carrots to Celina. This time Celina opened her mouth and accepted a spoonful. After that she willingly took some more. "See. They're good," said Miguel. "And they're good for you, too, aren't they, Mom?"

"Yes, they are," Mom agreed, "but babies don't realize that we know what's good for them, so they don't always want to accept what we offer."

Miguel turned to look at his mom. "Our youth pastor said we're something like that," Miguel told her. "He said God loves us and knows what's best for us, and he wants us to believe in Jesus as Savior and to serve him. But God lets us choose whether or not we want to accept him and serve him."

Mom nodded. "That's right. Just like Celina decided whether or not to accept the food you offered her, we decide whether or not to accept Jesus and receive the salvation God offers us," she said. "And after we do accept him, we have to decide whether to faithfully live for him and serve him." *GJT*

HOW ABOUT YOU?

Have you accepted Jesus as your Savior? Have you decided to serve him all of your life? Or are you turning your head—and heart—away? God loves you and knows it's best for you to not only have Jesus in your life, but also to spend your life serving him. Why not "open wide"? Decide today to receive him as Savior, and then give your life in service for him.

MEMORIZE:

"Choose for yourselves this day whom you will serve." Joshua 24:15, NIV

DECIDE TO LOVE AND SERVE JESUS

THE BEST ANSWER

Read: Romans 8:26-28

It hadn't been a good day for Michael. Nothing seemed to be any fun since his best friend, Daniel, had moved away. "Please, dear God," prayed Michael that night, "let Daniel come back and live here again."

"I know you miss Daniel very much," commented Dad as he tucked Michael into bed, "but I don't think his family is going to move back here."

"Yes, they will," Michael said confidently. "I asked God to bring them back, and he'll answer my prayer, won't he?"

"Yes," agreed Dad. "God always answers prayer, but his answer isn't always what we want it to be." After a moment, he asked, "Do you remember the time your puppy ran out the front gate and almost got hit by a car? Why do you suppose he did that?"

"I remember," Michael said. "Kipper came out because he wanted to be where I was."

"If that was what he wanted, why didn't you let him stay outside the fence with you?" asked Dad.

"Because he wouldn't be safe there," Michael answered promptly. "Kipper doesn't know enough to stay on the sidewalk like I do."

Dad nodded. "So even though Kipper wanted to be outside the fence, you knew better," he said. "That's the way God is. His answer to our prayers sometimes has to be 'no' because he knows what's best for us."

"But why wouldn't God want Daniel to come back?" Michael asked. "That couldn't be bad for me."

"But it might not be best for Daniel's family. His father had been out of work until he found a good job in another state," replied Dad. "Instead of praying that Daniel will come back, perhaps you should be asking God to help him and his family adjust to their new home."

Slowly Michael nodded. "And I'll ask God to help me find a new best friend, too," he decided. *KRA*

HOW ABOUT YOU?

Do you think God should answer all your prayers exactly the way you want? If things don't go your way, do you think God doesn't care? That's not true. He does care, and he knows what is best for you. So even when God's answer to your prayer is "no," trust him and believe that his way is best.

MEMORIZE:

"And we know that God causes everything to work together for the good of those who love God and are called according to his purpose for them."
Romans 8:28

ACCEPT GOD'S ANSWER

PRACTICE MAKES PERFECT

Read: 1 Timothy 5:1-4

"Hey, pass the gravy." Andrew interrupted the conversation at dinner.

Dad frowned. "Didn't you notice that your mother and I were talking?" he asked. "You interrupted us."

"Well, sor-*ree*," said Andrew, stressing the second syllable of the word. "But pass the gravy. I need some more."

Mom shook her head. "Whatever happened to saying 'please'?"

"Okay," replied Andrew. "*Please* may I have the gravy?" He rolled his eyes. "It's not like we're out in a restaurant or anything," he complained.

"Would you use better manners in a restaurant?" asked Dad.

"Well, yeah," answered Andrew, "or . . . like . . . if I was at somebody's house for dinner. You don't expect me to be all proper and everything around here at home, do you?"

"Actually," answered Dad, "yes, I do. You seem to think you should respect only people outside your own family—that you need to use good manners only when you're around other people. But the Bible says you are to honor your parents, and developing good manners is one way of showing honor and respect."

Andrew stared at his dad. "But . . . "

"Home is also the perfect place for you to learn to do good and make right choices," added Mom. "Home is where you should be practicing the right way to do things."

"A football player practices to get in shape for the Super Bowl," said Dad, "and a figure skater practices to get in shape for the Olympics. In the same way, here at home you should practice doing things right so that in school or in the neighborhood or wherever you are, you'll be in shape to behave correctly." He paused. "Do you understand what we're saying? Do you have any questions?"

Andrew looked thoughtful. After a moment, he grinned. "Yes," he said. "May I *please* have some more of that delicious gravy?" *BH*

HOW ABOUT YOU?

Does your behavior at home show that you honor your parents? You should be polite, thoughtful, and kind wherever you are, especially at home. That will please your parents, but best of all, it will please God. And it will prepare you to be polite wherever you are.

MEMORIZE:

"Children . . . should learn first of all to put their religion into practice by caring for their own family . . . for this is pleasing to God." 1 Timothy 5:4, NIV

PRACTICE GOOD MANNERS AT HOME

THE BEST COMPUTER

Read: Job 38:4-7; 41:11

Tyler stared at his dad's computer screen. "A boy in my class—Jared—says we're smarter than God," he said. "He says if we can invent computers, we can do anything. I told him we will always need God. Won't we, Dad?"

"Yes, but I'm afraid lots of people think the way Jared does," answered Dad. "Tyler, do you think this computer can give us the answer to the question you just asked?"

"Not unless somebody programmed it to answer that question," Tyler replied. "And the answer would depend on *who* programmed it. The computer can't think for itself."

Dad rubbed his chin. "So the computer can't be any smarter than the person who programs it?"

"Right," agreed Tyler.

"Do you know when the first computer was built?" asked Dad. Tyler shook his head. "It happened thousands of years ago," said Dad. "That first computer was built into Adam, and it was called a 'brain.' Who programmed it?"

"God did," answered Tyler.

"Right," said Dad. "Do you think the human brain could be smarter than the one who programmed it?"

"No," Tyler said.

"Right again," said Dad. "You know, Tyler, when the mechanical computer was first invented, people called it an electronic brain. They were copying God's idea. But God made it better than humans ever will. In fact, the human brain is still much more powerful than any electronic computer."

"Really?" asked Tyler. He sighed. "I can hardly remember my locker number, but this computer remembers everything."

"That's because we humans only use a very small percentage of our brain power," Dad told him.

"Why is that?" asked Tyler.

Dad looked uncertain. "I don't know. Maybe God decided we weren't responsible enough to use it all," he suggested.

Tyler grinned. "Yeah," he said. "If we did, maybe more people would get the idea that they were smarter than him." *HMT*

HOW ABOUT YOU?

Did you know that you own one of the most powerful computers in the world? Your brain is more wonderfully designed than anything humans can create. Nothing has been done that God hasn't thought of first. People believe they can do anything with computers, but the truth is, they can't do anything without God. He is—and always will be—the all-powerful and all-knowing God.

PEOPLE CAN'T OUTSMART GOD

WHERE'S GOD?

Read: Psalm 139:1-12

Joel lay on the sofa, his bald head a circle against the white pillow. Medical treatments had caused his hair to fall out. His mother looked over at him just as a tear slid down his cheek. "What's wrong, honey?" she asked. "Not feeling so good today?"

"I'm scared," replied Joel in a trembling voice. "It seems like God has gone away. Ever since I got sick, it feels as if he isn't here at all."

"It may *feel* like that," Mom said, "but God promises to always be with us. It's hard sometimes to keep praying and trusting him, but we need to do that." She sat down beside Joel. "The way you feel isn't surprising, though," added Mom. "It reminds me of something that happened to me when I was little."

"Were you sick, too?" asked Joel.

Mom shook her head. "No. I was with my family on a train trip," she said. "We stopped in a city, and my daddy got off the train. I remember watching for him to come back, afraid that the train would leave without him. I was so relieved when I saw him walk past the window. But a few minutes later, we started moving, and he wasn't yet with us. I was terrified because I thought we had left him behind."

"So did you?" asked Joel.

"No, but it certainly *felt* like it," said Mom. "Even though my mother kept saying she knew my daddy was on the train, I couldn't quite believe her. I cried until he walked back into the car. I would have saved myself a lot of worry if I had trusted my mom's word. And God's Word is more trustworthy than any person's. We can believe it when God says he'll never leave us."

"Show me where it says that," said Joel. "I want to read it for myself." *VEN*

HOW ABOUT YOU?

When bad things happen to you—you get sick, your dad loses his job, your friend moves away, or your family splits up—it may feel as though God has forgotten about you. It may seem like he doesn't care. But the Bible says he is near to those who know him. Instead of worrying, you can choose to trust that God's loving presence is near, no matter how you feel.

MEMORIZE:

"God has said, 'Never will I leave you; never will I forsake you.'"
Hebrews 13:5, NIV

GOD IS ALWAYS NEAR YOU

YOUR ACHILLES' HEEL

Read: Matthew 26:31-35, 69-75

"Mr. Simpson started to tell us a Greek myth about a warrior called Achilles," David told his folks one evening, "but then the bell rang. He said he'd finish the story tomorrow."

"Tell it to me, Davie," begged little Johnny.

"Okay, Johnny—but remember, it's not a true story," said David. "Anyway, Achilles was dipped in a magic river when he was a baby, and he became in-in-in . . . invulnerable!" he said triumphantly.

"What does that mean?" asked Johnny.

"It means he couldn't be harmed," explained David. "The magic river made Achilles so strong and mighty that no weapon could ever hurt him." David grinned. "I'd like to be like Achilles, so no one would ever be able to fight me and win!"

"Ah, but Mr. Simpson didn't finish the story," Dad reminded David. "Achilles wasn't as invulnerable as you seem to think."

"He wasn't?" asked David.

Dad shook his head. "When his mother dipped him into the river, she held on to him by his heel. Since his heel didn't touch the water, it wasn't invulnerable like the rest of his body."

"Oh, well," said David, "his heel was only a small spot."

"True," said Dad, "but the story says that Achilles died after being shot in the heel by a poisoned arrow. The term *Achilles' heel* is now used to describe the weak or vulnerable spot in a person's life."

"Wow!" exclaimed David. "Too bad his heel wasn't dipped, too."

"You know, David, it's possible for a Christian to think of himself as a *spiritual* Achilles," said Dad. "We may think we're so good and honest that Satan can't touch us. But he always seems to find our weak points— our 'Achilles' heel'—and he attacks us there. We need to ask God for his protection and strength in areas where we are weak." *MTF*

HOW ABOUT YOU?

What's your "Achilles' heel"? Is it pride? A tendency to lie? Greed? A hot temper? A desire to be popular? You may pride yourself on being a "good" Christian, but be careful! You also have weaknesses—weak points that Satan loves to take advantage of. Be honest. Ask God to show you your areas of weakness, and to help you guard against temptation in those areas.

DON'T BE OVERCONFIDENT

MEMORIZE:

"If you think you are standing strong, be careful, for you, too, may fall into the same sin." 1 Corinthians 10:12

ONE AT A TIME

Read: Matthew 11:28-30

Anthony bit on his pencil as he stared at a page in his math book. "Math's hard," he said. "I hope I pass this year."

Dad looked over Anthony's shoulder. "Page 117? You still have a ways to go in your book, don't you?" asked Dad.

Anthony frowned. "Yeah," he said. "And I've looked ahead; the problems only get harder."

Dad took the pencil out of Anthony's hand. "You need a study break," he said, "and I've got a dresser to move. How about helping me?"

Anthony nodded and followed Dad to the bedroom. Anthony went to one end of the dresser, and Dad went to the other. They pushed and pulled, but it wouldn't budge. "What have you got in there?" exclaimed Anthony.

Dad grinned. "It must be your mother's stuff," he joked. "Let's take out the drawers. That should make it easier." After they removed the drawers, Anthony went to the empty dresser and tried to move it by himself. It was still too heavy. Dad chuckled again and went to help.

Together, Dad and Anthony moved the dresser easily. "When we moved one part at a time and worked together, it wasn't so tough to move that dresser, was it?" said Dad as Anthony again sat down to work on his math. "You can solve your problem with math the same way. In fact, it's a good way to tackle all of life's problems."

"What do you mean?" asked Anthony.

"Deal with your math one part at a time instead of worrying about the whole year all at once. And don't tackle it alone—ask God to help you," said Dad. "Do the same thing when you face problems in life years, or even days, from now. Live one day at a time, and ask God to help you, not only with math, but with all kinds of problems." *SML*

HOW ABOUT YOU?

Do you have a problem that seems too big to handle? Maybe you have trouble with school-work. Ask God to help you learn what you need to know, little by little. Maybe you need God to help you improve a friendship. For example, you may need to apologize or just be a good listener. Whatever your problem, go to God for help—not next year, but today!

MEMORIZE:

"Give your burdens to the Lord, and he will take care of you." Psalm 55:22

WITH GOD'S HELP, SOLVE PROBLEMS ONE AT A TIME

SNIFF

Read: 2 Corinthians 2:14-18

"Oh, no!" Mom looked up when she heard the wail from upstairs.

"I bet Brianna broke something," said Tim. "She's always dropping things."

"Brianna," called Mom. "What's the problem?" There was no reply, so Mom headed up the stairs with Tim close behind. As they reached the top of the stairs, Brianna appeared at Mom's bedroom door.

"Phew!" exclaimed Tim, sniffing the air. "What's that smell?"

Brianna's eyes filled with tears. "I was dusting your room like you asked me to do, Mom, and when I was moving things on the dresser, my hand slipped and knocked over your perfume—that bottle Aunt Carolyn gave you," she explained. "It didn't break, but I guess it wasn't shut tight, and some spilled out. I'm sorry, Mom. I didn't mean to do it."

"Never mind," said Mom gently. "It was an accident."

Tim held his nose. "Ugh! Perfume! You smell," he told Brianna.

"I do not!" replied Brianna indignantly.

Tim sniffed again. "You do smell," he insisted. "Everything smells!"

Mom laughed. "Tim's right," she agreed.

"I guess so," admitted Brianna, "but it's a nice smell—not a bad one."

"I hope both you kids will always spread a nice, pleasing fragrance," said Mom.

Tim looked horrified. "What? Me smell like this? No way!"

Mom laughed. "I'm not talking about the aroma of perfume, Tim," she said. "I'm talking about the aroma of Christ."

Brianna and Tim looked puzzled, so Mom explained. "As Christians, we're called to fill our world with a sweet-smelling fragrance—not with designer-label perfumes, but with the love of Jesus," she said.

"Uh . . . I still don't get it," said Tim.

"When we're helpful, kind to others, forgiving, loving—in other words, when we live the way Jesus wants us to—we become the 'fragrance' of Christ to those around us," said Mom. *MTF*

HOW ABOUT YOU?

What kind of aroma are you spreading at home, in your school, at the mall, or on the playground? Are you spreading a sweet-smelling aroma by what you do and say? Although some people may criticize and turn away, to others you may be the fragrance that leads them to Christ.

MEMORIZE:

"Our lives are a fragrance presented by Christ to God. But this fragrance is perceived differently by those being saved and by those perishing."
2 Corinthians 2:15

SPREAD JESUS' AROMA

THE TELLTALE PRINTS

Read: Romans 16:19-20

Jason looked up as his sister Tara turned a page and showed the picture of Papa Bear to their little sister, Beth. Tara continued to read the story to Beth. " 'Who's been eating my porridge?' growled Papa Bear."

Jason spoke up. "Papa Bear could have found out who ate it if he had lifted fingerprints from his spoon," he told them. "We learned in school that everybody has a different set of prints. No two are alike—ever. Match the prints and you've got the criminal."

"Yeah, well, that's nice, Jason. Now let us finish this story," said Tara.

But Jason grabbed his magnifying glass and held it above Tara's fingers. "See those ridges?" he asked. "They leave a mark on everything you touch. Investigators use special powders to dust for fingerprints, and the powder sticks to the invisible ridge marks. The investigator carefully brushes away the dust between the ridges and then the print can be photographed and lifted with a print-lifting tape."

"Jason! We're not interested in fingerprints right now. We just want to read the story," said Tara.

"All right, but I've been practicing with my Junior Detective kit," said Jason, "so you'd better keep your fingers off my stuff!"

"Don't be rude, Jason," warned Mom, who had come into the room. "I hope you'll make sure you don't leave ugly 'prints' on people's lives."

"What do you mean?" asked Jason.

"Well, the impressions we make on others are something like fingerprints," said Mom. "People identify us by either the pleasant way we talk and act or by how rude we are. We develop a reputation. And of course, our words and actions should please God."

"Yeah, Jason," said Tara. "You better remember that, and . . ." She noticed Mom looking sternly at her. "And I'll remember it, too," Tara added. *LJR*

HOW ABOUT YOU?

Do the prints—the impressions—you make on others please both them and God? Make sure the reputation you gain is that of helpfulness, friendliness, and patience.

MEMORIZE:

"Choose a good reputation over great riches, for being held in high esteem is better than having silver or gold."
Proverbs 22:1

Read: Titus 2:11-15

"Look at those jellyfish!" exclaimed Robert. "They look like tiny parachutes!" He leaned forward, marveling at the shiny, silky-looking jellyfish that were floating in the fish tank.

Allison nudged her way closer to the tank. "Wow!" she cried. "Look at the colors—pink, white, blue, yellow, green, purple, and even striped!"

Dad was looking at the sign next to the popular attraction. "When out of the water," he read out loud, "jellyfish look like a glob of jelly dripping from your spoon. Jellyfish are invertebrates. They have no backbone and no central brain."

When Dad moved on, Allison continued to study the sign. "It says they float by opening and closing their bodies like an umbrella," said Allison. "They hardly move unless a current comes along."

That evening, the children talked about the things they liked best at the aquarium. "Those jellyfish were so pretty," said Allison.

"They're kind of carefree, too," said Robert. "They just float along, going with the flow of the current."

"That's like some Christians I know," commented Dad.

"Really?" asked Robert. "Like who?"

"Well," said Dad, "when Scott and Jonah were over yesterday, they were mocking Rebecca's lisp, and I heard you laughing about it, too—just 'going along' with whatever they said. I've been meaning to speak to you about it."

Robert looked down. "Those guys are so popular at school," he explained, "and . . . well, they've just started acting friendly toward me, so I didn't want to . . ." His voice trailed off.

"Jellyfish are beautiful, but they have no backbone," said Dad. "God didn't make you a jellyfish, Robert. He expects you to stand up for what is right. We sin when we just 'go along' with others who are doing wrong things—no matter what the reason." Robert nodded. *LJR*

HOW ABOUT YOU?

When friends watch a movie or listen to music that is not pleasing to God, do you refuse to participate? Do you protest if your friends make fun of others? Do you say no to cigarettes, drugs, or alcohol? Don't just "go with the flow" like a jellyfish. It not only has no backbone, it also has no brain. Ask God to fill you with his boldness to do what's right.

STAND UP FOR WHAT'S RIGHT

MEMORIZE:
"We should live in this evil world with self-control, right conduct, and devotion to God." Titus 2:12

January

12

"Dad, how do I change this print?" Stephen called from the study. He was using the computer for his homework.

"Here, I'll help you." Stephen's brother, Mark, sat down next to him. "The type of print is called the font," he said. "What font do you want?" He showed Stephen the various print types he could use. After Stephen chose one, Mark clicked the mouse a few times, and soon Stephen was finishing his homework.

When Stephen wanted to use the computer the next evening, there was the old font again. "Hey, Mark, why did you change this back, you dummy? Now set it up again!"

"I didn't change anything," said Mark.

"Don't lie! You fix it right now or I'll beat you up!" ordered Stephen.

"Not if you ask me like that," replied Mark. He let out a yell as Stephen came after him.

"What's going on here?" demanded Dad, coming into the room.

"Mark changed the computer, and now he won't fix it," said Stephen.

"I didn't touch it," Mark insisted.

"Stephen, I'll help you learn to fix it yourself," said Dad. "But understand that unless we change the default, the old font will come up again the next time we turn the computer on."

"The default?" asked Stephen. "What's that?"

"It's the way the computer is set to come on," said Dad. "Unless we make a permanent change, it will automatically come up with the old font."

"Let's change it then," said Stephen. Dad agreed, and soon it was done. "That takes care of one problem," said Dad, "but I'm afraid something else needs a change in its 'default setting.' Your angry reaction when things don't go your way indicates that a change is needed in your heart. You need to ask Jesus to help you make that change. And then you can show it by apologizing to your brother." *VEN*

HOW ABOUT YOU?

Do you often find yourself getting angry, telling lies, swearing, or doing other things you know are wrong? Only God has the power to change you. As he reveals to you various areas in your life that need to change, ask him to help you make the changes in your "heart's settings" to please him. You can have victory.

MEMORIZE:

"How we thank God, who gives us victory over sin and death through Jesus Christ our Lord!" 1 Corinthians 15:57

LET JESUS
CHANGE YOU

X-RAY MACHINE

Read: Psalm 119:9-16

"I don't see any cavities today," Dr. Post announced after checking Luke's teeth. "But I want to get a better look with some X-ray pictures."

As Luke waited for the X-ray to be developed, he looked around the dentist's office. On the wall he noticed a poster with instructions on how to brush teeth. And a giant stuffed tooth with a grinning face painted on it stood on a shelf. "You must like teeth," said Luke as Dr. Post came back into the room.

The dentist laughed. "Teeth are important, and we need to keep them healthy," he said. "Tell me, Luke—how often do you brush and floss your teeth?"

"Every day," said Luke. "Usually more than once! Mom makes me."

Dr. Post studied the X-rays of Luke's teeth. "Oops!" he said. "You do have a small amount of decay in one of your molars."

Luke groaned. "I almost wish X-ray machines didn't exist," he said.

"Whoa!" said the doctor. "You should be glad for them. Now we can clean out that decay before it gets worse. Relax. We can take care of that right away."

"Relax?" asked Luke as he watched Dr. Post prepare a drill.

Dr. Post smiled. "Sure," he said. "It won't take long to fix it." After he finished the drilling, the dentist spoke thoughtfully. "You know, Luke, that X-ray is something like the Bible."

Luke grinned. "Having my Sunday school teacher for my dentist means I get a lesson here, too."

"Right," said Dr. Post with a chuckle. "You see, the X-ray showed decay that I couldn't see with my eyes. And sometimes God's Word shows us sin—decay in our lives—that no one else can see. When that happens, we need to quickly drill it out; that is, we need to confess it and get rid of it before it gets worse." *LJR*

HOW ABOUT YOU?

Do you use God's X-ray machine—the Bible—to look at your heart and life? Sin may be hidden from others, but it's never hidden from God. Sometimes you may not realize that you're doing something wrong until it's pointed out to you. God's Word will make you more aware of any sin for which you need to ask his forgiveness.

LET GOD'S WORD SHOW YOU HOW TO LIVE

MEMORIZE:

"For the word of God is full of living power . . . cutting deep into our innermost thoughts and desires."

Hebrews 4:12

JUSTIN'S FAMILY

Read: Psalm 103:17-22

Justin looked at the paper his Sunday school teacher had given him. On it were written words she wanted him to remember. "This says, 'Jesus loves you, and he'll always take care of you,' " she told him.

Those words didn't make Justin feel especially happy. *I already have too many people taking care of me*, he thought. He had his parents, whom he didn't mind so much, but he also had two older sisters who were bossy sometimes. Now he'd learned that Jesus was watching over him, too.

His sisters were waiting when he came out of church. "How was Sunday school?" asked Miriam.

"Good," replied Justin. "We had a story."

"That's nice," said Miriam. "Don't forget to zip up your coat, or you might get sick. It's cold outside."

"Put on your mittens, too," added Deanne.

"Watch for oncoming traffic," warned Miriam as they crossed the street to the car.

"Hi, Justin," said Dad, as Justin climbed into the back seat. "Did you like Sunday school?"

"It was fine," answered Justin. "My teacher gave me this." He handed the paper to his mother.

"Jesus loves you. He'll always take care of you," read Mom. "That's a good message. I like to know Jesus is taking care of me."

"Is Jesus taking care of you, too?" asked Justin. Mom nodded, and he added, "I have too many people taking care of me!"

Dad smiled. "It must seem as if a lot of people are telling you what to do," he said, "but it's because we love you. One way Jesus takes care of us is by giving us a family so we can care for each other."

Justin thought about his dad's words and decided he should be glad to have a caring family. It wasn't every boy who had so many people giving him so much attention. *AK*

HOW ABOUT YOU?

Are you glad for all the family members God has given you? Do you thank him for parents, brothers and sisters, grandmas and grandpas? What other people has God sent into your life to help take care of you? Thank God for each one of them.

MEMORIZE:

"The righteous man leads a blameless life; blessed are his children after him." Proverbs 20:7, NIV

THANK GOD
FOR FAMILY

CLOCKS AND PEOPLE

Read: Deuteronomy 4:1-8

(Note: This story may not be suitable for very young children.)

"Mom," said Shawn, as he stirred his cornflakes slowly, "you said abortion is wrong, but my teacher says it's legal in America."

"Yes, it is *legal*," said Mom, "but sometimes people make up laws that go against God's laws. God says it's wrong to kill unborn babies."

As Mom was talking, Shawn's little brother, still in pajamas, appeared in the doorway. "Oh, Matt!" exclaimed Shawn. "You'd better hurry or you'll be late for school!"

"No, I won't," replied Matt. "The clock says it's only 7:00."

"But it's 7:30 already!" Shawn said. "The clock is wrong!"

"Jimmy set the time back last night," explained Matt.

"He did?" asked Mom.

"Yeah, because he didn't want to go to bed," said Matt with a grin. "So it's only 7:00, and I've got lots of time to get dressed."

Shawn stared at Matt, then burst out laughing. "That's silly!" he said. "It doesn't matter what the clock says if the *real* time is 7:30. You'd better hurry, little brother."

Mom nodded and gave Matt a gentle push. "Off you go, young man. Hurry and get dressed." She turned to Shawn, who was looking at the clock and giggling. "Shawn," she said, "Jimmy gave us a good example of what I was trying to explain about people making laws. He made the clock *say* the time he wanted it to be, but that didn't change the actual time. People may make a law that says abortion is all right, but God's law says it's wrong, so it *is* wrong—no matter what the law says."

Shawn nodded. "We need to live by what *God* says is right—not by what people say."

"Correct," agreed Mom. "Always consider what God's Word says about things, no matter what anyone else tells you." *MTF*

HOW ABOUT YOU?

Do your friends ever try to convince you that some wrong thing is right? Perhaps you've been told that cheating, lying, or disobeying your parents is sometimes okay. Even your country might have laws that go against God's Word—for example, people may make a law saying that abortion is okay; or they may make a law saying it's all right for men to marry men. Christians need to know what God says—and then they need to obey him.

MEMORIZE:

"Do not add to or subtract from these commands I am giving you from the Lord your God. Just obey them."

Deuteronomy 4:2

OBEY GOD'S LAWS

January

16

Read: John 3:3; 14:1-6

"What do you mean, not everyone gets to go to heaven?" Doug asked his friend Jacob. "Who gets to go?"

"Like my dad said," replied Jacob, "people who accept Jesus as Savior go to heaven."

"Well, I don't get it," said Doug. "Let's ask your dad about it."

Jacob's dad was in the living room. "Hey, Mr. Woods, everybody goes to heaven, right?" Doug thought he was asking the question in a way that would make it easy for Jacob's dad to say, "Yes, that's right."

Instead, Mr. Woods said, "No, Doug. Not everybody." After a pause, he said, "Doug, when you go home after school each day, do you ever wonder, 'Will I have a bed to sleep in tonight?' or, 'What will I do if my parents turn me away?' Do questions like that ever come to your mind?"

Doug laughed. "No, I'm their kid, so it's my home."

"Well, do any of your classmates expect to eat, sleep, and be taken care of in your home?" asked Mr. Woods.

"No," Doug said again. "They're not part of our family, so it's not their home."

"It's the same way with God's family," said Mr. Woods. "When you believe in Jesus as your Lord and Savior, you become a child of God—part of his family—and heaven is your future home. If you haven't received Jesus, you're *not* part of his family." Mr. Woods paused. "Are you part of God's family, Doug?" Doug shook his head. "You can be," said Mr. Woods. "You were physically born into your parents' family, so you're their son. Now God says you need to be 'born again'—into his family."

"Born again!" exclaimed Doug. "How?"

"By depending on Jesus alone to save you from your sin," replied Mr. Woods. He picked up his Bible. "Sit down and let me explain, okay?" Doug nodded. *NTB*

HOW ABOUT YOU?

Do you know where you will spend eternity? Will it be in heaven? Not everyone goes to heaven. The only way to make heaven your home is to be born into God's family. Accept Jesus today.

MEMORIZE:

"But to all who believed him and accepted him, he gave the right to become children of God." John 1:12

BE BORN AGAIN

A TRUE HERO

Read: John 15:9-15

Ethan stood on the sidelines in the crowded stadium, hoping to catch a glimpse of Buzz Howard—the greatest basketball player of all time! Ethan knew all the "stats" about Buzz by heart. He hadn't missed a single televised game. He had sent Buzz several fan letters, including pictures of himself, but he hadn't received a reply . . . yet. *Buzz is a busy guy*, thought Ethan, *but I'm sure he'll answer my letters after the season is over. I hope I get close enough to him so that he'll recognize me.*

The crowd cheered as the team appeared. One by one the players ran out. *Buzz is going to run right past here,* Ethan realized. "Hey, Buzz!" he called. "It's me, Ethan!" Ethan thrust his hand up for a "high five," but Buzz ran past, not even noticing him. "He ran right by! He didn't even look at me!" exclaimed Ethan, crushed.

"Yeah, so what did you expect, kid," said a tall boy behind him. "He's a celebrity; he doesn't know you." The boy chuckled, and Ethan walked back to his seat beside his dad.

"Hey, buddy, what's wrong?" asked Dad. "You did get to see your hero, didn't you?"

"Yeah," mumbled Ethan. "But even after all the letters and pictures I've sent, he doesn't know who I am."

"Well, Ethan, he's only human. He can't possibly know all his fans, even though they feel as though they know him. But I'm sure if he did know you, he'd want to be your friend," said Dad, putting his arm around Ethan. "That's the trouble with human heroes."

Ethan looked at Dad. "What other kind is there?"

"There's Jesus!" replied Dad. "He's not only a man, he's God—and he knows everything about you. He's the biggest hero and the best friend anyone could ever have." *BJP*

HOW ABOUT YOU?

What kind of person do you admire? Do you think talent or good looks make a person worthy of praise? The world is full of all sorts of heroes and celebrities, but there is only one person who is truly worthy of your praise. Jesus died to give you salvation! He is a true hero! He is a true friend!

MAKE JESUS
YOUR HERO

EARS AND ACTIONS

Read: James 1:22-25

"Have you boys cleaned your rooms?" asked Mom. "You know that's your Saturday chore!"

"Okay," replied Mark and Daniel as they reluctantly headed for their separate rooms. When Mark entered his room, he picked up a model car. "I'll just work on this a few minutes first," he decided.

Soon Daniel called out that he was finished. "Let's go sledding!" he said. Mark felt a twinge of guilt as he closed the door on his messy room, but soon he was having such a good time that he forgot about it.

Later, Mom reminded the boys to feed their pets. Daniel's job was to feed the fish, and Mark's job was to feed the dog. Daniel fed the fish immediately, but Mark decided to read the comics first.

"Bongo keeps begging for food!" said Mom later that evening. "Didn't you hear me tell you to you feed him, Mark?"

"Oh, I forgot!" Mark exclaimed as he jumped up to fill the dog's dish.

After dinner, Mom was working upstairs. "Mark!" she called. "Get up here! Didn't you hear me tell you to clean your room today?"

"I'm sorry," Mark replied, going quickly up the stairs. "I meant to do it."

Mom frowned. "Mark, you need to learn to obey me immediately," she told him. "You're all ears but no action. In other words, you're a 'hearer' of my word, but not a 'doer.' And that means you are a 'hearer' and not a 'doer' of God's Word, too, because he says to obey your parents. I can see that I'll have to help you learn that lesson."

Mark knew his mother was right. He had heard what Mom said and had even agreed to it, but he had not done it. He knew he deserved whatever punishment she was about to give him. *REP*

HOW ABOUT YOU?

Are you a "doer" of God's Word? He tells you to obey your parents, to be kind, to be honest, to love others, to forgive, and much more! Do you hear all this, perhaps even agree to it, and then forget all about it? Think of one area where you can be a doer of God's Word. Then go and do it now!

MEMORIZE:

"But be doers of the word, and not hearers only." James 1:22, NKJV

OBEY IMMEDIATELY

THE BEST JUDGE

Read: Romans 2:1-11

Danny looked up when he heard his mother sigh. "Oh, I just don't know what to do," she said, sitting down at the table. "I'm confused by the case I heard in court today." She had been chosen to serve on a jury.

"Tell us about it, Mom," said Danny. "Maybe we can help you."

"No . . . when you're a member of a jury, you're not allowed to discuss a case until it's over," Mom answered wearily.

"Why not?" asked Danny.

"Well," said Mom, "in America, a person has the right to a trial by jury."

"I know," said Danny, "and that means other American citizens are chosen to decide whether or not the person accused of a crime is guilty—but why can't a jury member talk about the case?"

"Someone else's opinion might sway a juror's thinking," explained Mom. "A jury member's final decision is to be based solely on the evidence given in court."

A week later, the case was decided, and then Mom explained the trial to her family. "I wondered if the defendant was telling the whole story," she said. "I prayed about it. I asked the Lord to give me the wisdom to make the right decision."

"It sounds as if you had an interesting week, Mom," observed Danny.

"Well, yes, I did," Mom admitted. "I learned a lot about trials and courtrooms that I didn't know before, and I also learned to appreciate the Bible and the Lord in a new way."

"What do you mean?" asked Danny.

"Well, no matter how just those of us on the jury tried to be, we're still human," explained Mom. "Only God is all-wise and always right in his judgments. I'm glad he's my judge." *LMW*

HOW ABOUT YOU?

Have you ever had the experience of sitting in a courtroom during a trial? Have you watched a trial on television? Judges and jury members try to do the best job they can in deciding who is right or wrong. Still, they are only human and mistakes can be made. Only God is all-knowing. Only God is a completely just judge. Aren't you glad he's the one in charge?

GOD IS THE
BEST JUDGE

MEMORIZE:
"Shall not the Judge of all the earth do right?" Genesis 18:25, NKJV

JUST ONCE WON'T HURT

Read: Hebrews 10:19-25

For several weeks, Cesar had been attending church with Javier. Then he began to skip church in order to do other things. "You don't have to go to church to worship God," he told Javier. "You can worship him anytime, anywhere."

"Yes, but skipping is a bad habit," answered Javier. "The first time you skipped, you said just once wouldn't hurt. Now it's been more than once. Remember that Bible verse we had from Hebrews? The one about Christians meeting together? In Bible times, Christians met together often—sometimes every day. Seems like we should be at church at least one day a week."

"Well, maybe," said Cesar, "but there are so many good things to do on Sunday!" And so he continued to miss most of the time.

As Javier and Cesar walked home from school one day, Cesar surprised his friend by saying, "Hey, Javier, I'll be going to church this week."

"Oh, good!" exclaimed Javier.

"In fact, my whole family is going," Cesar said. "My dad hopes it will help my sister and I to stop fighting."

"What have you two been fighting about?"

"The math test I flunked."

"But that wasn't your fault—you were absent when we had lessons on how to do a lot of those problems," said Javier. "Even Mrs. Jimenez said you could make it up."

"Yeah—but Dad didn't know that—at least not till my sister blabbed about it," Javier replied. "See . . . I told Mrs. Jimenez I was sick the day I missed, but I really skipped school that day. Dad was really mad when he found out about that. When I told him I didn't think it would hurt to miss just once, he got a funny look on his face and he said, 'Maybe all of us have been missing some important lessons by not going to church!' " *AGL*

HOW ABOUT YOU?

Have you skipped church? Have you skipped your Bible reading time? You might think that skipping "just once" won't hurt, but it can easily get to be a bad habit. Be faithful in Bible reading, in prayer, and in going to church.

MEMORIZE:

"Let us not neglect our meeting together, as some people do."
Hebrews 10:25

BE FAITHFUL

IS IT TRUE?

Read: Deuteronomy 18:18-22

"Dad, look at this!" Yuri pointed to the newspaper. "The paper says this lady is a prophetess, and there's a whole list of things she says are going to happen."

"Don't believe it," warned John, Yuri's older brother. "She's a fake."

"Is she a fake, Dad?" asked Yuri. "The predictions sound as if they could happen. She says there'll be a war in Africa and that we'll have a cold winter and . . ."

"There are always wars, and every winter is cold," interrupted John. "Even I could predict that!"

"That's true." Dad nodded. "People like to think they can forecast the future, but they can't. Before the Bible was written, God used prophets to give out his message, but now he speaks to us through his Word—the Bible."

"Aren't these people ever right?" asked Yuri.

"Sometimes—but it's probably a matter of good guessing," answered Dad. "We read in Deuteronomy that if a prophet makes even one mistake, he is not of God. Also, remember that Satan is very powerful, and he may sometimes give people special knowledge. That makes the whole thing very dangerous."

"But if these people can't really tell the future, how come they pretend they can?" wondered Yuri.

"They like the feeling of power it gives them," answered Dad, "and they like the money they get from doing it. Gullible people will pay lots of money to know the future."

Yuri was quiet for a few minutes as he read the list of predictions. "I guess anyone could have predicted most of these things," he agreed. "It is pretty silly to believe this lady has some kind of special power. I'm glad I know the true God who really does know and care about the future of my life." *LMW*

HOW ABOUT YOU?

Have you read predictions in the newspaper or heard someone predict the future? These people don't know for sure what's going to happen. Only God knows the future completely. And you have God's Word to lead you through whatever lies in the future.

ONLY GOD KNOWS THE FUTURE

MEMORIZE:

"In the past God spoke to our forefathers through the prophets at many times and in various ways, but in these last days he has spoken to us by his Son." Hebrews 1:1-2, NIV

Read: Proverbs 18:1-8

"Mom!" shouted Luis, as he bounded in from school. "Did you hear the fire engines today? The fire was at a place close to our school, and we're pretty sure who started it."

"Really?" asked Mom in surprise.

"Yep—Bryan Blaine," said Luis. "I told my teacher about him . . . you know—the things his mother told you about him liking fires and going to the firehouse so often. I overheard her when she was here the other day. Bryan was called to the office, and he was crying when he came out."

"Luis!" gasped Mom. "When Mrs. Blaine came to ask me to pray for Bryan, she didn't expect you to listen in and then talk about it! Why did you do such a thing?"

"I . . . I don't know," stammered Luis.

"Well, other than the few things you overheard, did you have any reason at all to believe Bryan might have set that fire?" asked Mom. Luis shook his head, and Mom continued, "You should have checked with me before talking about Bryan to your teacher. Luis, words are like feathers. Once they're out in the air it's hard to get them back again. You need to apologize to Bryan and his mother for what you've done. I'll go with you. Let's hope that in time they will forgive you."

As Luis reluctantly started out with his mother, his friend Marshall came running up. "Did you hear?" he called. "A short circuit caused the fire today. It wasn't Bryan after all." *AGL*

HOW ABOUT YOU?

Have you ever repeated something you heard, then realized what you repeated was false? Words can hurt people deeply and ruin friendships. The next time you're tempted to repeat something that would hurt someone else, ask yourself if God would be pleased with what you're about to say. If the answer is no, don't tell.

MEMORIZE:

"What dainty morsels rumors are— but they sink deep into one's heart." Proverbs 18:8

EYES OF LOVE

Read: Matthew 18:11-14

All evening Otto was restless and unhappy. Snowflake, his pet lamb, was missing, and it was a cold, wintry night. Dad had gone to search for the lamb but without success. Otto wished Dad would go with him to look for Snowflake once more, but Dad was in his comfortable chair before the fireplace, reading the newspaper. Knowing Dad had had a busy day, Otto hated to bother him, so after thinking it over, Otto quietly put on his warmest clothes and slipped out by himself.

Out to the mountain pastures Otto went. *B-r-r-r-r!* He shivered. *I didn't know it could be so cold!* "Snowflake!" he called over and over. "Sno-o-owflake! Where are you?" He ignored bruised knees and hands as he stumbled over rocks.

At last, Otto heard a tiny cry, and following the sound, he made his way to the lamb. It had fallen over the cliff and broken a leg. Gathering Snowflake in his arms, Otto stumbled back home.

After Dad had set Snowflake's leg, he and Otto sat at the kitchen table while Mom poured hot chocolate. Mom bandaged some of Otto's wounds as well. "They don't hurt much," Otto told her. "Honest. Just so I found Snowflake—that's all that counts."

Dad shook his head. "You know, Son," he said, "when I discovered that you had gone to look for Snowflake, I was ready to punish you. But I guess I shouldn't, since you were acting like the kind of boy we hoped you'd be. What puzzles me is why I didn't find Snowflake when I was up there looking for him."

"Maybe it was because Otto was looking with eyes of love," suggested Mom. "Love keeps on when everyone else gives up. Somehow, the way Otto searched for and found Snowflake reminds me of Jesus and his search for those who don't know him yet." *HCT*

HOW ABOUT YOU?

Otto left his warm home to find Snowflake, but Jesus left heaven's glory to find you. Otto suffered cuts and bruises for Snowflake. Jesus gave his life for you. He did all this because he loves you.

JESUS, THE GOOD SHEPHERD, LOVES YOU

24

GONE FROM MEMORY

Read: Psalm 25:4-9, 16-19; Isaiah 43:25

"Dear Jesus, I'm really sorry for my sin. Please forgive me and save me," Jerry prayed as he and Dad knelt by his bed one evening.

When he had finished praying, Dad smiled at him. "Jerry," he said, "I believe you asked Jesus to save you a couple of times before, didn't you?" Jerry nodded. "Did you really mean it before?" asked Dad.

Again, Jerry nodded. "Yeah, but I just wanted to make sure," he said.

Dad looked thoughtful. "Jerry, you're ready for bed a little early, so before you jump in, how about showing me the new computer program Grandma gave you?" he said.

Jerry's face brightened. "Sure!" He liked doing things on the computer. He put in the disk and showed Dad how he could type the answers to math problems, then delete the answers and do the problems again.

"That's great, but what happens to your answers when you erase them?" asked Dad.

"Why, they just disappear," Jerry answered quickly.

"Make them come back again," suggested Dad.

"I can't, Dad. When the computer erases them, they're gone," Jerry explained. "You can't call them up again because they're gone from its memory."

"That's right," Dad said with a nod, "and, Son, that's exactly what happens to your sin when you confess it to the Lord Jesus. It's gone forever, and he never calls it up again. He doesn't remember it anymore."

Jerry thought a minute. "That's a load off my mind," he said with a big sigh. "I'm glad to know my sin is gone from God's memory—just like my answers are gone from the computer's memory. I think I'll sleep better tonight." *DK*

HOW ABOUT YOU?

Have you sincerely confessed your sin and asked God to forgive and save you? Do you wonder if he has really done that? He does forgive you, and he forgets your sin, too. His Word says your sin is removed as far as the east is from the west and buried in the deepest sea.

MEMORIZE:

"I will forgive their wickedness and will never again remember their sins."
Jeremiah 31:34

GOD FORGIVES
AND FORGETS

A TRUE INVESTMENT

Read: Luke 12:15-21

On their birthday, the twins, Jana and Nick, visited their grandparents, and Grandpa gave them a personal tour of the bank where he worked. Just before leaving the bank, he took them into his office and gave each a personal savings account book. "I deposited some money into an account for each of you," he said. "Be sure to spend your money wisely—and I advise you not to spend all of it. Save some."

"I will," Nick stated firmly. "I'll save it all. Then it earns interest, doesn't it? Soon I'll have more and more and . . ."

"And you'll be a miser and an old man!" interrupted Jana. "I'm going to save some of mine, but I'm going to use some to buy a piece of fake fur and eyes to make puppets. I'll sell them at Mom's yard sale next month. In a few weeks I'll probably have way more than you'll have in years!"

Grandpa chuckled. "Our family has always had bankers and businessmen," he said. "You have that heritage, and it sounds like you two fit right in. But our family has another heritage—a more important one. Can you guess what that is? It has nothing to do with money or investments."

"Oh, I know!" exclaimed Jana, after thinking about it. "I've heard Dad say that we have a 'godly' heritage!"

"Oh, yeah," agreed Nick. "That's because Dad's a preacher, and Aunt Ellen's a Christian teacher at a college in Africa, and Uncle Ed's a Christian businessman."

"And all our grandparents believe in Jesus, too," added Jana.

Grandpa relaxed in his chair. "They've all invested their lives in serving God," he said. "I give you this money with my blessing, but remember that committing your life—including your money—to Jesus is the greatest and most satisfying investment any person can make." *RG*

HOW ABOUT YOU?

Does making a lot of money seem important to you? Never forget that money is only temporary. Unless you use your money for the Lord, it has no lasting value. Don't allow yourself to get caught up in accumulating the things of this world. Invest your life in what will last.

MONEY DOESN'T LAST

MEMORIZE:
". . . be rich in good works, ready to give, willing to share."
1 Timothy 6:18, NKJV

Read: Philippians 2:13-16

"There's a parking space," said Seth. He pointed. "Right there by the door."

"Great!" said Maria. Mom had allowed her to take the car to school, and she had to stop for some groceries before heading home. But as Maria drove toward the empty spot, she saw a blue and white sign. "We're not allowed to use a handicapped space," she said.

"Oh, come on!" whined Seth. "We're in a hurry." Just then another car pulled into the space. "That guy doesn't look handicapped," exclaimed Seth as they saw a man get out of the car and walk toward the store. "We could just as well have parked there!"

"You can't always see a person's handicap," said Maria, "and he does have a sticker." She drove on and soon found another place to park.

When they reached home, Maria told Mom about the parking spaces. "I don't see why we couldn't park there," Seth grumbled. "That man didn't look any more handicapped than I do. He didn't have a cane or anything!"

"Oh, Seth! You've been grumbling all afternoon," said Maria. "Like I told you, some handicaps don't show."

"That's true," said Mom as she saw Seth scowl. "And there are also handicaps such as bad attitudes."

"Bad attitudes?" asked Seth.

"When Christians display bad attitudes and actions, they're handicapped in their witness for the Lord," explained Mom.

Seth was sure Mom was thinking of him, so he tried to make a joke of it. "Maybe *they* should have handicap stickers and special parking places, too," he mumbled.

"I don't think so," said Maria dryly.

Mom shook her head. "It certainly would not be a sticker we'd be proud of," she said. "We need to *tell* people we're Christians, and we also need to *show* it by our actions." *SN*

HOW ABOUT YOU?
Do your actions and attitudes show that you love Jesus? Do you cheerfully put others before yourself and act unselfishly? When you show others you love Jesus by the way you treat them, it makes your witness more credible.

MEMORIZE:
"For God is working in you, giving you the desire to obey him and the power to do what pleases him."
Philippians 2:13

TELL—
AND SHOW—
THAT YOU
LOVE GOD

FOR YOUR PROTECTION

Read: 1 John 5:1-5

Justin slid into the car and closed the door. He set a large birthday present on his knees and smiled.

Mom fastened her seat belt and turned to Justin. "You don't have your seat belt on," she said.

"It's only two blocks to Cameron's house," said Justin. "I don't need the seat belt for such a short trip."

"Oh, yes, you do," disagreed Mom.

"But I can't reach it while I hold this present!" complained Justin peevishly.

"Here, let me help you." Mom reached over, pulled the seat belt down, and snapped it into the buckle. "There. Now we can go." She started the car and backed out of the driveway. "Seat belts were put into cars to protect us, and the law says we have to use them," she added.

"The law," repeated Justin, remembering a recent Sunday school lesson. "Are the Ten Commandments like seat belts? Miss Chin says God gave them to us to protect us."

"I like that thought," said Mom. "When you obey God's commands—which are summarized in the Ten Commandments—it's like putting his seat belt around your life." As she spoke, a soccer ball bounced into the street in front of them. Mom braked quickly and the car jerked to a stop—inches away from a little boy who dashed after the ball. Justin lurched forward, but his seat belt tightened, holding him back. The little boy grabbed the ball and ran back into his yard.

"If you hadn't insisted that I wear my seat belt, I might have smashed into the dashboard," admitted Justin, reaching for the present, which had slid off his lap.

"Exactly," Mom agreed. "Seat belts help you only if you put them on, and God's laws help you only if you obey them." *ECM*

HOW ABOUT YOU?

Do you faithfully wear your seat belt? Wearing it can protect you from harm. Do you faithfully obey God's laws? Obeying them protects you, too. Obey your country's laws and put on your seat belt in the car. Obey God's laws and follow his commands.

LAWS ARE FOR YOUR PROTECTION

MEMORIZE:
"Loving God means keeping his commandments." 1 John 5:3

"Dad, what are those long ropes on the side of the road?" asked seven-year-old Emil as they drove down the highway.

"Those are called guardrails," Dad replied. "Sometimes guardrails are made of wide metal bands, and sometimes they're heavy wire ropes."

"Guardrails?" asked Emil. "What are they for?"

"They're there to make sure people on the highway stay on the road," Dad replied.

"Why would they want to leave the road?" asked Emil.

"Well, they wouldn't *want* to leave the road," said Dad, "but sometimes people have accidents. In winter, the road might get slippery and cars might run into each other and slide off the road. Other times, people may not pay attention to what they're doing, or they may get sleepy while they're driving. When things like that happen, they could swerve off the highway. Then those guardrails would catch the car before it could roll down the hill at the side of the road. The guardrails keep them from much more serious damage."

"Have they ever saved anybody on this road?" asked Emil.

"I'm sure they have," said Dad.

"Wow," Emil said. "I guess they're really important!"

"Yes, they are," agreed Dad. After a moment, he added thoughtfully, "You know, those guardrails protect us on this highway, and when we use God's Word, it acts as guardrails to protect us on life's highway."

"What do you mean?"

"By life's highway, I mean the way we live our lives. When we have questions or doubts about what is right, the Bible can guide us and show us the right thing to do," explained Dad. "As we obey God's Word, it keeps us from straying from the way God wants us to go. It keeps us from trouble and helps us through difficult situations."

"Just like the guardrails," agreed Emil. "Guardrails are good!" *RT*

HOW ABOUT YOU?

Do you check your Bible when you're not sure what is the right thing to do? As you trust and obey God's Word, it will work as a guardrail in your life and will help you stay on the right road. God's way is the best and safest way for you to go.

MEMORIZE:

"Take only ways that are firm. Do not swerve to the right or the left."
Proverbs 4:26-27, NIV

LET GOD'S WORD PROTECT YOU

LOST NOTEBOOK

Read: Matthew 5:43-48

"Randy—one of the kids at my school—is always picking on me," Joe complained to his dad one night. "He always calls me 'Dummy' because I'm not good at math." Joe scowled. "I'm tired of being picked on," he added. "I hate Randy!"

"Whoa!" said Dad. "Remember those verses you learned for Bible club last week? Didn't they say Christians should do good even to those who don't treat them well?"

"You mean be nice to Randy, even after he has been so mean to me?" Joe asked.

Dad nodded. "That's what Jesus said we should do," he replied. Joe frowned.

On the way to school the next day, Joe found a notebook. *Wow!* He thought. *Somebody lost a bunch of homework!* He looked at the name. *This is Randy's notebook.* Joe smiled to himself. *What if I hide it or tear it up? That will get Randy into plenty of trouble!* But when Joe got to school and shoved the notebook under some papers in his desk, he remembered the talk with his dad. It kept bothering him as he went back outside to play. When the bell rang, Joe went in, took out the notebook and gave it to Randy.

At recess, Randy found Joe. "Thought you were real cool to turn my notebook in, huh? Now I'm supposed to be your friend, right?" he asked sarcastically.

"No," said Joe. "I was only doing what was right."

"Well, I don't want to be your friend," growled Randy.

"Don't be then," replied Joe. "All I did was help you."

Randy was surprised! "You must be crazy," he said. He started walking away, then turned back. "Well . . . maybe you aren't so bad after all," he blurted. "You did keep me out of trouble." *JLH*

HOW ABOUT YOU?

Can you think of someone who's being mean to you? Do something kind for that person today.

BE KIND TO YOUR ENEMIES

MEMORIZE:
"If your enemies are hungry, feed them. If they are thirsty, give them something to drink." Romans 12:20

THE RIGHT SIZE (PART 1)

Read: 1 Peter 2:21-23

Ted waited until the last minute to get out of bed, and then he "poked" at his breakfast. "Hurry, Ted—the bus will soon be here," said Mom. "You wouldn't want to miss school today."

"Yes, I would," said Ted.

"You would? Why?" asked Mom. "Don't you feel well?"

"Yes . . . I mean, no," Ted stammered.

"Whatever is the matter?" Mom wanted to know.

"It's the kids at school . . . they tease me because I'm so small. They call me 'Stump.' " Tears shone in Ted's eyes.

"Try not to let their words bother you, Ted. Speak to your teacher if you think you need to do that," advised Mom. "And try to return kindness for meanness. Your attitude and actions are more important than your appearance."

"But today we're playing basketball in gym, and no one will want me on his team. I'm the wrong size," protested Ted.

Gently Mom put her arm around his shoulder. "Ted, you may be smaller than you want to be, but God made you just as you are. He doesn't make mistakes. Maybe you'll grow faster when you're older, and catch up," she encouraged, "but even if you don't, God has a plan for you. He knows what is best. Trust him. Now here comes the bus. You do your best in gym—I'll pray for you today."

As Ted expected, he heard some groans when the gym teacher assigned him to a team. Some of the kids teased him, but when he didn't get angry about it, he found they usually stopped. The day wasn't quite as bad as he expected, but he still wished that just once he could be the right size! *JLH*

HOW ABOUT YOU?

Are you teased about your size, skin, hair color, or freckles? Are you called names? Teasing sometimes hurts, but don't strike back. Learn from Jesus. People were unkind to him, too. He'll help you to move beyond the teasing.

MEMORIZE:

"He did not retaliate when he was insulted." 1 Peter 2:23

GET ALONG
WITH OTHERS

THE RIGHT SIZE (PART 2)

Read: Psalm 139:14-17

When school was over for the day, Ted inched his way through the crowded bus and wearily plopped down in a back seat. It would be good to get home to a warm house and a hot supper. It was getting colder outside and snowing hard.

As the bus started out, Ted closed his eyes. He was sleepy, because he hadn't slept much the night before—he'd been too worried about the basketball teams. The next thing he knew, he was suddenly shoved across the seat and thrown onto the floor. The bus had hit a slippery spot. It had skidded and landed on its side in a ditch. Glass broke, metal crunched, and children screamed. The door would not open, and they could not get out.

"We'll have to wait for help," said the driver. He did his best to calm the children and make them comfortable. But the passing minutes seemed like years, and no help came. "Hey, let's go out a window," suggested one of the kids. Several tried it but they were too big. Then they thought of Ted. "Ted, you try it! You're little," one of them said.

Ted wiggled. He squirmed. He twisted. Suddenly he was out the window. He climbed up the bank to the road, but nothing was in sight. He limped along. Cold and bruised, he finally made it to the nearest house, and soon help was on the way.

Several days later, Ted received a citizen's award. He was credited for his part in the rescue. "Wow! I guess God made me the right size after all," he marveled.

Mom nodded. "You were just the right size for the job you had to do," she said. "God never makes mistakes." *JLH*

HOW ABOUT YOU?

Are you happy with your size, your looks, and the color of your skin? You're a special person, made by God for a specific purpose. He has a plan for your life. Be content with the way he made you, and trust him to guide you.

YOU ARE GOD'S
SPECIAL
CREATION

February

1

Read: 1 John 2:3-6

Nathanael sat quietly as his father read a portion of Scripture. "Wow!" exclaimed Dad as he closed his Bible. "This says we're to be like Jesus who was absolutely perfect. What a goal!" Dad looked at his family. "Anybody want to share how that's happening in your life?"

After a moment, Nathanael grinned. "I don't get in fights as much as I used to," he said, "and I don't cheat on spelling tests anymore. I like Sunday school better, too." His expression turned thoughtful. "I'm not changing much lately, though. Should I be?"

"Well, we should never stop growing in the Lord," said Dad, "but often it's hard to pinpoint where the changes are taking place."

The next day, Nathanael's family left to visit his grandma, who lived several hours away. When they got there, Grandma hugged little Leah. "You've grown!" she exclaimed, "and you've lost some teeth!"

"Thwee teeth," lisped Leah.

"And you must be six inches taller, Nathanael," said Grandma, hugging him. "You're a young man now!"

As Mom tucked Nathanael into his sleeping bag that night, he said, "I didn't think I had changed much since the last time we saw Grandma, but she was surprised by how much I've grown up."

Mom laughed. "I know. I often don't notice how you and Leah grow, either—until someone points it out or until you grow out of your clothes. I guess I see you too much to notice the gradual changes." She gave Nathanael a hug. "Grandma saw some spiritual changes in you, too. She told me how you and Leah played together without quarreling, and how you took part in our discussion during family devotions and in prayer."

"Really?" asked Nathanael.

"Really," said Mom. "Let's ask God to show us where we still need to change and to help us not get discouraged as we strive to be like him." *HLA*

HOW ABOUT YOU?

Do you get discouraged because it doesn't seem like you're growing much spiritually? Growth takes time—it's a process. Be faithful in learning more from God's Word and in obeying and serving him. Ask him to help you grow daily to be more like him.

GROWTH TAKES
WORK AND TIME

MEMORIZE:
"But grow in the special favor and knowledge of our Lord and Savior Jesus Christ." 2 Peter 3:18

A WALRUS FAMILY (PART 1)

Read: John 16:7-15

"Listen to this, Bethany," said Seth. "My book says a walrus calf is fed by its mother. When it grows older, the mother walrus pushes her calf into the freezing water to make it learn how to search for its own food."

Bethany shivered. "Br-r-r-r! I'm glad I'm not a walrus," she said.

Mom appeared in the doorway. "It's time to leave for the nursing home, Bethany."

Bethany frowned. "I don't want to go," she said.

"I need your help," said Mom. "You promised to pass the cookies."

"But I don't like the way the nursing home smells," complained Bethany.

"Life isn't always pleasant," Mom told her. "This is one way we can bring some joy to the people there. God is pleased when we serve others."

"Why doesn't Seth have to go?" asked Bethany.

"He'll be going another time," said Mom, nudging Bethany out the door. "Let's go."

Bethany was in good spirits when she and her mother returned home later that afternoon. "You should have come, Seth," she said. "There's a man there that everyone calls Gramps, and he told one funny story after another!" Bethany turned to her mother. "When can we go back, Mom?"

"How about next Tuesday, after school?" suggested Mom. "You could go then too, Seth."

"No, thanks," answered Seth. He looked up when Bethany gave him a shove. "Hey, what did you do that for?" he said.

"Remember the mother walrus in your report?" asked Bethany. "Mom knew it would be good for me to go to the nursing home, but she had to push me—like that mother walrus. Now I'm pushing you." Bethany spoke to her mother. "Let's go bake more cookies, Mother Walrus."

Mom smiled. "The Holy Spirit gives us nudges, too," she told them. "He never forces us to do his will, but he finds ways to encourage us." *LJR*

HOW ABOUT YOU?

Have you felt that you should tell someone about Jesus? Who nudged you to speak up? God the Holy Spirit. Has he also nudged you to put a generous part of your allowance into the missionary offering? Don't be afraid of God's nudges—even if they seem to be difficult or uncomfortable things to do. When you obey him, he will reward you.

MEMORIZE:

"When the Spirit of truth comes, he will guide you into all truth." John 16:13

OBEY GOD'S NUDGES

A WALRUS FAMILY (PART 2)

Read: Proverbs 11:24-28

"I can't believe it!" remarked Seth. "I actually enjoyed going to the nursing home, and I'm thinking about helping at the city mission, too. Pastor Jim says a lot of the people who go there are homeless and don't have warm clothes. Our youth group is already collecting coats and thermal underwear to give them."

"That's great," said Mom. "I think you'll enjoy that, too, Seth."

"I hope so," replied Seth. He grinned. "Thanks, Mother Walrus, for forcing me to get started by making me go to the nursing home."

"I think I'm getting credit for something the Holy Spirit did," said Mom. "I think he has been working on you."

"Well, maybe," Seth agreed.

Mom gave Seth a hug. "Like I said, I think you'll enjoy the mission work," she told him, "and I *know* you'll be blessed. The Bible says we'll be rewarded when we help the poor."

"Rewarded with blubber, I guess," added Dad, laughing.

"Blubber!" exclaimed Bethany. "That sounds gross. I don't think I'll help with anything like that anymore." She looked at her father. "What do you mean by blubber?" she asked.

"Well, it sounded like this was a walrus family, and God gave walruses lots of blubber—or fat—to protect them from the freezing cold," Dad told her. "When we help the poor, God gives us what we need to protect us from the cold hardships of life." Then he quoted Proverbs 11:25. " ' The liberal soul shall be made fat' " (KJV). Bethany groaned, and Dad laughed. "Actually," he added, "a more recent translation of that verse says, 'A generous man will prosper' " (NIV).

Mom laughed, too. "Service for God never goes unrewarded," she said. *LJR*

HOW ABOUT YOU?

Do you know any poor people? How can you help? Could you offer to babysit—free—for a young family with limited finances? Could you go without a few candy bars to buy gloves and hats to send to a mission? Could you collect canned goods and give them to a community pantry? However you choose to help the needy in your community, you will be blessed.

HELP THE POOR

MEMORIZE:
"If you help the poor, you are lending to the Lord—and he will repay you!"
Proverbs 19:17

February

4

"Hi, Mom." Sean sat down with a heavy sigh.

"What's bothering you, Sean?" asked Mom as she added ingredients to the almond bars she was making. "Did something go wrong at school?"

"Not really. It's just that I don't seem to fit in," replied Sean. "I'm not much good in sports, so I can't make the soccer team. I can't carry a tune, so I can't join the choir. I'm not even much good at math or science. I don't belong anywhere."

"What about the help you give Mr. Martinez in the library?" asked Mom. "You belong there. Mr. Martinez depends on you to return books to the shelves. That's important. And then there's your after-school duty, guiding the smaller children to the right bus. You're a good helper."

Sean looked doubtful. "Aw, Mom, those little jobs don't count. Anybody could do them."

"But not quite like you can, Sean," said Mom. "I know you would be greatly missed if you left your jobs for somebody else to do."

That evening after supper, Mom's almond bars were served. "These don't taste quite right to me," observed Mom after trying one. She took another bite. "Almond!" she exclaimed. "I forgot to put the almond flavoring in these bars!"

Dad laughed. "The missing ingredient," he said.

"Just a little thing, but so important," said Mom. "Maybe we can learn from my mistake," she suggested with a smile. "Dad, me, and you, Sean—each one of us is like one of God's essential ingredients, and we each have our own special job to do. If one of us is missing, life lacks something important. These bars take only a little flavoring, but it's important. And even the things we consider to be 'little jobs' are important, too."

Dad nodded. "That's right," he agreed. "So be faithful where God has put you right now. Don't be a missing ingredient." *KJH*

HOW ABOUT YOU?

Are you eager to serve God where you are right now? Do you sometimes feel like you don't fit in—like you're not good at anything important? Today's Scripture points out that what your talents are is not as important as what you do with them. Even "little" tasks done for the Lord are important, and he will someday reward you for serving him.

MEMORIZE:

"Whoever can be trusted with very little can also be trusted with much." Luke 16:10, NIV

YOU ARE GOD'S SPECIAL INGREDIENT

REACHING THE GOAL

Read: Hebrews 12:1-2

Bailey threw the basketball as high as he could, but it fell far short of the goal. "I can't reach it," whined the four-year-old. "I don't like this game. I wish Grammie had brought me something else for my birthday."

"Let's see if I can help you," said Dad. He removed a bolt and lowered the basket on the pole. "Now with a little stretching and practice, you should be able make it. Try again."

Bailey picked up the ball and threw it. It hit the rim and bounced. "You almost made it," encouraged Dad. "Keep trying."

Bailey was still trying, and doing better, when Mom called them in. "Dinner's ready," she said.

As they ate, Bailey proudly announced, "I made seven-eighty points for my team." Everyone chuckled.

"You've got quite an imagination," said Stewart, grinning at his little brother. He buttered a slice of bread. "We have the neatest science project going," he said. "I like working in the lab. I'm going to be a research scientist when I grow up." He grinned. "I may be the one who discovers the cure for cancer."

Mom smiled. "I pray someone does that long before you graduate," she said.

Bailey stuck out his chest. "I'm gonna be a famous basketball player."

Stewart grinned. "You've got a lot of stretching to do first." He pushed away from the table. "May I be excused, please? I think I'll shoot a few baskets myself."

"Have you done your homework?" asked Dad.

Stewart shrugged. "No. I'll do it later."

"Better get at it now," said Dad. "If Bailey's going to be a famous basketball player, he'll have to do a lot of stretching first, and if you're going to reach your goal of being a scientist, you'll have to do some mind stretching." *BJW*

HOW ABOUT YOU?

What do you want to be when you grow up? Be open to whatever God has for you, and then work toward your goal. Some of the steps may not be fun, but each step is necessary. With God's help, you can become whatever he wants you to be.

STRETCH TO REACH YOUR GOAL

MEMORIZE:

"I strain to . . . receive the prize for which God, through Christ Jesus, is calling us up to heaven."
Philippians 3:14

LIFE-GIVING FLOOD

Read: Acts 12:5-7, 11-17

"Hey, Mom, can I have this old plant?" asked Claudio. "It was in the garage." He held a potted geranium plant that appeared to be dead.

"Why do you want it?"

"At school today, I saw desert pictures in a book," he said. "One picture showed a dusty, brown desert, with a cactus sticking up. Another showed the same scene after it rained, with green shrubs and flowers blooming. So . . . I want to see if this plant will come back to life if I water it good."

With Mom's permission, Claudio put the plant, pot and all, into a pan of water. After the dry soil absorbed a lot of water, he set it in a warm, sunny window. A few days later, he discovered that small green shoots had sprung out of the apparently dead stem.

That evening, while Claudio was telling his family about the success of his experiment, Mom answered the phone. "Carl Chavez has had a heart attack," said Mother when she had hung up the phone. "He's in serious condition, and all the church members are being asked to pray for him."

"Does it help to have lots of people pray?" asked Claudio. "Or is it best to pray a whole lot about something yourself?"

"Well," Dad spoke up, "we certainly need to stay in touch with Jesus regularly. Careful, consistent prayer helps us grow spiritually—just like regular, careful watering of that geranium would have kept it in better condition. But extreme circumstances call for extreme actions. The story of Peter's deliverance from prison demonstrates that. Just like your geranium needed a flood of water, sometimes we need 'floods' of prayer."

"Yes," agreed Mother. "God honors our urgent requests and large volumes of prayer when the need is great."

"And we need to pray for Mr. Chavez right now," added Dad. "Let's pray together." *NR*

HOW ABOUT YOU?

Have you prayed for someone who was sick or had an urgent need? Have you had a special need that you had no way to meet yourself? Remember to talk regularly to the Lord about all the things that happen in your life. And don't be afraid to ask other believers to join you in praying about special, urgent requests. He wants you to do that.

MEMORIZE:

"The earnest prayer of a righteous person has great power and wonderful results." James 5:16

PRAYER BRINGS RESULTS

THE PICTURE PUZZLE

Read: Romans 12:3-8

Marissa, Natasha, and Darren decided to work their new 500-piece picture puzzle. The cover showed a picture of three sailing boats out at sea. "Let's empty all the pieces onto the table and turn them up the right way first," suggested Darren.

"There sure are a lot of different colors in this puzzle," said Marissa as she tipped the box over and pieces of all shapes and colors tumbled onto the table. "Some of the pieces are black or a dull grey. I like the ones with the pretty, sunshiny yellow color."

"I like the reds and oranges, too," said Natasha. "Those are the ones I want to work with. The ones with a lot of brown and dark blue are dull and ugly."

"Maybe so, but they're all part of the puzzle, and we need them all to finish the picture," Darren told her. He pointed to the cover of the box. "We couldn't make a picture like that if all the pieces were red and orange!"

"Like people," murmured Mom, who was working nearby. The children looked at her curiously. "We're all so different—tall and short, thin and heavier, quick and slow—but if we know the Lord, we're all part of his family," she explained. "We all look different and we all have different abilities, but we're all needed."

"Yeah. Imagine if everybody was a teacher—who would there be to listen to them? And who would grow the food for us to eat?" asked Darren.

"It figures you would think about food!" teased Natasha.

"Well, I know what you'd think about!" said Darren, with a grin. "You'd worry about who would make you clothes." *MTF*

HOW ABOUT YOU?

What has God called you to be? You don't have to feel unimportant or inferior if he hasn't called you to be a preacher or teacher; nor should you think that only professions such as medicine or law are important. God calls different people to all different kinds of work. If you are faithfully carrying out the task he has assigned to you, then you are doing the most important work you can do!

CHRISTIANS
ARE NEEDED
IN ALL
OCCUPATIONS

MEMORIZE:

"He is the one who gave these gifts to the church: the apostles, the prophets, the evangelists, and the pastors and teachers . . . to equip God's people to do his work and build up the church, the body of Christ." Ephesians 4:11-12

February

8

(based on a true experience)

John stumbled into the house. "I don't want to die, Mommy! I don't want to die!" he cried. He was an MK (missionary's kid) who lived in Chicosa, a village deep in the Peruvian jungle of South America.

"John!" exclaimed his mother. "What happened?"

"A . . . s-s-snake bit me," John explained tearfully, showing his mother two fang marks on his right foot. A venomous bushmaster had done its deadly work, and he knew how serious the situation was. "Am I going to die?" he asked as his mom went to radio for help.

"Jesus will take care of you," Mom replied, more calmly than she felt.

When the Christians in the village heard what had happened, many gathered to pray while they waited for the rescue plane to arrive. As they thought about how much God loved John and about the fact that God was in control of the situation, peace came.

John's dad read to him about how God had preserved the life of the apostle Paul when he was bitten by a deadly snake. "We serve the same God that Paul served," Dad reminded him.

John nodded. "God was on the island of Malta with Paul, and he's also in Chicosa with me," he said faintly.

By the time the rescue plane arrived to take him to the hospital, John's foot was swollen, hard, and discolored. But within a few hours, he was receiving the medical help he needed.

After John had been treated at the hospital, he and his parents bowed their heads to thank the Lord for what he had done. "Thank you, Lord Jesus," prayed John, "that you took care of me and that I'm already getting better."

"Yes, thank you, Jesus," added Dad. "Thank you for rescuing John from death." *BJW*

HOW ABOUT YOU?

Has God ever delivered you from death? Maybe you almost had a serious car accident . . . or you were very, very sick, and God healed you. Sometimes God saves us from death, and we don't even realize it. Now would be a good time to thank the Lord for life.

MEMORIZE:

"Our God is a God who saves! The Sovereign Lord rescues us from death." Psalm 68:20

THANK GOD FOR LIFE

THE WINNING LOSERS

Read: Romans 8:35-39

Patting the pocket on his shirt and finding nothing, Ramon searched all his other pockets. "Mark, I lost it," he said, his heart sinking.

"Now what did you lose?" asked Mark.

"My brand new pen," Ramon answered. "Dad gave it to me for my birthday. I shouldn't have taken it to school."

"Not with your record for losing things," agreed Mark, as they continued walking home.

When Ramon reached his house, he went to find Mom. He was surprised to see his father home early. "I didn't know you were here," said Ramon. "Your car's not in the garage."

"I lost my car keys, so one of the men in our office brought me home to get another set," explained Dad. "He's waiting out in front."

Just then Laurie burst through the back door. "It's terrible," she wailed. "I'm losing my best friend! Samantha and her family are moving to Arizona next month."

"Wow!" said Ramon. "I guess everybody in this family is losing things today. How about you, Mom? Did you lose something too?"

Mom smiled. "Not me! At least not today!" she said. "As Grandma used to say, it's a good thing your heads are fastened on, or you'd lose them, too!"

"Yeah!" exclaimed Laurie. "That would be bad."

Dad nodded in agreement. "Well, I'm glad there are some things . . . some very important things that we can never lose," he said. "Take the love of God, for example. Each of us has accepted Jesus as Savior so the love of God is always ours."

"Hey, yeah," said Ramon. "So even though we're a bunch of losers, we're really winners! That's good!" *HAD*

HOW ABOUT YOU?

Do you often lose things? Losing some things can make life inconvenient. Losing other things, like a cherished friend, can be very upsetting. But the good news is that you can never lose God's love. You can count on it for the rest of your life and for all eternity.

MEMORIZE:

"Neither death nor life, neither angels nor demons, neither the present nor the future, nor any powers, neither height nor depth, nor anything else in all creation, will be able to separate us from the love of God that is in Christ Jesus our Lord." Romans 8:38-39, NIV

GOD'S LOVE IS FOREVER

Read: Psalm 4:3-5

"Mom never has time for me anymore," complained Ashley as she and her brother, Jeremy, cleared the table.

"Well, she's had to work long hours since Dad left," said Jeremy.

"I know," admitted Ashley, "but she could spend a *little* more time with us."

"Have you told her how you feel?" asked Jeremy.

Ashley shook her head. "If she really loved me, she'd know without my having to spell it out." She scraped some leftover fish into her cat's bowl.

Later, Ashley noticed her cat making choking sounds. "Mom, come quick!" she called. "Something's wrong with Oliver!"

Mother hurried to investigate. "Oh, my!" she said. "Let's get him to the vet."

After an hour they arrived back home. The veterinarian had discovered that Oliver was choking on a fish bone, and he successfully pulled it out.

"It's my fault," Ashley said, "because I gave him fish bones."

"It's okay, honey," said Mom. "Oliver couldn't tell you what his problem was, so you had no way of knowing about the bone in his throat." She looked at her watch. "Now, you kids should get to bed," she added. "I'm going to work in the den for a while."

At the door of his room, Jeremy hesitated. "Ashley, remember how you said that if Mom really loved you, she'd know how you felt without you explaining it to her?" he asked. "Well, you love Oliver and didn't mean to hurt him, but *you* couldn't tell how he felt without being told. Why is Mom any different from you?"

Ashley stood still. "Maybe you're right," she said. "Ollie couldn't tell me what was wrong, but since I can tell Mom about my problem, I should." She turned toward the den. "Thanks, Jeremy," she said. "I'm going to have a talk with Mom." *CW*

HOW ABOUT YOU?

Are you upset with someone? It's natural to get angry sometimes, and there are times when it may even be justified. But the Bible says you shouldn't go to bed angry. Don't hold a grudge; grudges generally get worse and often turn to hate if you don't stop them. Follow God's command by talking about the problem and settling it before you go to sleep.

MEMORIZE:

" 'Don't sin by letting anger gain control over you.' Don't let the sun go down while you are still angry."
Ephesians 4:26

DON'T HOLD
A GRUDGE

AUNT LILLIAN

Read: 2 Timothy 4:1-8

Mark and his mother were at the hospital to visit Aunt Lillian. She wasn't really anyone's aunt. It was just an affectionate nickname given to her by the many, many children she had taught in Sunday school in the past years. "How good to see you," Aunt Lillian said, greeting her visitors.

"How are you doing?" Mark's mother asked.

"Oh, just fine! I've been able to witness to the man across the hall and had a good opportunity to share my faith with some of the nurses, too," replied Aunt Lillian excitedly. "I know the Lord put me here for a purpose, and I figure that purpose is to be cheerful and share his love with others. But, oh, how I wish he'd come back! Wouldn't it be glorious if he came today?" Several times during their conversation, Aunt Lillian referred to her desire for Jesus to return.

"Aunt Lillian is surely 'fighting a good fight,' " observed Mom as she and Mark left.

"Fighting?" asked Mark, puzzled. "You always tell me not to fight."

"She isn't getting into any fist fights," Mom assured Mark with a smile. "What I mean is that she's working hard at serving the Lord, even in the hospital. She's doing all she can to be a witness for him."

"She sure is cheerful about everything," observed Mark.

Mom nodded. "Even her cheerful attitude is a testimony for Jesus," she said. "No wonder she's so eagerly looking forward to the Lord's return—she's living a life pleasing to him." Mom paused and shook her head. "She puts me to shame sometimes. I'm often so busy that I don't even think about his return for long periods at a time."

Mark was listening carefully to his mother. "Me, neither," he confessed. "I guess I should." *LMW*

HOW ABOUT YOU?

Are you living in such a way that you would be happy to have the Lord return today? Are you obedient, helpful, and witnessing for the Lord? Are you developing love, patience, kindness? In other words, are you "fighting a good fight" for the Lord? Consider making a poster to hang in your room as a reminder that he is coming. It could say "Perhaps today . . ." Make up your mind to live a life that is pleasing to him in every way.

LOOK FORWARD TO JESUS' RETURN

MEMORIZE:

"I have fought a good fight, I have finished the race, and I have remained faithful." 2 Timothy 4:7

12

FISH OUT OF WATER

Read: Psalm 146:1-2, 10

During family devotions, Travis was thinking about his ball game. Suddenly he realized that everyone was staring at him. "Travis! It's your turn," said Dad. "You haven't been paying attention again."

"My turn? Uh . . . for what?" asked Travis.

"We're taking turns telling specific things we want to praise God for," explained Dad.

"Well, let me see. . . ." Travis tried to think. His little sister sighed impatiently in the chair next to him. Finally, Dad called on someone else.

The next afternoon, Travis received a shock when he went to his room. "Mom!" he cried. "Oscar's dead!"

When Mom came into the room, Travis showed her a small jar with Oscar, his goldfish, lying at the bottom. The jar was almost dry. "Where's his water?" asked Mom.

"Well, I started changing it, and I had just scooped Oscar into this jar when Mark stopped for me on the way to school. I thought he could live in here for a while," explained Travis.

"Travis, you know fish have to live in water," said Mom.

"I know . . . but there *is* water in this jar," said Travis. "Why do they need so much?"

"That's just the way God made them," replied Mom. "The water in that little jar is not deep enough."

During family devotions that evening, Travis was again inattentive. Finally, Mom said, "Travis, remember when we talked about how God made fish to live in water? Without enough water, they will die. Well, God made his children to worship and praise him."

Travis's eyes opened wide. "You mean . . . if I don't praise and worship God, I'll die—like Oscar did?" he asked.

"No, but you will become weak spiritually," said Dad. "I think you need to ask God to help you worship and praise him with your whole heart." *NCH*

HOW ABOUT YOU?

Is your mouth filled with praise for God? Do you praise him at home, on the school bus, in your classroom, on the playground? Have you praised him today? Have you thought about what a great God he is and worshiped him? Take a few minutes right now to do that.

MEMORIZE:

"But you are a chosen people . . . that you may declare the praises of him who called you out of darkness into his wonderful light." 1 Peter 2:9, NIV

YOU WERE MADE TO PRAISE GOD

WHY WAIT SO LONG?

Read: Romans 10:11-17

For a long time, Tom had been trying to find courage to witness to his friend, Amal. Many opportunities slipped by while he sat tongue-tied, too scared to say a word. But he knew he should talk to Amal and one day he made up his mind that he was going to do it! So he called Amal and invited him to come over.

Amal came, and the very first time Tom saw a chance to witness, he took a deep breath and plunged in. To his great surprise, Amal was very much interested, and before the evening ended, Amal had asked Jesus to be his Savior. "Why didn't you tell me about this before?" Amal asked. "Since it's really important, seems like you'd tell me—your best friend—about it."

Tom blushed. "I'm sorry. I know I should have," he admitted. "But I sure am glad you're a Christian now."

"Me, too!" Amal grinned at his friend. He looked at his watch. "Well, I gotta go home—I'll see you tomorrow, Tom."

The next morning, Tom was up early for breakfast. "Oh, yummy! Pancakes!" he said, smacking his lips. Just then the doorbell rang. Tom opened the door and saw Amal standing there.

"Tom, you'll never believe what has happened. My grandfather has died and now my family will need to move back to India to take care of his business. We will be leaving by the end of this week. I am so glad you told me about Jesus. Now I can take him with me to India."

"I'm glad too!" Tom said. "But I'm sorry to hear that you'll be moving. Come in for breakfast, and I'll tell you more about Jesus!" *JLH*

HOW ABOUT YOU?

Have you put off telling someone about Jesus just like Tom did? Fortunately, he was able to share Jesus with Amal before Amal moved to another country. Pray and ask God to help you know what to say and when to say it. He will help you.

MEMORIZE:
"How can they believe in him if they have never heard about him?"
Romans 10:14

BE A WITNESS

DO I HAVE TO SMILE?

Read: Ephesians 4:32

Benjamin and his mother and brother were at the grocery store to pick out valentine treats for his first-grade class.

"How many kids are in your class?" asked his older brother, Eric, as they made their way to the candy aisle. Benjamin shrugged.

"There are 21 people, counting Benjamin and his teacher," said Mom.

Benjamin picked up a package of candy. "Can I get this one?"

Mom looked at the package. "If we get this, we'll need two bags. There are only 20 pieces in one bag."

"That's enough," said Benjamin.

"Ben, 20 treats won't be enough for 21 people," said Eric.

"I'm not giving one to Steven." Benjamin took the package and headed for the checkout. "He's mean to me and I don't like him."

Mom pulled Benjamin back into the candy aisle. "Benjamin," she said, "you will not take treats unless you share them with everyone—Steven, too."

"But I don't like Steven," he said stubbornly. "He can't have any of my candy."

Mom looked at him sternly. "Valentine's Day is supposed to be about love, Ben," she said quietly. "So, either get some treats for Steven, too, or put all the candy back."

Benjamin picked up another bag of candy. "Well, all right . . . Steven can have some, but I'll look mad when I give it to him."

"Doesn't sound very loving to me," Eric said, as he helped his little brother carry the candy to the checkout. "I learned a Bible verse in Sunday school last week that says if we're living for God, we must always be kind to everyone, not just to people we like."

"You mean I have to smile when I give Steven his candy?" asked Benjamin, making a face. "He probably won't even say thank you."

"Maybe not," said Eric, "but you should smile anyway."

"I agree," said Mom, "and I'm sure God agrees!" *LFC*

HOW ABOUT YOU?

Is it sometimes hard to be kind to a person who is not nice to you? Today's Scripture reading says, "Be kind and compassionate to one another, forgiving each other" (NIV). God doesn't say, "Be kind only to kids you like—to those who are nice to you." He says to be kind to everyone. Can you be friendly and perhaps even share with someone who has been unkind to you? Do it for Jesus' sake—with a smile!

MEMORIZE:

"Don't get involved in foolish, ignorant arguments that only start fights."
2 Timothy 2:23

BE KIND TO EVERYONE

WHAT SHALL I BE?

Read: Colossians 3:23-24

"Know what, Mom?" said Jack. "I think I'll be a preacher when I grow up."

Mom grinned at Jack. "Great!" she said. "Of course, if God wants you to be a doctor, a lawyer, a dentist, or a pilot, I hope you're willing to be that, too. As for now, I need you to be an errand boy. I need some things from the mall."

"Okay," Jack said cheerfully.

The first stop he made was at the shoe repair shop to pick up his mother's shoes. "Here you are," said Mr. Chin. "These shoes of yours have good soles now." He smiled at Jack as he added, "How is the soul within you? Have you asked Jesus to save your soul?" Jack replied that he had, and they had a nice visit.

Jack stopped at the bakery next. "Do you like to make all these good things to eat?" he asked. The baker nodded. "Flour, shortening, raw eggs, and salt don't taste good alone, but put them together with milk and sugar, and you can make something really delicious," he said. "It reminds me of the way God uses our life experiences to make something good. The Bible says, 'All things work together for good to those who love God' " (Romans 8:28, NKJV).

As Jack headed home, he saw Officer Pete. "Do you like to put people in jail?" asked Jack.

"No," answered the officer, "but the Bible says we should obey the laws and our rulers. God wants those who break the laws to be punished and the good people rewarded."

Jack walked home thoughtfully. "Mom," he said that evening, "I found out that even if God wants me to be a baker, a policeman, or anything else, I can still be a preacher, too. Everybody I saw today did a good job of preaching." *AGL*

HOW ABOUT YOU?

Are you willing to be whatever God wants you to be? He needs people who love him and are willing to serve him in every occupation.

WITNESS WHERE
YOU ARE

NEAL'S BARGAIN

Read: Isaiah 58:2-9

"I don't think I'm going to church or Bible club anymore! I don't think I believe the Bible anymore, either!" declared Neal loudly.

"Why, Neal! What's wrong?" asked Mom. "Why would you say such things?"

"Well, our memory verse last week was Psalm 37:4. It says if I delight myself in the Lord, he'll give me the desires of my heart," answered Neal, "so I decided to try it. You know how badly I want a new bike, so I spent this whole week reading the Bible and singing Bible verse songs and thinking nice thoughts about Jesus—you know . . . delighting myself in the Lord. And I still don't have a bike! God didn't keep his part of the bargain, so I don't think I'm going to believe the Bible anymore!" With that, Neal slammed the back door as he went outside.

Later that evening, Mom talked to him about it. "Neal, do you remember what you said earlier about not believing God's Word?" she asked. "Maybe you didn't really meet the conditions of the promise. Here—read these verses."

Neal took the Bible from Mom and read from Isaiah, chapter 58. He gave his mother a puzzled look.

"You see," Mom said, "delighting yourself in the Lord is more than reading the Bible and singing songs just for the purpose of getting your own desires."

As the weeks passed, Neal did continue to go to church and Bible club. "Neal, how's your bike fund coming along?" asked Mom one day.

Neal grinned. "Well, I saved enough to buy one now," he said, "but I think I want to use part of the money to help send that boy down the street to church camp next summer."

Mom nodded. "I think you've been learning to delight yourself in the Lord the Scriptural way," she said. *REP*

HOW ABOUT YOU?

Are you someone who "wants what he wants when he wants it"? You can't bribe God into giving it to you by pretending to "delight" in him. Instead, seek to please the Lord with your life and allow him to sometimes change your heart's desires.

MEMORIZE:

"I take joy in doing your will, my God."
Psalm 40:8

DELIGHT IN
THE LORD

RULES, RULES, RULES

Read: 2 Timothy 3:14-17

"No, Tom," Mom repeated firmly, "you cannot stay at John's tonight. You know that Friday night is our family night, and you have to be here. It's our rule."

"Rules, rules, rules," Tom grumbled. "I don't see why there have to be so many rules."

"Rules are a necessary part of life," replied Mom. "Besides, Dad is pouring cement tomorrow, and he needs your help."

The next morning, Tom got up early to help his dad with the driveway. First, they dug out the dirt and stones. Next, they carefully placed boards all around the area where they wanted the cement. These were called "form boards," and they would hold the cement in place until it dried. Finally, they mixed the cement, poured it into the area enclosed by the form boards, and smoothed it with a trowel.

During family devotions that night, Tom said, "Pouring cement with Dad today helped me learn something."

"What was that?" asked Mom.

"Well," said Tom, "if it weren't for the form boards, the cement would have run all over instead of staying where we needed it. I guess rules are like form boards. They help me to grow up the way I should."

"You're right, Tom," said Dad. "Tell me . . . what happens when we take the form boards out after the cement hardens?"

"Nothing," said Tom. "The cement will still stay in place when it's dry. It will be firm and hard and I can play basketball on it and it will hold the car and won't get rutted like the old dirt driveway did."

Dad nodded. "In the same way, as you become a mature Christian, some rules can be taken away, and you'll still live the way God wants a Christian to live," he said. *AD*

HOW ABOUT YOU?

Are you willing to follow rules that will help you to grow up and become strong? As you obey your parents, teachers, and others in authority, you're obeying God and becoming stronger for him.

RULES HELP YOU GROW

MEMORIZE:
"Train up a child in the way he should go, and when he is old he will not depart from it." Proverbs 22:6, NKJV

18

WONG'S HISTORY

Read: Psalm 78:2-8

Wong hated history! "Why study things that happened so long ago?" he'd complain. His dislike for history carried over into church, also. When it came to studying the kings and judges in the Old Testament, Wong thought it was boring.

"The Bible itself tells us that all Scripture is inspired by God and is profitable to us," said Pastor Phillips when Wong complained to him. "We can learn from the lives of the Old Testament saints." But Wong was not convinced.

One summer, Wong's family took a vacation to visit some famous historical spots. As they walked through places where history actually took place, Wong discovered that he *was* interested in learning about them. The tour guides and brochures were fascinating! After reading the information at one of the Civil War battlefields, he exclaimed, "Their battle plan didn't make any sense! They marched in lines across the open fields and shot at each other!"

Dad nodded. "I think Civil War generals should have studied the Revolutionary War more," he said. "They might have learned some better battle strategies."

At Washington, D.C., they visited various monuments. "I'm beginning to understand more about history," said Wong. "It's neat that someone built all these monuments to remind us of the great people and all they did."

Wong's father looked thoughtful. "You know what monuments I'd like to see?" he asked. "I wish we could go to Israel and see the monuments people built in Old Testament times to remind them of God and the wonderful things he did."

Wong grinned. "Hey, yeah! Let's go!" he said.

Dad laughed. "I wish we could, but we can't," he replied. "Some of those monuments aren't even there anymore. But the stories are recorded in the Bible, so at least we can learn from the lives of the people who built them." *REP*

HOW ABOUT YOU?

Have you ever wondered why so much of the Bible is the story of the history of the nation of Israel? If you'll study their successes and failures you can learn much from them. They will teach you about our great God and how to serve him better.

MEMORIZE:

"Do not steal your neighbor's property by moving the ancient boundary markers set up by your ancestors."
Proverbs 22:28

LEARN FROM
THE PAST

FRUIT OUT OF SEASON

Read: 2 Timothy 4:1-2; 1 Peter 3:15

Tony looked at the bowl of shiny, red apples on the kitchen table. "Can I eat one?" he asked.

Mom nodded. "Sure," she said.

Tony reached for the biggest apple and took a bite. "Wow, Mom, we haven't had apples like these for a long time!" he said. "They're so sweet and juicy!"

"I'm glad you like them," said Mom with a smile. "They certainly are expensive at this time of year. I guess that's because they're out of season."

"Out of season? What does that mean?" asked Tony.

"We call the time apples get ripe the 'season' for apples," Mom explained, "and that's in the fall. These apples had to be brought in by truck from another state farther south."

Dad had come in and overheard the conversation. " 'Out of season,' " he mused. "That makes me think of the Bible verse that says, 'Be prepared in season and out of season.' It means that we should witness when it's convenient, and also when it's not." He looked over at Mom. "Remember Mrs. Cranston?"

"Who's she?" asked Tony.

"She's the lady who led Dad to the Lord," said Mom. "And soon after he accepted the Lord, I did, too."

Dad nodded. "I was just getting started in the insurance business, and the Cranstons were among my first customers," he said. "They often witnessed to me, but I didn't pay much attention. Then one day Mr. Cranston died. I went to see his wife about his insurance policy—and before I left, she looked at me with a tearful smile and said, 'I'm glad I know Bob is with Jesus. Won't you accept Christ, too?' I was so impressed by her testimony at such a time that I did receive Christ soon afterwards. I'd say she was witnessing 'out of season'—at a time when she was so sad over losing her husband." *SLK*

HOW ABOUT YOU?

God wants you to be a witness to others—not only when it's easy or convenient, but also when you're busy, tired, or have other things on your mind. Pray and read the Bible daily. That will help you be prepared both "in season" and out!

BE READY
TO WITNESS,
EVEN IN
DIFFICULT TIMES

MEMORIZE:
"Preach the Word; be prepared in season and out of season."
2 Timothy 4:2, NIV

February

20

Ben Summers quietly slipped around the corner and out of sight as he heard a group of children laughing in the hall. They're probably laughing at me, he thought. The kids hadn't given him any reason to believe that, but Ben was too concerned about what others thought of him. Whenever he saw any of his classmates looking his way, he was sure they were thinking something bad about him. As a result, he was painfully bashful. When his teacher asked a question in class, Ben never raised his hand, even though he usually knew the answer. And although he was a Christian, he was too shy to tell anyone about Jesus. Ben was not very happy.

One day Ben's English teacher gave a writing assignment. "I want you to learn how to describe people—to tell what they are like," she said. "So pick out a student in our class and write a paper describing that person."

The following day the teacher returned the corrected papers. She suggested they read some of them aloud and asked if anyone would object if the papers were read. No one seemed to mind, so they began.

As the students took turns reading, Ben was amazed to discover that several had written about him! As he listened to what they said, he was further surprised. Someone mentioned that he had freckles—but said they were "nice" ones. Someone else actually said he was "cute"! Almost everybody mentioned how smart he or she thought he was. No one called him bashful, but most of them said he was "quiet." It sounded as if they really would like a chance to get to know him better.

I guess the other kids aren't so bad—they're people just like me, thought Ben. *Maybe I should stop thinking so much about myself, and start thinking about them for a change. SLK*

HOW ABOUT YOU?

Are you like "Bashful Ben"? Not everyone is outgoing and talkative. That's all right—but God still expects you to be friendly and to tell others about him. Everyone needs friendship, and everyone needs Jesus. Don't worry about whether or not others will like you. Just be kind and friendly to them. Think less about yourself and more about their needs and interests.

MEMORIZE:

"Whoever loves God must also love his brother." 1 John 4:21, NIV

BE FRIENDLY

LIFE'S PUZZLE

Read: Psalm 25:1-5

Steve twisted and turned the squares on his puzzle cube. No matter how he turned it, the colors never seemed to line up right. Finally he tossed it aside. "Any jobs for you in the paper, Dad?" he asked.

"Nothing promising," sighed Dad. Seeing the look of despair in Steve's face, he added, "Don't worry. Something will turn up. The Lord has never failed us."

Steve wished he had his dad's faith. Four months ago Dad had lost his job when the company he worked for had gone bankrupt. Then, when they did not have any insurance, Steve's little sister had to be hospitalized. And last week Dad had sold their second car to pay for the insurance on the first one.

Dad looked at the puzzle cube that Steve had thrown on the couch. "Having trouble with that?"

"It's hopeless," Steve shrugged.

Dad went to the hall closet. "I have something that might help you." He returned with a paperback book. "Picked this up at a used book sale."

" 'How to Solve Puzzle Cubes,' " Steve read. He took the book and the puzzle into his room. Later that evening, his dad heard him shout, "Whoopee! I did it!"

Dad went to Steve's room to check it out. "Congratulations," said Dad. "It's quite a puzzle, but when you follow the directions, it all falls in place. It reminds me of life—life is a bit puzzling at times, too."

Steve nodded. "Yeah, I know. Like, why do we have to have all this trouble?"

"Christians are not immune to problems," said Dad, "but we have a heavenly Father to help us, and we also have a book of instructions. God teaches us as we patiently follow this Book," he held up his Bible, "and everything in life will fall in place." *BJW*

HOW ABOUT YOU?

Is something puzzling you? Do you have problems that seem hopeless? Get out God's instruction book—the Bible—and be taught. Trust the Lord (don't fret or worry), and praise him as you patiently wait. In time the puzzle will take shape, and you'll be able to see the pattern God is making in your life.

THE BIBLE IS GOD'S INSTRUCTION BOOK

MEMORIZE:
"Lead me by your truth and teach me." Psalm 25:5

February

22

Arriving home in a huff, Nat slammed the door. When his dog ran to greet him, Nat pushed him aside. "Get away, Bo! I'm not in the mood," he snarled.

"Nat!" exclaimed Mom, "What's the problem?"

"Oh, it's that dumb play at school! I never get one of the big parts," Nat complained.

"Well, what part did you get?" Mom asked.

"None—but Ken and Greg did! All I get to do is work on scenery," grumbled Nat.

"Well, you are good in art," Mom reminded him. "I bet Ken and Greg would love to be able to draw like you do." But Nat just scowled and left the room.

All the time Nat worked on the scenery, he seethed with jealousy. He was glad when the play was over.

As Nat was roller-skating a few days later, he fell and broke his right arm and wrist. "There, now. You'll soon be good as new," said the doctor as he put a cast on the arm.

During the following days, Nat was surprised at how much the cast bothered him. He whined, "I'm sick of this cast, and it's only been a week."

"Maybe you can learn a lesson from this," Mom said. "Remember when you wanted to be the star of the play, but you were chosen to draw scenery instead?"

"What's that got to do with my cast?" Nat asked.

"Well, you don't function well without your fingers, do you?" said Mom. "And that play wouldn't have been good, either, if any part of it were missing. The scenery was as necessary to the play as your fingers are to you, Nat. It wouldn't work for every boy to be the 'star' of the show. You see, the Bible says we each have special gifts, or talents, which God wants us to use. Think about it!" *AU*

HOW ABOUT YOU?

Are you happy with your talents? Or do you wish you could sing as well as your friend? Or that you could play ball as well as a classmate? Do you wish the Lord had given you the ability to stand up in front of people and speak? Be willing to try various things and develop the talents God has given you. Don't waste time wishing for a different gift.

MEMORIZE:

"God has given each of us the ability to do certain things well." Romans 12:6

USE YOUR GIFT

EVERY STEP COUNTS

Read: Psalm 51:1-4, 10

"Dad!" called Sean as he hurried into the house. "Jon is in jail!"

Dad sighed. Jon, the older brother of one of Sean's friends, had been in trouble before. "What did Jon do?" Dad asked.

"Jon and another kid broke into a house and stole some money," replied Sean.

Dad shook his head. "His parents must be very disappointed," he said. "We need to pray for them." Dad stood up. "I was about to go running. Want to come along?"

"Sure!" agreed Sean, and soon they were running along the roadside.

When they came to the place where Dad usually turned to go back, Sean looked at him. "Let's go a little farther this time," suggested Sean.

"Farther?" asked Dad. "You sure?"

"Why not? Can't you hack it, Dad?" Sean teased him.

Dad grinned. "I've been training for weeks," he said.

As they went on, Sean's legs grew heavier. He soon felt as though his lungs were going to explode. Finally, Dad stopped. "Okay, that's enough," said Dad. "Let's head back."

"Yeah. This is . . . far enough," agreed Sean, panting heavily. "It'll take forever . . . to get back . . . from here."

"Well, that's the thing. For every step you go out, you have to take another one to go back," Dad said.

Sean was exhausted. "Why did I ever want to go so far?" he moaned.

"Jon's gone too far, too, hasn't he?" Dad asked as they started back. "It will take a lot of time and effort for him to make everything right again—with the law, with God, and with his folks. Always remember that for every step you go wrong, you have to take another one to go back." *MKN*

HOW ABOUT YOU?

Have you done something that you wish you hadn't done? Remember that the more wrong steps you take, the more difficult it may be to make things right. Start back right now. Ask God to forgive you and to help you.

ALL ACTIONS HAVE CONSEQUENCES

THE THINGS I REMEMBER

Read: Psalm 119:9-16

Marc looked up when he heard Grandpa Burns' question. "Ma, do you know where I left my glasses?" asked Grandpa as he reached for his Bible. Marc was spending the weekend with his great-grandparents.

"Now, Pa, did you lose those glasses again?" scolded Grandma. "You had them on when you paid the paperboy."

"That wasn't today. I paid him yesterday," said Grandpa. "Now . . . " He stopped a moment to cough.

"Your cough is worse," murmured Grandma. "You'd better order more medicine."

"I just got some," said Grandpa. "That's who came today—Leo!" Grandpa turned to Marc. "Leo lives next door, and he went and picked up medicine for me."

Just then Marc spied Grandpa's glasses lying on the table. "Here are your glasses, Grandpa," he said. He laughed when Grandma asked for help in finding hers. "They're on your head," he said.

Grandma laughed, too. "I declare!" she exclaimed. "I clean forgot putting them on."

Grandpa opened his Bible. "Do you memorize many verses, Marc?" he asked. "Your grandma and I learned Psalm 91 and Psalm 103," he said. "Sometimes when our eyes are tired, we just say some of them together."

"There's something I can't understand," said Marc with a puzzled look. "You can't remember things that happened just today—even just a little while ago—so how do you remember things from so long ago?"

Grandpa smiled. "The fact is that most of the things you'll remember are things you learn and do as a child," he said. "They might be good, or they might be bad. That's up to you."

"That's right," agreed Grandma. *HCT*

HOW ABOUT YOU?

Are you hiding God's Word in your heart? Did you learn some verses this past week? To truly learn them—to really have them in your heart—you need to obey them as well as memorize them.

MEMORIZE:

"I have hidden your word in my heart,
that I might not sin against you."
Psalm 119:11

MEMORIZE
BIBLE VERSES

THE BENCHWARMER

Read: 1 Samuel 23:14-18

"I'm quitting basketball," Theo announced.

"Quitting!" exclaimed Dad. "Earlier this year, you could hardly wait to join the team."

Theo frowned. "All I am is a benchwarmer," he complained. "Coach Adams hardly ever lets me play."

"Coach Adams told me that you have great potential," said Dad.

"If he thinks I'm so great, why doesn't he let me play in more games?" asked Theo.

"The older boys have more experience," said Dad, "and Coach Adams is naturally going to use his best players when it's necessary for a win."

"I can play just as well as they can," said Theo. "At least, I could if I got to play in more games."

"Learn to be patient," said Dad. "We need to be 'benchwarmers'—people who wait patiently—in many areas of life."

"I've waited long enough," grumbled Theo. "The basketball games are nearly over for this year."

Dad picked up a Sunday school take-home paper from Theo's desk. "I see you've been learning about David," said Dad. "He was a benchwarmer, too."

"David never played basketball!" protested Theo.

"No," Dad said, "but he was a benchwarmer. When David was just a boy, the prophet Samuel anointed him to be king, but he had to wait about twenty years before he actually became king."

"Yeah," said Theo, "but being king is important. I don't think God cares if I play basketball or not."

"Maybe not," said Dad, "but *basketball* is not so much the issue as *quitting* is. When God allows us to go through experiences like this, he expects us to develop important virtues—like patience."

"Okay," Theo said with a sigh. "I get the point." He stood up. "How about a little one-on-one, Dad?"

"You're not quitting after all?" asked Dad.

"Not me," said Theo. "I just hope it doesn't take me 20 years to get into more games." *JRL*

HOW ABOUT YOU?

Do you ever feel like giving up? Learn now, through everyday experiences, to develop patience and endurance. It's always hard to wait for things, but God rewards persistence. Don't be a quitter.

LEARN TO BE PATIENT

MEMORIZE:

"Follow the example of those who are going to inherit God's promises because of their faith and patience."

Hebrews 6:12

THE WHINING SISTER

Read: James 4:1-3

As Shane took out a pile of homework, he heard Kris, his three-year-old sister, loudly complaining about something. He began to work, but the noise his sister was making distracted him. "Mom, what's wrong with Kris?" Shane asked impatiently. "Her whining is driving me crazy. I have more homework than anyone should be expected to do, and she's not making it any easier." Kris made a face and threw a sock at Shane.

"She wants someone to put her socks on for her," Mom answered calmly.

"But she knows how to put her own socks on," said Shane. "Oh, well . . . I'll do it, just to quiet her down!"

"Just a minute, please," Mom said. "Kris also knows how to ask nicely for things. So far, all she's done is whine and throw her socks."

"Yeah," muttered Shane, "but I don't know if I can stand that noise much longer."

"I wonder if God ever feels that way when we complain and get angry instead of asking him for what we need," said Mom thoughtfully. "I'm sure you'll have to agree that we often complain about things instead of praying about them."

Shane frowned. "You mean like just now when I complained about my homework and Kris's noise?" he asked. "Does God even want me to pray about *those* kinds of things?"

Mom smiled. "I wasn't thinking of that," she said, "but, yes, God wants us to pray about everything." She smiled. "Why don't we pray now?" Mom and Shane bowed their heads. "Dear Father, thank you for caring about all the details of our lives. We recognize that you know what's best for all of us," prayed Mom. "Right now we ask you to help Shane with his homework and to help Kris learn to ask instead of whine. Please help us to do that, too." *DY*

HOW ABOUT YOU?
Do you pray only at mealtimes and bedtime, or do you pray about things all through the day? God cares about everything you care about, and he wants you to ask for his help. He is pleased to give it.

MEMORIZE:
"Keep on praying. No matter what happens, always be thankful."
1 Thessalonians 5:17-18

PRAY CONTINUALLY

WALKING HOME

Read: Psalm 23

Ryan looked at the frail form on the bed. He knew his great-grandfather was probably going to die. "Are you afraid, Grandpa?" he asked.

"No, Ryan," whispered Grandpa as he reached for Ryan's hand. "I'm not afraid to die. Jesus is with me. I am going home to be with him."

Later that afternoon, Ryan's friend Al called.

"Can you come over?" invited Al. "Mom says you can stay for supper." So Ryan walked across the field to Al's house.

After they ate, the boys played computer games. After a while, Ryan glanced out the window. "It's dark!" he exclaimed. "I've got to go!"

As Ryan started across the field, he could barely make out the path. The moon was hidden behind the clouds, casting weird shadows. Strange sounds frightened him. Ryan's heart thumped and his knees felt weak. *Don't be a baby,* Ryan scolded himself. *Shadows can't hurt anyone.*

"Ryan?" a voice called from the darkness. Ryan's heart almost stopped, but then he recognized the familiar voice.

"Oh, Dad, am I glad to see you!" Ryan's voice wobbled. "Well . . . at least I'm glad to *hear* you. It's so dark and shadowy, I can hardly see anything."

"I came to walk home with you," said Dad. "I thought you might like some company crossing this dark field." Ryan nodded.

When they reached home, Ryan went to Grandpa's room and told him about his experience. "Once I knew Dad was there, I wasn't scared anymore," Ryan said, "even though I couldn't see him. It was almost like I could feel him with me." He hesitated. "Is that why you're not afraid to die?" he asked.

"Exactly," said Grandpa. "Death is like a dark shadow, and I can't actually see Jesus—but I know he's there because he promised, and I feel his presence with me." *BJW*

HOW ABOUT YOU?

Do you know someone who is dying? Are you afraid of dying? Death is like a shadow. You do not have to fear it when Jesus is with you.

CHRISTIANS DON'T NEED TO FEAR DEATH

MEMORIZE:

"Yea, though I walk through the valley of the shadow of death, I will fear no evil: for thou art with me."
Psalm 23:4, KJV

WHY AM I GUILTY?

Read: Mark 7:20-23; Jeremiah 17:9-10

I've sure studied hard enough for my history test tomorrow, thought Joel, *but there are so many dates to remember! I hope I don't forget them.* As he closed his book, Joel remembered a trick his friend Eddie had told him. On a small piece of paper he wrote the dates that were hard to remember. The next morning, he slipped the paper up his long shirtsleeve. "I'll use this only if I have to," he muttered.

When Joel took the test, he found that studying had paid off. Still, those dates were confusing. He looked over the finished test. Then he glanced at Miss Wilmia. She was busy at her desk, so he slipped the paper out of his sleeve and compared it to his test answers. *Oh, good!* He thought. *I got 'em right.* As he slipped the paper back up his sleeve, he noticed someone standing beside him.

Miss Wilmia reached down for his test. "I'll have to give you a zero," she said.

When his parents learned what had happened, Joel defended his actions. "It's not fair," he insisted. "Eddie cheated lots of times, and he never got caught. Besides, I didn't even do it—I didn't change a single answer! Miss Wilmia could have just taken my paper and graded it. Since I didn't change any answers, how am I guilty?"

"God sees our hearts, Joel," Dad told him. "God knows you planned to change answers if they were wrong. The temptation to sin is not wrong. But when we want to sin—when we plan to sin—that is wrong."

Joel frowned. "But if it all begins with wanting to do something wrong, how do you get rid of the 'want to'?" he asked at last.

"Confess it to God and ask him to help you overcome the temptation," Dad told him. *AU*

HOW ABOUT YOU?

Do you desire to do what is right? Or do you wish you could get away with doing things you know are wrong? If you knew you wouldn't be caught, would you steal? Cheat? Disobey? If so, confess your sin to God. Ask him to help you control your mind and desires.

MEMORIZE:

"I the Lord search the heart and examine the mind." Jeremiah 17:10, NIV

DON'T PLAN
TO SIN

WHO CARES?

Read: Hebrews 2:14-18

Mom brought Tim some hot broth. "This will make you feel a little better," she said as she sat beside him.

As he began to eat, Tim had a question. "Mom, do you think Jesus was ever sick when he lived on earth?"

Mom smiled. "Well, he experienced a lot of the same things we do," she said. Picking up the Bible, she opened it to the book of Matthew. "Here, in chapter four, it says Jesus was hungry. That's something we experience often."

"I'm sure not hungry today," said Tim with a wry smile.

"Not today, maybe," said Mom, "but you will be when you're better. Do you think Jesus ever got tired?"

"One time he fell asleep in a boat during a big storm," remembered Tim. "He must have been really tired! It would be hard to sleep while the boat was bobbing around on big waves."

Mom nodded. "And I believe the Bible specifically mentions that Jesus was tired when he sat on the edge of the well and talked with the Samaritan woman. Now, do you think he was ever sad?"

"Yeah, I think so," said Tim. "He was sad when Lazarus died. The Bible says, 'Jesus wept.' That's the shortest verse in the Bible."

"Right again," said Mom. "So we know there were times when Jesus was hungry, tired, and sad. Although the Bible doesn't exactly say Jesus also experienced sickness, it does say that he became like us in all things—except for one."

"What was that?" Tim asked.

"Sin," said Mom. "Jesus never sinned. He was tempted to sin, but he never gave in to temptation. Because he never sinned, he could be our Savior."

Tim nodded thoughtfully. "It makes me feel closer to Jesus to know he was a lot like me when he was growing up," he said. *CEY*

HOW ABOUT YOU?

Do you ever wonder if Jesus really understands you and your problems? Think about him as a young boy. Jesus was God, but when he came to earth as a baby, he looked and acted like all babies do. While he was a boy, he did many of the same things you do. Jesus understands you.

JESUS UNDERSTANDS YOU

MEMORIZE:

"For this reason he had to be made like his brothers in every way."

Hebrews 2:17, NIV

RAISED EYEBROWS

Read: Philemon 1:3-7

Carl stared at his uncle, who was answering his question. Uncle Frank was moving his eyebrows up and down as he talked. It looked very strange. Carl hesitated, then ventured another question. "Are you glad to be back from the mission field for a while?"

Uncle Frank looked right at Carl and raised his eyebrows a few times. Then he smiled. "It is good to get back to America," he said, "but we do miss the people we've been working with. The small church we started means a lot to the new Christians in that area."

It was after supper when Carl finally got up enough nerve to ask the question to which he really wanted an answer. "Why do you raise your eyebrows so often when we ask you a question?"

Uncle Frank laughed out loud. "Have I been doing that?" he asked. "You see, in the village where we work, that's how we say yes, and now I do it without thinking. When a missionary goes to another country, he not only has to learn a new language, but new gestures as well."

"That must have been hard," Carl said thoughtfully.

"It wasn't easy. Many of the ways of the people seemed strange and difficult at first," said Uncle Frank. "But we knew we were where God wanted us, and I doubt that we'd be very happy anywhere else. Being in God's will is the most important thing to us. Besides, now we love the people there, and we love the work God gave us to do. We think we have the best job in the whole world!" *JAG*

HOW ABOUT YOU?

Do you know any missionaries? They often face difficulties in a foreign country with different languages, gestures, food, and customs. They may also face loneliness, sickness, and fearful situations. Learn as much as you can about your missionaries, and don't forget to pray for them. With the support of your prayers and encouragement, the Lord will bless them and use them as they do the work he sent them to do.

MEMORIZE:

"Every time I think of you, I give thanks to my God. I always pray for you, and I make my requests with a heart full of joy." Philippians 1:3-4

PRAY FOR MISSIONARIES

A LONG TIME

Read: Luke 23:32-34

"Mom!" called Jeremy as he ran into the house. "Mike did it again!"

Mom looked up from her work. "Did what?" she asked.

"He said if I'd play checkers with him, he'd let me use his basketball," Jeremy replied angrily. "But after we played checkers, he wouldn't give me the ball," he complained. "It's not fair! I'm never going to play with him again!"

"Never is a long time, Jeremy," said Mom.

"Yeah? Well, I don't care!" yelled Jeremy, and he ran to his room, slamming the door behind him.

Later his mother went to talk with him. "Are you still mad at Mike?" she asked.

"Oh course I am!" exploded Jeremy. "Wouldn't you be?"

Mom thought about it. "Maybe," she admitted, "but what happened to you reminds me of a Bible story."

"It does?" asked Jeremy.

"Yes, it reminds me of Jesus on the cross," answered Mom. "Jesus spent his entire life helping people. He talked with them and taught them important things. He healed many of their diseases—and even raised some back to life. He wanted to be their friend! But instead of being thankful, many people didn't treat him fairly at all."

Jeremy nodded. "A lot of people hated him, and finally they killed him, didn't they?" he said.

Mom nodded. "You know," she continued, "he had every right to hate those people and never talk with them again."

"Kinda like me and Mike, huh?" Jeremy asked.

"Yes," agreed Mom, "but instead of being mad at them, Jesus loved them and asked God to forgive them. He even died for them so their sins could be taken away."

"Mom," Jeremy said slowly, "can I go over to Mike's house?"

"I thought you were never going to play with him again," she said.

"Aw, come on, Mom!" said Jeremy. "Never is a long time!" *PG*

HOW ABOUT YOU?

Have you argued with someone? Or have you been treated unfairly? Has someone not kept a promise? How did you react? Follow the example of Jesus and forgive those who have wronged you. Love them anyway. Perhaps the Lord will use your example and testimony to bring them to Jesus.

FORGIVE AND LOVE

MEMORIZE:

"Instead, be kind to each other, tenderhearted, forgiving one another, just as God through Christ has forgiven you." Ephesians 4:32

March

4

Jim sat at the kitchen table turning the pages of his Bible. "What are you doing?" asked his older sister, Beth.

"Our Sunday school teacher gave us some homework," explained Jim. "He's going to give a reward to the one who finds the most names or titles for God. Hey, maybe you can help me. Don't you learn that kind of stuff in Bible college?" He looked at his sister. "Mr. Benson doesn't care where we get our information, just so we learn."

Beth smiled. "How about 'Good Shepherd?' " she asked. "Remember the sermon on Psalm 23 a few weeks ago?"

"Oh, I forgot about that!" Jim wrote it down.

"The book of John talks about Jesus being the True Vine and the Door," Beth added.

"Oh, yeah! Thanks, Beth!" exclaimed Jim. "I've already got some others from the book of John where Jesus says he is the Way, the Truth, and the Life."

"Don't forget Isaiah 9:6," said Beth. "In that verse God is called Wonderful, Counselor, the Mighty God, the Everlasting Father, and the Prince of Peace."

Jim scribbled the names down. "You're a big help," he said with a grin.

"Thanks," said Beth. "How about Alpha and Omega?"

"Alpha and Omega?" Jim asked doubtfully. "That sounds like Greek to me!"

Beth laughed. "It is Greek, Jim! Alpha and Omega are the first and last letters in the Greek alphabet. It means that God is the beginning and the end of everything."

"Wow, that's neat!" Jim said.

Beth nodded. "And since God is the beginning and the end, it means he always was and always will be. He's everything that each name suggests." *LMW*

HOW ABOUT YOU?

Did you know that God has many names and titles? Why not start a family project and see how many you can find? After you've made your list, write down what each title represents. For instance, the Counselor is someone who can help you when you're faced with a difficult situation. Studying the names of God and what they mean will help you realize how great he is.

MEMORIZE:

"Lord, there is no one like you! For you are great, and your name is full of power." Jeremiah 10:6

LEARN WHO
GOD IS

MATTHEW'S PROBLEM

Read: Psalm 19:12-14

Matt dropped his books on the kitchen table and then slumped down in a chair. "You must have had a bad day," said Mom. "You look like you have all the problems of the world on your mind."

"I do have a problem," Matt agreed. "A serious problem. So many of the kids at school say bad words, and once in a while one of those swear words slips out of my mouth by accident!"

"Why not stay away from those who use bad words?" suggested Mom.

Matt shook his head. "I can't. I hear them in gym class, at recess, in the lunchroom—everywhere, really."

Mom nodded. "I know how you feel," she said. "On the afternoons that I work at the store, customers often throw a couple of swear words into an otherwise normal conversation. I know that sometimes those words tend to stick in your mind."

"So what do you do?" asked Matt.

Mom sighed. "Well, when I have the same problem at work, I do two things. First of all, I pray that the Lord will help me put the word out of my mind. Secondly, I quote some Scripture or start humming a chorus, so that I'm concentrating on something other than the word I just heard. Of course, if someone continually uses bad language in my presence, I politely ask him not to do that."

Matt nodded. "Good idea!" he said. "Thanks, Mom. Next time I hear someone swear, I'll do those things!" *LMW*

HOW ABOUT YOU?

Do you often hear people using bad language? Have you found yourself saying one of those words without thinking? Try the suggestions mentioned in the story. Concentrate on good things.

THINK OF GOOD THINGS

MEMORIZE:

"May the words of my mouth and the thoughts of my heart be pleasing to you, O Lord, my rock and my redeemer." Psalm 19:14

WHY?

Read: Luke 2:41-52

"Mom, make Shawn leave me alone!" Morgan exclaimed as she pushed her little brother into the kitchen. "He follows me everywhere!"

Shawn's eyes clouded with tears. "I do not."

Mom hugged her son and turned to her daughter. "What's the problem?"

"He asks 'why' over and over and over," complained Morgan. "I get so tired of it."

Mom smiled. "I guess you don't remember all the questions you used to ask, do you?"

"What questions?" asked Morgan.

"Oh, there were a lot of them," Mom told her. "Like, 'Why do birds sing?' 'Why do your fingers have nails?' 'Why does Grandpa walk so slow?' Now Shawn is learning by asking questions just like you did."

Morgan laughed. "Well, in that case I guess I better try to be a little more patient," she decided. "But I hope he learns fast. It does get tiresome."

"I realize that," sympathized Mom. "You know, it just occurred to me that when Jesus was a boy, he asked questions, too. Get my Bible from the table." After Morgan brought the Bible, Mom turned several pages. Then she asked Morgan to read a verse.

" 'And it came about that after three days,' " read Morgan, " 'they found Him in the temple, sitting in the midst of the teachers, both listening to them, and asking them questions' " (Luke 2:46, NASB).

Mom took the Bible and closed it. "I've heard some preachers say that Jesus was teaching, but others have suggested that he was also learning," she said. "In any case, maybe it will help us have more patience if we remember that even Jesus asked a lot of questions."

Morgan nodded and held out her hand to her little brother. "Come on, Shawn. Let's go back outside."

Shawn went along happily. Mom smiled when, just before the door closed, she heard Shawn's voice begin, "Morgan, why . . ." *RG*

HOW ABOUT YOU?

Do you become impatient with someone who asks a lot of questions? God does not condemn honest questions, and neither should we. It's a natural way of learning. Ask the Lord to help you to be patient and to be a good teacher when questions are asked of you. When you don't know answers, be sure to ask questions yourself, and learn from the teachers God has provided for you.

MEMORIZE:

"A wise man will hear and increase in learning, and a man of understanding will acquire wise counsel."
Proverbs 1:5, NASB

LEARN BY ASKING
QUESTIONS

TO SIN OR NOT TO SIN

Read: Psalm 139:1-12

"Slow down!" gasped Nathan as he and Mark ran across the parking lot of the shopping center. "I'm tired! What's your hurry anyway?"

"Did you see anyone follow us?" asked Mark breathlessly.

Nathan looked around. "I don't think so. Why?" In reply, Mark pulled a magazine from under his jacket. "Where'd you get that?" Nathan asked. "I didn't see you buy anything."

Mark snickered. "I didn't," he said. "I took it."

"Took it!" exclaimed Nathan. "You mean you stole it? Why?"

Mark shrugged. "Take a look," he said, holding out the magazine to Nathan. "Would you dare walk right up to the counter and take a chance on someone seeing you buy a magazine like this?"

Nathan was shocked. "That's a filthy magazine, Mark! You'd better take it back!"

Mark sneered. "What's the big deal?" he asked. "Nobody saw me take it, and nobody will see me look at it, so nobody will know the difference—unless you're gonna go tell your mommy." He slipped the magazine back under his jacket. "C'mon," he coaxed. "Let's go over to my house and sneak up to my room. It's not going to hurt anything."

Nathan shook his head. "I'm going home," he said.

Mark frowned. "Well, keep your trap shut about it," he said. "I know, and you know, and nobody else better find out!"

As Nathan watched Mark leave, a thought came to his mind. "Hey, Mark," he called out, "you forgot somebody! God knows!"

Mark scowled and continued walking. *BD*

HOW ABOUT YOU?

Do you think nobody saw you cheat? Did you get away with eating a cookie when Mom said you shouldn't? Do you think no one knows the angry thoughts you have about your brother or sister? Or that deep inside you really enjoy dirty jokes? You're wrong! God knows all about you. That can be scary if there are things in your life that do not please him. Confess them and ask God's forgiveness. Ask him to help you be the kind of person he wants you to be.

MEMORIZE:

"Woe to those who seek deep to hide their counsel far from the Lord, And their works are in the dark; They say, 'Who sees us?' and, 'Who knows us?'"

Isaiah 29:15, NKJV

GOD KNOWS ALL ABOUT YOU

LIKE ANDREW AND PETER

Read: John 1:37-42

Rudy waited eagerly for the weekly Bible club to begin. He enjoyed the songs they were learning, and he looked forward to hearing the story his teacher would tell.

After song time, Mrs. Jackson told a story about some fishermen. Rudy leaned forward. He loved to fish! "Some of Jesus' disciples were fishermen," Mrs. Jackson said. "Jesus told them that if they would follow him, he would make them fishers of men."

Rudy raised his hand. "What does that mean?"

"It means to tell other people about Jesus Christ and bring them to him, just like Andrew did," explained Mrs. Jackson. "When Andrew became a follower of Jesus, he brought his brother, Simon Peter."

Rudy looked at the floor. His younger brother, Johnny, had wanted to come to Bible club with him, but Rudy wouldn't let him. "I don't want you tagging along with me," he had said. Johnny had been crying when Rudy had left for Bible club.

The next week, Johnny was amazed when Rudy grabbed his hand and said, "It's time for Bible club. Come with me." Together they ran down the street to the Bible club. This week Mrs. Jackson explained how everyone had sinned and how only the blood of Jesus can wash sin away. Johnny fidgeted in his seat and whispered something to Rudy, who nodded.

After Bible club was dismissed, Rudy took his brother to meet the teacher. "Mrs. Jackson, my brother isn't a Christian. He wants to become one. Would you tell him again how to do that?" asked Rudy. Mrs. Jackson was delighted to help.

"Can I go to Bible club with you next week, too?" Johnny asked as he and Rudy walked back to their home.

"You sure can," Rudy replied. "From now on we're going to follow Jesus together, just like Andrew and Peter did." *TMB*

HOW ABOUT YOU?

Do you have brothers, sisters, or friends who don't know Jesus Christ as their Savior? Have you invited them to Sunday school or Bible club? Have you told them that Jesus loves them and wants to save them from their sins? If you know Jesus, you should be a "fisher of men," working to bring others to him, too.

MEMORIZE:

"Come, follow me," Jesus said, "and I will make you fishers of men." Matthew 4:19, NIV

BE A "FISHER OF MEN"

THE ROPE

Read: Psalm 119:9-16

"Welcome to Preschool Family Day," said Mrs. King as she greeted Aaron's mom and his sister, Jasmine. "Thanks for coming."

Mom and Jasmine watched as Aaron and his classmates colored a picture, listened to the story of *The Little Engine That Could*, and found things in the room that were blue.

After enjoying cookies and juice, Mrs. King clapped her hands for attention. "It's time to line up to go to the playground," she announced. She took two long ropes out of the closet. The boys lined up on one rope, and the girls on the other. Each child held tightly to the rope. Mrs. King took a rope in each hand and led the way out. "Be sure to watch for cars," she reminded the children as they started across the parking lot. The three- and four-year-olds made their way past several parked cars and a big yellow school bus. Their feet kicked up small clouds of dust from the gravel, and they giggled as geese honked from above.

"I remember that rope when I attended this preschool," Jasmine told her mother as they followed the children. "I held on to it for dear life." Then she laughed and added, "The playground seemed much farther away then, and walking past all the cars scared me."

Mother smiled. "We may be older, but we still need to hang on to a rope," she replied. Jasmine looked puzzled, and Mother laughed. "Not a literal rope, but in a way, God's Word is like a rope. We don't have to hold on to it to keep our salvation—the Bible says we are 'kept by the power of God.' But the Bible also tells us to hold on to what is good."

"How do we do that?" asked Jasmine.

"By reading, memorizing, and obeying what God says in his Word," said Mom. *LJR*

HOW ABOUT YOU?

First Thessalonians 5:21 says, "Hold on to what is good." Do you do that? Do you "hold tightly" to what God says? No one can plant God's Word into your heart, except you. No one can make you memorize it. You must make the choice to study God's Word. It takes time and effort, but you will be rewarded. Make Psalm 119:16 your promise to God—"I will not forget your word."

"HOLD ON" TO GOD'S WORD

MEMORIZE:
"I will delight in your principles and not forget your word." Psalm 119:16

NEVER ALONE

Read: 1 Kings 19:1-3, 9, 14-18

"I hate school," cried Brad, throwing his books on the table. "Why did we have to move here anyway? I miss my friends!"

Mom turned from the sink, where she was peeling potatoes. "I know it's hard," she replied, "but you know the reason we moved, Brad."

"Yeah," he said with a sigh, "because Dad got assigned to a new military post."

"Things will be better after you get acquainted," Mom assured him.

Brad took his books to his room and plopped down on the bed. *No one understands how terrible it is to go to a new school,* he thought. *I feel so alone.*

Brad dreaded going to a new church, too. When he was directed to his Sunday school class on the following Sunday, he slipped into the room and sat down in the back row. He listened halfheartedly to the teacher telling a story about Elijah. "Elijah really felt sorry for himself," the teacher said. "He felt alone and forgot to trust God."

Like me, Brad thought guiltily.

"But Elijah wasn't alone," the teacher continued. "God was with him. And God told him that there were several thousand people in Israel who did not turn away from God. He told Elijah that he would be given a helper, Elisha, to train for God's service."

After Sunday school, Brad was greeted by a curly-haired, husky boy who sat near him in school. "Hi, remember me? I'm Tim," he said. "I'm glad you came to this church. Hey, maybe you can go with me to the Bible club we have after school on Tuesdays. Some others from our class go, too."

"Sure." Brad grinned. As he followed Tim into the church auditorium, he thought, *I was feeling sorry for myself—just like Elijah. And, all the time God had some new friends just waiting for me. TMB*

HOW ABOUT YOU?

Are you in a new school or church and feeling like you are all alone? Ask God to help you find a Christian friend, who will then help you make other friends. And, remember, you are not really alone. God is always with you.

MEMORIZE:

"God has said, 'I will never fail you. I will never forsake you.'"
Hebrews 13:5

GOD IS ALWAYS WITH YOU

HELPING DAD

Read: Psalm 127:1-5

Malcolm could not believe how cranky Dad had been lately. Mom said it was because his company had run into major problems with the construction of a building. She said something about the state inspector not approving the plans Dad had drawn for the electrical wiring. All Malcolm knew was that Dad was like a bear with a sore foot! The problem was beginning to affect Dad's health, too. He wasn't eating much, and there were dark circles under his eyes. Malcolm overheard Mom telling Dad he needed to get more sleep. Dad replied gruffly, "Doesn't do any good to go to bed. Can't sleep anyway."

Malcolm had been reading a psalm each evening for his devotions. When he came to Psalm 127, the first two verses seemed to jump right off the page. (Did you read today's Scripture?) Before going to sleep, he prayed that Dad would be able to relax and forget his problems.

In the middle of the night, Malcolm woke up. He saw a light in Dad's study. Sure enough, there sat Dad, staring at his plans for the wiring. Malcolm approached him. "Dad, can I show you a verse I read tonight?"

"Sure," said Dad. Malcolm found the verse and read it. " 'In vain you rise early and stay up late, toiling for food to eat—for he grants sleep to those he loves.' " Dad nodded as he read it for himself. "Thanks, Malcolm. Let's both go to bed."

The next morning Malcolm couldn't believe his ears. Dad was whistling! "Malcolm, this morning I found the error in my plans," he said. "I don't know why I never saw it before. Guess my brain was too muddled by worry and lack of sleep." He tousled Malcolm's hair playfully. "Oh—and look here at verse three of Psalm 127. This verse is certainly true, Son." *REP*

HOW ABOUT YOU?

Has there been a time when your parents seemed concerned over a particular problem—so concerned that they could not sleep? Perhaps you could gently remind them that the Bible says it is useless to lie awake and worry. God can give them sleep. Remember this in your own life, too. Study well for that big test; then trust God to help you with it. Get a good night's sleep.

DON'T WORRY; TRUST GOD

MEMORIZE:

"In vain you rise early and stay up late, toiling for food to eat—for he grants sleep to those he loves."

Psalm 127:2, NIV

SECOND CHANCE

Read: Matthew 18:21-22

"Look what Joshua did to my video game!" David's face was red with anger. "He's ruined it!" He turned toward his little brother, who sat at the table eating a snack. "Don't you ever touch my stuff again!"

"I'm sorry, David," Joshua said sadly. "It just broked."

"Things don't just break!" David argued. "You broke it." He threw the game in the garbage and shook his finger at Joshua. "From now on you leave my stuff alone!" he repeated as he went to his room to study.

The next afternoon Mom joined David in his room. "More homework?" she asked.

"Another math test tomorrow," David replied. "We had one today, but most of us messed up, so Miss Nelson is giving us another chance."

Mom smiled. "It's nice of her to give you a second chance."

David nodded. "Miss Nelson is a nice teacher."

"Joshua sure could use a second chance," said Mom.

David looked puzzled. "Joshua doesn't take tests in kindergarten."

"He needs a second chance with you," said Mom. "Don't you think you were a little hard on him yesterday? He gets so much enjoyment from playing video games with you. You never seemed to mind before, and yesterday was the first time he ever hurt anything."

Joshua, who had been in the hall listening, came into the room. "I'll save my money and buy you another game," he said.

As David hesitated, his glance fell on his math book. Remembering his second chance in math, he smiled. "You don't have to do that, Joshua," he said. "That was an old game anyway. I've played it a hundred times." He handed him another video game. "Here's a new one. Why don't you play this instead?" *BJW*

HOW ABOUT YOU?

Do you realize that God has often given you a second chance? How many times have you lied, cheated, or disobeyed? How many times have you failed him in one way or another? Yet when you confess your sin to God, he always forgives you. Are you holding a grudge against somebody? Don't you think that person deserves a second chance, too?

MEMORIZE:

"Forgive the person who offends you. Remember, the Lord forgave you, so you must forgive others."
Colossians 3:13

BE FORGIVING

TIE A YELLOW RIBBON

Read: Luke 15:11-24

Alex hated church, family devotions, and chores—so late one night, he ran away. His parents searched for him, but it was no use.

Life away from home was not wonderful. Alex went to a big city, did a lot of odd jobs, slept where he could, and got into trouble. Hungry and broke, Alex ended up at a Christian homeless shelter. There he again heard the familiar gospel story. That night, Alex humbly confessed his sins and trusted Jesus as his Lord and Savior.

"Dear Mom and Dad," Alex wrote in a letter to his parents, "It's been years since you've heard from me, and after the way I've treated you, I don't blame you if you never want to see me again. But I've accepted Jesus as my Savior now, and I want to come home. The bus route still goes right past the house, so next Friday I'll be on the 4:30 bus. If you can forgive me and want me to come home, tie a yellow ribbon around the trunk of the old maple tree out in front of the house. If it's there, I'll get off, but if it's not there, I'll stay on the bus and stay out of your lives."

Alex was very nervous on the bus. "Will you do me a favor?" he said to the man sitting next to him. "Will you tell me if there is a ribbon tied around an old maple tree in my front yard? The house is about a mile down the road." The man agreed, and Alex buried his face in his hands.

Suddenly the man gave a shout. "Look!"

Alex looked. He saw a yellow ribbon tied around the tree trunk—and more ribbons hanging from almost every branch! In front of the tree stood his parents waving a big sign saying, "Welcome home, Alex! We love you!" *CVM*

HOW ABOUT YOU?

The love of parents is great, isn't it? The love of God is even greater! Even if you haven't run away from home, you may be a "wayward child"—a Christian who is living in a way that does not please God. Yet Jesus is ready and willing to forgive you. Confess your sin, return to God, and he'll welcome you back.

RETURN TO THE LORD

THE DROPOUT

Read: Hebrews 10:22-25, 35-39

"Mr. Barnes lectured me about not practicing my trumpet," Connor told his dad as he climbed into the car. "So I'm dropping out of band Monday."

"If the going gets rough, drop out," mused Dad. "Is that your motto?"

Connor just shrugged his shoulders.

After dinner, Dad turned on the news. ". . . and the fire totally destroyed the rescue mission at Main and Archer," said the reporter. "Several men who had been staying at the mission were severely burned. . . ."

"That's terrible!" Mom said. "Isn't your Sunday school class collecting money for that mission, Connor?"

"I think so," Connor muttered. "But I'm tired of Sunday school. Wish I could drop out."

Dad raised his eyebrows. "Dropping out of band and Sunday school? Looks like we've raised a dropout, Mom."

Just then the phone rang. "That was the hospital," Dad said after hanging up. "An old school friend of mine was injured in the fire and is asking for me. I haven't seen Ted Storm in 20 years, but he called a few days ago and told me he was in town." Dad put on his coat. "Pray while I'm gone," he said. "Ted needs to know the Lord."

Just before Connor was ready to go to bed, Dad returned and told about his visit. Mr. Storm had told Dad how he had wasted his life and neglected God. Weakly, he had asked Dad to pray with him. "Ted was a sharp kid, with lots of things going for him," Dad said sadly, "but he never learned how to finish anything. He dropped out of school, and he stopped going to church—said it bored him. He never stayed with any job. When the going got rough, he quit."

Connor was very quiet. "I think I'll change my motto," he said finally. "No more dropping out for me." *BJW*

HOW ABOUT YOU?

Do you "drop out" when the going gets a bit rough? Make it a practice to finish what you start, no matter how small the job may be. Don't brand yourself a quitter. God is faithful. You be faithful, too.

MEMORIZE:

"I have fought a good fight, I have finished the race, and I have remained faithful." 2 Timothy 4:7

FINISH WHAT YOU START

A DIRTY MOUTH

Read: Psalm 17:1-7

"What song should we sing before I read?" Dad asked, as he opened his Bible.

"Let's sing 'Praise Him,' " said Troy. "We sing that in Sunday school." His little brother, Tyler, had just finished eating a bowl of chocolate pudding. But for some reason he did not join in the singing.

At the end of the song, Dad looked over at his younger son. "Why didn't you sing with us tonight, Tyler?" he said. "Don't you know that song?"

"Yes," said Tyler, solemnly. "But I can't sing with a dirty mouth." Everyone laughed, and Mom brought a wet washcloth to remove traces of chocolate from his face.

"That's a good lesson, Tyler," said Dad with a smile. "We all need to remember that we can never praise God with dirty mouths. Our mouths must not be 'sin-dirty.' "

"You mean like saying bad words?" Troy asked.

"Yes," Dad agreed. "But I also was thinking that we often say things to hurt one another."

Tyler spoke. "Sometimes Troy calls me names."

"Oops! Sorry," said Troy quickly. "I guess I have to be more careful about what I say when I'm mad at somebody."

Mom spoke quietly. "Everybody is included in the list of those who need to be more careful," she said. "Sometimes we parents are guilty, too—guilty of being critical, or angry, or just complaining. And we all brag now and then. That's wrong, too."

"Before we offer our prayers or our praises to a God who is holy, we must ask him to cleanse us from any sin we have committed," explained Dad. "And it's often our mouths that have gotten us into trouble."

Everyone sat thinking a moment before Troy spoke up. "I guess it would be okay for you to sing with pudding on your mouth," he said, grinning at Tyler, "as long as your heart is clean!" *NKP*

HOW ABOUT YOU?

Do you always pray and sing with a "clean mouth"? Don't allow the sins of anger, criticism, gossip, or boasting to stain your lips. Be sure to "wipe your mouth" each time it becomes smudged by wrong speech. Do this by confessing your sin to the Lord. Then you can pray and sing with a clean mouth.

GUARD YOUR
SPEECH

MEMORIZE:
"Take control of what I say, O Lord, and keep my lips sealed." Psalm 141:3

March

16

Read: 2 Chronicles 34:1-3, 31-33

One evening at dinner, Mike told the family about a friend of his. "Lance doesn't go to church or Sunday school anywhere," he said. "I've invited him before, but he never wants to come. But after school today, I invited Lance to our church youth group, and this time he agreed to come along!"

"That's great!" said Dad. "We'll pray that he'll enjoy it—and that he'll understand his need to be born again."

Mike's younger brother, Adam, nodded. "Yeah! And when I'm in high school, I'm going to the Bible study group just like you do, Mike. Then I can invite my friends, and they'll be able to learn about Jesus, too." Adam often talked about how great it would be when he was grown up. He wanted to be a pastor. Then he could talk to his friends about the Lord and teach from the Bible. The people in his church would call him with special prayer requests.

Mom smiled at him. "You sure do seem to be thinking a lot about growing up lately," she said. "Don't be in such a hurry."

"But, Mom," said Adam, "I'm too young to be a pastor, or a Sunday school teacher, or even to lead a Bible study. I just want to be bigger so I can start to serve God."

"Wait a minute," said Dad. "Did you know that one of the most godly kings in Bible times began his reign at the age of eight? He showed great respect for God's Word. He didn't let his age stop him from doing what the Bible said, and his example influenced many people to live for God."

"Wow!" Adam was surprised. "Will you read the story of that young king, Dad? If he could serve God, so can I. After all, I'm eight years old now!" *DLR*

HOW ABOUT YOU?
Do you ever feel too young to serve God? The things you say to others, the love and kindness you show on the playground or at school, and the helpful things you do for your family and others are all ways of serving him. Don't dream about being old enough to serve God. Instead, serve him now!

MEMORIZE:
"Don't let anyone think less of you because you are young. Be an example to all believers in what you teach, in the way you live, in your love, your faith, and your purity." 1 Timothy 4:12

SERVE GOD NOW

WORTH IT ALL

Read: John 12:24-26

"How was school today, big guy?" asked Grandma.

"Okay, I guess," Nate replied. "We had a spelling bee, and I goofed on the word *martyr*. I spelled it m-a-r-t-e-r."

"Do you know what a martyr is?" Grandma asked.

"Sure." Nate nodded. "A martyr is anyone who has given his life for what he believes. I know that the first Christian martyr was Stephen. He was stoned for preaching the gospel. We don't have any Christian martyrs today, though, do we?"

"Indeed we have!" said Grandma.

"But why would anyone kill Christians?" asked Nate.

"Well," Grandma replied, "some countries have godless governments that don't allow Christians to openly practice their faith. In places like that, Christians are often arrested if they take a stand for Christ, and some are killed."

"Have you known any martyrs?" Nate asked.

"Not personally," answered Grandma, "but when I was a girl, five brave young men and their families were trying to take the gospel to the uncivilized tribe of Auca Indians in the jungles of Ecuador. In fact, you have the same first name as one of them. While trying to make a friendly contact with the Indians, all five were killed."

"How terrible!" Nate said. "It seems like such a waste. Couldn't God have kept that from happening?"

"Yes," said Grandma, "but do you know what happened after those men were martyred? Hundreds of young people who heard about it dedicated their lives for Christian service. Later, other missionaries were able to go to that Auca tribe, and some of the very men who led the attack were won to Christ." She smiled at Nate. "God's plan wasn't the same as that of those five men, but he didn't let their lives be wasted." *CVM*

HOW ABOUT YOU?

Would you be willing to die for Christ? From people's point of view, such loss of life sometimes seems a waste, but God has promised to reward those who are faithful. If you could talk with those martyrs today, no doubt they would say, "It's worth it all!" Will you give yourself to God and be willing to live or die for him?

BE WILLING TO LIVE—AND DIE— FOR CHRIST

MEMORIZE:

"If you try to keep your life for yourself, you will lose it. But if you give up your life for me, you will find true life."

Luke 9:24

HYMN MEANINGS

Paul's aunt was a schoolteacher, and she often shared things that happened at school. "My class has been learning the first verse of 'America the Beautiful,' " she told Paul's family one day. "It refers to the 'fruited plain' of our country. Well, one little girl has an uncle who is a pilot, and she asked if the 'fruited plane' was owned by United Airlines."

Everyone chuckled about this. "Well, I must have been at least 11 years old before I realized the hymn, 'In the Garden,' was about Jesus," confessed Uncle Don. "The chorus says, 'And he walks with me, and he talks with me.' I always thought it said 'Andy.' To me, that meant the old church janitor whose name was Andy. He always walked and talked with us kids."

"You know," said Dad, "those stories are funny, but it's kind of sad to think about kids not really knowing what they're singing about in church."

"But some songs have hard words," said Paul timidly. "Like one we sang last week about raising an ebenezer. What does that mean? What's an ebenezer?"

Dad smiled and reached for the family Bible. "The prophet Samuel built a stone monument and named it 'Ebenezer,' which means, 'The Lord helped us,' " he explained. "We read about it in 1 Samuel." He turned to the passage and read some verses. "So, Paul, to 'raise an ebenezer' means to declare that the Lord is our helper," continued Dad. "Does that make sense to you?"

"Yes," said Paul with a grin. He was glad he had asked. *REP*

HOW ABOUT YOU?

Do you still sing the old hymns in your church? They're great, but some of them may have words you don't often hear anymore. Do you ever wonder what those words mean? If so, don't be afraid to ask. Today's memory verse suggests that it's natural and good for you to ask questions. (By the way, that verse comes from another Bible story you might like to read— why not look it up?)

MEMORIZE:

"In the future, your children will ask, 'What do these stones mean to you?' Then you can tell them." Joshua 4:6-7

KNOW WHAT
YOU SING

WHAT TO DO

Read: 2 Timothy 2:15-16, 19-22

"I don't know if I can go on the summer retreat this year," Glen told his friend Brett. "Depends on whether I can earn the money for it. My dad's been sick and can't spare the extra cash, so I'm praying and looking for a job."

As Glen walked past a used-book store a couple of days later, he saw a "Help Wanted" sign in the window. He went in to ask about it. "I need someone a few hours a day," the manager said, "to sort through old books, mend them, and put them in the bins for display. Interested?" Glen was, and he got the job. He thanked the Lord for it.

When Glen began working, he saw that many of the books he handled were about the occult, horoscopes, violence, and people cheating on their spouses.

Glen tried to ignore the fact that, as a Christian, he didn't feel right about putting these kinds of books out for people to read. After all, hadn't God provided this job for him? Yet, when he went home at night, he often felt guilty—kind of dirty inside. He thought about some of the covers on the books he had to put out for display. He felt sure God didn't really want him to have a part in selling those books. Besides, how could he keep his mind pure if he had to look at these books each day? Finally, he decided it would be better for him to quit the job.

"But what about the retreat, Glen?" asked Brett, when he heard that Glen had given up his job.

"If God wants me to go, he'll supply the money in some other way," Glen replied. "I just couldn't see paying for the retreat with money I made selling bad books to others." *JLH*

HOW ABOUT YOU?

Do you ever try to justify doing something wrong because you're doing it for a good cause? Putting money in the offering plate is wrong if you stole the money. Helping another student to pass a test is wrong if you cheat to do it. Choose to depart from evil.

CHOOSE TO DEPART FROM EVIL

"Yuck! What a mess!" complained Phil as he and his family worked to clean an old house that they had inherited. "We'll never get this place cleaned."

"It's just that it hasn't been lived in for such a long time," said Mom. "Why don't you go and work outside with Dad? Patti and I will work inside."

Phil and his dad began picking up sticks, stones, and trash from the lawn before starting to mow it. Suddenly they heard a scream. A second later Patti came running out. "Oh, Daddy, what a horrible place!" she gasped. "A mouse ran over my foot, and there are spiders! And it's all so dirty!"

"It's awful out here, too," agreed Phil. He scowled. "This is going to take forever!"

Mom, who had followed Patti, spoke up. "As we worked, I was thinking that this house is a good illustration for the Sunday school lesson I'm teaching next Sunday. We can see that it's necessary to do some cleaning in a house every day or it will look like this one. That makes me think about cleaning another kind of house—my 'heart house.' "

Dad nodded. "Good thought," he said. "To keep my spiritual house clean, I need to do some heart cleaning every day. If I don't, little 'spiders' of selfishness and little 'mice' of anger, as well as other sins, creep in."

"That's a good comparison," agreed Mom. *BJW*

HOW ABOUT YOU?
Is there selfishness, disobedience, or anger in your "heart house"? Each day, confess whatever sin you find there.

MEMORIZE:
"For we are the temple of the living God." 2 Corinthians 6:16

CHRISTIANS ARE GOD'S TEMPLE

READ IT AGAIN

Read: 1 Corinthians 2:11-16

Gino could hardly sit still during the assembly. All month long the students at Jefferson School had been writing stories and then drawing pictures to illustrate them. Each student put together his own book for the Young Authors' Day contest, and the winners would be special guests for a day at the local college. They would learn about writing, and they would meet John Prescott, an author of books about animals. Gino had read all of Mr. Prescott's books.

"And now, the winners of the contest!" the principal announced. "Sue Kilt, Pam Bruder, Tamisha Tate . . . "

Gino sighed as he heard more girls listed. Maybe he hadn't won, but then the principal ended the list with "Alan Smit and Gino Bellini." Gino perked up. He was a winner after all!

Attending the event at the college was even better than Gino had anticipated. Afterwards, he told his parents about meeting Mr. Prescott. "Know how come he knows so much about animals?" Gino asked. Without waiting for an answer, he continued, "He told us a lot about himself and gave us a booklet of information. He's a conservation officer, and he works around animals every day. He's neat! Meeting him has made me want to learn from him. I'm going to read his books all over again!"

"I'm glad you had a good time," said Dad with a smile, "and I daresay you'll enjoy those books more than ever now. Meeting Mr. Prescott personally will help you understand his books." After a moment, Dad spoke again. "You know, Gino, meeting this author is a little like meeting Jesus—the author of the Bible. And knowing Jesus personally as your Savior, helps you understand his book better."

Gino grinned. "Hey! I know two authors," he said. "How about that!" *JLH*

HOW ABOUT YOU?

Do you personally know Jesus? Then you'll want to learn more about him by reading the Bible. Study its messages, memorize verses, and practice its truths. Then your life will show that you really know the author—Jesus!

READ YOUR BIBLE TO KNOW JESUS

MEMORIZE:
"Looking unto Jesus, the author and finisher of our faith." Hebrews 12:2, KJV

SEED SOWING

Read: Matthew 13:3-8, 18-23

One weekend, at a youth retreat, Harrison accepted Christ as his Savior. He was glad he was a Christian, but he dreaded facing his old friends at school, for he had been a leader in a rather wild group. "I know that some things my friends and I have been doing aren't right," Harrison told his mother before school on Monday morning. "I don't want to be that way any more, but I don't know how to tell them that I'm a Christian."

"It won't be easy, I know," agreed Mom. "I'll be praying for you today—asking God to give you courage to witness to your friends."

Harrison's old group of friends was waiting on the playground. They had been talking about ways to goof off in class, and they expected him to take part as usual. During the morning, Derek threw paper wads, Rawi shot rubber bands, and Justin "accidentally" knocked over a classmate's books. Harrison didn't join in. Several times he noticed his friends staring at him.

At lunchtime, when Harrison bowed his head, Derek scowled. "What on earth has come over you?" he snarled.

"Well," Harrison began nervously as he prayed silently, "I'm a different person. I've become a Christian, and now I want to live the way Jesus wants me to live."

Most of the guys laughed and mocked him, but Justin snapped, "Leave him alone!"

Harrison burst into the house after school. "Oh, Mom!" he exclaimed. "Guess what! The guys noticed I was different, even before I told them. And God gave me enough courage to tell them what happened. Some of them made fun of me, but Justin seems interested."

"That's great, honey," said Mom with a smile. "You know, the Bible compares witnessing to seed sowing, and you've begun to sow seed in the lives of your friends." *AU*

HOW ABOUT YOU?

Do your friends at school know you're a Christian? Does it worry you that they may tease you and make fun of you? Ask God for courage to sow the seed—his Word—to those around you.

MEMORIZE:

"He that winneth souls is wise."
Proverbs 11:30, KJV

WITNESS BY LIFE AND WORD

BEHIND THE SCENES

Read: 1 Corinthians 3:5-9

Tim rushed onto the stage, set some props in place, picked up some others, and rushed off. He was head "prop man" for the Junior Youth Group Play, and this was the final performance.

Though everything went well, Tim felt a little "down" when it was all over. He was almost the last to leave, and he gave a big sigh as he walked out of the auditorium and started down the church steps. Pastor Weber, who was coming up the steps, greeted him. "Congratulations on the fine job you did on the play," he said. "But why the big sigh?"

"I was thinking about . . . some other stuff."

"Care to talk about the other stuff?" asked the pastor.

Tim shrugged, but then he told his problem—concern about his father. Tim and his mom were Christians, but not his dad. "Mom and I have prayed for Dad, and I know you and the people here at church have, too," said Tim. "But it hasn't done any good."

"Wait a minute, Tim," interrupted Pastor Weber. "How do you know our prayers have done no good?"

Tim was surprised. "I don't see any change," he said.

"But you can't see inside his heart. God could be doing a work that we can't see on the outside," reminded Pastor Weber. "For instance, think about the play you just worked so hard on. The audience couldn't see all the behind-the-scenes work that took place to make it a success." Tim remembered all the rehearsals and the rushing around to set the stage while the curtain was closed. He nodded as Pastor Weber continued. "God also does a lot of behind-the-scenes work. Don't give up on your dad yet!" *AU*

HOW ABOUT YOU?

Are you discouraged by the lack of results in your prayers for a loved one? Do you feel you've done your best to witness, but it hasn't helped? Don't quit. You don't know what God has been doing in that person's heart. It may take a very long time before he or she comes to Jesus, but trust God for the results.

GOD WORKS—
KEEP PRAYING

MEMORIZE:
"God . . . is the one that makes the seed grow." 1 Corinthians 3:7

As Philipe threw the newspaper down with a sigh, Dad looked up in surprise. "Something wrong?" he asked.

Philipe shrugged. "Oh, I don't know," he replied. "It's just that everything in here is bad news." He picked up the paper and showed Dad the front page. "Look—war, earthquakes, crime, and all kinds of rotten things are going on in the world. It kinda gets me down sometimes. How can we look forward to the future when it seems as though the world might blow itself up one of these days?"

"Well, Son, I agree that things do look pretty bleak for this old, sinful world," replied Dad. "But Jesus promised never to leave or forsake us. The Bible teaches that God will eventually destroy the powers of darkness that are making this world such a scary place. As world conditions get worse and worse, we should be eagerly looking for the return of Christ."

"Yeah," said Philipe. "But sometimes it's hard to remember that God is still in control. Satan seems pretty powerful."

"Satan is powerful," agreed Dad, "but not as powerful as God. Philipe, you remind me of the servant of the prophet Elisha. Once, when a great number of Syrian soldiers were about to attack Elisha, his servant was frightened—until God opened the servant's eyes, so that he could see the large number of angels God had sent to guard them."

"I remember that story," said Philipe. "The servant thought the Syrians would overpower them for sure, but God was in control."

"That's right," said Dad. "Things happen only as God permits them."

Philipe smiled. "I'm sure glad I'm on God's side!" *SLK*

HOW ABOUT YOU?

Are you bothered by things like hunger, disease, and terrorism? Do reports of wars and floods and earthquakes make you worry about the future? You shouldn't "close your eyes" to the problems of the world, but you should also "open your eyes" to the power and plan of God. He's still in control, and his victory is certain.

MEMORIZE:

"He who is in you is greater than he who is in the world." 1 John 4:4, NKJV

GOD CONTROLS THE FUTURE

THE TOASTER AND THE BIBLE

Read: James 1:21-25

"Mom, I can't get the toaster to work," called Jason. Receiving no answer, he went to the laundry room where his mother was working. "I can't get the toaster to work," said Jason.

"Is it plugged in?" asked Mom.

"Plugged in?" repeated Jason. "I guess so—it always is, but I'll go check." Jason went back to the kitchen. *Oops!* he thought. *No wonder it didn't work.* He plugged in the toaster, put two pieces of raisin bread into it, and soon was enjoying perfect toast.

In Sunday school the next morning, Jason's teacher held up his Bible. "I'm sure you all learned long ago that you should read your Bible every day, right?" asked Mr. Scott. Heads nodded. "Good," he said. "I hope you do that, but are you aware that just reading the Bible isn't enough? What you read there needs to be plugged into your life."

"What do you mean by that?" asked Samantha.

Jason raised his hand. "I have an example of something that needed to be plugged in," he said. "I was trying to make toast yesterday, but the toaster wouldn't work. When I checked, I found out that it wasn't plugged in."

"I know about plugging in toasters," said Samantha, "but I still don't get how we plug the Bible into our lives."

Mr. Scott smiled. " 'Plugging it in' means doing what it says," he replied. "God's Word was meant to change us. For instance, if you read 'Obey your parents,' but then you try to get out of doing your chores, you're not letting the Bible change you. You haven't plugged it into your life."

"But if we read 'Forgive one another,' and then we do forgive somebody who treated us badly, we've plugged in what we read," suggested Jason.

"You've got it!" agreed Mr. Scott. *JMJ*

HOW ABOUT YOU?

Do you read your Bible each day? Is it plugged into your life—does it change your behavior? It should. Be sure to put into practice what you read.

PUT BIBLE
TRUTHS
INTO PRACTICE

MEMORIZE:
"Anyone who listens to my teaching and obeys me is wise." Matthew 7:24

CREATION AND THE TRUTH

Read: John 17:17-19; 2 Timothy 3:14-17

"Are you ready for the test on evolution tomorrow?" asked Joshua as he and his friend Daniel walked home.

Daniel sighed. "I guess so," he replied. "I can explain evolution the way Mr. Jackson did, but I don't believe it. I believe God created everything."

"Mr. Jackson says he doesn't think God created everything," said Joshua. He shrugged. "What does it matter?" As another boy rode by on a bike and waved, Joshua scowled. "There goes Benjamin Norris. That's one guy I'll never believe again!" he exclaimed. "You know what he did? He promised me that when he got a new bike, I could buy his old one. After he finally got a new one, he told me he had sold the old one to Jeff for twice as much as he had said I could have it for."

"Well, you can't blame Ben for wanting the extra money," said Daniel.

"Maybe not, but I talked to Jeff last week, and he said he paid the same amount I was going to pay." Joshua frowned. "If Ben lies like that about the bike, he'll lie about other things, too."

"Wouldn't that be true about God and the Bible?" asked Daniel.

"God?" asked Joshua. "What do you mean?"

"Well, the Bible is God's Word, and the very first verse says, 'In the beginning God created the heavens and the earth,' " replied Daniel. "The whole chapter is about God making everything. If it's a lie, how can we believe anything in the Bible?"

Joshua looked thoughtful. "So . . . if we're going to believe in the Bible and God, we've got to believe he created everything?" he asked.

"Yeah, that's the way I see it," agreed Daniel. *VMH*

HOW ABOUT YOU?

Do you believe the Bible? All of it? Can you say, I know God created everything? To believe otherwise is to say that God does not always tell the truth—and that's wrong. God always tells the truth, for he is truth. All of his Word—the Bible—is true.

MEMORIZE:

"All Scripture is inspired by God."
2 Timothy 3:16

ALL OF THE BIBLE IS TRUE

WHAT IS GOD LIKE?

Read: Philippians 3:8-10

Brian sat on the step deep in thought. "Hi, Brian." Looking up, Brian saw
Meredith, a college student who lived in his neighborhood. "A penny for your
thoughts," said Meredith.

Brian grinned. "I was just wondering what God is like," he said. "Cole thinks
God is really strict. That's what Cole's dad is like. Harry's dad is just the opposite,
and Harry thinks God is always loving and kind and wouldn't punish anyone." He
looked at Meredith. "Do you know what God is like?" Brian asked.

Meredith smiled. "As a matter of fact, I do," she replied, "because I know
God." Brian's eyes opened wide as Meredith continued. "We can know what God is
like from studying the Bible. It tells us how great God is—that he made the world
and everything in it. The Bible says God is holy—he can't do anything wrong.
He's also perfect . . . and best of all, he loves us."

"Then Harry's right. If God loves us, he would never be mean to us, would
he?" asked Brian.

"No," replied Meredith, "not mean—but God is righteous, and he can't
stand sin. He punishes the wicked and rewards those who obey him. And he cares
about us."

"Wow!" exclaimed Brian. "I'll have to tell Harry and Cole."

"But, Brian, it isn't enough to know what God is like," said Meredith. "You
need to know him personally!"

"I can know him?" asked Brian.

"Yes," Meredith assured him. "God loves you so much that he sent his Son,
Jesus, to take the punishment for your sin. Jesus died on the cross so God could
forgive your sin and not punish you. Then Jesus rose from the dead. That's what
we celebrate on Easter. If you believe in Jesus and trust in him, God will forgive
your sin and make you his child." *AGL*

HOW ABOUT YOU?

Do you know a lot about God? That's good, but that doesn't make you a child of God—a
Christian. You need to know him personally, and you can do that by receiving Jesus as your
Savior.

YOU CAN
KNOW GOD

MEMORIZE:
"I want to know Christ and
the power of his resurrection."
Philippians 3:10, NIV

28

LIKE DESERT PLANTS (PART 1)

Read: Psalm 37:30-31; Matthew 12:34-35

Austin hunched over his books at the study table in the public library. Sitting next to him, his sister Hannah sighed. "Isn't this rain a bummer?" she whispered, looking out the window.

"Uh huh," he muttered, not looking up. "Now leave me alone."

"This rain will ruin our family reunion," Hannah complained. "We'll be stuck inside listening to Uncle George's stupid jokes. We—"

"Will you shut up?" Austin demanded loudly. The librarian gave him a stern look.

At the supper table that evening, Hannah continued to complain about the rain. "I wish it never rained!" she said.

"Places where it never rains are called deserts, Dum-dum," Austin told her. "That's what my report is about. Deserts are so dry that hardly any plants can grow there. The mesquite tree sometimes sends its roots hundreds of feet into the ground to search for water. When it does rain, the barrel cactus swells with water and then shrinks again as it uses the water."

"Austin told me to shut up at the library," said Hannah, interrupting her brother. Austin kicked her under the table.

"Austin! You know better than to talk like that!" scolded Mom.

"Well, she's always a pest," grumbled Austin.

Mom frowned. "Austin, you should watch your tongue and both of you should be considerate of each other," she said.

"Yes, Son, maybe you need to be more like that mesquite tree and barrel cactus—maybe you need to 'drink' more deeply from God's Word," suggested Dad. "In fact, we should all have a thirst for his Word. It would be nice if we were as motivated to read the Bible as those desert plants are to get water. If we were swelling up with God's Word, good words would be coming out of our mouths and we'd have a desire to get along with one another." *LJR*

HOW ABOUT YOU?

What kind of words come from your mouth? Your words reflect what's in your heart. Read God's Word, think about it, and ask him to help you understand and obey it. As his Word fills your heart, good thoughts, words, and actions will come out.

DRINK DEEPLY FROM GOD'S WORD

MEMORIZE:

"Whatever is in your heart determines what you say." Matthew 12:34

LIKE DESERT PLANTS (PART 2)

Read: Isaiah 55:8-11

Hannah secretly gloated because her parents had reminded her brother Austin to learn to control his tongue. "Austin is always nasty to me," she complained out loud. "He's almost as bad as the rain!" she added, looking out the window. "I hate rain! I wish—"

"As for you, Hannah," said Dad, interrupting her, "you need to quit complaining. Remember what Austin said? Places where there is little or no rain are deserts." Hannah's smug, self-satisfied look disappeared from her face. "Without rain, you wouldn't have enjoyed the baked potatoes we had for supper tonight," Dad added.

"Or the apple pie we're going to have for dessert," said Mom.

"But rain always ruins our plans," whined Hannah.

"It doesn't ruin God's plans," said Dad.

Mom nodded. "I think those desert plants have a lesson for you, too, Hannah. Dad reminded us that we all need to 'drink' deeply from God's Word, remember? When we do that, it helps us to accept the 'rain' that falls in our lives, as well as the rain that falls outside."

"Rain in our lives?" asked Hannah. "What do you mean?"

"I mean the disappointments and difficult circumstances that we all must face at one time or another," said Mom. "We need to realize that God is working all things—even the bad things—for our good."

"Someone put it this way, 'Every cloud has a silver lining,' " said Dad. "God said it even better. In Romans 8:28, he says, 'We know that God causes everything to work together for the good of those who love God.' Whenever it rains—whether it's rain falling from the sky or difficult times in our lives—just remember that God is in control and knows what is best. When we remember that God uses rain to bring good things, we can stop complaining." *LJR*

HOW ABOUT YOU?

Do your difficulties seem like "rain"? Do you complain and grumble? Let rain remind you that God truly does know what is best for you. God uses rain to bring good things.

DON'T
GRUMBLE—
TRUST GOD

MEMORIZE:
"He . . . provides rain for the earth, and makes the green grass grow in mountain pastures." Psalm 147:8

CHANGE OF PLANS

Read: James 4:13-16

When Connor and his dad clapped their hands and shouted loudly, two barn swallows quickly flew out of the garage, their tails looking like forks against the blue sky. "Why can't we let them nest in the garage, Dad?" asked Connor as he watched the birds fly over a neighbor's house and disappear.

"For one thing, they'd make a mess," answered Dad. "For another, our garage wouldn't be a safe place to raise baby birds." As he spoke, Dad pressed a button to lower the garage door. Instantly, it became dark, and the cool breeze was gone.

Connor nodded. "Our garage would get too hot for them, wouldn't it?" he asked.

"Yes," replied Dad. "And when the door is closed, the mother and father birds wouldn't be able to go in and out and bring food for the baby birds." Dad opened the garage door and let the cooler air back in.

"I guess they'll have to change their plans and find a new home—just like we had to change our plans and find a new home when we moved here," said Connor. "But I liked our other house and my school there."

"Well, Mom and I liked it, too. We were surprised when my company wanted us to move to this town," said Dad, "but I'm sure we'll like it here, too." He thought for a minute. "We can make our plans, Connor, but it's really the Lord who directs our steps—and we want to follow him."

"You think God wanted us to move?" asked Connor.

"Yes, I believe he led us here," said Dad. "We may not know why—just like those barn swallows don't know why we shooed them out of our garage. But *we* know it's best for them to build their nest elsewhere, and *God* knows what's best for us." *MFW*

HOW ABOUT YOU?

Is it hard for you to accept a change in plans? When things don't go the way you'd like, look for lessons God might want to teach you. Be assured that he knows what's best for you, and trust him to work things out for your good.

MEMORIZE:

"The mind of man plans his way, but the Lord directs his steps."
Proverbs 16:9, NASB

TO SAVE HER YOUNG

Read: Romans 5:6-8; 1 John 4:9-10

"Hey, Brad, look!" Derek pointed excitedly. He and his brother were exploring the field behind their grandparents' home.

"Where?" Brad asked. "What do you see?"

"That bird! Over there! Sh-h-h!" Derek's attention was on a little bird floundering on the path ahead. It looked like it had a broken wing.

"Let's catch it," said Brad. "I bet Grandpa could set its wing so it will heal."

"Good idea," agreed Derek.

The boys walked quietly toward the bird, but it hobbled away from them, covering the ground quite quickly in spite of its handicap. After following the bird for a while, the boys were surprised to see it fly off with no sign of weakness or injury.

"Did you see that?" Derek asked, puzzled. "That bird wasn't hurt after all! I wonder why it acted that way?"

When they got home, Brad and Derek told Grandpa about the bird. Grandpa nodded. "Some birds protect their young that way," he said. "When anything gets too near her nest, the mother bird pretends to be wounded in order to distract the enemy. Then when the enemy is lured far enough away, she flies off to safety."

"Do you think a mother bird ever died doing that?" Derek asked.

"Quite possibly," Grandpa replied.

"Wow!" exclaimed Brad. "The mother bird is willing to risk her life for her babies!"

Grandpa nodded. "It reminds me of what Jesus did for us," he said. "He didn't just *risk* his life, he actually *died* for us! Jesus died so we could have eternal life." Grandpa smiled. "We receive that life when we accept Jesus as Savior," he added. "What he did causes us to love him, and let's be sure to thank him, too." *RRL*

HOW ABOUT YOU?

Can you imagine someone loving you enough to die for you? That's how much Jesus loves you! He died to take the penalty for your sins and to give you salvation. No one loves you more than that.

JESUS LOVES
YOU AND DIED
TO SAVE YOU

SOMEBODY'S FOOL

Read: 1 Corinthians 3:18-23

After school, Daniel took his Bible from his locker and looked around nervously. He knew that if certain kids saw him with a Bible, he'd be teased. "Hey! Daniel!" called James, a boy from his church youth group. "You dropped something." As Daniel looked down, James called "April fool!" and both boys laughed. "Want to shoot a few baskets with me and some of the guys?" asked James. Daniel hesitated, and James noticed the Bible in his hand. "You're not going to that Bible club, are you?" asked James.

Daniel nodded. "Why don't you come?" he asked.

"I get enough Bible lessons on Sunday," replied James. "Don't you?"

"Not really," said Daniel. "Besides, Pastor Drew said last week that if we attend Bible club, it might encourage other kids to come, too. He said it was one way to be a testimony." Daniel hesitated. "I don't always do so good at telling kids about Jesus," he admitted, "so I made up my mind that attending Bible club was one thing I was going to do." The boys headed for the door. "Why don't you come along?" urged Daniel. "You're a Christian, too, aren't you, James?"

"Yeah, sure," mumbled James, "but I don't think it's necessary to talk about it all the time." Actually, he felt rather guilty. "What I mean is . . . well . . . some of the guys already tease me about going to church. They'll think I'm really a geek if I go to Bible club instead of playing basketball."

Daniel thought it over. Then he shrugged. "It's funny," he said. "All day we've been playing jokes or having jokes played on us, and we've been called an 'April fool.' And Pastor Drew said the world will often make us its fool. I think I'd rather be a fool for Christ." *AU*

HOW ABOUT YOU?

Are you afraid to let others see that you're a Christian? Afraid of being considered a geek or a fool? Act in ways that are wise in God's sight. Live to please him, not the world. Be a witness and share the gospel with others.

BE A FOOL FOR
CHRIST

MEMORIZE:
"We are fools for Christ's sake."
1 Corinthians 4:10, KJV

2

Read: Ecclesiastes 3:1-11

"Look, Scott! Look what I've got!" exclaimed Jared. He held a yellow and black goldfinch. "I'm going to call him Chirpie and keep him for a pet."

His older brother looked doubtful. "That bird looks sick," Scott said.

"He's not sick!" objected Jared. "I'm going to see if Mom will let me keep him in the old bird cage."

After he showed the bird to Mom, she spoke softly. "He's a beautiful bird, Jared, but he doesn't look very strong. I'm afraid the bird might die."

"But, I can pray, and God will make Chirpie better," insisted Jared.

"God *can* make him better, Jared," agreed Mom, "but he might not."

Jared looked doubtful. "Then why did God give him to me, Mom?"

"Maybe it's because he needed a kind little boy to take care of Chirpie for a few days while he was sick," suggested Mom. "Maybe God was looking for someone—like you—with a big heart to love this little bird." She was quiet for a moment, then said, "Okay, Jared, I'll let you keep Chirpie, but you must agree to accept God's timetable and the number of days that he allows you to have him."

"Okay," said Jared, nodding his head. "But I'm still going to ask God to let Chirpie get well."

The next morning, Chirpie lay dead in his cage. Jared had tears in his eyes. "Mom, it looks like God gave me Chirpie for only one day," he said sadly. "It hurts that he died, but I'm glad God let me take care of him the last day he was alive." Jared wiped the tears from his eyes.

Mom hugged Jared. "Accepting God's timetable is an important part of the Christian life," she said. "We should learn to appreciate every moment God gives us—even if it's just one day." *MEC*

HOW ABOUT YOU?

Have you had a pet that died? Or has someone in your family died? Learn to appreciate the time God has given you with that person or with that pet. Realize that he has a timetable for every life. Accept with thanksgiving each day and moment God gives to you.

MEMORIZE:

"But I trust in you, O Lord; I say, 'You are my God.' My times are in your hands." Psalm 31:14-15, NIV

ACCEPT GOD'S TIMETABLE

THE WRONG SIDE

Read: Ephesians 4:29-32

Caleb and Jake watched as their little brother played soccer in the park. Their father soon arrived and took a seat on the grass next to them. "How's Cody doing?" asked Dad.

"Good," answered Caleb.

Dad smiled. "I'm glad to hear that. Cody has been so excited about belonging to the soccer team. It's been a long time since I've seen that kind of enthusiasm."

"Not me," Jake blurted out. "There's this boy, Nicholas, in my class, and he's about as excited over math as Cody is over soccer. Can you believe it? All the guys make fun of him and call him names."

"I hope you're not one of them," said Dad.

Jake swallowed. "Aw, we're not really mean to him," he mumbled.

Dad shook his head in disapproval. "I hope not," he said.

"Well, you gotta admit he's kinda . . ." began Jake, but he was interrupted by Caleb, who got up and started shouting.

"Stop, Cody! Stop!" Caleb turned toward his father. "Cody is kicking the ball toward the wrong side!" he exclaimed.

Jake jumped up, too. "Oh, no! Cody!" he yelled. "You're helping the wrong side!" Unfortunately, Cody didn't stop. He kicked the ball right into the opposition's goal, scoring a point against his own team. Jake sighed heavily as he dropped to his seat. "It looks like he forgot what team he belongs to."

Dad nodded, then asked, "You're sure you don't do that?"

"Me!" Jake was shocked. "No chance!"

"I hope not," replied Dad. "Just remember that any time you team up with kids who are cruel to others and mock them, you're forgetting that you belong on Jesus' team. Your actions show whether or not you're scoring points for his team or for Satan's team." *SML*

HOW ABOUT YOU?

Do you make fun of people or do unkind things because you're trying to fit into a certain group? Do you behave in ways that are not pleasing to God, just so you'll be accepted by the popular crowd? Many people score points for the devil by the way they act and the things they say. Jesus has called Christians to be on his team, and that requires treating people right. Don't forget which team you're on.

BE KIND TO ONE
ANOTHER

MEMORIZE:
"Be kind to each other, tenderhearted, forgiving one another, just as God through Christ has forgiven you."
Ephesians 4:32

THE SUN AND THE MOON

Read: 1 John 2:3-6

"The moon is really bright tonight, isn't it?" said Steve.

"Yeah . . . it's a great big ball of fire," said Eric.

"Not really," said Steve. "It's the sun that's a ball of fire. Sometimes the moon looks like that, too, but it doesn't really have any light at all. The moon reflects the light of the sun—that's why it looks bright. I learned about that in my science class."

"Come on in, boys!" called Mom. "It's time for bed."

"Okay," they both called back, and they headed inside.

"Mom, guess what!" said Eric as the boys went in. "Steve told me that the moon isn't really a big fireball. Did you know that?"

"Yes," she said. "I knew that. Now scoot along to bed, or morning will come before you're ready for it."

The next day, Eric asked a question that had been puzzling him. "Mom, my Sunday school teacher says people are supposed to see God's love when they look at our lives," he said, "but we aren't God, so how can they see his love? I don't get it."

"I know!" Steve spoke up. "Remember what I told you about the sun and the moon last night?"

"Sure," said Eric. "You said the moon reflects the light of the sun."

"Right," replied Steve. When people look at the moon, the light they see is really the light of the sun. And we're not God, but our lives should reflect him. When people look at the stuff we do, they should be seeing what Jesus would do if he were in our place. Get it?" Steve looked to Mom to help him explain.

"That's right," agreed Mom. "When we reflect God's love, we do the things God wants us to do—we behave in the way we believe Jesus would behave if he were still walking on earth."*AEB*

HOW ABOUT YOU?

Do others see the love of Jesus reflected in your life? As you face each day and each situation, ask yourself, "What would Jesus do?" As you follow his example, and as you practice the things he teaches, others will see God's love in you.

MEMORIZE:

"Christ, who suffered for you, is your example. Follow in his steps."
1 Peter 2:21

REFLECT THE
LOVE OF GOD

PUNISHMENT OR CELEBRATION?

Read: Luke 15:1-10

Evan stretched his neck to see Brad in front of the church, facing the congregation. "It's a joyous day in heaven when one of God's sheep returns to the flock," said Pastor Kerns. "This young man attended our church as a boy, and it was here that he accepted Jesus as his personal Savior. However, temptations came along, and he wandered away from God. But Brad has repented—praise the Lord! Let's celebrate his homecoming!"

When people stood and began clapping, Evan wrinkled his nose. *Why all this fuss for Brad?* he wondered. *I heard he joined a gang.* As Evan slid back in the pew, Mom tapped his shoulder and motioned for him to stand.

Later, Dad and Evan chatted. "I noticed that you seemed reluctant to stand up this morning and celebrate Brad's return," said Dad. "Didn't you want to encourage him? Weren't you glad to see him back at church?"

"He joined a gang, didn't he?" asked Evan. "Isn't that bad? Shouldn't Brad be punished instead of having everybody get all excited about him?"

"Well, let me try to help you understand," said Dad thoughtfully. "Do you remember the time a puppy appeared at our door?"

Evan giggled. "Yeah, he was so cute! I wanted to keep him, but he was wearing a tag, so you called his owners."

"Did the owners punish the puppy for running away?" asked Dad.

"No." Evan said, smiling. "They hugged him and fed him doggie treats. They were so happy that he was found."

"Brad is something like that puppy," said Dad. "In a way, he was lost—he was a Christian, but he was living far from the Lord. However, God loves Brad even more than the puppy's owners loved their puppy. God is happy that Brad has confessed and forsaken his sin. We celebrate, too, because this is a victory over Satan." *RRZ*

HOW ABOUT YOU?

Are you happy when someone confesses sin and turns to God? It's easy to be led astray; it's hard to admit sin. When someone does that, there's rejoicing in heaven. Christians should rejoice, too.

REJOICE WHEN SINNERS REPENT

MEMORIZE:

"There is joy in the presence of God's angels when even one sinner repents."

Luke 15:10

THE RIGHT ANSWER

Read: Genesis 11:1-9

"In music class today, Miss Armstrong taught us a silly song about a man who tried to go to heaven in a hot air balloon. When that didn't work, he tried a kite," Mario told his family one night. "I felt bad singing that song because it was making fun of the Bible."

"It doesn't sound like a very good song," agreed Dad.

"Then Angie raised her hand and asked Miss Armstrong how to really get to heaven," added Mario. "Miss Armstrong didn't answer, so Xavier piped up and said you had to die to go to heaven. Altaf said your good deeds had to outweigh your bad deeds, and then Samantha said you had to be a member of her church to go to heaven. So I raised my hand and said I knew the real way to heaven. I started to say that you have to believe Jesus died for your sins and that he rose again, and you have to accept him as your Savior."

"Good for you!" said Mom. "How did Miss Armstrong respond?"

"She ended the discussion before I could finish!" said Mario. "She taught us that song, and she let the other kids talk, but when I wanted to tell what the Bible says, she interrupted me and changed the subject!"

Dad shook his head. "People often will talk about the Bible as if it's fiction—or a good-luck charm—but they refuse to listen to the truth."

"And people have been trying to get to heaven on their own for a long time," said Mom. "Think about the tower of Babel. Way back then, people thought they could reach heaven through their own works."

"Well, I'm sure glad I know the real way to get to heaven!" Mario exclaimed. "Tomorrow I'm going to talk to Angie and give her the right answer to her question." *LMW*

HOW ABOUT YOU?

Do you know the one, true way to heaven? God's Word is true, and it says that the only way is by accepting Jesus Christ as your personal Savior. Have you done that yet?

MEMORIZE:

"There is salvation in no one else! There is no other name in all of heaven for people to call on to save them."
Acts 4:12

JESUS IS THE WAY TO HEAVEN

DISAPPEARING PEAS

Read: Psalm 5:4-7

Robby sat at the table long after his brother Jason had gone out to play. It didn't seem fair! His mom had told him he couldn't leave the table until he had eaten all his supper—including his peas. Robby pushed the peas around on his plate so it would look as if he had eaten some. "Can I go now?" he asked, showing the plate to his mom.

Mom shook her head. "You were given only a few peas," she said, picking up the last of the dirty dishes. "The rule is that you have to eat all of them."

As soon as Mom's back was turned, Robby slipped the peas into his pocket. He figured he could dump them later, and Mom would never know.

"Oh, Robby, good for you!" exclaimed Mom when he showed her his plate again. She gave him a hug. "I'm proud of you. It wasn't so bad, was it? Now you can play."

Robby left the table and went to the backyard. He didn't feel very happy as he tossed the peas under a bush. Somehow he didn't enjoy playing with Jason either. His conscience was really bothering him. He knew he had lied to his mom by his actions, if not with his tongue—and he also knew God was not pleased.

"Boys, would you like to have a piece of fudge?" Mom called. "Children who finish their suppers deserve a treat."

Robby followed slowly as Jason dashed toward the house. He knew he would have to tell the truth. He could not live with this lie on his heart.

"I'm glad you told me," said Mom after Robby confessed what he had done. Robby was glad, too. And strangely, eating leftover peas while Jason ate fudge seemed to make him feel even better. *DLS*

HOW ABOUT YOU?

Are you careful to never tell a lie with your lips? How about with your actions? Have you thought that as long as you didn't actually lie with your tongue, it was okay to fool your parents or a teacher? That's called deceit. God hates lying, but he hates deceit, too. If you've been deceitful, confess it. Make up your mind to be honest in every way.

ALWAYS BE HONEST

MEMORIZE:

"You will destroy those who tell lies. The Lord detests . . . deceivers." Psalm 5:6

April

8

Read: 1 Timothy 2:1-3

Tyler heard the back door slam as his dad came into the house. Lately Dad had been so short-tempered and grumpy that Tyler didn't know what to expect. Tyler was almost afraid to be around him now, so he gathered his homework from the coffee table and headed for the bedroom. It made him sad. He felt as if he'd lost his dad.

After finishing his homework, Tyler headed to the kitchen for something to eat. To his surprise, he found his parents sitting at the table, holding hands! He could tell they had been crying. He felt embarrassed and turned quickly to leave, but Dad called him back. "Don't go, Tyler," he said. "Please sit down. I need to talk to you." Nervously, Tyler sat down. "I know I haven't been a very pleasant person to be around lately," said Dad, "and I'm really sorry. I've had an awful lot of pressure at work, and I'm afraid I've been taking it out on the ones I love the most. I'm so sorry. I know that's a poor excuse for my behavior, and I know God isn't pleased with the way I've been acting. I've asked him to forgive me, and he has. Mom has forgiven me, too—and now I'm asking you to forgive me and to pray for me, Son. With God's help I'm going to do better. I want to be a real father to you again."

With tears in his eyes, Tyler jumped up from his chair and hugged his dad. He was so happy to have Dad back again, and he would be glad to pray for him. *I should have done more of that sooner,* he thought. *DJS*

HOW ABOUT YOU?

Do you expect your parents to be perfect? Remember, they're human just like you. When they act in ways you don't understand, what do you do? Do you pray for them? They need your prayer support. Will you give it?

MEMORIZE:

"I urge you, first of all, to pray for all people. . . . Plead for God's mercy upon them, and give thanks." 1 Timothy 2:1-2

PARENTS NEED PRAYER

OLDER BROTHER

Read: Hebrews 2:9-13

Scott pushed a hand-held lever, and his battery-powered car sped away down the sidewalk. "Wow, look at it go!" exclaimed Scott's friend, Mike.

The boys took turns with the car. One pushed the lever while the other got the car when it went off the sidewalk. Then Taylor, a bigger boy, stopped to watch. When Scott went to pick up his car, the bigger boy pushed him. "Let's see this car spin out in the sand," Taylor said, reaching for the car.

"No!" said Scott, trying to get it back. "That will clog the gears."

"So what? Let's see what happens," said Taylor.

Scott was worried, but Taylor was so much bigger and stronger than he was. He didn't know what to do. Just then a new voice spoke behind them. "Any trouble here?"

Scott turned around and saw his older brother. "Hi, Sean," he said in relief. "Mike and I were running my car on the sidewalk. It'll be ruined if it goes in the sand."

Sean glanced at the car in Taylor's hand. "How about giving my brother's car back to him," he said.

Taylor handed Scott the car. "It's a dumb car anyway," he said, then shuffled away.

"Thanks a lot, Sean," said Scott.

"Oh, anytime, little brother," said Sean as he walked away whistling.

"Good thing Sean came along," said Mike. "I wish I had an older brother to watch out for me."

Scott placed the car on the sidewalk and pressed the lever. "You kinda do," he said. "You're a Christian, aren't you? I learned in Sunday school that when we're born into God's family, we're children of God and we're all like brothers and sisters—and Jesus is sometimes called our older brother."

"Hey, I learned that, too, but I forgot," said Mike. "I guess I do have a very special older brother!" *CEY*

HOW ABOUT YOU?

Have you ever thought of Jesus as your brother? If you're a child of God, he's even closer to you than a brother, although you can't see him. A human brother or sister can't always be around, but Jesus is.

JESUS CARES FOR YOU

EXCUSES, EXCUSES

Read: 2 Thessalonians 3:7-13

"Clint, please take out the trash," called Mom.

"I'll do it later," replied Clint from his bedroom. "I'm busy studying."

"Clint," Mom said sternly, "I asked you to do a job. I expect you to do it right now." Clint grudgingly went to take out the garbage. As his mother watched him, she thought of a way to teach him a lesson.

"Mom," yelled Clint the next day, "where's my red shirt?"

Wearing a new shirt, Mom came from her room. "I was going to wash clothes last night, but I didn't get it done. I wanted to finish sewing my shirt," she said.

Clint glanced at a pile of dirty clothes in the corner of his room. He chose something else to wear and then hurried downstairs. Finding nothing on the table, he stopped in surprise. "Mom, what's for breakfast?" he asked.

Mom was drinking a glass of juice. "I didn't make breakfast," she said.

"But I'm hungry," whined Clint. "You usually make breakfast." He looked around. "And where's my lunch bag?"

"Sit down, Clint," said Mom, pointing to a chair. "You're right—God has given me the responsibility of taking care of you, but there are certain responsibilities that he has given you, too . . . such as the responsibility of obeying your parents. You were supposed to clean your room, take out the trash, and set the table yesterday. You thought you had some pretty good excuses for not doing those things. Aren't my excuses just as good?"

Clint remembered how he often made excuses to avoid helping his mother. "I'll try harder to obey right away," he promised.

"Good." Mom nodded and gave him a hug. "Now, I'll make you a quick breakfast and help you get your lunch bag ready. After school you can clean your room, and I'll do the washing!" *JK*

HOW ABOUT YOU?

Do you willingly and promptly do your share around your home? Do you help with things like washing dishes or mowing the lawn? Or do you expect your parents to do everything while you just do as you please? God says that everyone—including you—should work. Stop making excuses and get on with the tasks God has given you.

MEMORIZE:

"Whoever does not work should not eat." 2 Thessalonians 3:10

NOT A COWBOY

Read: John 10:11-15

Wayne had just moved to Pennsylvania from Texas, and his Sunday school teacher had been trying to make him feel at home. "Why the frown, Wayne?" Mr. Markley asked. "Can I help?"

"I was just thinking about our lesson today," he replied. "Why did Jesus call himself a good shepherd? I'd like it better if he had said, 'I am the good cowboy!'"

Mr. Markley laughed. "Oh, Wayne, I know you loved your Texas ranch. But I think Jesus knew what he was doing when he compared himself to a shepherd. Suppose you tell me—what does a cowboy do?"

"Aw, that's easy." Wayne's eyes lit up. "He drives the cattle where he wants them to go. They used to do it on horses, but now they often use pickup trucks and sometimes helicopters."

"Well, how about sheep?" asked Mr. Markley. "How do you get a sheep to go somewhere in particular?"

Wayne grinned. "Sheep are so dumb you can't drive them. You have to lead them wherever you want them to go. If there isn't a shepherd for them to follow, they just wander away and get lost. That's why I'd rather have—"

"Ah," Mr. Markley interrupted, "but think about the way people act, and I think you'll see why Jesus compared himself to a shepherd. People are more like sheep than cattle. Without Jesus, we're lost and just wander around. We're probably 'too dumb'—as you would put it—to be driven. God doesn't force us to go his way, like a cowboy would drive the cattle. God is like a loving shepherd, ready to help us and lead us."

"I never thought of myself as a sheep, but I guess I do sometimes act like one," admitted Wayne. "And I sure know a sheep needs a shepherd." *REP*

HOW ABOUT YOU?

Are you like a lost sheep? Are you wandering around—lost in sin? Jesus, the Good Shepherd, invites you to follow him. Admit that you are a sinner and are helpless without him. He gave his life to pay for your sins. Won't you come to him today?

FOLLOW JESUS, THE GOOD SHEPHERD

MEMORIZE:
"I am the good shepherd. The good shepherd lays down his life for the sheep." John 10:11

THE HOPELESS CASE (PART 1)

Read: 1 Corinthians 15:57-58; 16:13-14

"Poor Mrs. Martin," said Mom, shaking her head. "Last week she was robbed again."

"You mean the old lady who lives alone above the drugstore downtown?" Jeff asked.

"Yes. She wasn't at home at the time of the robbery," Mom said, "and I'm glad about that. What an awful experience! I was planning to visit her this afternoon. Why don't you come along?" Since Jeff had nothing better to do, he agreed. He thought it might be interesting to see where she lived.

When Mom knocked on Mrs. Martin's door, a shaky voice called out, "Who is it?"

"It's Mrs. Adams," called Jeff's mother. "We met in church when you visited several weeks ago, remember? My son Jeff and I are here to see you, and we brought some homemade bread. May we come in?"

There were several seconds of silence before Jeff heard a chain lock, a bar lock, and a bolt lock being opened. "Just have to be careful," said Mrs. Martin. "Those crooks may come back. Can't feel safe in your own apartment." She invited them in and accepted the bread from Mom. The rest of their visit was spent listening to Mrs. Martin's angry talk about "crooks" who rob innocent people.

"Whew!" exclaimed Jeff as they headed back home. "Am I glad to be away from Mrs. Martin and her 'crooks'! That's all she talked about. I can't believe you want to go back. She's a hopeless case!"

"Oh, today was just the beginning. Mrs. Martin needs Jesus, and we took the first step to introduce him to her. We listened," explained Mom. "The next steps will be to continue to pray and then make another visit. I hope you'll be my partner in this."

Jeff looked at Mom uncertainly, then shrugged his shoulders. "Maybe," he said.

"You won't be sorry, Jeff," Mom said softly. *JAG*

HOW ABOUT YOU?

Do you know a "hopeless case"? Did you feel your first attempts to witness to that person were worthless? Don't give up. First be a friend to the person. Perhaps he or she needs to know someone is interested enough just to be a listener. Then, as God gives opportunity, tell that person about Jesus.

MEMORIZE:

" 'You are my witnesses,' declares the Lord, 'that I am God.' "
Isaiah 43:12, NIV

WITNESS WITH FRIENDSHIP

THE HOPELESS CASE (PART 2)

Read: Isaiah 55:10-12

The next few visits to Mrs. Martin's were almost repeats of the first one. Sometimes Jeff went along, and he thought very little was accomplished. But Mom wasn't discouraged and continued to bring Bible tracts and homemade goodies. Then, during one visit, Mrs. Martin stopped talking about "crooks" and turned to Mom. "Why do you keep coming to see me?" she asked. "Even my own children don't visit this often!"

Mom smiled and looked over at Jeff as if to signal that the time had come. "We care about you, and so does Jesus," she told Mrs. Martin. "We visit and bring a few things, but he did so much more for you. You see, sin disqualifies everyone from heaven, but Jesus never sinned. So he voluntarily died on the cross for your sin. But that isn't all! Jesus rose again, and he wants you to live in heaven with him someday. To do that, you must accept what he has done for you."

Mrs. Martin listened quietly. Jeff noticed that, for the first time in all their visits, she was not thinking about crooks.

"I'd like to show you a special verse from my pocket Bible," Mom said, pulling it out of her purse. "Jeff, why don't you read John 3:16."

Jeff took the Bible and found the verse. "Here, Mrs. Martin," he said. "This verse tells you how much God loves you." Mrs. Martin looked at the verse, and Mom explained more about the need to believe in Jesus Christ as Savior. She gave her a Bible tract that explained the way of salvation. Mrs. Martin barely looked up as they got ready to leave. Her eyes were on the verse.

The next time they called on Mrs. Martin, Jeff was surprised at the smile on her face. "Jesus loves me," she said simply, "and I love him, too." *JAG*

HOW ABOUT YOU?

Do you continue to pray for and witness to the "hopeless case" you know? Sometimes it may take weeks, or even years, before you see any results, but don't give up. Keep on praying and presenting God's Word. He promises that it will accomplish his purpose.

KEEP ON
WITNESSING

MEMORIZE:
"My word . . . will accomplish all I want it to, and it will prosper everywhere I send it." Isaiah 55:11

Read: Hebrews 4:14-16

During the next few weeks, the word crooks was mentioned less and less when Mom and Jeff visited Mrs. Martin. Her questions about God and his Word increased more and more.

One day Mom showed Mrs. Martin how to begin a prayer list. "Make a list of people and things you want to pray about," instructed Mom, "and then behind each item leave room to record how God answered your prayer."

When Mom suggested that she pray about her fears, Mrs. Martin looked surprised. "Jesus is interested in things like being afraid of crooks?" she asked.

"Yes, he is," Mom said, smiling. "He really is." Mrs. Martin looked at her prayer list and wrote "crooks" at the bottom.

Just before school began in the fall, Jeff and his mother once again visited Mrs. Martin. "I hope you'll still visit me after school starts, Jeff," said Mrs. Martin. Then, turning to Mom, she continued. "I prayed about those fears I had—you know, the 'crooks.' Look at the answer Jesus gave me." She offered Mom her prayer list.

Mom took the list. There, after the word "crooks," Mrs. Martin had written "caught."

"They caught the young men who robbed my apartment, but I didn't get back any of the things they took," Mrs. Martin explained. "They're in jail, and now I'm praying that they'll find Jesus, just like I did."

"We'll pray with you," said Mom. "We'll be prayer partners." Mrs. Martin smiled and nodded her head. *JAG*

HOW ABOUT YOU?

Have you learned that Jesus cares about your fears—fears of the night, robbers, or bad dreams? He cares about your problems as well as your joys. Do you bring everything to him in prayer, trusting him for an answer? A prayer list is a good idea, and a prayer partner is, too. Learn to bring all your concerns and requests to Jesus, along with your thanksgiving.

MEMORIZE:

"Don't worry about anything; instead, pray about everything. Tell God what you need, and thank him for all he has done." Philippians 4:6

PRAY ABOUT EVERYTHING

SPILLED MILK

Read: Luke 17:1-5

"How could you be so careless, Tatianna?" cried her brother, Travis. "Now my brand new sweater has milk all over it. Leave it to my dumb sister to spill her cereal on everything!"

"I really am sorry, Travis," she said tearfully. "I didn't mean to get your sweater dirty."

Travis scowled and turned away. "Travis, don't you think you're being a bit harsh with Tatianna?" asked Mom. "She did apologize. How about trying a little bit of forgiveness?"

But Travis stormed out of the kitchen and up to his room to change. "Being sorry doesn't make my sweater clean," he said.

At school, Travis was glad when it was time for art—his favorite class. He hoped it would help him forget the upsetting morning. But on the way to the art table, Travis accidentally knocked into Emily's desk, causing her paint brush to sweep across the corner of her picture with paint. Travis gasped. "Oh, Emily, I'm so sorry! I've ruined your beautiful painting."

Emily looked sadly at her picture. "I know you didn't mean to do it," she said. Then her face lit up. "I think if I paint over it with another color, it will cover it right up."

That evening, Travis told his mother how Emily had covered the smudge on the picture. Mom nodded. "You know," she said, "there's a verse that I'm reminded of—one I learned when I was about your age. It's Proverbs 10:12. 'Hatred stirs up strife, but love covers all sins' (NKJV). Emily showed love when she covered the smudge you made—and I think it would have been good if you had done that this morning when Tatianna spilled her cereal." Soberly, Travis nodded. *DLR*

HOW ABOUT YOU?

Do you find it difficult to forgive others? If you're a Christian, the Bible says your sins are covered by the blood of Jesus. He does not hold one thing against you! And the Bible teaches that Christians are to practice that same kind of loving and forgiving with others.

FORGIVE
OTHERS

MEMORIZE:

"Above all, love each other deeply, because love covers over a multitude of sins." 1 Peter 4:8, NIV

FENCE OF PROTECTION

Read: Psalm 27:1-6

"Oh, Steve, can't we take Elm Street to the park?" said Rachel as she walked along with her brother.

Steve shook his head. "That would make it too much farther," he answered, "and it's far enough already." Rounding the corner they could see the park about three blocks away.

"Well, I hope that big dog doesn't come out to chase us," Rachel said as they approached a fenced yard.

"Did you forget all the stuff we talked about yesterday?" Steve asked bravely. "We don't have to be afraid, because Jesus is with us, remember?" Suddenly a large mean-looking dog began to growl. He was near the back of the yard but turned toward the children as they walked by. Then, showing his teeth, he started in their direction. "Run!" yelled Steve, and both children dashed down the street. The dog ran too—right into the chain-link fence that surrounded the yard. Then he stood there, fur raised, barking loudly. Steve and Rachel didn't slow down until they were several houses away. When they finally turned to look at the dog, he was still watching them, growling.

Later they told Mom about it. "Steve forgot all about how God was protecting him—you should have seen him run," Rachel said, teasing her brother. "We didn't really have to be afraid, though. That fence kept the dog away from us."

"Yeah," said Steve, "but all I saw was the big dog." He laughed a little sheepishly. "I didn't even notice the fence."

Mom nodded. "Jesus has a 'fence of protection' around us all the time," she said, "but often the things that frighten us keep us from remembering that. From now on, every time you're afraid, think of the fence. Let it remind you that Jesus has promised to take care of you." *JAG*

HOW ABOUT YOU?

Did you know Jesus has a "fence of protection" around you? Fierce dogs, a hard math test, a raging thunderstorm, or giving an oral book report cannot tear down that "fence of protection." This doesn't mean that bad things will never happen to you. But it does mean that God will allow only as much as you can handle—and he'll help you handle it. If you belong to Jesus, he will keep you in his care.

MEMORIZE:

"But the Lord is faithful; he will make you strong and guard you from the evil one." 2 Thessalonians 3:3

JESUS' CARE
SURROUNDS YOU

HE'S ALIVE

Read: 1 Thessalonians 4:13-18

Cory stood in the funeral home and wondered if he would ever forget the telephone call that brought the dreadful news that Grandpa Connors had died of a heart attack. Cory felt almost sick every time he looked at the casket. That cold, lifeless body lying there couldn't be the wonderful Grandpa who had taken him fishing just last month! His parents and grandmother puzzled him, too. When people came to see the family, Mom and Grandma often cried all over again— but they always ended up smiling! *How can they smile with Grandpa gone?* he wondered. *I sure don't feel like smiling! Will I ever be happy again?*

Finally, it was time for the funeral. Cory had been trying to block all the sadness out of his mind, but as he listened to the quiet organ music, an awful thought struck him. *I'll never see my grandpa again!* he thought. *After this service they'll close the casket and bury him under the ground, and I'll never see him again!* Tears came to his eyes.

Just then the pastor stood up and began to speak. His first words were, "Some of you are sorrowing today because you heard that Brother Jim Connors is dead. It's not so! He's alive! He has left his earthly body and gone to heaven. Don't sorrow without hope, for if you know Jesus as your Savior—like Jim Connors did—you'll see him again in heaven someday." The pastor went on to quote verses from John, chapter 11, but Cory had already heard what he needed to hear most. He realized that his parents had been saying the same thing, but only now did it sink in. *Thank you, God,* he prayed silently. *Thank you that I'll see Grandpa again! REP*

HOW ABOUT YOU?

Has someone died who was dear to you? It made you sad, didn't it? It's all right to feel sadness, and it's all right to cry. Even Jesus cried (read John 11:35). But if that person was a Christian—and if you are, too—your sorrow should be mixed with joy because that loved one is alive and happy in heaven. Someday you will meet again. Praise the Lord!

**BELIEVERS
DIE TO LIVE**

MEMORIZE:

"Jesus said to her, 'I am the resurrection and the life. He who believes in me will live, even though he dies.'"

John 11:25, NIV

"You don't really believe what that preacher said, do you, Linda?" In the backseat of the car, Greg listened as Uncle Larry questioned his mother. Uncle Larry had gone to church with them, and it was the first time Greg could remember his uncle going to church.

"Yes, I do believe what Pastor Grange said, Larry," Greg's mother answered.

"Ahhhh, now, Linda," protested Uncle Larry, "Granddad Casey used to preach about the end of the world when we were kids. Nothing's happened yet."

"A lot has happened," Mom countered. "A great deal of prophecy has been fulfilled."

"Like the prophecy of Ezekiel and Daniel?" Greg joined the conversation.

His mother looked surprised. "What do you know about Ezekiel and Daniel?"

"Quite a lot," Greg answered with a smile. "We've been studying the major prophets in Sunday school."

Uncle Larry grinned. "Tell me about it, kid." Greg knew his uncle was making fun of him, but he didn't care. People had made fun of Isaiah, Jeremiah, Ezekiel, and Daniel . . . and Jesus, too.

"People laughed at Jeremiah," Greg said. "They called him the 'weeping prophet.' Guess they were the ones weeping when his messages came true."

Uncle Larry blinked, and Greg's mother nodded. "If you'll read the newspaper, Larry, along with some Bible prophecies, you'll find God's Word is still being fulfilled."

"I'd rather not think about it," Uncle Larry said. "It sounds spooky to me."

Greg started to tell his uncle about the way the people had treated Jeremiah and Ezekiel, but when Uncle Larry refused to talk about it anymore, Greg decided he had said enough. He would just pray for Uncle Larry. God would take care of him. All Greg could do was deliver God's message. BJW

HOW ABOUT YOU?

Do you get discouraged because people don't like the messages that are in God's Word? Do you find that they don't want you to talk to them about God? Don't give up. Continue to give them God's message, just as the prophets did. Don't let their hard looks discourage you.

MEMORIZE:

"Do not say, 'I am only a child.' You must go to everyone I send you to and say whatever I command you."
Jeremiah 1:7, NIV

TELL GOD'S MESSAGE

THE FAD TRAP

Read: Matthew 6:28-33

"Mom, can I use a needle and thread?" asked Tom one evening.

Mom looked up in surprise. "I guess so," she said.

As Mom passed the door of Tom's room a bit later, she saw him sitting on his bed, trying to sew something onto his sweater. "What in the world are you doing?" she asked as she walked over, picked up the sweater, and examined it. "Hmm—so this is what the thread and needle were for. Where did you get this little emblem, and why are you sewing it on your new sweater?"

Tom blushed. "I took it off an old shirt. The cool kids wear something like that on their shirts and sweaters."

Mom shook her head. "Sounds like you're caught in a fad trap," she said. "Brand name clothes are nice, but isn't it a matter of pride when you have to have the label on the outside of your clothes so everyone will think you have the popular kind?"

"Aw, Mom," protested Tom, "there's nothing wrong with wanting to be in style, is there?"

"No," Mom replied, "unless it becomes so important to you that you're willing to spend far more than you should just to get a certain label—or you're willing to try to deceive others in order to impress them. God would not be pleased with that."

Tom sighed. Then he looked at Mom and grinned. "Oh, well . . . I hated trying to sew anyway," he said. "It won't take me long to rip this back off—it's not sewed on very well." *SLK*

HOW ABOUT YOU?

Is it important to you to wear clothes and shoes that are "in style" and that will impress others? Watch out! It's wrong to judge people by the brand of clothes they wear—and it's dangerous to let your friends' opinions mean more to you than the principles of God's Word. Next time you go shopping for clothes, make sure you're not caught in a "fad trap."

FADS CAN
TRAP YOU

MEMORIZE:

"Therefore do not worry, saying . . .
'What shall we wear?' "
Matthew 6:31, NKJV

THE EASTER PICTURE

Read: Mark 16:1-7

Preston worked carefully on his drawing for the Easter picture contest. As he was sketching, his friend Mark looked over his shoulder. "Easter eggs? Got them a little out of shape, didn't you?" scoffed Mark. "Wait till you see my picture—Peter Cottontail with a whole basketful of eggs! Hey, what color are you going to paint your eggs?"

Preston shook his head. "These aren't eggs. This one's a big stone. And look—see this? It's the opening of a cave. The big stone was rolled away from there," he explained, pointing to his drawing.

"Stone!" Mark exclaimed. "What's that for? This is supposed to be an Easter picture. You're supposed to draw Easter rabbits or maybe some chicks—stuff like that."

"This *is* an Easter picture," Preston insisted. "I'm drawing the empty tomb. I thought I might try to draw an angel or the disciples or something." Preston paused. "I don't think I can draw them good enough to win the contest though," he added doubtfully.

Mark was puzzled. "I don't get it," he said as the bell rang. "What are you talking about? What's that got to do with Easter?"

Preston looked at him in surprise. "Don't you know about Jesus?" he asked.

"Jesus?" repeated Mark. "Well, I know he was born at Christmastime. Oh . . . I guess maybe I did hear a story once about him dying or something. Is that what you're talking about?"

Preston did some quick thinking as they put on their jackets to go home. "Look," he said, "why don't you come to my house? I can show you the real Easter story in my Bible storybook. It's time you learned what Easter is all about!" *AU*

HOW ABOUT YOU?

Do your friends know what Easter is about? Will you tell them? Ask the Lord to help you to share the real meaning of Easter with at least one friend this week. Then do it!

MEMORIZE:

"He isn't here! He has been raised from the dead, just as he said would happen." Matthew 28:6

EASTER MEANS JESUS ROSE FROM THE DEAD

WHAT YOU WATCH

Read: Psalm 101:2-7

As they waited for Sunday school to begin, the junior high students talked about their favorite television programs. "Did you see *High and Mighty* last night?" asked Brad.

"Sure did," replied Brenda.

"I liked when Rusty got drunk," said Brent, "and then he knocked those two cops right through the nightclub window. Wham-o! Two dead ducks!"

"Yeah. I'd love to be one of his girlfriends on the show," added Sue, "like that blonde he was kissing at the dance club. Wasn't it funny when her husband showed up?"

Suddenly the children realized that their teacher was standing in the doorway. The subject was quickly changed, and Mr. Miles began the lesson. At the end of the session he said. "Don't forget the party next Saturday."

When the kids arrived for the party, there was a big television set at the front of the church sanctuary. "What's that for?" they asked.

"It's Saturday night, and I thought you might want to watch *High and Mighty*," replied Mr. Miles. "I'll turn it on."

The kids looked at each other uneasily, but the first few minutes of the program weren't too bad. When one of the characters swore, everyone felt uncomfortable. When an actress appeared wearing skimpy clothing, some of the kids exchanged uneasy glances. Soon Sue called out, "Let's not watch this!"

Mr. Miles rose and turned off the set. "I thought you liked this show," he said.

"Yeah, but . . . well, church is God's house, and somehow it seems wrong to watch that kind of program here," said one of the kids.

"I agree," said Mr. Miles.

"And if it's wrong to watch it at church, then it is probably wrong to watch it at home, too," added Brent.

"That's right," said Mr. Miles. "We need to live for God all the time—not just when we're in church." *SLK*

HOW ABOUT YOU?

Would you be comfortable watching your favorite TV programs if Jesus was watching them with you? If a program makes you uncomfortable, then switch the channel or turn the TV off. Ask God to help you resist the temptation to watch programs that make sin look good.

TURN OFF
BAD TV

MEMORIZE:
"I will refuse to look at anything vile and vulgar." Psalm 101:3

Read: Titus 3:4-7

As Charlie and his dad passed the high school, they saw kids holding signs for a "free car wash." As Dad stopped for a traffic light, one young man leaned toward the open window. "May we wash your car?" he asked eagerly. "It's free!"

"Oh, sure it is," said Charlie's dad. He chuckled.

"No . . . it really is free!" insisted the young man. But Dad didn't believe him.

"The car does need washing," said Charlie as they arrived home. "Why don't we wash it?"

"Okay," agreed Dad, and they hauled out the garden hose and rags.

Just then Charlie's mom came out. "Why don't you take the car to the high school?" she asked. "They're giving free car washes."

"You fell for that line, did you?" asked Dad with a smile. "There's got to be a catch to it."

"No, there isn't," his wife assured him. "I heard it on the radio. One of the school clubs has gotten people to pledge money for every car they wash. The more cars they wash, the more they make, but it won't cost you one penny."

"Really!" exclaimed Dad. "Come on, Charlie." They jumped in the car and drove back to the school. As Dad pulled into the parking lot, a girl walked up to the car. "I'm sorry, Sir, but we're closed," said the girl.

"Was it really free?" asked Dad, and the girl assured him that it was.

"You missed a free car wash," said Charlie.

Dad sighed as they drove away. "You're right," he said, and then a thought struck him. "This is exactly the way it is with God's gift of salvation," he told Charlie. "Many people think there's a catch to it—that they must in some way pay for or work for their salvation. But God says it's a 'gift'—it's free." *CVM*

HOW ABOUT YOU?
Do you think you have to earn salvation? Believe God when he says it's free. If you have questions, talk to your parents, to Christian friends, or to a trusted adult.

MEMORIZE:
"By grace you have been saved, through faith—and this not from yourselves, it is the gift of God—not by works, so that no one can boast."
Ephesians 2:8-9, NIV

SALVATION IS FREE

CAPTAIN MIDNIGHT

Read: Hebrews 12:1-2

Eight-year-old Craig planted himself in front of the TV to watch cartoons. His favorite was Captain Midnight, and he often pretended to be Captain Midnight with his black cape and hood.

"Mom," said Craig's sister one morning, "I put a dollar on my dresser yesterday, and now it's gone!"

Mom questioned Craig about it. When she didn't get his attention, she tried again. "Okay," Mom chuckled, then chanted, "Earth calling Captain Midnight! Come in, Captain! Carolyn is missing a dollar. Can you help us?"

Craig loved this game, and he answered in his deepest voice, "Can solve mystery easily. Captain Midnight takes from the rich and gives to the poor. I, Captain Midnight, gave dollar to boy in class who needed to buy school supplies." With this admission, he shouted, "Up, up, and away," and he spread his arms to "fly" to school.

"Hold on there," said Mom, catching hold of his arm. "You've taken this Captain Midnight thing too far. While he does many good things, he does not always do what is right. Your wanting to help a friend is a good thing, but the way you did it was wrong. Would Jesus have stolen from one person to help another person?"

"Well . . . no," Craig admitted. "But I did do something good with the money."

"Yes, you did. But the money wasn't yours to give," replied Mom. Craig admitted he'd known that stealing, for any reason, was wrong. "Craig, you'll have to pay Carolyn the dollar out of your allowance," said Mom. "And I hope you've learned a lesson. Trying to be like Captain Midnight is okay some of the time, but following Jesus is the best way to live our lives." *REP*

HOW ABOUT YOU?

Is there a "superhero" whom you idolize—a cartoon character, an athlete, a musician, or some other well-known person? Make Jesus your hero, or pattern for living. He'll never lead you wrong.

MAKE JESUS YOUR HERO

MEMORIZE:
"Let us fix our eyes on Jesus, the author and perfecter of our faith."
Hebrews 12:2, NIV

NO STRINGS ATTACHED

Read: 2 Corinthians 9:6-11

Arthur stared long and hard at the money bank in his hand. Soon he would have enough money to buy the bike he wanted—he'd have enough, that is, if he didn't give the money to Daniel Chin. Daniel was Arthur's best pal, but in one more week, Daniel would be leaving with his family to go to the mission field. Arthur was going to miss Daniel for sure! Arthur looked at the contents of his bank once more. "I guess I'll give it all to Daniel," he decided. He put the money in an envelope to take along to the farewell party for the Chin family.

When Arthur had a chance to talk to Daniel alone, he handed Daniel the money. "I want you to have this," he said.

Daniel's eyes opened wide. "Thanks!" he exclaimed. "But isn't this the money you were saving for . . ."

"Yeah," interrupted Arthur, "but I want you to have it. Buy anything you'd like with it."

Several days later, Arthur's father had a talk with him. "I can't help noticing your gloomy expression lately," Dad said. "Do you miss Daniel so much, or is it something else?"

"It's the money I saved for a bike," Arthur admitted. "I gave it to Daniel, but I thought God might have someone give me a bicycle or something because I gave my money away."

"I thought you gave your money with no strings attached," said Dad.

Arthur frowned. "What does that mean?"

"It means you give without expecting anything in return," explained Dad. "That's the kind of giving God wants us to do. I think you need to ask the Lord to change your attitude. Ask him to help you to be a generous, cheerful giver."

Arthur was ashamed. "I really do want Daniel to have the money," he said. "I really do." *AGL*

HOW ABOUT YOU?

Do you give with "no strings attached"? Or do you think first of what you might get in return? Ask God to help you give in a way that pleases him. It's not always an easy thing to do.

MEMORIZE:

"Don't give reluctantly or in response to pressure. For God loves the person who gives cheerfully." 2 Corinthians 9:7

GIVE CHEERFULLY

A NEW NAME

Read: 1 John 4:7-11

"Marcus, how would you like Felipe to be your father?"

As his mother asked the question, Marcus frowned. "My father?" he asked. "He's my stepfather, but he can't be my real father. My real father died."

"But, Marcus," said Mom, "Felipe loves you very much, and he would like to adopt you."

"I don't want to be adopted. I just want to be Marcus Bruka!" he exclaimed. Then he stomped off to his room.

Later that week, Felipe, Marcus's stepfather, talked to him. "I'd love to have you call me 'Dad,' " he said.

"A person can only have one dad," Marcus told him. "Adopting somebody doesn't really make him your kid."

"Oh, I don't know about that," said Felipe. "Tell me—do you want to go to heaven someday, Marcus?"

"Of course," answered Marcus.

"But you know that only those who are children of God can go to heaven," Felipe told him. "And no one is automatically born a child of God. We must be born again, or adopted, into his family, right?"

"Well . . . yeah," agreed Marcus.

"God becomes our Father," continued Felipe. "He gives us a new name, and he even gives us a new home in heaven—because he loves us. Marcus . . . I would like to adopt you—to make you my son, give you my name—because I love you."

"B-b-but I . . . I don't love you," stammered Marcus.

"I know," replied Felipe, "but I'm hoping you will. You know, the Bible says we love God because he first loved us. Somebody had to start loving—so God did. But he adopts us into his family when we decide we want him to. And unless you decide you'd like me to adopt you, I won't attempt to do that. But I hope you'll think about it." *HCT*

HOW ABOUT YOU?

Do you know that God loves you and wants to adopt you? He wants to give you a new name—Christian. That's why he sent his only Son, Jesus, to die for you. But God won't force his way into your life. He'll come only if you respond to his call. Will you ask him to be your heavenly Father?

YOU CAN BECOME GOD'S CHILD

MEMORIZE:
"We love because he first loved us."
1 John 4:19, NIV

April
26

"What on earth are you doing?" exclaimed Toby's mother as she rushed down the basement stairs after hearing a loud "bang" coming from there. "Look at the mess you've made."

"Aw," mumbled Toby, "I was just experimenting with my chemistry set. I didn't know this stuff would blow up."

"Well, I don't like these experiments," said Mom, frowning.

"But if you don't experiment, how are you going to find out about things?" protested Toby.

Mom sighed. "Well," she said, "maybe it's better not to know about some things. I'm afraid that lately you've been doing some other experimenting, too, haven't you?"

Toby was surprised. "Like what?" he asked.

"Well, you were smoking the other day, weren't you?" Mom asked. As Toby began to deny it, she continued, "Your breath smelled like smoke."

"Aw, well . . . some of us just tried it," admitted Toby, "but we didn't like it much. It doesn't hurt to experiment with stuff as long as you don't go overboard. You can't know anything for yourself unless you try it."

Mom reached into a cupboard and took out a bottle of floor cleaner. Toby watched as she poured some in a glass and handed it to him. "Have a drink," she invited.

"Mom," he gasped, "that's poison!"

Mom nodded. "But you don't really know that, do you? You haven't tried it for yourself. Sure you wouldn't like to try some?" she said.

"No, thank you!" exclaimed Toby. He looked at her curiously. "Were you really going to let me drink that?"

"Of course not," said Mom. "I just wanted to show you that it isn't necessary to try things to know they are bad for you. That principle is true regarding sin, too. It's never safe to experiment with sin." *HCT*

HOW ABOUT YOU?

Do you feel you must try everything for yourself? That could be dangerous. Listen to your parents and to others who have "been there." Above all, listen to God's Word. Leave sin alone.

MEMORIZE:

"Do not do as the wicked do or follow the path of evildoers." Proverbs 4:14

DON'T
EXPERIMENT
WITH SIN

FORGIVE ME MY SINS

Read: Psalm 32:1-7

Reuben and Tyshaun were eager to see Flash, Uncle Roosevelt's new pony. "I have some pictures of him," said Aunt Millie as the children traveled with their uncle and aunt on their way to spend a weekend at the farm. She took an envelope from her purse. "Here they are."

"Let me see!" said Tyshaun eagerly. "Wow! He's neat!" Reuben wanted to see, too. He grabbed a picture, but Tyshaun held on tight. Reuben hung on, too, and after a short tug of war and some angry words, Tyshaun slapped Reuben. "There!" he said. "That will teach you!" Reuben began to cry.

"Just a minute!" interrupted Uncle Roosevelt. "Let Aunt Millie have the pictures, and you both just sit back in your seats for a bit."

By the time they arrived at the farm, the fight was forgotten, and they enjoyed a delicious lunch. As Reuben helped wipe the dishes after lunch, one of the plates slipped from his hands and crashed to the floor. "Oh, Aunt Millie, I'm so sorry!" he exclaimed. "I'll buy you a new one."

"That won't be necessary, Reuben," said Aunt Millie.

Just before bedtime, Uncle Roosevelt read a chapter from the Bible, and each one led in prayer. Both Tyshaun and Reuben ended their prayer with, "Forgive my sins for Jesus' sake, Amen."

Uncle Roosevelt had a question. "What sins do you want God to forgive?" he asked.

Tyshaun looked surprised. "I . . . I . . . well, any wrong thing I did."

Uncle Roosevelt nodded. "Anything specific that you should confess to God?" he asked.

"We quarreled in the car," remembered Tyshaun. "I guess we should confess that."

"Reuben, when you broke one of my dishes, you were sorry and told me about it right away," said Aunt Millie. "That was good—and when you sin against God, it's also good to immediately confess it to him and ask his forgiveness." *AGL*

HOW ABOUT YOU?

Have you ever told a lie? Talked back to your parents? Been unkind to someone? You need to tell God (confess) the things you do wrong. Be specific. Ask God to help you not to repeat those actions that dishonor him.

MEMORIZE:

"But if we confess our sins to him, he is faithful and just to forgive us and to cleanse us from every wrong." 1 John 1:9

CONFESS YOUR SIN TO GOD

April

28

Read: 1 Corinthians 12:4-11

Tim noticed that sports seemed to be the big thing at Oak School, where he was a newcomer. He figured if he could be good at sports, he'd be accepted by his classmates. So Tim became an enthusiastic "joiner." He worked hard at baseball, basketball, track—whatever was the current sport. But in each sport, he was clumsy! Tim got "out" the most in baseball, made the most fouls in basketball, and his long jumps were the shortest. "I'm a born loser," Tim would complain. "Whenever the guys choose teams, I'm chosen last." Fifth grade was not a happy experience for him.

"Tim," said his gym teacher one day, "we're going to begin interclass competition in baseball, and we need a statistician—someone to keep score at the games and figure batting averages. Your math teacher tells me you're a whiz at math. Would you like the job?"

"Hey, yeah!" exclaimed Tim. He was soon established as the official scorekeeper, and for the first time in his life, he felt liked, appreciated, and needed. He felt like one of the gang—not because he was just like them, but because he had a talent too. His enthusiasm returned. Not only was he the scorekeeper at the games, but he cheered the loudest as well! *PMR*

HOW ABOUT YOU?

Are you trying to become one of the gang by being just like everyone else? God made you a unique person with special gifts and abilities that he wants you to develop and use. Don't compare yourself with everyone else. Don't measure your abilities by your friends' abilities. The Bible tells us this is not wise.

MEMORIZE:

"When they . . . compare themselves with themselves, they are not wise."
2 Corinthians 10:12, NIV

YOU ARE UNIQUE

I HATE WORK (PART 1)

Read: Proverbs 6:6-11

Aaron and Kevin wanted to go to the school baseball game, but first they had to clean the garage. Aaron knew he was working slowly, but he just couldn't get excited about cleaning the garage. By the time he finished his share, the ball game was half over.

"Mom, I'm done. Will you drive me to school?" he called.

"No, Aaron," Mom answered. "You should have been ready when I took Kevin. Now I'm baking cookies."

Aaron sniffed the air. "May I have a cookie?" he asked.

"Yes, but be careful," cautioned Mom. "They're hot!"

After taking a bite, Aaron smacked his lips. "Yummy! Super good!" he exclaimed. "You must love to bake."

Mom looked up. "Not really," she said. "Most of the time I bake because your father—and you and Kevin—like baked goods." Her eyes twinkled. "To see you happy makes me happy," she added.

Aaron looked surprised. "I sure wouldn't do all that work if I didn't have to."

"Aaron," said Mom, "if you had your way, you wouldn't work at all. But did you know that work is part of God's plan for happiness?"

"It is?" Aaron asked.

Mom nodded. "You should read the verses in Proverbs about the lazy man and the sluggard," she told him. "They don't please God. The one who pleases God is the faithful and diligent worker."

"That's happiness for God—not for the person who's doing the work," said Aaron.

Mom smiled. "Don't be so sure. Psalm 128:2 says, 'You will enjoy the fruit of your labor. How happy you will be!' It's rewarding to see the fruit—the good things that result from the work you do."

"I suppose you're right," admitted Aaron. "I'll try to think of that the next time I'm working. Then maybe I'll enjoy it more." *AGL*

HOW ABOUT YOU?

Do you hate work? Do you complain about it? Or do you cheerfully wash dishes, make your bed, and mow the lawn? Your willingness to work and do your best pleases God. It brings happiness, too, as you see the good results of serving God and others.

WORK BRINGS HAPPINESS

MEMORIZE:

"Whatever your hand finds to do, do it with all your might."
Ecclesiastes 9:10, NIV

I HATE WORK (PART 2)

Read: 2 Thessalonians 3:10-13

"Hi, Mr. Mitchell!" Aaron greeted his Sunday school teacher. "I thought you'd still be in bed." Mr. Mitchell had fallen from a scaffold and hurt his back. After surgery and a few days in the hospital, he was back home. So Aaron and his dad stopped by for a visit.

"You can't keep a good man down," Mr. Mitchell joked. "I'm thankful that I don't have much pain now. I may never be able to go back to construction work, though—or even lift anything very heavy."

"That's too bad," said Aaron's father. "I know how you loved your work."

Mr. Mitchell nodded. "I was afraid I wouldn't find any work that I could do," he said. "But just a couple of days ago, God provided work for me."

"Wonderful!" exclaimed Dad. "Where will you work?"

"For right now, my boss gave me two accounts to work on right here at home."

"What an answer to prayer!" marveled Dad.

Mr. Mitchell nodded. "The Bible says if a man refuses to work, he shouldn't eat! So as long as I can do something, I want to work—after all, I love to eat!" They all laughed. "I also experienced the truth of Ecclesiastes 5:12—'People who work hard sleep well,'" added Mr. Mitchell. "Since I've been working again, I sleep like a log." He looked at Aaron. "I'm looking forward to teaching again, too. I'm so glad the Lord saved me from my sin that I want to serve him all I can."

On the way home, Aaron was thoughtful. He had never really thought about how it would feel if he were unable to do work. He decided that he was glad he could help with chores. "Work is good after all," he told his father. When Dad looked at him in surprise, Aaron chuckled and added, "I like to eat, too!" *AGL*

HOW ABOUT YOU?

Do you enjoy work? Have you considered how it would feel if you were unable to do any work? Make a list of things God has done for you. Truly thank him, and then you, too, will work more joyfully. (If you're still tempted to grumble about work, remember how much you like to eat!)

MEMORIZE:

"Whoever does not work should not eat." 2 Thessalonians 3:10

THANK GOD FOR WORK

OUT!

Read: Acts 3:11-12; 4:10-12

Josh sat on the couch watching a baseball game with his dad. "It's too bad Pete isn't here," said Josh. "He loves baseball."

"Who's Pete?" asked Dad.

"He's a new kid at school," Josh answered. "I like him."

Dad smiled. "I talked to a new family at church last week," he said. "They have a son named Pete. I wonder if that's him."

"I doubt it," said Josh. "Our church talks a lot about Jesus dying on the cross for us, but Pete doesn't believe it. He believes in God, though, and he's a really good kid."

Dad sighed. "Pete's missing out on salvation by not believing in Jesus and what he did for us on the cross," he said.

Dad's reply was muffled by loud cheering. The batter had just slammed the ball far into right field. The player already on first base started running to second. "Go! Go!" yelled Josh, jumping up. The runner passed second base and raced to third. "He'll score for sure!" said Josh as the player rounded third base and headed for home. But Josh's cheer turned to a groan as the runner got tagged out. The game was over.

"For all that effort, it's too bad he didn't make it home," said Dad. "He reminds me of your friend Pete."

Josh's eyebrows shot up. "Why?" he asked.

Dad clicked off the TV. "In baseball, you don't score unless you make it to home plate. Passing first, second, and third base isn't enough. That's a little like your friend Pete. He may be nice and believe there's a God. He might even admire Jesus, but that's not enough. Pete doesn't believe in the cross—he doesn't believe that Jesus died for him. He's missing Jesus, the Savior. Unless he changes, Pete won't be saved. He'll be considered out."

Joshua frowned. "Tomorrow I'll tell that to Pete." *SML*

HOW ABOUT YOU?

Do you know anyone who's really nice but who refuses to believe that when Jesus died on the cross, he paid the penalty for sin? It's not enough to just believe that there's a God. Don't come to the end of your life and find that you're "out"—out of heaven. God sent his Son to die on the cross for you. Believing on him is the only way to heaven.

BELIEVE IN JESUS

May
2

STIFF COMPETITION

Read: Psalm 147:10-11

In the final lap of his practice run, Matthew pushed hard. *If I can run this fast tomorrow, I'll get the gold medal for sure,* he thought. As he ran through the imaginary finish line, he slowed down and grasped his side to relieve a cramp.

"Hi, Speedy," a voice called from beside the track.

"Dad!" Matthew puffed, jogging off the track. "You been here long?"

"Not long," answered Dad. "It's time for dinner."

"Not yet! I need to run just a little longer, okay?" begged Matthew.

"Matt," said Dad, "nourishment is just as necessary as running practice. And I'm also concerned that your running has kept you away from other important activities. I'm wondering if we made a mistake in letting you join the track team. You've missed family devotions, and you've not had time for your regular church activities, either. There's a youth service tonight, right?"

"Yeah," said Matthew, "but the track meet is tomorrow, and I just *have* to beat Tony."

"Are you aware that you have another opponent?" Dad asked. "One who is trying to beat you just as hard as Tony is?"

"Who?" asked Matthew, glancing around the track.

"He's not on the field," Dad said. "He's not even interested in your track record. He's interested in your heart, your soul, and your mind." Matthew knew now who Dad meant. "Satan doesn't care if you win or lose this meet," said Dad, "but he does want you to neglect fellowship with God and with other believers. Just as you can't beat Tony without strengthening your body, you cannot beat the devil without strengthening your heart, mind, and soul."

"You're right," admitted Matthew. Then he had a thought. "After we pray for my heart and soul and mind at family devotions tonight, could we pray for my legs, too?"

Dad smiled as they walked home together. "We sure can." *HMT*

HOW ABOUT YOU?

Is there something in your life that takes away from time spent with God? Even great activities such as sports, hobbies, or time spent with friends can't replace your time with God. Think of your life as one great competition. God wants to give you the winner's prize, but Satan wants to beat you out of it.

MEMORIZE:

"So think clearly and exercise self-control. Look forward to the special blessings that will come to you at the return of Jesus Christ." 1 Peter 1:13

TRAIN TO WIN
AGAINST SATAN

THE MYSTERY SEEDS

Read: Galatians 6:7-10

Jordan and his sister Jackie had been given permission to plant a small vegetable garden. While Jordan ran to his room to get the seeds, Jackie mapped out, with paper and pencil, where she wanted everything planted.

"What's taking you so long?" asked Jackie a little later.

"I put the seeds right here on my desk, but they're gone," said Jordan. "Let's ask Mom if she's seen them."

They found Mom washing dirt off their little sister's arms. "How'd Debbie get so dirty?" asked Jackie.

"Playing in the sandbox," said Mom.

"No, I wasn't," said Debbie. "I was planting the garden. I found the seeds on Jordan's desk, so I planted 'em."

"You what?" yelled Jordan. "You don't know how to plant a garden!"

"Do, too," said Debbie. "I dug a hole and dumped the seeds in it."

"Those were not your seeds! You're a thief!" yelled Jordan.

"That's enough, Jordan," said Mom sternly.

"Well, it's true!" exclaimed Jordan. "And I hate thieves!" He turned and went to his room.

Mom followed later. "Jordan," said Mom, "do you remember our Bible reading this morning?"

"We . . . uh . . . yeah, it was about reaping what we sow," he mumbled.

"Yes," said Mom. "It was wrong of Debbie to plant those seeds, but what you planted was worse."

"I haven't planted anything," said Jordan.

"You've planted a seed of hate in your sister's heart," said Mom. "I'm sure you don't want to reap hate from Debbie."

Jordan sighed. "I . . . I didn't mean what I said. I was just mad. I'm sorry, Mom."

"All right," said Mom. "You'll need to apologize to Debbie."

"Okay," Jordan said. "Then can we go buy more seeds? I'd like to teach Debbie how to plant them the right way."

"Great idea," said Mom. "*You'll* be learning how to plant seeds the right way, too—seeds of kindness." *TAS*

HOW ABOUT YOU?

When people do things you don't like, do you sow seeds of hate or seeds of kindness? The Bible says we are not to repay evil with evil, but with good. And remember that whatever it is you sow, that's what you'll eventually reap.

YOU'LL REAP
WHAT YOU SOW

MEMORIZE:
"You will always reap what you sow!"
Galatians 6:7

BIRD IN A CAGE

Read: Proverbs 1:1-9

"Dad, may I go to the ball game with Matt?" asked Cory.

"I'm sorry," replied Dad, "but the answer is no. Last time you went, you stayed out past your curfew. The rule is that if you can't get in on time, you stay home the next week."

"Oh, all right." Cory stalked out of the room. "Dumb old rules."

Cory switched on the TV in the den. He was embarrassed when one of the actors swore just as Mom walked into the room. "Cory," she said, "you know it's against the rules in this house to watch that kind of show."

Cory turned off the TV. "Nobody wants me to have any fun."

The next day, Cory was again complaining. "We've got another new rule at school," he said. "We're not allowed in the halls without a written permission slip. I'm sick of all the rules—at home and at school . . . even at church. Can't a guy ever be left alone? I feel like I'm caged up, the same as Pepi." Cory glanced at the birdcage in the corner. "Hey, Pepi's missing!"

Mom sighed. "I know," she said. "When I opened his cage to give him fresh water, he zipped out right past me. He dropped to the floor and Smokie grabbed him. I rescued Pepi from the dog's mouth, but it was too late. I'm sorry, Cory. Pepi is dead."

Cory stared. "That dumb bird!" he exclaimed. "We had him in his cage for his own good."

"Cory, you're a lot like Pepi," said Mom. "You think rules keep you 'caged'— and in a way, they do. But they're for your protection." Mom paused. "Pepi's cage was good for him, and God's rules—and ours—are good for you. They allow you to enjoy life and be protected, too. I just wish Pepi had learned to be content." *MRP*

HOW ABOUT YOU?

Do you get tired of obeying rules? If left to yourself, you'd probably follow the desires of your sinful nature right into disaster. Thank God that you have the Bible to show you how you should live. Thank him, too, for parents and teachers who care enough to make rules for your good. Obeying them leaves you free to enjoy a safe, happy life.

MEMORIZE:

"He who despises the word will be destroyed, but he who fears the commandment will be rewarded."
Proverbs 13:13, NKJV

OBEY RULES GLADLY

ALL WET

Read: Luke 16:10-13

Reuben threw a fastball to Tommy at the other end of the yard. Tommy returned it to Reuben's baseball mitt with a thud. "I sure hope we both make the team," Tommy yelled.

"Me, too," Reuben agreed.

When Mom called Reuben for dinner, he tossed his mitt on the grass. Tommy pedaled off on his bike.

After dinner, thunder began rumbling through the sky and rain began to fall. Soon it was pouring!

The next day, Reuben searched for his mitt. "Oh, no!" he exclaimed. He ran to the backyard. Water dripped from the mitt as he picked it up.

"You left your mitt outside in the rain?" asked Dad when he saw Reuben with the wet mitt. Reuben nodded unhappily. "How many times have I talked to you about taking care of your things?" asked Dad.

"I needed a new mitt anyway," said Reuben. "See how worn this is?"

Dad took the mitt and shook his head. "No new mitt as long as you're so careless with the one you have," he said.

"But, Dad!" cried Reuben. "The tryouts for the team are next week. I need a mitt to practice."

"You'll have to make do with this one," said Dad. He dropped the soggy mitt into Reuben's hands. "The Bible says that all we have is from God. He expects us to take the best possible care of what he's provided—even baseball mitts. Learning to take care of such things trains us to take care of more important things, too." Dad paused at the porch steps. "Hang the mitt out on the clothesline," he suggested. "It'll dry out more quickly there. Then you'll need to use vegetable oil to soften the leather again. It's a good reminder that taking care of things in the first place will save you a lot of trouble and work." *JW*

HOW ABOUT YOU?

Do you take care of your things? The Bible says you should be faithful (or trustworthy) in caring for them. Doing so pleases God and also teaches you the responsibility needed for taking care of "true riches"—for handling spiritual responsibilities.

TAKE CARE OF THINGS

MEMORIZE:

"And if you are untrustworthy about worldly wealth, who will trust you with the true riches of heaven?"

Luke 16:11

THE GOOD HIDING PLACE

Read: Psalm 104:16-25

Michael stood at the window, watching a rabbit kick dirt with its strong hind legs. *What's he doing that for?* wondered Michael. *I'll ask Jeff when he gets home.* His older brother usually knew the answers to Michael's many questions about nature.

The rabbit, noticing movement at the window, suddenly sat still. After watching a while longer, Michael returned to his play, forgetting all about the rabbit.

When Michael was mowing the grass a few days later, he noticed a small bare spot with a little dried grass over it. It was where the rabbit had kicked up the grass and dirt. "Jeff, look here," he called.

When Jeff came, he carefully lifted the dried grass, and Michael saw fur in the little hole. With a smile on his face, Jeff pulled out a handful of the fur. Peering into the hole, Michael saw four tiny rabbits. "So that's why the rabbit was digging here!" Michael exclaimed.

"The babies are called kittens, and the nest is called a form," Jeff explained. "The mother rabbit pulls fur from her chest so her kittens will stay warm even when she's not with them." He carefully put the fur back over the baby rabbits, then covered everything with the dried grass so it looked just as before.

"I ran the lawn mower right over that spot and didn't even see the nest . . . uh, I mean the form!" Michael was amazed. "How did the mother rabbit know how to make such a good hiding place for her kittens?"

"God made his creatures in a wonderful way," Jeff said. "Each kind of animal has its own type of protection, each eats the kind of food God intended for it, and each cares for its young in just the way God planned. God's wisdom is shown in all his creation." *CEY*

HOW ABOUT YOU?
What can you find today that shows how wonderfully God made the world? All around you are signs that he made the world in a very wise way. Each of his creatures have special habits, and each brings glory to God in its own way.

MEMORIZE:
"O Lord, what a variety of things you have made! In wisdom you have made them all. The earth is full of your creatures." Psalm 104:24

NATURE SHOWS
GOD'S WISDOM

KEEP THE FIRE BURNING

Read: Hebrews 10:23-25

"Oh, Dad! Camping is so much fun!" exclaimed Brad as he roasted a marshmallow over their campfire. "I wish we didn't have to go back home early to go to church. I don't see why it's so important to go every week anyway."

"Hmmm," said Dad, "let's see if I can show you." Brad watched as Dad took a long stick and pushed a burning coal away from the crackling fire. "Keep an eye on that red-hot coal for a while," Dad advised.

A little later, Brad noticed that the coal was no longer burning. He pointed it out to his dad. Dad nodded. "When you remove a coal from a fire, it loses its glow and its warmth," he explained. "The same thing can happen to a Christian who doesn't meet with other believers."

"But lots of people are sick and can't go to church," said Brad. "Do they lose their glow and warmth?"

Dad smiled. "Always remember that there's a great difference between being unable to attend church and choosing not to go. I think the Lord provides other ways to keep the 'embers glowing' for those who can't go. Can you think of some?"

"Well, I guess by hearing sermons on television or radio, or by reading the Bible," suggested Brad.

"Right." Dad nodded. "It also helps to talk with other Christians and to read Christian books."

Brad looked thoughtfully at the ember. "What happens if you put it back in the fire?" he asked.

"Let's find out." Dad pushed the ember back into the fire, and soon it was glowing brightly. Dad smiled. "The real danger in skipping church is that it's easy to make a habit of it," he said. "Now do you understand the importance of church and of being there regularly?" Solemnly, Brad nodded. *VLC*

HOW ABOUT YOU?

Is going to church and Sunday school important to you? It should be. It's part of God's plan for your growth in spiritual things. Whenever possible, be there. When you must miss, listen to God's Word on the radio if you can, and spend extra time studying it for yourself. Don't just skip church.

MEMORIZE:

"And let us not neglect our meeting together, as some people do, but encourage and warn each other, especially now that the day of his coming back again is drawing near."
Hebrews 10:25

ATTEND CHURCH
FAITHFULLY

May
8

"It's just not fair," stormed Troy as he and Peter came into the kitchen after school. "I'm your own brother!"

"What are you two quarreling about?" asked Grandma.

"Peter asked another kid to do his paper route for him while he's at school camp," Troy told her. "He could have asked me. He knows I need the money. He's just being . . ."

"Hey! I asked you to help me not long ago," broke in Peter. "I told you that you had to put the paper on the porches, out of the rain. But you were in such a hurry to finish, you just tossed them toward the houses, not bothering to see where they landed. My customers complained about that."

"I guess it's no wonder he doesn't want to give you the responsibility of his paper route for three whole days!" said Grandma. Troy stalked off.

After dinner that evening, Dad picked up the Bible for family devotions. He read about some servants who were faithful in a responsibility they had been given. As a result they were given even greater responsibility. But one of the servants had not been faithful, and all responsibility was taken from him. "It's good for us to consider how we're handling *our* responsibilities," said Dad when he finished reading.

Troy's thoughts went back to what had happened regarding the paper route, and he felt guilty. Dad's voice cut into his thoughts. ". . . and so Jesus wants us to always do our very best in whatever job we're given, whether it's some kind of employment, school work, a job in the church, or whatever tasks come our way as we live the Christian life each day."

No more sloppy work for me, Troy decided. *I'm going to do my best to be a faithful worker—in everything. CEY*

HOW ABOUT YOU?

Do you try to get finished with your jobs as quickly or as easily as possible? If you can be trusted with doing a small job to the very best of your ability, people will also trust you with bigger and better jobs. And God will, too.

MEMORIZE:

"He who is faithful in a very little thing is faithful also in much."
Luke 16:10, NASB

GOOD WORK
BRINGS
REWARDS

GRASS HUTS AND BASEBALL

Read: 1 Thessalonians 3:6-9

Greg tossed his pen down on the table and crumpled up another piece of paper. "What should I write about, Dad? I've never written a letter to a missionary before, but I have to do this for homeschool."

Dad looked up from the letter he was writing. "What would you like to hear if you were spending four years in another country?"

"I'd want to know how the teams were doing in baseball or soccer or whatever," said Greg with a grin. "And I'd like to know what new model planes are out. But I'm just a normal kid, not a missionary kid!"

Dad raised his eyebrows. "And you think a 'missionary kid' wouldn't be interested in those things?"

Greg shrugged his shoulders. "Well, when I think of missionaries, I picture grass huts, wild animals, and people who don't wear many clothes. I don't even know if missionaries know how to play baseball."

"Hmmm . . . maybe you better put that letter aside until later," Dad suggested. "We're scheduled to hear from a missionary family in church tomorrow. They have a son about your age, and they'll be here for Sunday dinner."

The next week, Greg couldn't stop talking about his new friend. Peter had grown up in South America where his folks were missionaries. "He goes to a big school with other missionary kids," Greg said. "They have a baseball team, and Peter likes to play shortstop, just like me. And they have a really good soccer team. He has a model ship collection, too. Missionary kids are a lot like me!"

Dad grinned and nodded. "When he goes back to the mission field, maybe you can keep him posted on how your favorite teams are doing!" *DLR*

HOW ABOUT YOU?

Have you ever written to, or gotten to know, a missionary family? Why not write to one and maybe exchange pictures and share hobbies? Paul, who was the first missionary sent out by the Christian church, was encouraged when he heard good reports about his Christian friends. (See today's Scripture.) A letter from you could really brighten someone's day.

ENCOURAGE A
MISSIONARY

MEMORIZE:
"Good news from far away is like cold water to the thirsty." Proverbs 25:25

NEVER TOO YOUNG

Read: 1 Samuel 3:1-10

During supper, Mom and Dad told Ryan and Meg about their new neighbors. "We helped them move in, and it was hard work," said Dad. "I sure am tired tonight. I know your mom is, too." But the work was not yet done. Ryan volunteered to help with the dishes. Afterwards, Ryan went out to help Dad wash the car.

When the work was finally finished, Dad read the paper and Mom relaxed in her favorite chair, reading a book. Ryan was sitting at the table drawing an airplane when Meg complained that her shoe was untied. Quickly Ryan jumped up to tie it for her. A little later, Meg wanted someone to read her favorite story to her. Noticing how tired Mom looked, Ryan volunteered. Shortly before going to bed, Meg wanted someone to play dolls. "Oh, no!" groaned Ryan. "Not dolls!" But he went with her so that Mom could rest after the long, hard day.

After Meg was in bed, Ryan got back to his drawing. He noticed Dad yawning. "You sure are nice people, Mom and Dad, for helping the neighbors move in and all," Ryan observed. "When I grow up, I want to be helpful—just like you."

Dad smiled as he answered. "Oh, you don't have to wait until you're older. You've accepted Jesus as Savior, and he expects you to begin right away to serve him. You serve him by serving others. You're already doing that now."

"I am?" Ryan asked.

"Sure," said Mom. "Tonight you helped with the dishes."

"And you helped me wash the car," Dad chimed in. "I noticed you did an extra good job on the windows, too."

"You also took care of Meg," Mom added. "You are very helpful, and Dad and I are pleased. I know the Lord is, too." *MMB*

HOW ABOUT YOU?

Do you think you're too young to help? You're not. God uses children as well as adults. Ask him to use you. Start serving him by serving at home. There are many things you can do to help around the house, such as keeping your room clean, helping with the dishes, running errands, or watching your younger brother or sister. You're never too young to help!

MEMORIZE:

"And the boy became the Lord's helper."
1 Samuel 2:11

BE A
HELPER NOW

THE WALLET

Read: Luke 15:3-10

Chris looked everywhere for his wallet. He was sure it had been in his pocket just before he gave a vigorous whack to a ball and then had to slide into third base. He went out and searched all around the ball diamond. No wallet. He looked in the area where the kids at school hung their coats. It wasn't there. He asked his friends if they had seen it. They had not. When he got home, he looked all through the house, even though he was sure it wouldn't be there. He was right.

The next day when Chris went to school, he checked the Lost and Found box. "There it is!" he exclaimed in delight. "And it still has a couple dollars in it!" He smiled broadly as he tucked it securely into his back pocket.

When Chris told Dad about his wallet, Dad smiled. "Your lost-and-found wallet reminds me of a woman in the Bible who lost a coin and searched until she found it. She was so happy; she called her friends to let them know her coin was found."

Chris grinned. "I think we should celebrate that my wallet is found too," he said. "How about some ice cream, Dad?"

Dad laughed, then he got a carton of ice cream out of the freezer and scooped some into two bowls. "Do you know who else is happy when something is found?" he asked. "The Bible says there is joy in the presence of God's angels when a lost sinner repents and turns to Jesus."

"You mean when I accepted Jesus as my Savior, the angels knew about it and were happy?" asked Chris.

Dad nodded. "Yes, but I believe Jesus is the happiest of all when someone is saved," he said. "He loves us all so much." *JAG*

HOW ABOUT YOU?

Have you ever lost a book, toy, or wallet and searched for a long time before finding it? Jesus, too, has waited a long time for you to come to him. Believe that he died on the cross for your sins and receive his gift of eternal life. Even the angels in heaven will rejoice.

SALVATION BRINGS JOY

MEMORIZE:

"In the same way, there is joy in the presence of God's angels when even one sinner repents." Luke 15:10

SNOWCONES AND EGGS

Read: Luke 19:1-8

John raced home from the snowcone stand. He had saved money all week for this icy red-white-and-blue treat. What a day! To have a snowcone like this, and then to have the girl at the stand give him too much change! Now he had enough money for another snowcone tomorrow! He did feel a twinge in his conscience, but after all, it wasn't his fault he had been given too much money. He didn't steal it! He eased his conscience with that thought.

As Mom read the paper that afternoon, she gave an exclamation of surprise. "Mr. Mullins died," she said.

"Who's he?" asked John.

Mom put the paper down. "He's someone I knew long before you were born," she said. "When I was a little girl, we raised chickens and sold eggs. One day a man came to buy eggs. After he left, I noticed he had given me a five-dollar bill instead of a one. I knew I should return his money, but I didn't do it. Well, the years went by, and from time to time the memory of the money I owed to that man came back to disturb me. Finally, I asked God to forgive me, and he did. In fact, he did even more than that. He allowed me to find that man and repay what I owed him."

"Was it Mr. Mullins?" asked John when Mom paused.

Mom nodded. "After I repaid the money, I forgot all about it until just now. Believe me, John, if the Lord pricks your conscience about anything you've done, it will save you a lot of distress if you make it right immediately."

John had a huge lump in his throat. He knew what he must do. He would never be able to enjoy a snowcone tomorrow, knowing how he had gotten the money. *DS*

HOW ABOUT YOU?

Have you kept money or a toy that isn't really yours? Or have you told a lie, cheated, or disobeyed—and it seems like you got away with it? Do you feel guilty or uneasy every time you think about that? You should! God gave you a conscience to make you aware of wrong things in your life. And if you're a Christian, you have the Holy Spirit to guide you. Zacchaeus made "wrong" things "right." You need to do that, too.

MEMORIZE:

"Confess your faults one to another, and pray one for another." James 5:16, KJV

MAKE WRONG THINGS RIGHT

THE DOG AND THE GATE

Read: 1 Timothy 6:11-14

Chris and his father were out walking when Dad stopped to chat with a man who was working on a car. While they talked, Chris wandered through a gate and into a large yard. Suddenly, he heard a loud growling noise. A large, mean-looking dog was coming toward him! As Chris turned and started running, the dog chased him, barking furiously. Frightened, Chris ran this way and that—and around bushes—trying to escape the dog. He heard the owner calling the dog. Then he heard Dad's voice. "Over here, Son! Here's the gate!" Immediately, Chris dashed toward his father. As he ran through the gate, Dad slammed the gate shut before the dog could follow.

"Whew! That was close!" gasped Chris as the owner came up. "I'm sorry," said Chris breathlessly. "I shouldn't have gone in there."

Soon Dad and Chris were on their way again. "You know, Son, I've been thinking about a question you asked the other day—about why Christians can't seem to stop sinning," said Dad. "Think about how you ran from that dog."

"I have been," said Chris. "I wouldn't have gotten away if you hadn't stood by the gate, showing me the way to go."

"That's right." Dad smiled. "That's how it is in the Christian life, too. We not only have to 'flee' from sin, but we also have to 'follow' righteousness. We must think about the Lord Jesus and the kind of person he is. As Christians, we have a 'goal' to run towards—the goal of being like Christ!" *SLK*

HOW ABOUT YOU?

Do you find it difficult to get rid of sin in your life? It's important to recognize sin and try to avoid it. But you must also keep Christ in your mind as a positive example of righteousness and obey the commandments in his Word. Look to Jesus. He'll "show you the gate"!

FLEE SIN;
FOLLOW CHRIST

MEMORIZE:
"God is faithful, who will not allow you to be tempted beyond what you are able, but . . . will provide the way of escape." 1 Corinthians 10:13, NASB

THE PROCRASTINATOR

Read: James 4:13-15

Drew looked at his watch, surprised to see how fast the time had gone. He had to get down to the store to pick up the decorations for the party the church young people were having, and he would have to move fast to make it. But by the time Drew got downtown, the store was closed.

The party was held without decorations. No one was happy about the way Drew had put off his responsibility until it was too late. He heard Sasha complaining to Alyssa about it. "Should have known better than to give the job to the procrastinator," Sasha said.

Putting things off was a habit of Drew's, and everyone, including Drew, knew it. He was that way about everything—school, church activities, and even chores at home. He always meant to get right at his assignments, but there never seemed to be any real hurry. Then, all of a sudden, it would be too late.

One week a message at church tugged at his heart. The pastor's sermon was about being ready for the coming of Christ. Almost as long as he could remember, Drew had known that he needed to be saved. He intended to talk to somebody about it, but he always put it off till later. Today, however, the lesson soaked into his mind and heart. *What if I put it off too long?* he wondered. *What if I die . . . or what if Jesus comes? I wouldn't be ready!*

This time he listened carefully as the minister explained how to be saved. Right in his seat, he quietly bowed his head and asked Jesus to save him. Then when the invitation was given he went forward to make a public commitment to the Lord. "This was one decision I didn't want to put off any longer," he confessed. *RIJ*

HOW ABOUT YOU?

Have you surrendered your life to Jesus Christ? Or are you putting it off until later? The Bible warns that life can end at any time. For you, tomorrow on earth may never come. Admit today that you have sinned. Ask Jesus to forgive you and take over your life.

MEMORIZE:

"Don't brag about tomorrow, since you don't know what the day will bring."
Proverbs 27:1

DON'T WAIT
TO BE SAVED

DON'T FORGET

Read: Luke 17:11-19

"Good-bye, Mrs. Nelson." Brad hopped out of the van. "Call me later, Eric."

"Okay," Eric replied as he moved into the front seat beside his mother. "That was fun, Mom," he said. "I wish we could have a Bible club picnic every Saturday."

"I don't," Mom said wearily. "After all the work that was involved, I'm exhausted."

As they turned into the driveway, Eric's dad met them. He opened the door. "Let me carry in the leftovers—if there are any. Did everyone have a good time?"

"I suppose they did," Mom said as she handed Eric the volleyball equipment, "but nobody said 'thank you.' I picked them up, planned the games, furnished the food, and then took them back home. And not one said 'thank you.' "

"They forgot, Mom," Eric said, defending his friends. "They had such a good time, they forgot to thank you. They think you're a great teacher."

"Where do you want this ice chest?" asked Dad.

"Just set it on the cabinet," Mom replied. "I'll take care of it later. I really am concerned about the poor manners of my students."

Eric frowned. Then he grinned. "Aren't you forgetting something, Mom?"

Mom looked puzzled. "I don't think so. You brought in the games. Your dad brought in the ice chest."

"I know," Eric said with a chuckle. "And you forgot to thank us."

Mom blushed, and then she laughed with her husband and son.

At that moment the telephone rang. Mom picked up the receiver. "Hello. Yes, this is Mrs. Nelson. Oh, Brad, you're very welcome. I'm glad you had a good time. I did, too. Thank you for calling. Good-bye." Mom smiled as she hung up the phone.

Dad winked at Eric. *BJW*

HOW ABOUT YOU?

Do you have trouble remembering to say "thank you"? Tie a string around your finger for one whole day, as a reminder. And while you are minding your manners, don't forget how much the Lord Jesus has done for you. Why not stop right now and tell him thanks?

REMEMBER TO SAY THANK YOU

MEMORIZE:

"Always giving thanks to God the Father for everything, in the name of our Lord Jesus Christ." Ephesians 5:20, NIV

YOU CAN'T DO IT

Read: Ephesians 2:13-19

Brad and his friend Tim watched from the front row as Mr. Blair, the "gospel magician," held up three wooden blocks, each with a hole through it. On one block was the word "God," on another "people," and on the third "sin." Mr. Blair threaded the block marked "sin" onto the middle of two ropes. Then he tied a knot to make sure the block couldn't come off. Next, he threaded the block marked "people" onto one end of the ropes, and the block marked "God" onto the other end.

"In the Garden of Eden, people and God had beautiful fellowship until sin entered the picture," said Mr. Blair. "Sin separated people from God." He held up the ropes to show the block marked "sin" between the other two blocks. "God and people are still separated by sin, and they can only be brought together if sin is removed. 1 Peter 3:18 tells us that Jesus suffered and died to bring people to God."

Mr. Blair covered all three blocks with a large red cloth, which represented the blood of Jesus, then called Brad and Tim to come up as volunteers. Each grasped an end of the ropes and pulled. The block marked "sin" dropped unbroken to the floor! Then he removed the red cloth to show the other two blocks—"people" and "God"—together.

After the program, Brad wanted to know the secret to the trick, but Mr. Blair had a better question. "What have you done about the sin in your life, Brad?" he asked.

"Me? I'm not so bad," said Brad. "I've always gone to church."

"The Bible says that won't help because only the blood of Jesus can remove sin," Mr. Blair replied. "You need to confess your sin and let God wash it away. Until your sin is removed, you cannot have fellowship with him." *CVM*

HOW ABOUT YOU?

Do you try to please God by going to church and doing good deeds? Do you think the good will outweigh the bad? Before you can have fellowship with God, your sin must be removed, and you can't remove it yourself—only Jesus can. If you've never done so, confess your sin and accept Jesus as your Savior right now.

MEMORIZE:

"But now . . . you have been brought near to him because of the blood of Christ." Ephesians 2:13

CHRIST'S BLOOD REMOVES SIN

PITCHING STRAIGHT

Read: Proverbs 12:17-22

Peter wound up for the pitch and let the ball go, but it was too high. It sailed through the air over Danny's head—and right into Benjamin Wood's store window! Danny gave a quick backward look over his shoulder. "Come on, Pete!" he urged. "Let's get out of here!" Peter took off after Danny, who was tearing across the playground and down the street. "Whew!" Danny gasped when they were out of sight of the store. "That was a close shave, but we're safe now."

Peter hesitated. "Shouldn't we have stayed and owned up to it?"

Danny looked at him sharply. "Are you crazy, Pete? I'm going home. See you tomorrow."

"Okay," Peter mumbled. He had just recently accepted Jesus as his Savior at the same church Mr. Wood attended. He knew Jesus would want him to own up to what he had done. So Pete headed back to Mr. Wood's store.

Mr. Wood was outside, looking at the damage when Peter approached him. "Uh, Mr. Wood . . . I just wanted to tell you that I was the one who broke your store window! I . . . was trying to pitch a curve ball, and . . ."

Mr. Wood looked down sternly at Peter. "There's only one thing to do," said Mr. Wood, and Peter trembled. "Learn to pitch straight!" Mr. Wood began to chuckle and patted Peter on the back. Peter suddenly realized that Mr. Wood was joking with him!

"Always be as honest and straightforward as you are now, and with the Lord's help, you'll be a strong Christian," said Mr. Wood. "Now, about the window . . . do you think you could come and do some sweeping and cleaning for me and work off the price of replacing it?" Gladly, Peter nodded his head. *HMP*

HOW ABOUT YOU?

Do you face your problems honestly? Or do you make excuses for the things you do that are not pleasing to God or to your parents and friends? Do you try to hide them? Confess your sins and stop sinning, with God's help. Then your actions will be a testimony for the Lord.

ALWAYS BE
HONEST

MEMORIZE:

"The Lord hates those who don't keep their word, but he delights in those who do." Proverbs 12:22

I WISH IT WERE MINE

Read: Exodus 20:1-5, 17; Colossians 3:5

When Rico saw the brand new baseball mitt Gregory brought to school, he felt envious. Gregory always had something new! This time it was the very mitt Rico had seen in the sports store.

Rico wished that mitt was his! All day he kept thinking about it. *It isn't fair!* he thought. *Gregory's father is rich, so he gets everything he wants. Why can't I have what I want for once?*

As Rico left school that afternoon, his eyes widened as he passed the baseball diamond. There, close to the backstop, lay Gregory's new mitt. Rico picked it up, glancing around to make sure no one saw him. He'd return it to Gregory in the morning, but tonight he'd pretend it was his.

That evening Rico played catch with his brother. When Dad asked where he got the mitt, Rico stammered a bit. "Well . . . one of the guys loaned it to me," he said.

In the morning, Rico decided to keep the mitt another day. When Gregory asked if anyone had seen his mitt, Rico didn't answer.

A week passed, and still the mitt lay in his room. Rico couldn't play with it because Dad might ask questions again. And since it would be embarrassing to return it to Gregory now, Rico just shoved it to the back of his closet. That's where Mom found it. She asked Rico about the mitt.

"I just wanted it so much," Rico confessed, "so I brought it home to try it out. I never meant to keep it."

"But you did keep it," said Mom. "The real trouble started when you kept thinking about wanting something that belonged to someone else. This led you to lie and to steal. Now you'll have to return the mitt and talk to Gregory. But I think first you need to talk to God." *HWM*

HOW ABOUT YOU?

Does someone have something you really want? Do you keep longing for it and wishing it were yours? Careful! While it is okay to desire certain things, it is not okay to become obsessed with getting those things. If you find yourself thinking too much about certain things, ask God to help you to think about other things.

MEMORIZE:

"Beware! Don't be greedy for what you don't have." Luke 12:15

DON'T BE GREEDY

BASEBALLS AND BUSHES

Read: Romans 14:7-13

"Oh no!" groaned Brad as he and his sister, Sandi, waited for Mom outside the grocery store. "Here comes that old grouch!"

Sandi looked up and saw Mrs. Blake approaching. "Be quiet," hissed Sandi.

Mrs. Blake greeted the children pleasantly. "By the way, Brad, I found a baseball in my yard," she said. "Is it yours?" Sandi gasped when Brad said that it was.

After Mrs. Blake was gone, Sandi turned to Brad. "You know that ball's not yours," she scolded. "How can you lie like that?"

"Aw, what's the difference? Mrs. Blake doesn't know whose it is, so I might as well have it," argued Brad.

When Mom heard the story, she told Brad that he could not have the ball. "Sandi's a tattletale," Brad declared angrily. "My having that ball wouldn't hurt anyone."

That evening, Brad answered the door when Mrs. Blake came over. "Did you bring my ball?" he asked in a low tone, hoping his mother wouldn't hear.

"Here it is," answered Mrs. Blake, handing a ball to him. "It landed on my prize rose bush and broke it. I shall expect you to pay for it!"

Just then Mom appeared in the doorway. "Brad, you must tell the truth," she said sternly. "You know that ball is not yours."

"Well!" snorted Mrs. Blake. "The ball belongs to the boy until you find out it has done some damage. Then it isn't his!" Brad and his mother tried to explain, but Mrs. Blake stomped off.

"You thought you weren't hurting anyone, Brad, but now I'm being blamed because of what you did," Mom said, taking the ball from Brad. "I don't know if it will help now, but you will have to pay Mrs. Blake for the rose bush and return the ball," she told him. "And always remember that your actions do affect other people." *AGL*

HOW ABOUT YOU?

Are you aware that when you lie or do wrong things, your actions may hurt others too? Ask God to help you live rightly for him.

YOUR SIN CAN HURT OTHERS

MEMORIZE:

"For none of us lives to himself alone and none of us dies to himself alone."

Romans 14:7, NIV

Liang laughed when his friend Brayden invited him to Sunday school. When Brayden told Liang he'd be praying for him, Liang laughed louder. In spite of that, Brayden was nice to Liang. He helped Liang with math and invited him over to his house. But nothing seemed to make Liang interested in church or God.

"Why doesn't your dad buy you a bike, Sunday school boy?" taunted Liang. "Then you wouldn't have to walk to school."

Brayden just shrugged. "Dad got hurt and has been out of work for a while, so I haven't asked him about it," he explained. "I'm saving my money to buy one."

"Yeah? Well, you'll probably never make it," taunted Liang. "You probably put all your money in the collection plate on Sunday!"

Brayden shook his head. "No, but I wish I could put more in the offering," he said quietly.

Liang laughed. "Well, a used bike doesn't cost so much, and you've been working after school," he said. "So what's taking so long? Where's your money going?"

Just then Brayden's little sister, Jaime, came out of the house with a cast on her foot. "Hi, Liang," she said with a smile. "Look! I'm getting my foot straightened! Mommy said that since Daddy's out of work, I'd probably have to wait longer . . . but Brayden helped to pay for it." She grabbed Brayden's hand. "He's my big brother!" she added proudly.

"Whew!" Liang whistled and the grin faded from his face. "You have had problems, haven't you? But you never complained! Maybe there is something to that religion of yours. Maybe I will go along with you next Sunday to find out more." *AGL*

HOW ABOUT YOU?

Are you witnessing for Jesus by your life as well as by your words? Do you keep your temper under control? Are you uncomplaining when things go wrong? Do you offer help when you can? Sometimes it takes a long time to win a person to the Lord, but if your life and your words are faithful witnesses for Jesus, you can trust God to use them for his glory.

MEMORIZE:

"My word . . . will accomplish all I want it to, and it will prosper everywhere I send it." Isaiah 55:11

WITNESS
THROUGH
ACTIONS

THE COVER-UP (PART 1)

Read: Psalm 51:1-4

Ahmad didn't see the warning signs, and he rode his bike right into some recently poured cement. Quickly he took off a shoe and frantically used it to try to make the cement smooth again. *How could I be so dumb?* he wondered. *The people who live here are going to be awfully mad if I don't get this fixed up. At least they're not home yet.*

But when Ahmad tried to fix the mess, he only succeeded in making it worse by getting pebbles and grass mixed into the cement, which was already starting to harden. *Maybe I can do a better job if I use some of Dad's tools,* he thought. Then he noticed that his bike tires were coated with concrete. So before heading home, he took off his shirt and used it to clean them.

Back home, he got a clean shirt, but then Mom saw him and sent him on a couple of errands. Just as he was about to leave, she discovered his dirty shirt and demanded an explanation. When she heard Ahmad's story, she shook her head. "You should have told someone right away," she said. "Instead, you tried to cover up what you did. As a result, you ruined this shirt. And your shoes and bike should have been washed with water while the cement was soft—I just hope they're not ruined, too! But now you'd better hurry back and find the people who live there. Perhaps there will still be time for them to fix the cement." *JLH*

HOW ABOUT YOU?

If you do something wrong, do you confess it or try to cover it up? When you try to cover up wrongdoing, it usually gets you into more trouble. God wants you to confess your sin and receive forgiveness. Then, of course, you should do what you can to make things right.

MEMORIZE:

"Finally, I confessed all my sins to you and stopped trying to hide them."

Psalm 32:5

DON'T HIDE SIN

THE COVER-UP (PART 2)

Read: Psalm 95:6-11

Ahmad hurried as fast as he could, but by the time he got back to the cement, it had hardened just the way he had left it—a mess. A man was coming from the house as Ahmad rode up. "I . . . I'm sorry, Sir. I wasn't paying attention, and I . . . I messed up your cement," Ahmad stammered. "I didn't mean to. And I did try to patch it. Honest I did."

"I can see that you did," the man replied. "I'm Mr. Olson, and I live here. Why didn't you come and tell me what happened right away? I could have fixed it then."

Ahmad stared at his feet. "I didn't want anyone to know I did it," he admitted. "I wanted to fix it like new, but when I tried to make things better, they just got worse. And now the cement is set. I waited too long, and it got hard."

"That's right," agreed Mr. Olson. "It is hard now. You know, people's hearts are something like the cement."

Ahmad was startled. "What do you mean?" he asked.

"Jesus Christ died for sinners, but some people put off becoming Christians until, like cement, they get hardened into a wrong way of living," explained Mr. Olson. "They wait too long, and allow their hearts to get hardened against God's love and forgiveness."

Ahmad nodded. "I know about that," he said. "My friend, Scott, took me to his church. The teacher said that we must not harden our hearts to Christ."

"That's right," Mr. Olson said. "It's important to keep your heart soft toward the Lord. Now, I've got to get to this cement. Perhaps you can help me." *JLH*

HOW ABOUT YOU?

Have you put off finding out more about Jesus? Do you have questions? Talk to your parents, your pastor, or a trusted Christian friend.

MEMORIZE:

"Today you must listen to his voice.
Don't harden your hearts against him."
Hebrews 3:15

ACCEPT JESUS

THE PRIZE

Read: 1 Corinthians 9:24-27; Philippians 3:13-16

Terry's dad looked into Terry's room. "I thought you were writing your testimony," said Dad.

Terry shrugged and tossed a paper airplane into the air. "I was, but I can't seem to concentrate," he said. "I'd rather run. I can't wait for the cross-country meet tomorrow."

"Well, there are some things you have to do—including that paper you're writing—even if they aren't as exciting as racing," said Dad. "Now get busy." Reluctantly, Terry got to work.

The next day was clear and cool—perfect for the race. The starting whistle blew, and Terry got an early lead. Since it was a cross-country race, the sounds of the crowd that had gathered to see the runners off soon quieted in the distance. Terry ran on. The cool breeze was not enough to counteract the bright sun, and he began to tire. After a time, his legs began to feel very heavy. *Why am I doing this?* he wondered. *This is hard work, and no one can even see me!* Then he remembered that his family would be waiting for him at the finish line. "Do your best," Dad had told him.

Terry's stride picked up. He raised his head. The prize at the end of the race was worth working for. And besides the prize, he wanted to do his best for the Lord.

After the race, Terry and his family celebrated his second-place finish. "When I was all by myself on the track, I got tired and didn't feel like going on," said Terry, "but I remembered the prizes."

"Right," agreed Dad. He paused, then added, "That's also true in the Christian life—like in the case of the testimony you were writing last night. You may not even see the prize for that—the prize of someone accepting Jesus as Savior." *NR*

HOW ABOUT YOU?

Do you depend on the praise of others to help you get a job assignment done? Or do you work faithfully, even when tasks are very hard and no one seems to see or appreciate your work? There are rewards waiting in heaven for faithful workers, and Jesus watches when no one else does.

KEEP WORKING FOR GOD

MEMORIZE:

"I strain to reach the end of the race and receive the prize for which God, through Christ Jesus, is calling us up to heaven." Philippians 3:14

A SNEAKY TRAP

Read: 1 Corinthians 11:13-15

Ryan and his sister Sarah sat close to Grandpa, waiting for a story.

"Hairy Bee knew his job," began Grandpa. "He knew he had to fly to the clover patch, collect pollen, and bring it back to the hive in the barn. But poor Hairy got bored and decided to go exploring. On one trip, he found the flower garden. He sniffed the daisies and buzzed in and out of the daffodils. It wasn't long before all Hairy's trips to the clover patch were interrupted by a stop in the flower garden.

"Lucky Ladybug had a wonderful family, but she was bored. *I'm sick of going back and forth to get food from the food bin,* she thought. *It's a long trip. I bet I can find a shortcut.* So each time Lucky made the trip, she tried a different path, hoping that the new one would be shorter than the last.

"Now Hairy and Lucky were being carefully watched by a spider named Sneaky. He smiled each time he saw Hairy stop in the flower garden. He grinned as Lucky went around and around, searching for a shortcut. 'I'll trap them,' Sneaky snickered. 'All I'll have to do is attach to my web a brightly colored flower for Hairy and make my web look like a shortcut to Lucky.'

"The spider did just that, and Hairy and Lucky became Sneaky's dinner."

Grandpa looked at the children and added one final thought. "Satan can be just as sneaky as the spider," he warned. "He can make sin look good. Avoid his traps by reading and obeying the Bible." *AHG*

HOW ABOUT YOU?

Do you like to take the easy way instead of doing the things you know you should? Do some things that are wrong look good to you? Is there a bad habit in your life? Don't let Satan trap you.

MEMORIZE:

"Resist the Devil, and he will flee from you." James 4:7

AVOID SATAN'S TRAPS

BRAIN POWER

Read: Proverbs 3:5-7

Joel had only one more experiment to do and his science project would be complete. It would take three days, and then he'd be finished. Joel was sure his display would win first prize. He'd won many other contests—the spelling bee, the math quiz bowl, and others, too. His classmates teasingly called him "Brain Power," and he liked the nickname.

Joel read over the science fair rules once more. To his horror, he saw that the fair would be held the next day. "Oh, no! I thought it was next week!" he exclaimed. "I won't have time to do the last experiment."

As Joel sat with his head in his hands—quite upset with himself—he suddenly thought of a way he could win. *I can fake the last part. I'm sure I know how the experiment will turn out,* he told himself. *I can write that down and just say I actually did it. The judges will never know.*

After the students set up their displays in the library, they waited anxiously while the judging took place. Finally they were allowed back in. Joel expected to see a beautiful blue ribbon on his display—but instead, there was a note that read, "Results of last step are not likely to be right. Cannot award any prize."

Joel held back his tears until he reached home. Then he poured out his story to Mom.

"Joel, you wanted to be wise in the eyes of the judges and of your friends—and yourself," she said quietly when he finally calmed down. She opened her Bible and pointed to a verse. "Fear of the Lord is the beginning of wisdom," she read, then looked up. "Doing what is right before God is where real wisdom begins."

"I need to remember that," Joel said. "I guess that's using real brainpower." *CEY*

HOW ABOUT YOU?

Do you put God's laws first in your life? It's fun to have friends admire you for getting good grades or for winning contests. But never put earning the attention of others before doing what is right. Real brainpower lies in fearing God and keeping his commandments.

BE WISE!
OBEY GOD!

MEMORIZE:
"Fear of the Lord is the beginning of wisdom." Proverbs 9:10

THE BASEBALL DIAMOND

Read: Psalm 139:1-3, 23-24

Dad and Umit were on their way to Umit's baseball game. "Look at the map we got from Coach Baronski, and tell me where to find the ball field, Son," Dad said.

"Well," Umit replied, as they moved slowly past the school, "Let's see, turn into the north drive, then curve around left through that parking lot. Okay, now curve right—go close to the school—then left again. Now turn right and go up the hill between those two tennis courts."

They followed the directions on the map and finally passed the tennis courts. "But the road ends right here," Dad said in a puzzled tone, "and I don't see any baseball field yet. Does the map say anything else?"

Umit looked at the map again. "There's a note at the bottom that says, 'Keep going, even when you think you're at the end of the road. Take the trail through the grass and go over the hill. At the bottom of the hill, near the lake, you'll find the ball field and parking lot.' "

Dad laughed at the directions. "Okay, Son, it sounds goofy, but here we go." Bumpity, bump . . . through the grass and up over the hill they drove. There it was—a beautiful little lake, lush green grass . . . and the ball field, too.

"It didn't seem like this crazy road could possibly be the right way, did it, Dad? We couldn't see the playing field until the last minute, but we followed the map and it got us where we needed to go."

"That's right," agreed Dad. Then he said, "You know, it reminds me of life. There are a lot of twists and turns, but if we make decisions based on the directions and rules God gives in the Bible, things will turn out right." *CG*

HOW ABOUT YOU?

Will you follow God's way even when it seems difficult? When God allows things to happen that you can't understand, continue to trust and follow him.

MEMORIZE:

"Teach me to do your will, for you are my God." Psalm 143:10

TRUST GOD'S WAY

HIDDEN WEEDS

Read: Hebrews 12:12-15

Ronnie was uprooting some dandelions in his front yard, when his friend Kevin walked up. "Hi," said Kevin. "Want to go swimming?"

"Can't," answered Ronnie. "My mom says she's sick of seeing yellow dandelions instead of green grass. I have to get rid of them. She showed me how to work around the plant with this tool and pull out the whole root." He wiped his brow with a dirty hand. "It's awful hot, too."

"Yeah." Kevin nodded. "Much too hot to do them that way. Why not just cut the tops off? Here—I'll help you. You hold the leaves, and I'll hit 'em with the point of the hoe. We'll be done sooner, and then we can go swimming."

"Okay," agreed Ronnie, "but be careful not to mess up the grass." So the boys got busy, and soon they were finished and were off to the creek to swim.

Several times in the next few weeks, Ronnie had to "pull" dandelions again. Each time, he used the hoe to cut off the tops. One day Mom stood at the window and watched. She went out to talk to him. "I didn't understand why we couldn't get rid of those weeds," she said, "but now I see the problem. You aren't pulling them the way I showed you."

"Oh," said Ronnie looking at the leaves in his hand. "I didn't think it mattered, as long as you couldn't see them."

"But it does matter. As long as the roots are still in the ground, the dandelions spring right back," explained Mom.

That evening, Dad heard about the dandelions. "That's a good example of the way we sometimes treat sin," he said. "We tend to think that if it isn't seen by other people, it doesn't matter. But unless the sin is rooted out—removed—it shows up again." *AU*

HOW ABOUT YOU?

Do you find yourself committing the same old sins over and over? Don't try to hide. Living God's way is possible through Christ—and it's well worth the effort.

ROOT OUT SIN

"I had a good time," said Sam as he and his parents were on their way home from a visit with Grandma Price. "While you grown-ups discussed the economy, I wandered around in that cemetery down the street. There sure are some interesting things carved on the grave markers. What do you want on yours, Dad?"

"Hmmm . . . a Bible verse, maybe," said Dad. "The carvings often express the thing for which the person is remembered, and I want people to remember that I was a Christian."

"People had put fresh flowers on some of the graves. Why do they do that?" asked Sam.

"Perhaps it comforts them to bring flowers and to remember good times they once had with the person they loved," suggested Mom. "They do it in memory of the one who died."

Dad nodded. "That reminds me of the memorial service we have at church," he said.

"Memorial service? What service is that?" asked Sam.

"That's the communion service," Dad told him. "The Bible tells us to observe it in remembrance of Jesus and all he did for us—how he lived, died, and rose again."

"That's right." Mom nodded. "We should be thinking of how holy he is, yet he died for us. Just think . . . he took *my* sins and died for *me*."

"It's an awesome thing, and yet we so often just take it all for granted," said Dad thoughtfully. "It's good that we do have a memorial service to remind us of all Jesus means to us." *AU*

HOW ABOUT YOU?
Does your mind wander during the communion service? Learn to keep your thoughts fixed on Jesus and what he's done for you. Use this service as a time to realize again how precious Jesus is.

MEMORIZE:
"For as often as you eat this bread and drink this cup, you proclaim the Lord's death till He comes." 1 Corinthians 11:26, NKJV

REMEMBER ALL JESUS HAS DONE FOR YOU

ALL DRESSED UP

Read: Matthew 24:37-44

Silas eagerly jumped out of bed one Saturday morning. This was the day he had been waiting for. His scout group was going to the zoo. Quickly, he made his bed and got dressed. After breakfast, he cleaned his room. Then he cleaned the fish bowl without waiting to be told. He was going to make sure there would be no possibility that he'd have to miss the outing because his work wasn't done. He even willingly took a shower before dressing for the club excursion. He proudly put on his club shirt with the new award patch his mother had sewn on for him. He was ready early!

"Can I go out and play while I wait?" Silas asked his mother.

"Sure," agreed Mom, "but stay close by so you'll be ready when it's time to leave."

The wait seemed long, and Silas wandered off to watch some boys play baseball at a nearby park. After a while, he returned home. "When are we leaving, Mom?" he asked.

"We're not," said Mom emphatically. "I went out and called and called you. I even honked the horn, but you didn't come."

"I was all ready to go," wailed Silas.

"Sorry," said Mom, "but it's too late now." Silas was heartbroken!

For family devotions that evening, Dad read aloud from Matthew, chapter 24 (see today's Scripture). Mom turned to Silas. "It made me very sad that you didn't get to go to your club outing today," she said. "You were all dressed up and had your work done, but because you didn't answer my call, you missed the trip to the zoo. It reminds me of the people who are 'all dressed up' in good works, but they won't be ready when Jesus returns." *AU*

HOW ABOUT YOU?

Are you all "dressed up" in good works—attending church and doing all sorts of good things? Don't stop, but remember it is only through faith in Jesus that we are saved.

BE READY WHEN
JESUS COMES

TIDAL WAVE

Read: Matthew 7:24-29

The kitchen door slammed shut behind Jon. After greeting his mother, he poured milk into a glass and plopped down in a chair. "You won't believe what happened to my project today," he said. Jon had worked for two weeks creating an ancient Mayan city that included a temple, a palace, and several small buildings.

"Tell me about it," said Mom.

"After you dropped me off at school, Mike came over and started asking questions about the project," said Jon. "Well, he was carrying a bowl of water to use on his own project. Before I had two words out of my mouth, someone else bumped Mike, and my Mayan city was hit by a tidal wave."

"Oh, dear!" exclaimed Mom.

"It washed the ground right out from under the main temple," continued Jon. He frowned. "When I was working on it, somebody suggested that I should use plaster for the ground instead of sand. I should have listened."

"Well, I'm sorry your project was messed up," sympathized Mom.

"Me, too," said Jon. He laughed. "But my teacher said it was the most realistic disaster project she'd seen. And she said I should always remember that sand doesn't make a firm foundation, and things don't last unless they stand on a strong foundation."

Mom nodded. "Your story reminds me the Bible passage that talks about the importance of building our lives on the right foundation," she said. "If we trust in anything or anybody other than Jesus, it's as though we're building on sand. The only lasting foundation is the Lord Jesus Christ."

"Yeah." Jon nodded. Then he grinned. "Well," he said, "I chose the wrong foundation for my project, but I have the right one for my life, and that's more important!" *JW*

HOW ABOUT YOU?

Do you have the right foundation for your life? Have you trusted Jesus as your Savior? Any other foundation—things you may trust in like being kind, doing good works—will be swept away some day. Accept Jesus.

MEMORIZE:

"For no one can lay any other foundation than the one we already have—Jesus Christ." 1 Corinthians 3:11

BUILD YOUR LIFE ON JESUS

DEAD, BUT ALIVE

Read: 2 Corinthians 5:1, 6-9

Stretching sleepily, Jimmy wondered why he had that strange, empty feeling in the bottom of his stomach. Then it all came back to him. He glanced over at the other bed. Yes, it was empty. It really was true—his big brother, Jack, was gone. It was almost two weeks since Jack had left for school in the morning and had not come back. Tears rolled down Jimmy's cheeks as he remembered. There had been an accident, and Jack had been killed. Mom said he had gone to heaven.

The door to Jimmy's room opened, and his mother came in. "Good morning!" she said. Noticing his tears, she sat beside him on the bed. "You're thinking of Jack, aren't you?" she asked. "Daddy and I miss him, too, but we also try to think of how happy he is with Jesus."

"But, Mom, how do you know he's happy?" asked Jimmy.

"I know because Jack accepted Jesus as his Savior," Mom replied, "and the Bible says that when those who trust in Jesus leave this life, they go to be with him."

Jimmy nodded "Yes, but I still don't understand," he said with a sob. "You always say Jack's in heaven, but he was right there in the casket, and then he was put in the ground at the cemetery." Jimmy covered his face with his hands.

"Jack's body is in the grave, but his soul, or his life—the real Jack—is with Jesus," explained Mom. "Your body is just a house in which the real you—your soul—lives. Your body may die, but not your soul. It lives. Jack's body died, and we buried it, but God took Jack's life—his soul—to heaven. So when I think of Jack, I think of him in heaven." *AU*

HOW ABOUT YOU?

Do you know that your life, or soul, lives forever? When a Christian dies, his soul goes to be with Jesus.

BODIES DIE;
SOULS DON'T

PREPARATION NEEDED

Read: Colossians 3:23-25

"Can I sign up for a Little League team?" Phil begged. He could just see himself in the team uniform!

"Well, if you sign up, you'll have to get up early every Saturday for practice," warned Dad. "You might have to sacrifice other activities, too. Are you willing to do that?"

"Oh, sure," Phil said confidently.

"Okay," said Dad. "If you're willing to give it your all, you can sign up."

The practice sessions were fun at first, but as the weeks went by, Phil found it harder and harder to get up early on Saturday mornings. "Practice! Practice! Practice!" he'd mutter when he heard Mom call. "If it were a real game, I wouldn't mind getting up." Then he'd turn over and go back to sleep till Mom called again.

One morning, Dad knocked on Phil's bedroom door. "Get going," Dad insisted. "You're going to be late."

"I'm not going today," Phil murmured sleepily.

"Not going?" Dad asked in surprise. "Why not?"

"All we do is practice," mumbled Phil. "I want to play—not work."

"Anything worthwhile takes work," said Dad. "And if you want to do your best then you have to work at it." Phil sighed. He knew he might as well get up. Phil threw off the sheet. "I'm on my way, Dad," he said. He grinned at his father. "You should have been a preacher," he teased, and Dad grinned back. *AU*

HOW ABOUT YOU?

Are you willing to prepare and to work for things you want? The Bible gives many examples of times when preparation was needed. Noah prepared the ark for a place of safety; Solomon prepared material for building the temple; even God is preparing a place for his children. Practice, study, and faithfully prepare for the things in which you are involved. Then you can do them "as to the Lord."

PRACTICE
WILLINGLY

PAY ATTENTION!

Read: Psalm 25:4-10

"I'll watch the map and tell you where to turn, Dad," said Brett as he and his father packed the car for their fishing trip.

"Okay," agreed Dad, "but I'd better check to see where we have to turn off the highway."

"No, I see it, Dad," said Brett, scanning the map. "I'll let you know when we're getting close," he promised. So while Dad drove, Brett took charge of the map. "This map shows some other lakes that might be good for fishing, too," said Brett after a while. "Let's fish in these other lakes sometime," he suggested.

"Perhaps we can do that," said Dad, "but you *are* going to tell me where to turn to get to Glen Lake, aren't you? It seems to me we should have come to the road by now."

Brett took a closer look. "I think I missed our road, Dad," he admitted. Dad stopped the car, checked the map, and turned the car around. Soon Brett spotted the sign for the road to Glen Lake. "There it is!" he exclaimed. Dad nodded and made the turn. Before long, they were fishing at the lake.

After a delicious fish dinner that evening, Dad read some Bible verses. Brett wasn't really listening. In his imagination, he was landing a huge fish when he heard Dad say, "Amen."

"Like a map, the Bible gives directions," said Dad. "It gives directions for living." He grinned at Brett. "We found out that maps help us only if we pay attention to what they tell us, didn't we?" he said. "I wonder how often we miss out on important lessons in Christian living—or on blessings God wants to give us—because we don't pay attention when his Word is read or taught. It's easy to daydream when we should be listening. Let's guard against that, shall we?" Solemnly, Brett nodded. *CEY*

HOW ABOUT YOU?

Do you listen carefully while the Bible is being read or while Bible lessons are being taught? If you're in the habit of letting your thoughts drift during those times, make up your mind to break that habit. Begin paying close attention so you won't miss out on what God has for you.

MEMORIZE:

"Show me the path where I should walk, O Lord; point out the right road for me to follow." Psalm 25:4

PAY ATTENTION TO GOD'S DIRECTIONS

HELPFUL ANTS

Read: 1 John 4:7-11

"I'm thirsty," said Sam as he and his dad detached water bottles from their bikes and sat down on a park bench beside the trail. Both drank in companionable silence. Then Dad handed a granola bar to Sam.

As Sam removed the wrapper, a piece of granola fell to the ground. A tiny ant appeared immediately and tried to whisk it away. He tried again and again, but the piece was just too large for him to handle. As Sam watched, a mass of scurrying ants appeared. They worked together, lifting and dropping the chunk several times until it fell apart. Then each ant seized a small piece, and they all ran off in the same direction.

"Did you see that?" asked Sam. "That ant needed help—and he got it!"

"He sure did," replied Dad. "That was a wonderful example of how God wants Christians to behave."

Sam looked at Dad. "What do you mean?"

"Well, watching those ants reminded me of what happened when that big storm ripped shingles off our garage roof last summer," replied Dad. "Remember how several people from church helped us repair it?"

"Yeah," replied Sam. "With all their help, it didn't take long before it was fixed. A big job became a small one, just like with the ants."

"Right," said Dad. "I'm sure they didn't think about it at the time, but those people were actually demonstrating to the neighborhood the love that Christians should have for each other—giving evidence that we belong to Christ. Mr. Lawrence, next door, was so amazed at the way they helped us. He asked me why they did that, and I had the opportunity to tell him that we love one another because we love Jesus. He wanted to know more about it. I'm praying that he'll soon know Jesus, too." *ECM*

HOW ABOUT YOU?

Can people see that you love others? Do you show love by willingly helping your mother or father clean the house? Do you cheerfully help with the yard work? Are you available to help neighbors or classmates as much as you can? When people see that you have a helpful attitude and love God, perhaps some of them will want Jesus in their lives, too.

SHOW GOD'S LOVE

MEMORIZE:
"Your love for one another will prove to the world that you are my disciples."
John 13:35

RAIN, RAIN, RAIN

Read: Psalm 51:1-10

"I thought vacation was supposed to be fun," grumbled Jonathan. It felt damp and chilly inside the tent as rain beat against the canvas sides. "Why does it have to rain today?"

"God didn't promise us sunshine for the trip," replied Dad. "We'll just have to make the best of the rain and try to think of some good things about it." He grinned. "It's giving our dusty van a much-needed washing," he added. But Jonathan didn't smile.

"I want you and Dylan to get your pajamas on," Mom told the boys. "Then we'll have devotions and sing some choruses. That will help us forget about the rain."

Soon the boys were inside their warm sleeping bags. "Maybe the rain will be gone by the time we wake up tomorrow," said Dylan.

"Maybe," agreed Dad, "and then we'll go fishing. Now . . . what shall we sing tonight?"

"I know," exclaimed Jonathan. "Let's sing, 'What can wash away my sin?' "

Dylan laughed out loud, and Dad chuckled. Jonathan was puzzled. "What's so funny?"

Mom smiled. "We've got all this rain, and you want to sing about sin being *washed away*," she said.

"Oh," said Jonathan. "I guess that is kind of funny."

"Actually," said Dad, "it's a very good song to sing tonight. Remember how dirty our van was? The rain washes away the dust and dirt, and the blood of Jesus washes away our sins. Instead of being unhappy about the rain, maybe we ought to let it remind us of Jesus and what he did for us when he died on the cross."

"Right," said Mom. "Thanks, Jonathan, for choosing the perfect song."

As the family sang the old hymn, Jonathan remembered that every one of his sins was washed away by the blood of Jesus. How wonderful that God would forgive the bad things he did! *CA*

HOW ABOUT YOU?

Have your sins been washed away? Have you confessed them to Jesus? He died and shed his blood on the cross so you can be forgiven. Every bad thing you've done can be washed away.

MEMORIZE:

"The blood of Jesus, his Son, cleanses us from every sin." 1 John 1:7

JESUS WASHES
AWAY SIN

NO!

Read: Hebrews 4:12-16

As soon as he heard that his cousin Julio was coming to visit for the weekend, Pedro knew there would be trouble. It wasn't that he didn't like Julio. It was just that Julio often had ideas that Pedro knew displeased his parents—and the Lord. It's so hard to always tell him no, thought Pedro, but I'm going to do it. He reminded himself of a recent Sunday school lesson about the time Jesus was tempted. Jesus never gave in, and I'm going to ask him to help me not give in, either, decided Pedro. Jesus was tempted, too, so he'll understand the problem.

As Pedro expected, from the moment Julio arrived, he was full of plans. "Hey, Pedro," whispered Julio, "those kids next door are having a picnic. Let's take the hose and squirt water over the fence. Boy, will they be surprised!"

Pedro grinned and started to pick up the hose, but then he stopped. He knew his parents had been witnessing to those neighbors, and besides, it was wrong anyway. "No, Julio," he said, shaking his head, "we shouldn't do that."

All weekend, Julio suggested various things. Some sounded like fun, but Pedro knew they were wrong. For instance, it would be wrong to secretly paint pictures on the neighbor's sidewalk. That would be hurting someone else's property. It also would be wrong to read his sister's diary. Pedro knew they should respect the privacy of other people. So Pedro continued to say no.

"Wow," Pedro said after Julio had gotten on the train to go home. "I made it! I didn't yield to Julio's tempting once. I asked God to help me say no, and he did!" *LMW*

HOW ABOUT YOU?

What do you do when a friend tries to get you to do something wrong? Giving in to temptation might seem like fun at the moment, so sometimes it's hard to say no. Next time you're tempted to play nasty tricks, to cheat just a little, to read something not meant for your eyes—or whatever the temptation is—tell Jesus about it. If you sincerely ask for help to overcome the temptation, he will give it.

MEMORIZE:

"God is faithful, who will not allow you to be tempted beyond what you are able, but with the temptation will also make the way of escape, that you may be able to bear it."
1 Corinthians 10:13, NKJV

DON'T YIELD TO TEMPTATION

WHERE IS HE? (PART 1)

Read: Ezekiel 33:6-11

"I dare you to jump over that mud puddle without getting wet," said Pete.

"Okay," said Andy, as he backed up a few steps and then began running. Just before he jumped, he hesitated a little and ended up landing right in the middle of the puddle.

Pete laughed. "What made you miss?" he asked. "I thought maybe you were going to make it after all."

"A mosquito flew in my face," he said, "and it threw me off balance." He eyed his muddy clothes. "I sure hope my mom doesn't get mad when she sees me," he said.

"Yeah . . . but better you than me," said Pete. "Your mom is so understanding . . . and peaceful." He sighed. "What good are mosquitoes, anyway? Sometimes I even wonder what good *I* am." Andy just stood there, not sure what he should say. "Well, I've got to get home," added Pete, "or I'll be in trouble even if I'm not muddy." Andy laughed, as the boys parted for home.

"Pete and you are together a lot," said Andy's mom when she saw his muddy clothes and heard about the dare. "Have you ever told him about Jesus?"

"No," said Andy. He felt guilty as he remembered his conversation with Pete that afternoon. There had been opportunities to witness, but he had let them slip by. He could have told Pete that one reason his mother was calm and understanding was because she was a Christian. He could have said that God had a purpose for everything, even mosquitoes. He could have shared that God had a plan for Pete's life, too. But he had kept silent.

"May I call Pete and invite him over for supper?" he asked. "There are some things I have to talk to him about."

Mother smiled. "Sure," she said. *JLH*

HOW ABOUT YOU?

Do you witness to your friends? Watch for chances to speak a word for Christ. Pray about it, and you'll be surprised how many opportunities come your way. Don't be silent when you have a chance to share the gospel.

MEMORIZE:

"We cannot stop telling about the wonderful things we have seen and heard." Acts 4:20

USE
OPPORTUNITIES
TO WITNESS

WHERE IS HE? (PART 2)

Read: James 4:13-15

Andy was determined to witness to his friend, Pete, though he didn't really know just what to say. But he was surprised to find that when he opened his mouth to tell Pete about Jesus, it wasn't as hard as he expected it to be. He was further surprised to find that Pete was interested. It wasn't long before Pete was attending Sunday school with Andy, and only a little longer before Pete accepted Jesus as Savior and Lord. He continued to attend church each week with Pete.

Early one morning, Andy's mother came into his bedroom, and he could tell by her face that something was wrong. "I have something sad to tell you," she said, sitting down on the edge of his bed. "Pete died last night."

"What?" Andy sat up straight. He couldn't believe his ears.

"Pete's mom just called. While Pete was playing near the river in the woods, he lost his balance and fell in. He apparently drowned."

"It can't be!" sobbed Andy. "We have plans for today." His mom hugged him. "Mom, where is Pete now?" Andy asked.

"I think you know the answer to that," said Mom. "Was Pete a Christian?"

"Sure," said Andy. "So he's gone to heaven, right? He asked Jesus to save him after Sunday school a month ago. Don't you remember?"

"I remember," Mom nodded. "Since Pete trusted Christ as his Savior, his soul is in heaven now."

"And if he hadn't . . . he'd be lost—he'd be in hell now." Andy shuddered at the very thought. "Oh, I'm so glad I finally told him about Jesus." He took the tissue Mom handed him and wiped his eyes. Mom put her arms around him as he again broke into great sobs. "I'll miss him so much, but I'm so glad I'll see him in heaven someday." *JLH*

HOW ABOUT YOU?

If you suddenly died today, where would you go? If Christ is your Savior, you'd go to heaven, but if he isn't, you'd be lost in hell. That's not at all pleasant to think about, but it's true. Make sure you are ready—that you are among those who will go into "eternal life." Receive Jesus today.

MEMORIZE:
"And they will go away into eternal punishment, but the righteous will go into eternal life." Matthew 25:46

BE READY TO DIE

June
8

The darkness of Mikey's bedroom was broken by brilliant flashes of lightning, accompanied by loud crashes of thunder. Mikey was trying to sleep, but the storm just would not let him. First, he covered his ears with his hands and squeezed his eyes shut. Then he buried his head under his pillow and scrunched way down under his blankets, but the noise of the storm just crept around his huddled form. Finally, he could take it no longer. "Mom!" he called. "Mom!"

Soft footsteps hurried down the hall. Mom came into the room and gently pulled back the covers. "It's okay, honey—I'm here," she said.

"I'm afraid! The storm is so loud." Mikey's voice quivered.

"Yes it is," agreed Mom. "I couldn't sleep, either."

"You mean you were afraid like I was?" Mikey asked.

Mom smiled. "Well, not quite," she replied. "I was awakened by the storm, and I must admit I didn't care for all the noise and flashing light. What helps me a lot is to realize that God knows all about the storm. In fact, he controls it. I began to pray and thank Jesus for the rain—we really need it to help our garden grow. In fact, lightning helps the garden too. As I prayed, I remembered how Jesus loves and cares for me, and my fear went away."

"Really?" asked Mikey.

"Really," said Mom. "Would you like to thank Jesus for taking care of you and ask him to help you to not be afraid?" she asked. Slowly, Mikey nodded. *JAG*

HOW ABOUT YOU?

Are you afraid when you're awakened at night by a thunderstorm? Remember Jesus is with you, and he's in control of the storm. Ask him to help you not to be afraid, and then trust him to do it. He wants to help you.

MEMORIZE:

"He calmed the storm to a whisper and stilled the waves." Psalm 107:29

DON'T FEAR; TRUST

BEFORE THE SUN SETS

Read: Ephesians 4:25-32

"A fine friend you turned out to be!" Jimmy accused Joe, turning his back on him in anger. "You promised to help me work on my bike, and then you went to play ball instead!"

"I had to!" Joe shouted back. "They needed a pitcher. Bill was sick, and they asked me to take his place. You know I can throw some good curves!"

"Well, this is the last time I'll ever believe you!" said Jimmy, his face clenched in anger. With those words he stomped off.

When Dad read the Bible after supper as usual, Jimmy's mind kept wandering back to the angry exchange of words between Joe and himself—but suddenly some words from the Scripture caught his attention. "Don't sin by letting anger gain control over you. Don't let the sun go down while you are still angry." The words hit Jimmy like a thunderbolt. They were meant for him! He could hardly sit still. "May I be excused? I've got to do something real quick!" he blurted out as soon as Dad finished reading. "The sun will be going down soon, but it won't take me long!"

"Uh . . . okay," said Dad.

In a flash, Jimmy was up and out of the house, running toward Joe's house. His bewildered parents looked at each other in surprise. "What in the world has happened?" asked Mom.

In less than fifteen minutes, Jimmy came back, whistling happily. "Jimmy, what's up?" Dad asked.

Jimmy grinned. "I had a deadline to meet, and a friendship to patch up!" As he told them what had happened, his parents looked at each other with smiles on their faces.

"Nice going, Jimmy," said Dad. "That's putting Scripture into action!" *HMP*

HOW ABOUT YOU?

Do you lose your temper easily? Are you willing to ask forgiveness and make up with someone you may have hurt by your harsh remarks? Don't put it off until tomorrow. Do it now. Ask the Lord to help do this, and then ask him daily to help you keep your temper under control.

MEND FRIENDSHIPS TODAY

MEMORIZE:

" 'Don't sin by letting anger gain control over you.' Don't let the sun go down while you are still angry."

Ephesians 4:26

"Thank you for your prayers and support." Star was reading part of the Carlsons' prayer letter to her Sunday school class. "The Brazilian children love to hear the Bible stories. Please join us in prayer for money to buy a copy machine. Our old one is broken and can't be repaired. Thank you. In his service, the Carlsons."

When Star finished, Dan spoke up. "Isn't there some way we could help them buy a copy machine?" he asked.

"Be practical, Dan," Star answered. "Those things cost a lot of money, and we don't have any. All we can do is pray."

"But why couldn't we have a class project to earn some money?" Dan persisted.

Mr. Adams, their teacher, thought it was a good idea and asked for some suggestions. Scott raised his hand. "My neighbor is looking for strawberry pickers," he said.

The class agreed that picking strawberries would be a good project for earning money toward the purchase of a copy machine. All 10 raised their hands to indicate that they would help.

Mr. Adams was pleased. "You may be working in a strawberry patch, but you will be having a part in God's work of reaching the unsaved," he said. "Since I work every day, I won't be able to help you, but I'll give a reward to those who are faithful. All who pick berries every day this week are invited to my house on Saturday for a pizza party. Now, we'd better begin today's lesson." *JLH*

HOW ABOUT YOU?

Are you willing and available to serve the Lord? Do you sometimes say, "All I can do is pray"? Prayer is important and necessary, but perhaps God wants to answer the prayer for workers by using you! Look around. Can you earn money for the Lord by baby-sitting or mowing lawns? Can you serve him by cheerfully serving others—washing dishes, running errands, removing trash? There is much you can do. Go to work today!

MEMORIZE:

"We work together as partners who belong to God. You are God's field, God's building." 1 Corinthians 3:9

SERVE THE LORD

THE MISSIONARY PROJECT (PART 2)

Read: Luke 16:10-13

Early Monday morning, 10 sixth-graders came to Mr. Barton's strawberry patch. Chris was enthusiastic at first, but he soon grew tired of picking berries and left early. Luke complained of mosquito bites and said he needed to "be somewhere."

On Tuesday, eight of the students were working hard when Clarence and Brett began throwing berries at one another. Mr. Barton heard the commotion and came over to investigate. "What's going on here?" he asked gruffly. "I thought you came to work."

"We want to have some fun, too," Brett said. "Since that's over, I guess I'll leave!"

"Me, too," said Clarence, and the boys walked off.

By Saturday, the number of workers had dwindled to three—Scott, Dan, and Star. The others all had excuses to keep them from working. Some complained about the weather or the dirt. Others decided that shopping, swimming, or playing ball was more important to them than earning money for a missionary project.

Mr. Adams was eagerly waiting to hear about their week when the three arrived for the party. "How did the picking go?" Mr. Adams asked. "Did you meet your goal?"

"No." Dan shook his head. "But Mr. Barton said we could pick again next week, so we figure we can earn the rest of the money we need then."

"I see. Well, where's everybody else?" Mr. Adams asked. "Aren't they coming?"

"They dropped out," said Star. "At first everyone pitched in and helped, but then they started quitting. Dan and Scott and I were the only ones who worked today."

"I'm sorry to hear that," said Mr. Adams, "but I'm glad the three of you were faithful in finishing the job you had to do. Now, what kind of pizza would you like?" *JLH*

HOW ABOUT YOU?

Are you faithful in your youth group, your Sunday school class, the junior choir, or some other church activity in which you've become involved? Jesus is counting on you to do your part in his harvest field. Don't make excuses for not being there faithfully, and don't quit. Get the work done.

DON'T BE A QUITTER

MEMORIZE:

"Therefore, my dear brothers, stand firm. Let nothing move you. Always give yourselves fully to the work of the Lord." 1 Corinthians 15:58, NIV

Todd and Brett were excited. They were visiting their Uncle Jim and Aunt Ellen in Kentucky, and they were going on a tour of a big cave nearby. Uncle Jim had planned to take the day off and go with them, but an emergency came up, and he had to go to work after all. "I suppose you can go, anyway," he decided, "but be sure you behave yourselves and stay close to the guide."

Early in the afternoon, the boys joined a large tour group waiting outside the cave. The guide led them down a cement staircase into the cool atmosphere of the cave. She pointed out interesting things along the way. "The temperature in this cave always remains at 55 degrees," she announced. "Notice the rock formation on your right. It took 12,000 years for the dripping lime-water to produce that shape. In fact, this cave is more than 6 million years old."

"Not necessarily," mumbled a quiet voice behind Brett. The boys turned to look at the elderly man.

"What do you know about caves?" asked Todd. "Are you a scientist?"

The man smiled. "Yes, I am. I'm Professor Ryan from the University. I'm also a Christian, and I believe that God created the world literally as it's recorded in the Bible."

"Why did you say that the cave might not be 6 million years old?" asked Brett curiously.

"No one knows just how old it is, except the Lord," replied the man quietly. "He could have created the cave when he made the world, or it might have been produced during the flood of Noah's day. What I'm saying is that people shouldn't be so positive about theories for which there is no real proof." *SLK*

HOW ABOUT YOU?

Do you like to explore? Do you enjoy watching nature programs on TV, visiting scenic places, and reading books about the wonderful world God made? Perhaps you have heard or read things that contradict the teaching of Creation as found in the Bible. Don't let your faith be swayed by "experts" who use their influence to attack God and his Word. Only God really knows all things.

MEMORIZE:

"By faith we understand that the entire universe was formed at God's command." Hebrews 11:3

GOD MADE THE WORLD

NO TIME TO WAIT (PART 1)

Read: Lamentations 3:22-28

Micah flopped down on the porch step next to Jamal. "Wait, wait, wait!" muttered Micah. "That's what she always says."

"Who?" asked Jamal, popping a cookie into his mouth.

"Mom," groaned Micah. "I'm starving to death, and she won't let me have any cake."

"My mom wanted me to wait, too," confided Jamal, "but she let me have some cookies now."

Later that week, Jamal came whizzing down the street on a new bicycle. "Jamal always gets what he wants," complained Micah to his folks. "Like that bike. How come I have to wait for everything?"

Micah's father smiled. "For one thing, money in this family is limited," he said. "Besides, the Lord wants us to learn to wait for him to work things out for us. He wants us to develop patience."

The years went by, and the pattern remained the same. Whatever Jamal wanted, he seemed to get. After graduating from high school, Micah worked in a restaurant and saved money for college. Jamal, on the other hand, promptly got married. "Why should we wait?" he said. "We want to be together. Now I just gotta find a good job."

But this time Jamal didn't get what he wanted right away. He couldn't find the kind of job he wanted. Also, his new bride wasn't used to pampering him the way his parents had. So, instead of trying to work things out, Jamal immediately decided a divorce was the answer to his problems.

Micah sighed when he heard what was happening in his old schoolmate's life. "You know," he said to his parents, "I remember how I used to envy Jamal because his folks seemed to just hand him everything. But I wonder if Jamal would handle life better now if he hadn't always had his way while he was growing up. Thanks, Mom and Dad, for teaching me to wait." *BJW*

HOW ABOUT YOU?

Do you always want your wishes granted immediately? Learn to wait patiently for things—even for simple things. Learn to enjoy looking forward to God's plan for your life. Learn to receive things in his time.

MEMORIZE:

"But you, O man of God, flee these things and pursue . . . patience."
1 Timothy 6:11, NKJV

BE PATIENT

June

14

As Micah was walking to church one day, he met his old friend Jamal. "Hi, Jamal!" he said.

"Hey, Micah," called Jamal, "what are you doing these days?"

"Well, I'm about halfway through dental school," Micah replied. "I'm home for the summer, and I'm on my way to church now. Why don't you come along? You'll hear a life-changing message."

"Me? Go to church? You kiddin'?" mocked Jamal. "I haven't been to church since I went with you as a kid."

"Well, come with me again now," pleaded Micah.

"I've got other things to do," retorted Jamal. "I'll go to church when I'm too old to do anything else."

"You know, Jamal," said Micah, "you've never waited for anyone or anything . . . but now you are waiting to do the most important thing in life—getting straight with God."

Jamal shrugged. "Yeah, well, I've got lots of living to do before I start thinking about being a Christian," he said.

"But living without the Lord isn't really living, Jamal," responded Micah.

"So you say," grunted Jamal. "Been nice seeing you, Micah—sermon and all. I've got to run now. See ya around." With a wave of his hand, Jamal jumped into his car and drove away.

The next day, the newspaper reported a terrible car accident. Jamal had apparently decided he couldn't wait for a train. He tried to beat it, but he didn't make it. Amazingly, though, Jamal had not been killed. Micah decided to visit his friend in the hospital. *Perhaps if I spend time with Jamal as he recuperates, God will open a door for me to talk more about Jesus*, thought Micah. *BJW*

HOW ABOUT YOU?

Have you been waiting to give your life to Jesus? Do you have questions? Talk to your parents, your pastor, or a Christian friend.

MEMORIZE:

"Seek the Lord while you can find him.
Call on him now while he is near."
Isaiah 55:6

LOOK FOR THE OPPORTUNITIES

Read: Romans 9:1-3; 10:1

"Mom, may I go skateboarding with Jon?" asked 10-year-old Philipe.

Mom smiled. "Jon, Jon, Jon," she replied. "Ever since you met him, all I hear is 'Jon.' Why don't you bring him home sometime? And have you invited him to church?"

"I forgot," admitted Philipe, "but I will. May I go now?"

And so it went for most of the summer. Almost daily, Philipe talked about Jon. "Have you found out if Jon goes to church anywhere?" Mom would ask from time to time, and Philipe would reply, "I keep forgetting to ask him. I'll do it tomorrow."

One day Jon didn't show up at the skateboard park. Philipe became upset as the days passed, and he still didn't see Jon. One evening, Dad said, "I'm afraid Jon won't be coming around anymore. I heard that his dad is wanted by the police. They don't believe he committed any crime, but he won't tell what he knows about one. Somehow he learned they were on his trail, and he took off. Seems he's been on the go like that for a couple of years."

"Oh, no!" groaned Philipe. "I'll probably never see Jon again. I'm going to miss him." Philipe sighed. "I wish I had talked to him about how Jesus wants to be his Savior and his friend. Jon needs someone like Jesus who can go with him wherever he goes."

"Why don't we pray for Jon now?" asked Philipe's dad. "Telling our friends about Jesus and praying for them are great ways to show love." *AGL*

HOW ABOUT YOU?

Do you have a friend that you love and care about? Have you watched for opportunities to talk to your friend about Jesus? Ask God to help you be bold when the opportunity arises.

CARE ENOUGH
TO WITNESS

MEMORIZE:
"How can they believe in him if they have never heard about him?"
Romans 10:14

June

16

NOTHING BUT THE TRUTH

Read: Ephesians 4:21-25

Bailey and Ben were identical twins. When they came home from their ball game earlier than usual one day, Mom looked at them suspiciously. "Mr. Sanchez, from the hardware store, just called," she told them. "He said his window was broken by a baseball. Do either of you know anything about that?" The twins shook their heads. "That's funny," said Mom. "Mr. Sanchez said he noticed that one of you was batting when the window was broken."

"Scott did it," said Bailey.

"Yeah. We saw him," added Ben.

Mom raised an eyebrow. "I thought you didn't know anything about it," she reminded them. She looked at them sternly. "Now, which one of you did it?"

"I did," mumbled Bailey after a moment.

Mom sighed. "Your lying bothers me much more than the broken window," she said. "Last week, Bailey, you said you didn't know how Tobin got a black eye, but later I found out you hit him. And, Ben, you told me that the dog must have eaten some of my chocolate cake, but there were cake crumbs around your mouth as you said it."

"Oh, Mom!" protested Bailey. "We were just fibbing—not lying."

"Yeah," agreed Ben.

"And what's the difference?" asked Mom.

"Well . . . a little fib isn't as bad as a lie," said Bailey.

"Do you *really* think there's any difference?" asked Mom. "No matter what you call them, all lies are equally bad in God's sight. You both say you are Christians, yet you haven't obeyed God's instruction in Ephesians to 'put away lying.' That's a very serious matter." *HCT*

HOW ABOUT YOU?

Do you ever tell lies to avoid being punished, to please others, or to impress people? All lying is wrong. If you are a Christian, let God's Holy Spirit help you tell the truth—all the time.

MEMORIZE:

"The Lord detests lying lips, but he delights in men who are truthful."
Proverbs 12:22, NIV

TELL THE TRUTH

BIG ENOUGH

Read: Proverbs 3:5-7, 13

Don and Lisa were spending the summer with their parents in a desert area where their dad was working as an archaeologist. They could see the tall jagged pinnacles of rock from their camper, which was parked close to the place Dad worked. The pinnacles fascinated Don. "Never go out among those alone," Dad warned the children. "You could get lost, or you might be bitten by a rattlesnake."

"I'm no baby," grumbled Don when he and Lisa were exploring one day. "I'm big enough to look after myself, and I'm going to climb that tall pinnacle you can see in the distance over there. Come on."

Lisa knew better, but she went along with Don. When they reached the pinnacle, Don began to climb. It was quite a struggle, but he was nearing the top when suddenly a stone let loose. Down he fell, all the way down to the bottom! "O-o-ohh," moaned Don when he tried to get up. "My leg! Oh, it hurts awful bad!" He was unable to stand on it, and Lisa had to go back alone and get Dad.

Don was embarrassed and ashamed. "I . . . I'm awful sorry I didn't obey you, Dad," he said when he was safely back home and resting on the couch. "I . . . I just thought I was big enough to do what I wanted."

"None of us ever gets too big for guidance," Mom told him as she tightly wrapped his sprained ankle. "God gave you parents to guide you, and he expects you to obey them."

Dad nodded. "That's right," he agreed. "And all of us need to look to God for guidance and obey the guidelines he has set down for us in the Bible. No one ever gets big enough to get along without God." *HCT*

HOW ABOUT YOU?

Did you read today's Scripture passage? It contains good advice for anyone who thinks he's big enough to get along without God. Allow God to direct your decisions and your direction in life.

YOU WILL
ALWAYS
NEED GOD

MEMORIZE:
"Don't be impressed with your own wisdom." Proverbs 3:7

GO AHEAD—JUMP!

Read: 1 John 4:15-19

Niko and his dad were hiking toward their summer cabin, which was located at the top of the mountain. They weren't far from the cabin when they came to a river and found that the bridge had collapsed. "I guess we'll have to jump across the river," Dad observed.

"Oh, no! It's too wide," cried Niko. "I'll never make it!"

"I'll get you across," Dad assured Niko. "Get the rope and those leather straps from the backpack."

At the riverbank Dad fixed a makeshift harness with the straps and fastened the rope to it. After attaching it to Niko, Dad moved to the edge of the river and jumped with all his might. He scrambled to safety. "Now toss me the lose end of the rope," he called, then caught the rope easily. "Your turn to jump now, Son," said Dad.

"But I can't jump that far!" moaned Niko.

"Just trust me," said Dad. "Go ahead—jump!"

Niko stepped to the edge of the riverbank, hesitated a moment—then jumped! Missing the other bank completely, Niko landed in the river. He would have been swept away by the wild water, but Dad quickly began pulling him out. "You did it, Dad! You did it!" shouted Niko as he struggled up the bank. He was wet, but unharmed.

They continued their hike up the mountainside to the cabin. Before long, Niko was drying out in front of a roaring fire. "You know, Niko," reflected Dad, "our adventure in crossing the river reminds me of trusting Jesus."

Niko looked at Dad curiously. "How?" he asked.

Dad nodded. He smiled at Niko and asked, "First, answer this question. Why did you trust me?"

"Because you're my father," replied Niko. "And I know you love me."

"It's the same way with Jesus," said Dad. "I can trust him because I know he loves me." *CH*

HOW ABOUT YOU?

In what ways has God shown his love for you? Knowing his love for us helps us to trust him with our lives. Remember, he knows what is best for you.

MEMORIZE:

"There is no fear in love; but perfect love casts out fear." 1 John 4:18, NKJV

YOU CAN TRUST GOD

REWARDS

Read: Matthew 10:38-42

"Dad! Dad!" Joe yelled. "Come quick! My lamb won't get up!"

Dad came over quickly and inspected the lamb. He frowned and said, "I'm afraid it's pneumonia, Joe. I guess I'd better call the vet."

"Will Woolly die, Daddy?" Joe asked.

"We'll do our best to see that he doesn't," said Dad. "You've worked hard to get Woolly ready to take to the fair, and we'll work hard to get him well again."

Joe did work hard after the vet came—giving his lamb its medicine and keeping the stall clean so sores wouldn't develop on its body. But Woolly refused to eat for days and lost weight. Joe couldn't walk his lamb, so its muscles didn't develop. When the day of the fair came, Joe's lamb was well and looked good, but was so underweight and poorly muscled, it didn't win any ribbons.

"I'm proud of you, Joe," his dad told him. "You didn't give up on your lamb, and you worked so hard. We didn't see the result we hoped for, but I'm going to reward you for your efforts. Here's some extra money to spend at the fair."

"Joe," said Mom, "your efforts for Woolly remind me of your efforts to get Sammy interested in knowing Jesus."

"What does Woolly have to do with me inviting Sammy to church?" he asked. "I keep asking him, but he hasn't accepted my invitation yet."

Mom smiled. "Your heavenly Father rewards you for your efforts, too—even if there are no results."

"That's right," agreed Dad. "It's up to us to be faithful. The results are in God's hands."

"Just keep inviting Sammy," said Mom. "Your faithfulness saved your lamb's life. Someday your faithfulness in witnessing to Sammy may result in his salvation. God will reward you anyway. He knows your heart." *NIM*

HOW ABOUT YOU?

Do you give up when your friends aren't interested in joining you in church or Sunday school—or do you continue to share your testimony? Jesus wants willing workers who are faithful, even when it seems as though nothing is working. Don't give up on your friends, and God will reward you.

BE FAITHFUL IN WORKING FOR JESUS

MEMORIZE:

"For I, the Son of Man . . . will judge all people according to their deeds."

Matthew 16:27

GLAD TO GO TO CHURCH

Read: Psalm 122

It was late Sunday afternoon when there was a knock on the side door. It was two of Jim's friends—Francisco and Everardo. "Hey, Jim," said Francisco, "we're starting a ball game in the lot at the end of the street. Come on out."

It sounded like a great idea to Jim, but before he had a chance to reply, Dad spoke. "Not now, Son," he said. "It's time to get ready for church."

"Phooey!" thought Jim. "Why do I always have to go to church and miss the fun?"

The next day, Jim's school was buzzing with the latest news. Kurt, one of Jim's classmates, had been arrested, along with his older brother, for selling drugs at the ballpark. Jim and Francisco were talking about it on the way home. "Can you believe it?" said Jim. "I do feel sorry for Kurt, though. I mean . . . his folks never seem to care what he does, or how late he's out, or anything. And they never take him to church."

"Pooh," muttered Francisco. "Just because you don't go to church doesn't mean you're gonna be a criminal. I don't go to church much, but I've never touched drugs in my life!"

"Yeah," murmured Jim, "but I'm glad I go anyway."

That evening Dad read Psalm 122 during family devotions. "I was glad when they said to me, 'Let us go to the house of the Lord,'" he began. When Jim laughed a little, Dad looked up and frowned. "What's so funny, Son?" he asked.

"It isn't really funny," Jim answered. "But as you read that verse, I was thinking, 'I am glad that Dad says to me, you have to go to the house of the Lord.' It might be keeping me out of a lot of trouble." *AU*

HOW ABOUT YOU?

Do you attend church regularly? Do you sometimes wish your parents wouldn't make you go? Perhaps going to church won't keep you out of trouble today. But learning God's principles and following them will help keep you out of trouble throughout your life. Be glad to go to church.

MEMORIZE:

"I was glad when they said to me,
'Let us go to the house of the Lord.'"
Psalm 122:1

ATTEND CHURCH
GLADLY

ENOUGH ICE CREAM

Read: Exodus 16:14-15; Numbers 11:4-6

"What's for supper, Mom?" shouted Eddie as he came in from baseball practice. "I'm starved!" Soon they sat down to eat, and Dad thanked the Lord for the food.

As the dishes were passed, Eddie said, "No, thank you. I don't care for salad." Then, "I don't like rice." His parents were quiet until he said, "Yuk! I don't want any broccoli, either. It's gross!" Mom sighed wearily. She was trying to be patient, but this nightly criticism of the food bothered her.

"Eddie," Dad began quietly, "you remind me of the children of Israel in the Bible. They complained that they were starving, so the Lord supplied them with manna. After a while, they also complained about the manna! We need to learn to be thankful for what we have to eat."

"I'd be satisfied to have just one thing all the time—but instead of manna, I'd choose strawberry ice cream," replied Eddie. "I could live on that!"

A few weeks later, Eddie had to have his tonsils out. After the surgery, his throat was so sore! "Here, Eddie," said the nurse, "have some ice cream." The cold ice cream soothed his throat and tasted so-o-o good. And when Mom was ready to take him home, he heard the nurse tell her to let him have all the ice cream he wanted!

In a few days, Eddie was almost back to normal—and he was starving! After putting the meat and vegetables on the table, Mom set a large bowl of strawberry ice cream in front of Eddie. He watched hungrily as the meat was being passed, but nobody suggested that he take any. "Can't I have just a little of that?" he asked hesitantly. "I never want to see strawberry ice cream again." *AU*

HOW ABOUT YOU?

Are you ever guilty of complaining about the food that is served to you? Notice the Bible verse for today. It does not say, "If we have our favorite food." It just says, "If we have enough food." Ask God to make you content with whatever food he provides for you.

BE THANKFUL
FOR FOOD

MEMORIZE:
"So if we have enough food and clothing, let us be content."
1 Timothy 6:8

TOMMY AND OLD ASAPH

Read: Psalm 73:3-7, 12-14, 21-28

Tommy often envied his friend, Hoku, because it seemed like everything always turned out right for him. Hoku's parents let him do just about anything he pleased. And although Hoku never went to church, he seemed to receive all the "blessings" that Tommy figured should go to "good" boys and girls. For instance, Hoku had just gotten a new 10-speed bike.

Tommy was beginning to feel bitter whenever he thought of all Hoku had. He knew that wasn't right, so he asked Dad about it. "I thought God would treat people who love him better than he treats those who don't love him," said Tommy. "But Hoku isn't a Christian, and yet he's got things a lot better than I have! How come?"

Dad smiled. "You sound exactly like Asaph," he said.

"Like who?" Tommy wanted to know.

"Like Asaph . . . a man who wrote some of the Psalms," said Dad. "Come . . . I'll show you." Tommy and his Dad sat down at the kitchen table, and Dad turned to Psalm 73. "Look here, Tommy," he said. "At the beginning of the psalm, Asaph is complaining to the Lord because evil people are prospering and being successful, while everything dreadful happens to him."

"Wow . . . I know just what he means," said Tommy. "Did he feel that way by the end of the chapter, too?"

"No." Dad shook his head. "He realized that those who know Jesus have the best future waiting for them."

Tommy thought about that. Then he grinned. "I guess I don't have it so bad after all," he decided. *AU*

HOW ABOUT YOU?

Are you a Christian who is sometimes jealous of unbelievers who have more things, and perhaps less trouble, than you do? Don't forget—unless they become Christians, they don't have a bright future ahead like you do. Thank the Lord for what you have, and don't complain about what you don't have!

MEMORIZE:

"But the wicked . . . they have no future. . . . The Lord saves the godly."
Psalm 37:38-39

CHRISTIANS HAVE A BRIGHT FUTURE

A PLACE OF ESCAPE

Read: Psalm 71:1-5

Nathan and his dad were sitting near their tent when a flash of red crossed the sky. Nathan's gaze followed the little red bird's swift flight as it landed on a nearby rock. "Wow! What kind of bird is that?" he asked.

"It's a cardinal," said Dad.

Seconds later, the cardinal flew into a huge maple tree. Nathan tried to locate the bird through his binoculars. "I can't see it anymore."

"That's because it's completely shielded by leaves," replied Dad. Then he pointed to the sky. "Look! That's a hawk circling in the air."

"Oh, no!" exclaimed Nathan as the hawk hovered over the maple tree. "I bet he noticed that cardinal because it's so bright. I hope the cardinal won't become lunch for him."

"Don't worry," said Dad. "I think the hawk would rather catch a field mouse for lunch." Nevertheless, Nathan sighed with relief when the hawk finally glided out of sight.

"This world is scary sometimes," observed Dad, "and as Christians, we're similar to bright cardinals because we stand out in a dark and gloomy world. Our brightness—our cheerful testimony or peace-filled heart—often catches the enemy's roaming eye. Satan is our adversary, and he tries to destroy us. But we can always escape."

"By hiding in a tree, like the cardinal?" asked Nathan with a grin. He knew that wasn't right.

Dad smiled. "No," he said, "but by fleeing to God. He hides us in the powerful fortress of his presence. In almighty God, we always have a place of escape."

"Yeah, but what does it mean to flee to God?" Nathan asked slowly. "How do we do that?"

"Good question," said Dad. "I'd say we do that by calling on him to help us when we face temptations or troubles. We also do it by trusting him to take care of us and to watch over us." *SML*

HOW ABOUT YOU?

Are there things that you're afraid of? Are there situations that are difficult to go through? Are there temptations that are hard to resist? Remember that Satan is no match for almighty God. Ask God to help you in every situation. Take shelter in him, and take courage. Trust him at all times.

GOD TAKES CARE OF YOU

MEMORIZE:

"God is our refuge and strength, always ready to help in times of trouble."

Psalm 46:1

DANGER! STAY AWAY!

Read: Psalm 1

"This is great, Uncle Minke!" exclaimed Toby as he helped his uncle with the chores. "I'm glad Mom sent me to spend the summer with you here on the farm." He frowned. "Mom worries too much, though," added Toby. "She doesn't like some of my friends—she thinks they're too rough. Just because I hang around with them, it doesn't mean I'll do the stuff they do."

Uncle Minke frowned. "Yes, but friends of that kind will often tempt you to sin," he said. "Instead of seeing how far you can go along with the crowd without sinning, you should keep clear of situations where you'd be tempted." Toby just shrugged.

Uncle Minke cautiously opened the door to another room in the barn. It contained a heavily constructed stall in which there was a mean-looking bull with long horns. "As you know, this animal is the reason I don't let you play in this section of the barn," said Uncle Minke. "If this critter should get loose, he'd be very dangerous. The man I bought him from told me he nearly gored a man to death."

"He did?" asked Toby. "How did it happen?"

"Well, the man knew the animal could be mean and dangerous, but he had taken care of this bull from the time it was a baby. He figured he knew it well. As he was putting clean straw in the bull's pen one day, he turned his back," explained Uncle Minke. "The bull rushed him and gored him." Uncle Minke shook his head. "If that man had stayed out of the bull's reach, he wouldn't have been hurt. Sin is like that. The only way to be safe is to stay away from it. Choose close friends who won't lead you into sin." *HCT*

HOW ABOUT YOU?

Do you think it won't hurt you to have close friends who like to do wrong things? Do you think you can take care of yourself? Satan is very clever. He likes you to think you can get close to sin and not be harmed. Don't let him fool you. Stay away from those who would tempt you.

MEMORIZE:

"Blessed is the man who does not walk in the counsel of the wicked." Psalm 1:1, NIV

CHOOSE FRIENDS WHO HONOR GOD

THE BOSS

Read: Colossians 3:22-25

"Hey!" called Bryan as he ran into the backyard where his mom and dad were painting the new deck. "I got a job!"

"What kind of job?" Mom asked as she worked.

"I'm going to mow Mr. Das's lawn every week," said Bryan, "and he's going to pay me!"

"That's great," said Dad, "but right now, why don't you help us paint?"

"Are you going to pay me?" asked Bryan.

"Sure we are," said Mom. "We'll give you a bed to sleep in and clothes to wear and food to eat and . . . "

"Aw, Mom," murmured Bryan, but he picked up a paintbrush. He dipped it into the bucket and began to paint, working slowly and carelessly.

"Bryan," said Dad, "I was hoping you would show me that you're ready for your first job outside the family. Instead, I'm seeing that you aren't mature enough to work for someone else."

"Sure I am," said Bryan. "I'll do much better when I'm getting paid."

"Why is that?" asked Dad. "Will the work you do for Mr. Das be easier? Is he easier to work for?"

"No," said Bryan sheepishly, "but it's just different. Like I said, I'll be getting paid."

"I thought Mom pointed out that payment can come in different forms," said Dad. "Actually, it shouldn't really matter who is in charge of a job you're doing or what the pay will be. What is important is that you have one boss who is always watching. He doesn't pay you in dollars and cents, but he will have a far greater reward for you if you do good work."

"Do you mean God?" asked Bryan.

"I sure do," said Dad. "That's who you're really working for, no matter who pays you—or who doesn't pay you." *HMT*

HOW ABOUT YOU?

Does your attitude toward work depend on the circumstances—on whether you're getting paid or for whom you're working? Remember that God is the boss who really matters. His rewards are great.

DO YOUR WORK
FOR GOD'S
APPROVAL

MEMORIZE:

"Work hard and cheerfully at whatever you do, as though you were working for the Lord rather than for people."

Colossians 3:23

Rick, who was spending a couple of weeks with his grandfather, was helping Grandpa hoe the garden. *This ground sure is stony*, thought Rick as his hoe hit something hard. It glistened in the morning sun, and Rick picked it up. "Grandpa," he called, "come and look at this. I never saw a stone this shape before." He wiped the dirt from the pointed stone and handed it to his grandpa.

"Oh, ho!" Grandpa exclaimed. "This is interesting! You just dug up an arrowhead."

"Cool! We talked about arrowheads in history class," said Rick. "Native Americans used them to hunt game."

"Yes," said Grandpa. "Just think—this one was hidden in the ground for a long time—possibly a hundred years or even more."

"I'll show this to my history teacher," said Rick as Grandpa handed the arrowhead back to him.

As Rick continued hoeing, he was more interested in his task than he had been earlier. *Maybe I'll find another arrowhead,* he thought as his eyes carefully searched the ground. But there were no more to be found that day.

After supper, Grandpa reached for his Bible. "We'll read from the seventeenth chapter of Acts tonight," he said, handing the Bible to Rick. "Read verses 10 through 15." Rick found the verses and began reading. When he reached verse 11, which says that the Bereans "searched the Scriptures daily," Grandpa smiled. "That verse reminds me of the way we dug around in the garden," he said.

"The garden?" asked Rick. "What does the garden have to do with the Bible?"

"Well, I've dug in that garden many times, but never found the arrowhead you dug up. I've also 'dug' into God's Word many times. It contains valuable treasures—we can find many important instructions and promises and much wisdom as we search the Scriptures," explained Grandpa. *LAW*

HOW ABOUT YOU?

Do you feel like you have learned all there is to learn from familiar Bible stories? Keep on "digging." Read the Bible for yourself, and listen when your pastor, Sunday school teacher, or parents talk about it. Get to know God better and see what treasures he has for you in his Word.

MEMORIZE:

"In him lie hidden all the treasures of wisdom and knowledge." Colossians 2:3

FIND TREASURE IN GOD'S WORD

GOD'S LIGHT

Read: Matthew 5:14-16

"What are you doing, Dad?" asked Jared.

"Mom and I decided we'd like a window here," said Dad, "so I'm measuring the wall and marking it where I need to cut the hole for the window."

"Why do you want a window there?" asked Jared. "We won't have a very good view from it."

"The view may not be great, but just wait and see what a difference a window here will make," said Dad as he put the tape measure back into his toolbox.

The next day, Dad carefully cut a hole in the wall and fit a new window into place. "Wow!" exclaimed Jared as he came into the room. "I think I'll like having a window there after all. The view is better than I expected. We can see sky, trees, birds, some of the lawn—and we have a really good view of the side of the Reeves' garage." Dad smiled. "But you know what's the best thing of all about this new window?" continued Jared.

"What's that?" asked Dad.

"All the light it lets in," replied Jared. "It's so much brighter in here!"

"Quite different, isn't it?" agreed Dad. "We should be like this window."

"How would we be like a window?" asked Jared.

"The window lets light into our house, and we can bring light—the light of Jesus—into the lives of others," explained Dad.

"I can see the light that comes through the window," said Jared, "but you can't really see the light Jesus gives, can you?"

"In a way, I can see it. I saw the change in your life when you accepted the Lord," said Dad. "I'm thinking of when you invited Samuel to come to church with you or the time you volunteered to take Mr. Freeman's dog for a walk. That's bringing light into people's lives." *DMM*

HOW ABOUT YOU?

Do you share the light and love of Jesus with others? Sharing God's love will make the world a brighter place to live! Let your friends know that God's love is also available to them.

SHARE
GOD'S LIGHT
WITH OTHERS

MEMORIZE:
"Let your good deeds shine out for all to see, so that everyone will praise your heavenly Father." Matthew 5:16

BIG BROTHER

Read: Acts 16:19-25

"You're getting married?!" yelled Mike. "To Jim Ford? Mom, how can you? He's got two kids already. Why don't you marry Dad again?"

"Mike, you know that after your dad left us, he married someone else. He won't be back," said Mom quietly. "I thought you liked Jim."

"Not for a father!" exclaimed Mike. He turned and ran out the door and into his neighbor's backyard. "Mom's going to marry a man with two little boys!" Mike told Mr. Jones angrily. "I don't want someone else's dad! I've got to get away. I'd never be happy here." He sat down on a porch step.

"Do you think you'll find happiness someplace else?" asked Mr. Jones.

Mike shrugged. "I sure won't find it here!"

"Mike," said Mr. Jones, "happiness isn't something you *find*. It's something you *make* by trusting God. The Bible tells us that Paul and Silas sang even though they were in prison. You can be happy, too, even when things aren't particularly pleasant." Mr. Jones put an arm around Mike. "You're a Christian, Mike. Won't you trust God to help you?" he asked.

"But I . . ." Mike began to protest.

"I know this is a difficult time for you, but what about your little brother and sister?" asked Mr. Jones. "Would it be right to run off and let them face things alone? They'll need their big brother. Your new brothers will need help too—it will be difficult for them as well. You can be a witness for the Lord to all of them."

Mike hesitated. "Well, maybe," he said. Then he sighed. "Okay, I'll stay."

"Good," said Mr. Jones. "Let's both pray that God will help you make happiness for all of you." *AGL*

HOW ABOUT YOU?

Does something in your life make you unhappy? Do you wish you could leave it and go your own way? Happiness comes from trusting God, even in difficult times. Ask God to help you accept things you cannot change. Work hard to make life happy for those around you.

MEMORIZE:

"Those who trust the Lord will be happy." Proverbs 16:20

FACE YOUR
PROBLEMS AND
TRUST GOD

HOOKED

Read: Psalm 10:1-4

The house was quiet as Marty listened. *Dad and Lewis and Rich are in the garage, getting ready for a fishing trip, and Mom is gone shopping,* thought James. *Here's my chance.* He quickly turned on the computer, then dialed up the Internet. *This is it!* he thought after a moment. *That's the Web site all the guys were talking about. It's gross! If Mom and Dad knew I was looking at this, they'd . . .* A scream pierced the air—then another!

James jumped to his feet and ran to the garage, where Lewis stood, holding a fishing rod. The line went from it to Rich, and the hook was embedded in the back of Rich's neck. "I'm hooked! I'm hooked!" Rich screamed as tears rolled down his cheeks. When he saw his big brother, he sobbed, "Get me unhooked, James."

James looked around. "Where's Dad?"

"He went next door," explained Lewis.

At that moment, Dad walked into the garage. When he saw what had happened, he examined the hook in Rich's neck. It was soon removed, and the wound was cleaned and bandaged. "You'll be fine—just be glad Lewis didn't get it higher and hook your brain," teased James.

Rich laughed, and the little boys went down the hall to the den. "Wow! Look at this! It's gross!" Lewis's voice floated back to the kitchen. Startled, James realized that he had forgotten to turn off the computer.

Later that evening, Dad and James had a little talk. "I warned you not to play around with the Internet, James," said Dad. "You told Rich to be glad Lewis didn't hook his brain. There was no danger of the fishhook doing that, but on the Internet there are things that will do exactly that. Pornography will hook your brain. It can ruin your life." *BJW*

HOW ABOUT YOU?

Do you use the computer? It's wonderful for many things, but it also can be very dangerous. Never play around with sites that you know your parents wouldn't allow. Never look at sites that God would disapprove of. If you accidentally see one, turn it off immediately. Watch out! You could easily get hooked.

DON'T GET
"HOOKED"
BY EVIL

MEMORIZE:
"Keep away from every kind of evil."
1 Thessalonians 5:22

THE FIREFLIES

Read: Galatians 5:13-15

As their parents sat on the patio, Ashley and Zac ran across the dark lawn, trying to catch fireflies. Zac's voice rang out. "Leave that one alone! That's my firefly!"

Mom sighed. "There are a thousand fireflies out there, but they want the same one," she said. "They argue so much lately."

Through the dark, they heard Ashley shouting, "Stop it, Zac! Don't put your firefly in my jar!"

Dad stood up. "Ashley! Zac!" he called. "Bring your firefly jars and come here." Still arguing, the children came through the darkness to the patio.

"Do we have to come in?" Ashley whined. "We're just starting to have fun."

Zac lifted his jar. "How many did you get, Ashley?"

Ashley held up her jar and started to count, "One, two, three . . . oh no! What is that firefly doing?"

Zac peered closely at Ashley's jar. "It looks like . . ." he paused. "Mom! Look, Dad!" Ashley held the jar so her parents could see. "It looks like one firefly is eating another one."

Dad nodded. "Fireflies do that," he said.

"Yuck!" said Ashley.

"That's gross." Zac agreed.

"I don't know why that should bother you," Dad said. "You kids bite and devour each other, too."

"We what?" Ashley said.

"You bite and devour each other," Dad repeated.

Mom nodded and explained. "Just today, Ashley, you were crying because Zac said some ugly things about you to his friends—and Zac was hurt when you laughed at the birdhouse he was building."

"You're destroying each other's self-esteem and your love for one another," said Dad.

Ashley put her jar down. "I can't watch this," she said and turned to her brother. "Zac, I'm sorry."

"Me, too," mumbled Zac as he took the lid off his jar and released the fireflies. *BJW*

HOW ABOUT YOU?

Do you show love to your brothers and sisters? It's the opposite of "biting and devouring" one another. Don't constantly fuss and quarrel. Instead, try to work things out together.

MEMORIZE:

"If you keep on biting and devouring each other, watch out or you will be destroyed by each other."

Galatians 5:15, NIV

LOVE ONE ANOTHER

A SURPRISING RETURN

Read: Luke 12:37-44

"I'll do it later," said Ryan as he stretched out on the couch. "Mr. Blake won't be back until Saturday."

Mom took the TV remote control from Ryan. "I thought Mr. Blake said he might be back anytime this week," she said.

"I know," said Ryan, "but what are the chances he'll come back early? Practically none."

Mom clicked off the TV. "Go mow his lawn right now."

"Oh, all right," grumbled Ryan.

As Ryan got out the mower, his mother left for the store. Ryan watched her drive away. *I need a drink before I start mowing,* he told himself. He returned to the house and got a glass of lemonade. Then he plopped down on the couch and watched TV while he sipped his drink.

Some time later, Ryan heard a knock on the door. He opened the door and stared in surprise. "Mr. Blake! I didn't know you'd be back so soon!"

"I can see that by looking at my lawn," Mr. Blake replied with his arms crossed.

"I'm sorry, Mr. Blake," said Ryan. "I'll mow it for you right away. You don't even have to pay me."

Mr. Blake shook his head. "Too late now," he said. "I can take care of it myself."

Later, Ryan admitted to his mom what had happened.

"Aren't you glad it was just Mr. Blake who came back?" she asked.

Ryan was puzzled. "What do you mean?"

"You weren't ready for Mr. Blake to return, and I'm afraid you weren't ready for Jesus to return, either," said Mom. "Going back on your promise to Mr. Blake—and also disobeying me while I was gone—are things that are not pleasing to God. Mr. Blake's surprising return should remind us all that Jesus could come back at any moment, too—and we need to be ready." *SML*

HOW ABOUT YOU?

If Jesus Christ came back today, would he find you faithfully living for him? Or would he find you uninterested in learning about him and pleasing him? Even more importantly, would you be among those who go to be with him when he returns? Have you trusted Jesus as your Savior? Don't put it off. Always remember . . . Jesus may come today!

BE READY FOR JESUS' RETURN

MEMORIZE:

"You also must be ready all the time. For the Son of Man will come when least expected." Matthew 24:44

July

2

BEGINNING TO FLY

Read: Ephesians 4:22-24

"Leave my stuff alone!" Jason shouted at his younger brother. "And get out of my room, you little pest!"

His mother entered Jason's room just as five-year-old Carson ran out. "Jason! What's the problem?"

Jason's eyes flashed with anger. "Carson *knows* he's not allowed to touch my things, but I caught him holding my model airplane!"

"I can understand why you're frustrated," said Mom. "I'll have a talk with Carson."

"Well, I'm going to do more than *talk* to him if he touches it again," threatened Jason.

After a moment, Mom asked, "Remember that colorful butterfly we saw earlier today?"

"Yeah," Jason mumbled. "So?"

"Do you think it ever tries to crawl back into its old cocoon?" she asked.

"Of course not," said Jason. "Why?"

"I was thinking about that evening a few months ago when you trusted Jesus as your Savior and Lord and gave him control of your life," said Mom quietly. Jason stared at the floor as she continued. "It's been so neat to see God's Spirit working in you to become more obedient, more respectful, more patient. Watching you change has been like watching a new butterfly emerge from its cocoon and then begin to fly."

Jason looked thoughtful. "I guess I haven't been flying very well today," he admitted. "But Carson *is* supposed to leave my desk alone."

Mom nodded. "That's true," she said, "but don't you think he listens better and learns more from you when he sees Jesus in you?"

Jason breathed a heavy sigh. "You mean when I don't shout or call him names?"

"Exactly," said Mom. "God doesn't plan for butterflies to return to their old cocoons, and he doesn't want *you* returning to your old ways of thinking and acting."

Jason paused in thought, then his face brightened. "I'm going to find Carson. And don't worry, Mom. I won't lose my temper this time." *LCA*

HOW ABOUT YOU?

Are you "flying" lately? Ask God to help you develop kindness and patience and to become more like Jesus each day. The changes may seem slow to you, but those around you will be excited to see God working in your life.

MEMORIZE:

"Therefore, if anyone is in Christ, he is a new creation; old things have passed away; behold, all things have become new." 2 Corinthians 5:17, NKJV

JESUS MAKES YOU
A NEW PERSON

BRETT'S PLAN

Read: 1 Peter 4:7-11

"Mom, guess what I just did!" said Brett.

"What did you do?" she asked, smiling.

"Well, Grandma and Grandpa will be home tomorrow, so even though we mowed their lawn a few days ago, I mowed it again," said Brett. "Now they won't have to work so hard right away."

"Good job, Brett!" said Mom. "I know they'll appreciate it."

Later, Brett sat at the table with his homework. He frowned. "This takes way too long!" he complained. "My teacher gives us too much work! She doesn't want us to have any fun."

"Oh, I'm sure that's not true," said Mom, sitting down beside Brett. "Remember how excited you were this afternoon?" she asked. Brett nodded. "Usually you don't like mowing lawns," said Mom, "but you had fun mowing Grandpa's. Why was that?"

"Well . . . I know it will make him and Grandma happy," said Brett.

Mom nodded. "Did you know that doing your homework makes someone happy, too?" she asked.

"Who? My teacher?"

"Yes," said Mom. "And doing a good job on your homework makes me and Dad happy, too. But most importantly, it makes Jesus happy."

"Jesus?" Brett questioned doubtfully.

Mom nodded. "God's place for you right now is in school," she said, "so don't you think he wants you to do your best?" Brett was silent. "If you knew that doing your homework would make Jesus very happy, wouldn't it be easier to do?" asked Mom.

"I guess so," he said.

Mom smiled. "We all sometimes have to do things we don't feel like doing," she said. "Right now I don't particularly want to cook dinner. But it's my turn, and I know it makes you and Dad happy. So I'll go do it!"

Brett laughed. "And you don't want us to starve!" he added. "Besides, it will make Jesus happy, too!" He turned to his books. "Okay, I'll get this homework done." *KRL*

HOW ABOUT YOU?

Work—even schoolwork or chores around the house—can be fun if you're doing it for someone you love. If you really love Jesus and believe you're doing those things for him, you won't be so tempted to complain.

PLEASE JESUS IN ALL YOU DO

A WALK IN THE WOODS

Read: Romans 5:1-6

Although Mike was happy to be back on his grandparents' ranch in Wyoming, everything was different this summer. In late May, his grandmother had become ill and had to be in the hospital. Then one day when Grandpa was going to see her, a lady had crashed into his car. Grandpa wasn't hurt, but the car had been totally wrecked. That same week the pine forest behind the stables had burned down. Now Grandpa looked tired, and Grandma, who was back home, looked older. Even the ranch seemed different with the blackened trees in the background.

Mike was glad to be able to help with the many chores around the ranch. As he groomed the horses or picked beans in the garden, he often thought about his grandparents' attitude. He had noticed that they still trusted the Lord.

One evening his grandfather said, "Let's take a walk so you can see firsthand the remains of the forest fire."

Together they walked across the field to the woods. Mike pointed to the ground. "Look! Those pine cones don't even look burnt," he said.

Grandpa picked up one of the cones. "This is from a lodgepole pine," he told Mike. "The Lord created them to produce two different kinds of cones. This kind opens only when exposed to heat. Through his marvelous handiwork, God ensures that even a fire will result in good."

"God thought of everything, didn't he?" asked Mike.

"He sure did," Grandpa said thoughtfully. "It's been a rough summer. Sometimes it's easy to get discouraged, but when I look at these pine cones, I'm comforted. I know that God can bring good out of the 'fiery trials' we face. He cares for us, Mike, and wants the best for our lives."

Mike nodded. It was good to know that God was in control—both in the forest and in the lives of his children. *LMW*

HOW ABOUT YOU?

Has something "bad" happened in your life? Maybe you've faced a divorce, illness, or even a death in your family. Remember that the Lord is there for you. He cares about the forest enough to create a special type of pine cone. He cares about you even more.

MEMORIZE:

"These have come so that your faith—of greater worth than gold, which perishes even though refined by fire—may be proved genuine and may result in praise, glory and honor when Jesus Christ is revealed."

1 Peter 1:7, NIV

GOD CARES
FOR YOU

LOST IN THE WOODS

Read: Psalm 66:16-20

"We're lost," Karl said, as he and James faced a fork in the trail. "I don't know which path leads back to camp."

James groaned. "I knew we shouldn't have gone hiking without permission."

"Well, they shouldn't make such strict rules," grumbled Karl. "Let's pray for help," he suggested, and James nodded. After praying that God would help them find the way back to camp, Karl studied each of the two paths again. "Hey, look," he called. "This is the one we came on!"

"How can you tell?" James asked.

Karl pointed. "There's the compass you accidentally dropped."

When the boys arrived at camp, everyone was relieved to see them back safely. They had been missed, and a search party was being organized to look for them.

Mr. Heston, the camp director, called the boys into his office to talk with them. They were a little nervous, because they knew they had broken the rules, but they decided to tell how they had prayed and God had answered. "Maybe that will make Mr. Heston forget we disobeyed," they told each other.

Mr. Heston listened soberly. Then he said, "I'm not sure God answered your prayers." Karl and James could hardly believe what they heard. "I didn't hear any indication that you boys were sorry you broke the rules," Mr. Heston continued. "You didn't ask me to forgive you, and as far as I know, you didn't ask God to forgive you, either. God says that if we 'regard iniquity' in our hearts—that is, if we aren't sorry for our sin, or if we refuse to give it up—he will not hear us."

"But after we prayed, we found the right path," argued Karl.

Mr. Heston nodded. "While you prayed out there in the woods, the counselors and I prayed here at camp," he said. "I wonder if God answered your prayers—or ours." *TMB*

HOW ABOUT YOU?

When you get into a tight spot, do you quickly pray for help? That's good, but as you pray, be sure to examine your heart. If there's unconfessed sin there, ask God's forgiveness and turn from it. Then you will be ready to pray.

CONFESS SIN; THEN MAKE REQUESTS

MEMORIZE:
"If I regard iniquity in my heart, the Lord will not hear me."
Psalm 66:18, KJV

A MEASURE OF FAITH

Read: 2 Peter 1:2-4

"We're finally in Philadelphia!" said Steven and Julie after a long car trip with their parents. They toured Independence Hall, and Steven was fascinated by the Liberty Bell. "It would've been neat to hear that bell ring every day!" he exclaimed.

"That peal of freedom was dear to the hearts of many," agreed Dad. "We owe a lot to our Founding Fathers. They had the faith and the vision to fight for our freedom. It didn't come easily, but they never gave up. They knew the importance of fighting for what they believed in."

Julie pointed to a plaque on the wall. " 'Philadelphia, the city of brotherly love,' " she read. "Why is it called that?"

"William Penn founded the city," explained Dad. "History books tell us that the settlement in this area was kind of an experiment in holy living. Under William Penn's plan, peace, goodwill, and brotherly love were to be extended to all, including the Indians."

"Hey, we studied that in school," said Steven. "William Penn treated the Indians fairly, and they trusted each other. When the Indians promised certain things, he believed them."

Dad nodded. "He took them at their word and acted upon it," he said. "They had faith in one another."

"Mr. Penn must have been a smart man," Julie decided.

"Yes, he was," agreed Dad. "He realized the importance of trust between people—and we all can learn from his example. But you know . . . there are promises more dependable than those of either Mr. Penn or the Indians. God has given us all kinds of promises, and we need to have faith in him. Just as Mr. Penn had faith in the Indians and acted upon their promises, we must have faith in God and act upon his promises. It takes faith and trust in God to be victorious Christians." *JLH*

HOW ABOUT YOU?

Are you claiming God's promises by faith? God says, "I will supply all your need." Do you trust him to do that? When you are in doubt, do you pray for the wisdom he promises to give you? When you are afraid, do you remember his promise that he will never leave you? Start claiming God's promises by faith.

MEMORIZE:

"He has given us all of his rich and wonderful promises." 2 Peter 1:4

CLAIM GOD'S PROMISES

RASPBERRY RIOT

Read: 2 Thessalonians 3:7-12

Mom was going to make raspberry jam, so Brandon and Dave had to pick the raspberries. "Come on, Dave," urged Brandon. "We each have a row to pick. Dad said he'd take us fishing when we're done picking berries, so let's get it finished."

"It's too hot to pick berries," grumbled Dave as he wandered out to the patch. He took his time picking berries, and soon he stopped and said a few mean things to his brother. He enjoyed bugging Brandon, but Brandon didn't respond.

The boys had been picking for about 20 minutes when Dave's friend Kevin walked by. "Hey, Kevin, look here!" Dave yelled as he tossed a raspberry over the fence at his friend. Kevin came through the gate and grabbed some raspberries himself, tossing them back at Dave. Soon raspberries were flying everywhere! Dave's T-shirt was stained with splotches of red, and smashed berries covered the ground.

"Cut it out," Brandon said. "Mom needs these berries."

Reluctantly, Dave went back to his job, but by this time Brandon had finished his row.

"Hey, no fair," Dave whined. "Come help me with these."

"Not today," Dad said, walking up behind him. "I've been watching you boys. Dave, your behavior is unacceptable. The Bible teaches us to work hard and to quietly go about our own business. I don't think that describes your attitude or actions this morning, does it, Son?"

"No, Sir," mumbled Dave, head down.

"Right now you'll have to finish your job while Brandon and I get ready to go fishing. I'm sorry, but you won't be able to join us this time. When your work is done, you might take a look at those verses I was talking about—they're from 2 Thessalonians 3:7-12. Next time you're given work to do, remember what God says about it." *LMW*

HOW ABOUT YOU?

When someone gives you a job to do, do you do it quickly, in a responsible manner? Do you put forth your best effort, or do you often "goof off"? Do you waste a lot of time when you're supposed to be working? The Bible tells us we are to be an example to other people through the good job that we do.

DO YOUR
JOB WELL

MEMORIZE:

"Make it your ambition to lead a quiet life, to mind your own business and to work with your hands, just as we told you." 1 Thessalonians 4:11, NIV

HIGH-FLYING SPARKS

Read: Ephesians 5:8-16

It was Friday night, and Raul was camping out with his Sunday school class. They had a wonderful time fishing, swimming, and cooking out. After supper, they roasted marshmallows and told jokes. From time to time, they poked at the logs on the fire. When Mr. Juan, their teacher, poked a particularly big log, sparks flew up into the sky. "Wow! That almost looked like fireworks!" said Raul.

Mr. Juan smiled. "Did you notice that some of the sparks went up just a few feet before they died out?" he asked. "Others went much higher before burning out—and some went up and up till they were out of sight." He looked around at the kids. "Can you think of ways those sparks are like Christians?" he asked.

Raul yawned. "No," he said. Nobody else offered any suggestions, either.

"Well," said Mr. Juan, "some people make professions of faith and live for the Lord a few weeks, and then it's almost like their light goes out. From then on, other people can't even tell they're Christians."

"Yeah," said one of the kids, "and some people believe in Jesus and live for him for a longer time."

Mr. Juan nodded. "Maybe till some problem discourages them," he said.

"And other Christians are like the high-flying sparks. Their lights burn for Jesus forever!" suggested Raul.

"Now you've got it," agreed Mr. Juan. "The question is: What kind of spark are you? Think about it." He stood up. "Now let's douse this fire and get into those sleeping bags."

Soon the fire was out. "Good night, all of you," said Mr. Juan. "See you in the morning. And remember—God wants you to be like those 'high-flying sparks'!"
REP

HOW ABOUT YOU?

Is your "light" burning brightly, or has something discouraged you so that your light has grown dim? Acknowledge your discouragement and ask God to help you let your light shine despite the discouragement.

MEMORIZE:

"Let your light shine before men, that they may see your good deeds and praise your Father in heaven."
Matthew 5:16, NIV

SHINE FOR JESUS

HIDE AND SEEK

Read: Psalm 139:7-12

"Forty-eight, forty-nine, fifty. Ready or not, here I come!" As Rick heard the words ring out, he scooted a little higher in the tree. *This is the best hiding place I ever picked*, he thought. Looking down at the thick green leaves, he could barely see the ground.

Rick heard the game go on below. "Free! I got in free," someone sang out. Then after a few minutes he heard, "One, two, three on Mary, behind the lilac bush."

A katydid began singing, and a soft breeze stirred the leaves. Rick drew a deep breath, enjoying the warm summer air. He looked at the bright blue sky and thought about God—as he had often done lately. His Bible club teacher had explained that God had sent Jesus to earth to seek and save sinners. *I'm not really all that much of a sinner,* he often told himself. *Now, up here in this leafy old tree, my friends can't find me,* he thought, *but God knows where I am—and he knows all the things I've ever done. I can hide from my friends, but I know I can't hide from God.*

Right then and there Rick quietly admitted to God that he was a sinner and needed salvation. He asked Jesus to come into his life and save him.

Suddenly Rick heard voices and remembered the game. "Come out! Come out, wherever you are. We give up," the children called. Rick slid down the tree and walked over to the other kids. "Oh, there you are," they greeted him. "We were ready to start a new game. We've been calling and calling you. It's about time you came."

"Yes," Rick agreed with a smile as he thought of his prayer. "I'd been hiding too long." *CEY*

HOW ABOUT YOU?

Have you been putting off coming to God? Do you have questions? Talk to a trusted adult, your parents, or your pastor to find out more.

YOU CAN'T HIDE
FROM GOD

MEMORIZE:
"For the Son of Man has come to seek and to save that which was lost."
Luke 19:10, NASB

July

10

Ignoring the barking of his dog, Skip, Jacques hopped on his bike and sped down the road to go swimming. When he arrived home a few hours later, he got himself a big glass of juice. He noticed that Skip was still barking, but not as loudly. Jacques recalled his promise to take good care of Skip. "Pets depend on humans for care," Dad had told him. Jacques knew he should check his dog, but he decided to finish reading an article in his sports magazine first.

During the evening meal, Jacques drank two tall glasses of cool lemonade. "I've been so thirsty all day," he said.

"So was I," nodded Dad. "And it's no wonder—it's a hot day!"

When Jacques finally went out to feed his dog after dinner, he was shocked to see Skip lying on his side, tongue hanging limp, and eyes half closed. "Skip! What's wrong?" cried Jacques, kneeling down beside his dog. "Ben! Come here!" Jacques shouted to his older brother.

Seeing the dog, Ben exclaimed, "Skip needs water!"

Jacques ran for water, but Skip was too weak to lap it up. Ben took a rag, dipped it in the bowl, and squeezed some water into the dog's dry mouth. Skip swallowed weakly as Ben continued to give him water from the wet rag. It took a long time, but Skip finally grew stronger and sat up.

"Jacques, Skip could have died," Ben scolded.

Ashamed, Jacques hung his head. After Ben went into the house, Jacques put his arms around Skip. "I'm so sorry, Skip," he murmured. "I should have known you'd be thirsty, because I was so thirsty myself. I'm going to take better care of you in the future." Jacques was glad to see the dog wag his tail as if he was saying thank you. *CEY*

HOW ABOUT YOU?

God loves people and all his creatures. Take care of your pet in a way that pleases Mom and Dad—and God.

MEMORIZE:

"A righteous man cares for the needs of his animal." Proverbs 12:10, NIV

CARE FOR
YOUR PETS

VISIT FROM A COUSIN

Read: Romans 12:3-10

Vincent, who lived in a large city, was spending a weekend at his uncle's farm. This was his first visit to the farm, and he expected to be bored. Vincent's cousin, Andrew, wasn't sure how to entertain him.

"You mean you don't have a computer?" Vincent said. "What do you do around here?"

Andrew answered, "For one thing, we work. In my spare time, I go hiking, or swimming in the pond, or . . ."

"We have a pool in our backyard," Vincent bragged.

Andrew took a deep breath and continued, ". . . or go horseback riding."

Vincent looked interested. "Can I go riding?"

"Sure," Andrew agreed. Later, as he watched his cousin attempt to mount, he grinned. Evidently, his smart cousin knew nothing about horses.

As the boys rode away, Vincent asked, "What are we going to do tomorrow?"

"We'll be going to church," Andrew answered. "It's Sunday."

"Oh, no," groaned Vincent. "Church is boring." At that moment his horse took off at a gallop, but Vincent hung on! When the horse finally slowed down, Vincent's eyes were wide. "Boy," he gasped, "that was more frightening than riding the Big Ben Tube at Lakeshore Water Park."

Andrew laughed. "Life on the farm can be exciting," he said.

After supper, the family gathered around the table for devotions. Vincent seemed to listen as Andrew's dad read the Scripture and led in prayer. But he didn't comment until he and Andrew were in bed with the light out. "When I came here, I thought you wouldn't know anything cool," he confessed. "But you know lots of things." After a moment's silence, Vincent said, "Maybe going to church tomorrow will help me learn a few more things I need to know." *BJW*

HOW ABOUT YOU?

Do you look down on others who don't know all the things you know, or who don't have everything you have? Be careful! God warns about being the kind of proud person who puts other people down.

LEARN FROM OTHERS

DAVID'S MEAN MOMMY

Read: Proverbs 6:20-23

"Mommy! Cassie looks funny!" cried David. Hearing the anxiety in her five-year-old son's voice, Mom dropped the dish towel and ran into the family room where David's baby sister stood holding tightly to the playpen railing. She was trying to cry, but no sound came, and her usually pink lips had a dusky blue color. Her eyes were wide and frightened. "What's the matter with her, Mommy?" the little boy asked anxiously.

Mom lifted Cassie quickly and began to thump her on the back. After a moment, a bright green marble popped out of Cassie's mouth, and she burst into tears. David began to sob, too. "You hurt her, Mommy! It wasn't her fault. I gave her the marble."

While comforting the crying baby, Mom also drew David close. "How many times have I told you not to give Cassie any of your small toys?" she said. "It's nice that you want to share, but she's not ready for some things yet."

When the children had calmed down, Mom continued talking to David, "Last week some of the kids wanted you to play down by the creek. Remember?" David nodded. "When I said 'no,' you told me I was a mean mommy," continued his mother. "Just now, you cried when I was getting the marble from Cassie. You thought that was mean, too, but it made her stop choking, didn't it?"

David nodded solemnly. "But she didn't like it," he said.

"No, but it was something I had to do to help her. You see, Jesus has given you parents who love you very much, and we're trying to do what's best for you," Mom said tenderly. "Sometimes you may not understand, and it may even hurt—but I want you to learn to trust us and obey us, just as we trust Jesus to help us do the right things." *PIK*

HOW ABOUT YOU?

Do you sometimes feel like yelling at your parents? You need to obey, honor, and respect them, even when you don't understand why they have had to do or say certain things.

MEMORIZE:

"Keep thy father's commandment, and forsake not the law of thy mother."
Proverbs 6:20, KJV

HONOR AND
OBEY PARENTS

EVERY SECRET THING

Read: Matthew 6:1-6

Mark's mother noticed that he recently was spending more and more time alone in his tree house. When she asked why, he just smiled and said, "Oh, I like to be alone sometimes."

That afternoon, Mom said to Dad, "I'm curious about what Mark does out in that tree house. He seems very secretive about it."

Four-year-old Jana popped into the room. "I know," she squealed. "I know."

"You do?" Mom was surprised. "What is it?"

"Can't tell. Big girls don't tell secrets," Jana reminded her parents. They sighed. "Besides," Jana continued, "Mark said that if I tell, I can't pray in his tree house when I get big, like he does."

"Pray? You mean 'play,' Jana," Mom corrected.

"Unh-uh. I mean pray," insisted Jana. "Mark prays and reads the best stories. I heard him, but he made me promise not to tell or . . . Oh, no! I told!" She burst into tears.

After the sobbing little girl had been comforted and sent out to play, Mom smiled. "Mark is following Jesus' instructions to enter into a secret place of prayer," she said. "I'm glad."

Dad nodded. "We talk so often about how God sees and knows all things and how someday he'll reveal and judge all the bad things we do. We tend to forget that he'll also reveal the good things we do in secret, and he'll reward us. Mark will be rewarded for what he's doing."

"Yes," agreed Mom, "but meanwhile I guess we had better keep his secret— it's a good one." *AU*

HOW ABOUT YOU?

Do you have a secret time of prayer, or do you just pray when everyone else does? If you were to be rewarded today for the good things you have done in secret, would you get any reward? If you're a Christian, try to do one good thing every day—secretly. Someday you'll be glad you did.

GOD GIVES REWARDS

14

Read: Psalm 37:3-8

Joel and his dog ran out to the old 80-year-old barn where his father was rebuilding a wall. As they approached, Joel saw the wide ditch that had been dug so Dad could replace the foundation that had cracked.

As Joel eyed the ditch and got ready to jump, Dad slapped down a wooden plank. "Here's a bridge for you," he said.

"But I want to try a running jump to see if I can make it across on my own," laughed Joel.

"Yes, you want to," said Dad, "but you'd better listen to someone who knows better."

"Well, okay," agreed Joel, and he gingerly made his way across the plank. After reaching solid ground, he turned to call the dog. "Come on, Rusty," Joel called. Rusty came running up to the plank, then stopped. "Aw, don't be afraid, boy. Come on," encouraged Joel. Rusty just sat on his haunches.

"Cross the bridge, Rusty," Dad called and after a moment said, "Looks like Rusty's afraid to follow."

"Why would he be afraid, Dad?" Joel asked.

"Well, I guess he's never had to walk across a plank before," replied Dad.

Joel chuckled, "He wouldn't make a very good pirate hound!"

Dad wiped the sweat from his brow, "Encourage him a little more and he will follow because he trusts you."

Joel tapped lightly on the bridge, "This way, Rusty." The dog edged forward, sniffed the board and looked up at Joel. Slowly he placed a paw on the board, then timidly scooted toward Joel's outstretched arms. Joel patted Rusty's head as the dog reached him.

Dad lovingly thumped Joel on the head. "This reminds me of God and us. Sometimes when we get scared we have a hard time trusting that his way is best. But it always is!" *KC*

HOW ABOUT YOU?

Do you trust God's ways when times are difficult? Always remember that God desires the best for you. It isn't always easy to trust him, especially when his ways might seem scary or risky.

MEMORIZE:

"Put your trust in the Lord."
Psalm 4:5, NKJV

WELCOME

Read: John 14:1-3; 17:24

"All right!" exclaimed Garret as they pulled into Grandma's driveway. "We're finally here!" Grandma Peck lived so far away that they had been traveling for two days.

"Yeah," said Sarah. "I'm glad we're here."

Dad grinned. "Me, too," he said. "I want to relax with a nice, tall glass of iced tea."

Garret laughed. "Well, I bet Grandma has a pitcher of it all ready so that you can have some right away." He pointed. "Look! There she is at the door to welcome us," he added, "and she's got a glass of something in her hand. It's probably your iced tea."

Garret was right. "I knew you'd want this right away," said Grandma. She had also been thinking of the others. She had baked Garret's favorite pie, made fudge for Sarah, and fixed a "nibble tray" with snacks that she knew Mom especially liked. In addition, the house had been scrubbed, clean sheets were on the beds, and a special meal was in the oven. There were new books for the kids to read, and new games for them to play.

"It must have taken you a long time to get ready for us to come," said Sarah when she realized all that Grandma had done.

"Oh, well, I enjoyed preparing for you because I love you," said Grandma, giving Sarah a hug.

"Sounds like my Sunday school lesson all over," said Garret with a grin. "It was about how Jesus loves us and is preparing a place for those who love him."

"I'm so thankful to know that each one here loves Jesus and that we'll all enjoy heaven together," said Grandma. "What a wonderful place that will be!"

Dad nodded. "You've given us a great welcome here," he said, "but you're right. We can't even imagine how very special God's welcome will be!" *LMW*

HOW ABOUT YOU?

Have you helped prepare for company—getting everything just right for those who are coming to visit? If you're a Christian, the Lord Jesus is preparing a place in heaven for you. It's hard to imagine what a very special, wonderful place that will be—and it won't be just for a visit. It will be for all eternity!

JESUS IS PREPARING A PLACE FOR CHRISTIANS

MEMORIZE:
(Jesus said) "I go to prepare a place for you." John 14:2, KJV

CROOKED SHINGLES

Read: Psalm 32:1-5

Sergei enjoyed helping his dad with shingling the roof. Dad showed him how to place the shingles, making sure to line them up with the row below. After they had worked a while, there was a phone call for Dad. "This may take a while," said Dad. "Want to take a rest?" But Sergei was sure he could manage by himself. "Okay, but keep your eyes on the row below, or you'll start to put them on crooked," Dad warned. "And the farther you go, the worse it will get."

"I'll watch," said Sergei.

After Dad left, Sergei worked hard. He wanted to show his dad how much he could do alone. But as he hurried, he became less careful, and when he started a new row, he found that the previous row ran just a little crooked. "It's not enough to make any difference," he decided. But it did make a difference, and each row got "off" a little bit more. Soon it was easy to see that the shingles were quite crooked.

"Let me see if I can guess what happened," said Dad when he got back and noticed the crooked rows of shingles. "First, you went too fast, and one of the shingles didn't get nailed up quite right. Then, instead of taking time to do it over, you tried to cover it . . . only things got worse."

"What can we do to make it right?" Sergei groaned.

"We'll have to take the shingles off—all the way to where they start to go wrong—and nail them back correctly," said Dad.

As they removed the crooked rows, Dad spoke, "You know, Sergei, there's a spiritual lesson here," he said. "When we stray away from the Lord, we can't make things right by trying to cover up the wrong things we've done. We need to confess our sin." *AU*

HOW ABOUT YOU?

Do you think one little sin isn't so bad? Have you tried to cover up wrong things that you've done? Don't do that. As soon as you know you've done something wrong, that's the time to make it right with God.

MEMORIZE:

"But I confess my sins; I am deeply sorry for what I have done." Psalm 38:18

CONFESS SIN
RIGHT AWAY

SALTED LEECHES

Read: Matthew 5:10-16

Jen and Mark came laughing and splashing out of the water and onto the beach near their family cabin. The cool water felt wonderful on such a warm day, but as Jen began toweling off, she suddenly stopped laughing. She shrieked in horror and pointed at her ankle.

Mom came running from the cabin. "Are you hurt?" she asked.

Jen pointed at her ankle again and began to cry. "It's a leech! Get it off!" she exclaimed.

"Calm down, honey," said Mom. "Mark, go into the cabin and get the salt shaker."

Mark headed off to get the salt. Soon he was back and handed the salt shaker to Mom. "Watch this," she said. Kneeling down, she poured salt on the leech. Immediately, the slimy little black blob curled up into a ball and fell to the sand. "There. All better," said Mom.

Jen sniffed and tried to smile. "How did you know that salt would make it let go?"

Mom grinned. "Old trick I learned as a kid. When you live near a lake, you learn how to take care of leeches," she said, "and my church teacher taught a lesson one day that has always helped me to remember this little trick."

"What lesson was that?" Mark asked.

"My teacher was explaining a verse in the Bible that talks about Christians being the salt of the earth," replied Mom, "and I remembered how we used salt on leeches. I told my teacher about it, and she said we can think of sin as a leech clinging to people. We can think of ourselves as the salt that will help release those people from the sin 'leech.' We can help people want to be free from their sin. We do that by living the way God wants us to and telling them about Jesus." *KMS*

HOW ABOUT YOU?

Do you know people who need to be set free from their sin? Have you told them about Jesus and his gift of salvation? As the salt of the earth, Christians need to get out God's message—that Jesus sets sinners free.

BE A "SALTY" CHRISTIAN

FUEL ON THE FIRE

Read: 2 Timothy 2:22-26

As Blake and David were studying, their father came to their room, waving a rusty hammer and nails. "I found these down in the woods by the fort you were building," Dad said sternly.

"We're sorry," said David quickly. "We won't leave your tools out again, will we, Blake?"

"No, you won't," growled Dad, "because you are forbidden to use them again!" Blake began to protest that he was not to blame, but Dad didn't seem to hear as he went out to the garage.

Blake glared at David. "You're the one who took them and left them outside," Blake said angrily.

David shrugged. "You use Dad's tools as often as I do," he said. "Besides, I'm not about to take the blame by myself."

As Blake raised a clenched fist to punch his brother, in the back of his mind he remembered his youth leader kneeling down by a small fire at a recent campout. "What happens, guys, when I place wood on the fire?" Pastor Bill had asked.

"The fire gets bigger," someone had answered.

"That's right," agreed Pastor Bill. "What will happen if no more wood is added?"

"The fire will go out," came the quick response.

"Right." Pastor Bill nodded. "I want you to remember that Proverbs 26:20 compares a fire to an argument or a quarrel. Without wood a fire goes out, and without angry words or attitudes, a quarrel dies down. God commands us to be gentle when possible and to love one another."

Blake knew a big fight would erupt if he continued arguing with David—it had happened many times before. In fact, he could see that David was braced for an angry confrontation now. Blake hesitated only a moment. Then he turned and walked away muttering quietly, "This time I'll do what God says I should." *GDF*

HOW ABOUT YOU?

If someone does or says something you dislike or that hurts your feelings, what do you do? If someone starts a quarrel with you, do you add "fuel to the fire" by saying something nasty in return? If possible, be gentle, kind, and patient.

MEMORIZE:

"The Lord's servant must not quarrel; instead, he must be kind to everyone."
2 Timothy 2:24, NIV

STOP QUARRELS

THE MIME

Read: Matthew 7:16-20

As Rob and his mother got off the Ferris wheel, he pointed to a crowd of people. "Can we go see what's going on over there?" he asked. Mom nodded, and they walked over.

Rob was fascinated as he watched a man with a white painted face acting out various skits. The crowd laughed as the man pretended to be learning to ride a bike. "Mom, why doesn't he talk?" asked Rob.

"Because he's a mime," Mom replied. "They never talk, but you can always tell what they're doing. Just watch—you'll see."

Next, the mime pretended to wash a window. He acted as though he bumped his head on the pretend ladder. Then he pretended he was eating an ice cream cone and the ice cream fell off. The crowd applauded as he acted out one scenario after another. The show ended with the mime making a sad face and waving good-bye.

Rob turned to his mother. "Wow! He never said a thing, but I could follow the whole story."

"That goes to show you how loudly actions—even facial expressions—speak," said Mom. "It's good to remember that our actions really do speak louder than our words."

"Do my actions ever tell you anything?" asked Rob.

"Sure they do," said Mom. "For instance, just yesterday I told you to clean your room. When you agreed and then rolled your eyes, I knew what you were saying."

"Oh, Mom!" protested Rob. "I did clean my room!"

"Yes, you did," agreed Mom. "Your actions showed me two things. First of all, they told me that you didn't really want to clean your room. They also told me that you are an obedient son, because you cleaned it anyway." She smiled. "What I really want to point out is that as Christians, we should be especially careful how we act." *ASB*

HOW ABOUT YOU?

Are you aware that your actions speak loudly? Show consideration, kindness, and God's love in actions as well as in words.

ACTIONS ARE IMPORTANT

MEMORIZE:
"Even children are known by the way they act, whether their conduct is pure and right." Proverbs 20:11

GAZELLES AND THOUGHTS

Read: Psalm 18:28-36

Jerry and his mom munched their popcorn as they stood in front of the gazelle exhibit. The sleek and powerful animals stood quietly on the grass behind a chain-link fence. Jerry guessed the fence was only about as tall as his dad was. "Mom, can't those gazelles jump over the fence?" he asked.

Mom smiled. "They probably could," she replied. "Can you guess why they don't try?"

"Not really," said Jerry.

"Do you see how the top of the fence leans toward the gazelles?" asked Mom, and Jerry nodded. "Well, an article I read says gazelles have poor eyesight and that when a fence leans into their area, it creates an illusion—a false idea—that the fence is much higher than it really is. According to the article, that's why they don't try to escape."

"Really? I guess they need glasses," joked Jerry.

Mom smiled as they moved on toward the monkey exhibit. "The way the fence keeps the gazelles from running free is a little like the way our thoughts sometimes keep us from being free," she said.

Jerry was curious. "What do you mean?" he asked.

"The way the fence is built gives the gazelles a false idea, and our thoughts can give us false ideas, too," explained Mom. "When we listen to thoughts that tell us we'll never be good students or that we're too clumsy, or when we think God doesn't love us, we get false ideas that keep us from being the best we can be."

"So . . . if the gazelles knew the truth, they could jump over the fence," said Jerry thoughtfully, "and if we know the truth and believe what God says, we can break free from false thoughts." *RSM*

HOW ABOUT YOU?

Do thoughts that you are a failure or bad or not valuable to God create false ideas that keep you from being the person God wants you to be? Don't be trapped by illusions. Believe God and become the kind of person he wants you to be.

MEMORIZE:

"For I can do everything with the help of Christ who gives me the strength I need." Philippians 4:13

BELIEVE GOD

CALL WAITING
Read: 1 Samuel 3:1-10

"Hold on, Pete." Matt spoke into the telephone receiver. "Something's wrong with our phone." He looked up and called, "Mom! The phone is beeping!"

Mom came into the kitchen. "Oh," she said, "I ordered call waiting. Push the flash button and say hello."

Matt did so and was surprised to hear Dad's voice. "Hi, Matt," said Dad. "Let me talk with Mom, please."

Mom took the phone and pressed the flash button. "Pete, Matt will call you back in a minute," she said. Once more she pushed the button. Then she began talking with Dad.

When she was finished, Matt grinned. "Cool!" he exclaimed as he called Pete's number.

Matt was telling Pete a joke when he heard the beeping tone again. *I'll get it after I finish this joke*, he thought, but before he was through, the beeping stopped.

That evening, the phone rang again, and Mom answered it. She returned a few minutes later. "That was Grandpa," she told Matt. "He called this morning to see if you wanted to go fishing today. Since nobody answered, he assumed no one was home."

Dad looked surprised. "That's odd," he said. "You were home all day. And since we have call waiting, you should have gotten the call."

"I did hear a beep," admitted Matt. "I guess I waited too long before I answered it." He sighed.

"It's too bad you didn't answer his call," said Dad. Then he added, "I hope when God tries to get your attention you will be careful to listen and not ignore him."

"How does he try to get our attention?" asked Matt.

"Through pastors, Sunday school teachers, parents, or friends," said Dad. "Other times he speaks to us through verses we read in his Word—or perhaps simply through the urging of the Holy Spirit in our hearts. If we don't respond, we might miss a blessing." *SLK*

HOW ABOUT YOU?
Have there been times when you knew God was warning you about something or was urging you to do some work for him? Have you quickly responded and followed his leading? Answer his "call" right away!

ANSWER GOD'S "CALL" IMMEDIATELY

MEMORIZE:
"Speak, for your servant is listening."
1 Samuel 3:10, NIV

Read: Psalm 37:23-28

Josiah shuffled through the pieces of the jigsaw puzzle. "Wow! I've never tried to work a puzzle with so many pieces before!" he exclaimed.

"I know it looks hard, but I'm sure you can do it," replied his mother. "Want some help? I could turn the pieces right side up for you."

"Okay," agreed Josiah. "I'll work on the barn." He started to sift through the jumbled pile, looking for the red pieces.

"Josiah, do you know what this jigsaw puzzle reminds me of?" asked Mom as she turned pieces.

"Ahhh . . . my room, I guess. A big mess," answered Josiah with a laugh.

Mom chuckled. "It does look a lot like the clutter under your bed," she said, "but what I had in mind was something else—our lives. Sometimes life seems to be filled with overwhelming problems. We can't see how the pieces of our lives can possibly fit together, but God knows how they will fit perfectly. Isn't it wonderful that he has a plan and purpose for everything that happens in our lives, even when we can't see what it is?"

"Do you mean like the time I didn't make the Jackson soccer team?" asked Josiah.

Mom nodded. "Yes," she said. "You were so disappointed. You didn't see how that 'piece' of your life fit—you said you thought you might as well give up playing soccer. Then Mr. Constantine called and asked if you'd like to play the goalie position on the Greenwood team, which he was coaching. You found that you really liked playing with that team."

"Yeah, that was pretty awesome," agreed Josiah.

"I think God wanted you on Mr. Constantine's team so we could get to know their whole family," said Mom. *ASB*

HOW ABOUT YOU?
Are you a Christian who is in the midst of disappointment? Does your life seem like a jumbled mess that will never fit together? Trust God. He has a plan and purpose for all things in your life, and he will work them together for your good.

MEMORIZE:
"And we know that God causes everything to work together for the good of those who love God and are called according to his purpose for them."
Romans 8:28

GOD HAS A PURPOSE FOR EVERYTHING

Read: Acts 16:22-25

Aaron threw himself onto the couch and wiped away an angry tear. He listened to the rumble of thunder and the pattering of raindrops against the picture window. "This weather is the worst!" he declared as his father walked into the living room.

Dad stood with his hands on his hips, looking out the window. "Well, we certainly won't be going to the amusement park today," he said.

"We won't be doing anything but wasting a day of vacation," snapped Aaron.

"Whoa there!" exclaimed Dad, holding up both hands toward Aaron, like a policeman stopping traffic. "This rain may dampen everything outside, but let's not allow it to dampen our spirits."

"How can we help it?" asked Aaron as he sat up.

"Easy!" replied Dad. "We change our point of view. You're thinking of all the things we can't do because of the rain, Aaron. Let's look at all the things we can do in spite of the rain. For instance, we could play Monopoly. And the last time we played Taboo, your mother and sister blew us away. Do you think we could get revenge today?"

Aaron leaped to his feet. "Sure we can!" he said. "Good idea, Dad! We've got some other games we haven't played for a long time, either. Let's get them out, too." He paused. "I suppose Beth will want to save some time to read—but then can you maybe help me with my new model ship, Dad? And tonight we could have popcorn and pop." Suddenly, Aaron looked troubled again.

"What is it now?" asked Dad.

"What if we run out of time before we get finished with everything?" asked Aaron.

Dad laughed as he put his arm around Aaron's shoulder. "Well, then I guess we'll just have to pray for rain tomorrow, too," he said. "Come on—let's go find the competition." *MLR*

HOW ABOUT YOU?

When things don't go as you want them to go, do you grumble and pout? Ask God to help you display the kind of attitude Paul and Silas had. Ask him to help you discover the good things in your situation. Ask him to change your point of view.

LOOK AT THE BRIGHT SIDE

LEARNING THE HARD WAY

Read: 1 Corinthians 10:6-11

"Hey, Ryan," said Ben, walking into Ryan's backyard. "I've got something I want you to try. It's a—" Suddenly Ryan jumped up to grab his little brother.

"Toby!" yelled Ryan. "Don't touch that flower! There's a bee on it!"

"Bug purdy," Toby cooed, as Ryan pulled him away from the flower. "I want to pet it."

"The bee is pretty," agreed Ryan, "but bees can hurt you. Don't touch it, okay?" He watched Toby toddle off to see another flower.

"Sorry, Ben," he said. "What did you want me to try?"

Ben looked around, then pulled something from his pocket. "Here . . . try this," he said. "It gives you a real buzz."

Startled, Ryan asked, "Is that marijuana? I don't want anything to do with that—or any other cigarette. Drugs harm your body and mind."

"How do you know if you don't try them?" declared Ben.

"They've been proven to be bad," Ryan said. "That's a fact, and I don't have to *try* drugs to learn that."

Just then, Toby let out a wail. "Wyan," he called as he held up his hand. "Wyan, it hurted me!"

Ryan ran to help his brother. "I told you not to touch that bee!" exclaimed Ryan. As he looked at Toby's finger, a car drove into the yard. "Oh, good! Mom's home," said Ryan. "Come on, Toby."

After taking Toby to his mother, Ryan went back out to the patio where Ben was waiting. "Toby is a good example for you, Ben," said Ryan. "I told him that bee could hurt him, but he had to try touching it anyway. He learned about bee stings the hard way. We've been warned that drugs are dangerous and that trying them could lead to getting hooked on them. I'm not going to learn about drugs the hard way—and I hope you won't either, Ben." *VMH*

HOW ABOUT YOU?

Do you think you have to try things for yourself? Don't learn the hard way. Often you can avoid sin and its dreadful consequences by learning from the examples of others. If in doubt, ask yourself, "What would Jesus do?" Then do your best to follow his example.

MEMORIZE:

"Such things were written in the Scriptures long ago to teach us."
Romans 15:4

LEARN FROM EXAMPLES

LADDIE'S ENEMY

Read: Luke 6:27-36

"Mr. Wilson kicked at Laddie!" said Chad angrily. "He tried to hurt him. I know we agreed to pray for Mr. Wilson, but I don't want to pray for a dog hater!"

Mom frowned. "Chad," she said quietly, "Jesus said we should pray for our enemies."

"I know," Chad said, "but it's hard to do."

The next day, Mr. Wilson called. "That vicious dog of yours got loose from your yard and bit me!" he said. "I've a good mind to report you to the authorities."

Chad and his parents discussed what they should do. Chad finally agreed reluctantly to find a home in the country for Laddie. "Don't you think you also should go and see Mr. Wilson, Chad?" Mom asked.

Chad was dismayed. "You mean go in his house?" he asked.

Mom nodded. "He's hurt, and apparently your dog did it," she said. "I'll go with you."

When they arrived, Mr. Wilson was as grumpy as ever. "That beast of yours almost killed me!" he said.

"I'm sorry," said Chad. "I don't know how he got out, but since he bit you, Mr. Wilson, I'm . . . I'm going to get rid of him."

Mr. Wilson stared at Chad. "You are?" Chad nodded.

"Well . . ." Mr. Wilson cleared his throat. "Actually, I let the dog out, hoping he'd run off," he admitted. "When I tried to drag him by the collar, he bit me. It . . . it wasn't the dog's fault—don't get rid of him." Chad stared in surprise. "Didn't mean to tell you that," muttered Mr. Wilson, "but there's something different about you folks."

Mom spoke up. "It's the Lord Jesus," she said. "And we'd love to tell you more about him."

Chad's eyes were wide with amazement. *It does work to pray for your enemies,* he thought, *just like the Bible says. BP*

HOW ABOUT YOU?

Is there someone who doesn't like you? Who mistreats you? Do you try to get even? Don't! Instead, pray for that person and try to find something nice to do for him or her. Even if nothing changes right away, keep praying. Leave the results up to the Lord.

PRAY FOR YOUR ENEMIES

MEMORIZE:

"But I say, love your enemies! Pray for those who persecute you!"

Matthew 5:44

DANGEROUS THORNS

Read: Hebrews 12:1-3

"It kinda feels like we're deep in a jungle!" declared Shawn as he hacked at the hedge of large, sprawling bushes in their backyard. Helping tear out the hedge seemed like an adventure to Shawn and Alexandra.

"These bushes have big thorns," Dad warned them. "Be careful!"

"We will," they agreed—but frequently one of the thorny branches would cling to a shirt or prick or scratch an arm. Then Dad had to gently and carefully remove it from someone's clothes—or skin!

For almost two hours, they clipped, sawed, and pulled on those stubborn bushes—even crawling into the thicket now and then. "Look at us!" exclaimed Alexandra when they finally finished pulling out the prickly growth. "We're all scratched up and bleeding—even you, Dad."

"Those bushes were terrible," declared Shawn. "They were a lot more dangerous than they looked."

"Yeah—they didn't look so bad. I even thought they were kind of pretty," said Alexandra, "but when we weren't careful, the branches stuck to us and scratched really bad!"

Dad nodded. "They're an example of bad things that look pretty good," he said. "Sometimes we forget that some wrong things—such as sins—may not look so bad. But sin always hurts us. It causes more pain and harm than those prickly bushes."

"What are some bad things that might look good, Dad?" asked Alexandra. "I can't think of any."

"Well . . . things like TV programs or movies that promote lifestyles that aren't pleasing to God," Dad said. "Listening to certain types of music might cause wicked lyrics to stick in our minds. Even wanting to please other people can cause us to do wrong things and get tangled up in sin. If we give in to sinful things that don't look so bad, they cling to us like those thorny branches, and will eventually cause pain and hurt in our lives." *RT*

HOW ABOUT YOU?

What do you watch on TV? What do you read or listen to? Do you hang around with kids whose values and standards are not those that God gives in his Word? Things that don't look so bad are bad if they tempt you to do things that are wrong. Be careful! Don't allow them to entangle you in sin.

MEMORIZE:

"Let us strip off . . . the sin that so easily hinders our progress."
Hebrews 12:1

DON'T GET ENTANGLED IN SIN

Read: Revelation 21:10, 22-27

Tai sat at the table, while his mother mopped the floor. "Mom, how do you explain salvation to someone?" he asked. At that moment, the screen door flew open and Tai's brother Mi-lee stepped in.

"Stop!" Mom hollered. "Don't come in one more step with all that mud on you."

"But I'm thirsty," objected Mi-lee. "I don't want to stay out any longer."

"I'm not asking *you* to stay out," Mom told him. "I'm asking you to leave all that mud at the door, and come in clean." She helped Mi-lee pull off his dirty shoes and brushed the mud off the back of his jeans. Then she let him in, and Mi-lee got a drink and headed to his room.

"What just happened here is an example of what happens in salvation," Mom told Tai. "God loves us very much, and he wants to take us to heaven—but not covered in dirt."

"When you say *dirt,* you mean *sin,* don't you?" asked Tai.

"Exactly," agreed Mom. "When we admit that we're sinners and we ask Jesus to save us, he'll clean off the dirt—he'll wash away our sin—so that we can live with him in heaven someday."

"It's really quite simple," said Tai thoughtfully. "You'd think everyone would want to be saved."

"Yes," said Mom, "but look out the window." She pointed to Mi-lee's friends, who were still climbing the dirt piles. "They're having a lot of fun out there, and they will all complain when their parents make them take a bath. Sometimes getting clean doesn't seem as fun as getting dirty."

"I think I get it," Tai said. "I guess we have to help people understand how good it is to be clean—and especially how good it is to have God remove the dirt of sin. Right?"

"Right," agreed Mom. *HMT*

HOW ABOUT YOU?

The gospel message is simple. Sin is "dirt" and cannot be allowed in heaven. God wants to clean sin out of your life so that someday you can live with him in heaven. Do you have friends who need to know about that? Share the message with them.

LET GOD CLEANSE YOU FOR HEAVEN

MEMORIZE:

"Wash me clean from my guilt. Purify me from my sin." Psalm 51:2

July

28

"I don't like camp! Don't go! Stay with me!" Four-year-old Joy sobbed, as she clung to her big brother.

"I'm not going to be gone forever," Mark told her. "I'm just going for a couple of weeks."

"No! Stay and play with me," the little girl insisted. Gently, Mom pried Joy's hands loose from Mark's leg and picked her up. "Next Saturday we're going to camp for Family Day. Mark will do fun things with you there, and we'll have a picnic," she promised.

"Can we have marshmallows?" Joy asked.

Dad laughed. "Yes, we can have marshmallows," he said. "Get your stuff, Mark. It's time to go."

As the door closed behind them, Dad and Mark heard a little girl's voice. "How long is it until Family Day?"

On Saturday, they all went to the camp, and Joy had a wonderful time. "I like camp after all," she decided.

A couple of weeks after camp ended, Mark's parents got the call they had been dreading. As Mom hung up the phone, her eyes were wet with tears. "Poppy is gone," she said.

"Gone?" Mark repeated. "Gone where?"

"Gone to heaven," Mom answered.

It took a minute for Mark to grasp the fact that his grandfather had died. "But I asked Jesus to heal him," Mark wailed. "I didn't want him to leave us."

Dad put his arms around Mark and Mom. "We are never ready to give up our loved ones," said Dad, "but we know it's not forever."

"Not forever?" Mark sobbed. "Death *is* forever."

"Oh, no!" Dad said. "Death is just a door leading into another world. Someday we're going where Poppy is. We'll see him again in heaven."

Joy tugged at her father's arm, wanting him to pick her up. "Don't cry, Markie," she said. "We'll see Poppy when we go to Family Day in heaven." *BJW*

HOW ABOUT YOU?

Has someone that you love gone to heaven? When you feel sad and lonely, remember that the separation is not forever. You can see your loved one again. What a wonderful Family Day that will be!

MEMORIZE:

"Do not . . . grieve like the rest of men, who have no hope."
1 Thessalonians 4:13, NIV

FOR THE CHRISTIAN, DEATH IS NOT FOREVER

OCEAN OF LOVE

Read: Romans 8:33-39

The Akanbi family put up sun umbrellas in their favorite spot at the beach. Mary and Rachel dashed for the water, but Philip stayed behind. "The waves are so big today," he said.

"Come on in, Phil," called Mary. "It's fun! Don't be so scared."

Phil shook his head, then sat down on the beach and began to build a sand castle. "Dad," he began after a little while. "I feel rotten inside. I think God has quit loving me."

"God has never quit loving you for a minute in your whole life," Dad assured him. "What makes you think he has?"

"Well, my Sunday school verse was, 'Keep yourselves in the love of God,' " he said. "But I . . . I lied to you and Mom the other day, so I just know I haven't kept God loving me."

"I remember the incident," said Dad, "but you confessed that to us, and we forgave you."

"That's right," said Mom. "And when you confess your sin to God, he forgives you, too."

Dad nodded. "But all through this time, God has never quit loving you, Philip," he said. He waved a hand toward the ocean. "God's love is something like the ocean," he added. "Just think of all the water out there, and you're not enjoying any of it. Why not?"

"Because I'm afraid," said Phil.

"Exactly," agreed Dad. "Your fear of the big waves keeps you from enjoying the water. And unconfessed sin kept you from enjoying the love of God. But the Bible doesn't say, 'Keep God loving you.' It says, 'Keep yourselves in the love of God.' "

"But how do you do that?" asked Phil.

"To 'keep yourself in the love of God' is to do the things God loves—to live the way he wants you to," replied Dad. "Then you can enjoy the love that's there for you." *MRP*

HOW ABOUT YOU?

Have you wondered if God still loves you? Perhaps you've disobeyed, been unkind, used bad language, or allowed some other sin to come into your life. Make things right with God and with others and enjoy the love that is there for you. God always loves you, but sin will keep you from enjoying his love.

DO THE THINGS GOD LOVES

MEMORIZE:
"Keep yourselves in the love of God."
Jude 21, KJV

SINK OR SWIM

Read: Romans 3:20-24, 28

Down under the water Caleb went! He came up sputtering. "What did I do wrong?" he asked Aunt Sue. He and his sister Leslie were spending a week with their aunt at her lakeshore cottage, and she was teaching them to float. Caleb looked over at Leslie. "She's just lying on the water!" he exclaimed in surprise. "Why can't I do that?"

"You tried to help yourself float, so you sank," said Aunt Sue. "Try again—just relax and lay back on the water and don't try so hard." So Caleb took a deep breath and tried again, but once more . . . blub . . . gasp . . . gurgle. He sank a second time. "Relax," advised Aunt Sue.

After several tries, Caleb finally floated. "I'm not doing anything!" he exclaimed. "I'm just letting the water hold me up."

That evening, Caleb was thoughtful. "Why so quiet, Caleb?" asked Aunt Sue.

"Well," said Caleb, "I was just thinking. As long as I tried to do something to make myself float, it didn't work. I had to just lay back in the water."

"That's right," agreed Aunt Sue. "You had to trust the water to hold you up."

Caleb nodded. "It's kind of like what my teacher told us in Sunday school yesterday," he replied. "He says we can't do anything to help ourselves be saved—we just need to trust Jesus."

"That's what the Bible says, too," said Aunt Sue. *HCT*

HOW ABOUT YOU?

Are you trying to do something to save yourself? It won't work. The only way to be saved is to trust Jesus to do it all. Won't you trust him today?

MEMORIZE:

"Believe on the Lord Jesus Christ, and thou shalt be saved." Acts 16:31, KJV

TRUST JESUS TO SAVE YOU FROM SIN

THE WAY TO GROW

Read: Matthew 5:14-16

As Mom came down the stairs and headed for the kitchen, she heard the voices of her sons. "That's not fair! You've got your shoes on, Ravi. That makes you a little taller," wailed Andy. "Take them off!"

"All right," came the answer from Ravi. Mom heard shoes plop onto the floor. As she reached the kitchen, she saw what the commotion was all about. Andy and Ravi were measuring each other's height against the doorpost. "See there! I'm still taller than you!" boasted Ravi. "And I'm a year younger!"

The children turned as Mom came into the room. "We wanted to see how much we had grown," Ravi told her. "And I'm taller than Andy! See!" He pointed to the mark on the doorpost.

"That may be true," said Mom, "but you never know—in another year Andy may pass you again. And don't forget, there are more important things to be concerned about than just growing physically. I was pleased to see from your last report cards that both of you are growing in knowledge."

The boys grinned, and Mom spoke again, "There's another way in which I hope you two are growing. Both of you have received Jesus as your Savior. You know him, but are you growing spiritually—'growing in grace, and in the knowledge of Jesus' as the Bible says?" asked Mom.

"I probably could do better," confessed Ravi.

"Me, too," Andy admitted.

"Do you know what makes you grow taller and stronger?" asked Mom.

"Eating good food and exercising," replied Ravi.

"And I know I grow in knowledge by studying hard," added Andy.

"Right," agreed Mom, "and you grow 'in grace and in the knowledge of Jesus' by studying God's Word and obeying it." *HMP*

HOW ABOUT YOU?

Do you know Jesus as your Savior? Do you grow spiritually by studying his Word and obeying him? Does your life glow for him by the things you do and say?

KNOW, GROW, AND GLOW

DIRTY FOOTPRINTS

Read: Ephesians 2:1-9

"Dad!" called Sam as he stood at the back door. "Can you bring me a towel? I've been swimming in the creek, and I'm dripping wet." Sam waited for a few moments, wiggling his toes, which were caked with mud and grass. He called his father again, but he didn't come. "I'll have to get a towel myself," grumbled Sam, swinging open the screen door and stepping onto a freshly mopped kitchen floor. He hesitated. Then, taking long steps, he carefully tiptoed across the sparkling tiles to the bathroom. In spite of his best efforts, he left behind a trail of dirty, grassy footprints.

Minutes later, Sam stood in his bedroom in clean, dry clothes. A soiled towel lay crumpled on the floor next to his bed. "Samuel J. Smith!" he heard his father call sternly. "Get in here right this minute!" Sam ran to obey. He found his father standing in the kitchen doorway, pointing to Sam's muddy footprints on the clean floor. "Just look what you did!" he scolded. "You know you can't come into the house with such filthy feet."

"But I tried to walk carefully," protested Sam.

Dad pointed to the mop behind the door. "You have some cleaning to do," he said.

Sam got busy with the mop. "You'd think I'd trudged mud into heaven itself!" he muttered under his breath. Then he grinned at his father. "I bet they'll make you head janitor when you get to heaven, Dad," he teased.

Dad smiled as he watched Sam wipe up the dirt. "Well, muddy feet won't keep anyone out of heaven," he said, "but a sinful, unchanged heart will. Some people think they can 'tiptoe carefully' into heaven, but all their good efforts add up to nothing better than dirty footprints on a clean floor. Unacceptable! Only a clean heart qualifies a person for heaven." *JRG*

HOW ABOUT YOU?

Are you trusting in your own good deeds to get you into heaven? That won't work. Even your best deeds are not good in the sight of a holy God. You can receive the new, clean heart he requires only by accepting Jesus, who is perfect and holy, as your Savior and Lord.

GOOD DEEDS
WON'T GET YOU
TO HEAVEN

MEMORIZE:
"All of us have become like one who is unclean, and all our righteous acts are like filthy rags; we all shrivel up like a leaf, and like the wind our sins sweep us away." Isaiah 64:6, NIV

GOD'S PROTECTIVE GEAR

Read: Ephesians 6:13-18

Bill walked into the house and dropped a pile of football gear on the table. "Mom, I'm all signed up for football," he said.

"Great!" said Mom, picking up the mouthpiece. "This protects your teeth, and your helmet protects your head and face."

Bill grinned. "And these pads protect my shoulders, and these shin guards protect my shins. I'll be well-protected."

"Right—and be sure to wear all of this protective gear," Mom said firmly. "Don't forget."

"I won't!" Bill assured her. "I've learned my lesson. I forgot my mouthpiece when I went to practice the other day. The coach said I had to go and get it if I wanted to play, so I did. Good thing, too. When I got back, I got a good knock on my chin in the very first play. I might have been hurt without it."

That evening, Bill showed Dad all his football gear. Dad smiled. "Did you know that God has protective gear for us to wear, too?" he asked. "It's called the 'armor of God,' and each piece is important. Who can remember what those pieces are?"

"I'll start," said Mom. "We need to wear the belt of truth. That means we have to be honest in everything we do. And if we're wearing the breastplate of righteousness, it means we are right with God."

"We need the helmet of salvation," said Bill. "And . . . uh . . . our feet must be ready to take us to share the gospel with others. And we need our sword, which is the Word of God."

"Good!" said Mom. "We also need the shield of faith to trust God in times of trouble and temptation."

Dad nodded. "Just as it's important to wear your football gear, Bill," he said, "it's even more important to wear the armor of God." *DB*

HOW ABOUT YOU?

Do you faithfully put on God's protective gear? Living without just one piece of God's armor opens you to the attacks of the devil. Think about each piece daily, and make sure that it's a part of your life. Use it when you're tempted.

MEMORIZE:

"Put on all of God's armor so that you will be able to stand firm against all strategies and tricks of the Devil."
Ephesians 6:11

WEAR GOD'S
ARMOR

THE BROKEN WINDOW

Read: 1 John 1:9-10; 2:1

Austin and Matt were playing catch in the vacant lot behind Mrs. Randall's house when . . . crash! The baseball went right through a glass window. Hardly believing what had happened, the boys looked at each other and made a dash for home.

"It's just an old storage shed," said Matt when they'd finally stopped running. "They don't even use it anymore."

"Yeah," agreed Austin, his tennis shoes scuffling slowly in the dirt. Both boys were Christians, and they knew they should admit what they had done. "We have to go back and tell her," Austin said after they had gone a couple blocks. Matt nodded, and they turned around and headed back.

Mrs. Randall listened patiently at the door as the boys explained what had happened. "O-h-h-h," she said. "I certainly forgive you, but that window is still your responsibility. Do you have money to pay for it?" Austin and Matt shook their heads. "I'll tell you what," said Mrs. Randall, "my rose garden needs weeding, and I don't have time to do it. Why don't you boys work on that for a while?" Relieved, Austin and Matt got to work.

The boys had just finished when Mrs. Randall came out carrying a plate of cookies and three glasses of cold milk. As she set the plate down, she said, "I know it was hard to come back and tell me what you had done, but you made the right choice." She waved a hand toward the roses. "It's like my rose garden," she said. "Weeds were choking the flowers, but you got rid of them and made the garden beautiful again. When we confess to Jesus what we have done wrong, he removes the weeds of sin and makes our lives beautiful again." She smiled at the boys. "I believe you've more than paid for that old window. Now how about a cookie?" *RV*

HOW ABOUT YOU?

Do you need to "go back" to someone and to God and confess something you've done wrong? Are there "weeds of sin" that need to be rooted out? Only Jesus can remove them. He'll do that when you're sorry about them and confess them. Do it today.

MEMORIZE:

"But if we confess our sins to him, he is faithful and just to forgive us and to cleanse us from every wrong."

1 John 1:9

CONFESS SINS

DOOR TO HEAVEN

Read: John 10:1-9

"Hey, Mom, can Brandon and I go for a hike in the park? He's the nicest boy I've ever met! I bet he's a Christian."

"That will be fine, Tony," Mom said. "Brandon does seem very nice. Have you asked him if he knows the Lord?"

"Yeah," said Tony. "He said he tries his best to be real good."

"I see. But you know that doesn't make a person a Christian," replied Mom. Tony just shrugged and ran out to meet Brandon.

The boys had a great time hiking, but soon, it was time to head for home.

"Hey, look," Tony said. "From up on this hill you can see your neighbor's house."

"Wow, yeah!" said Brandon. "Let's take a shortcut across the valley. It should bring us right to our road."

"Okay, let's go!" agreed Tony.

The boys soon came to the road on which they lived. "Oh, no!" groaned Tony. "I forgot about the high chain-link fence between the road and this park. There's barbed wire at the top."

The boys followed the fence for a while, looking for a hole, but there was none. They had to go all the way back to the path which led out of the park.

When Tony finally reached home, he explained what had happened. "We were so close, but we couldn't get here. The only way home from the park was through the entrance gate."

Mom nodded. "That reminds me of what we talked about earlier. Brandon is a nice boy. And just as both of you were so close to home, Brandon may be close to the kingdom of heaven. Yet the only way to get into heaven is through the gate. And Jesus is that gate."

Tony nodded. "I'm going to pray for Brandon and tell him about Jesus," he said. "Maybe he'll come to church with me, too." *KL*

HOW ABOUT YOU?

Have you come through the "gate" for salvation? The good things you do are not good enough to get you into heaven. Only Jesus, the Son of God, lived a perfect life, and only Jesus died for your sins. He is the only way to have eternal life. Do you believe this? Trust him as your Savior today.

MEMORIZE:

"Yes, I am the gate. Those who come in through me will be saved." John 10:9

JESUS IS THE WAY TO HEAVEN

THE FISHING TRIP

Read: Luke 10:29-37

"Jack, wake up! Time to go after Ol' Mossback," Dad whispered. "Uncle Bill is here."

Jack jumped out of bed and quickly got into his fishing clothes, already imagining himself pulling in the big fish. It was still dark when they started traveling in the pickup truck toward the lake.

"Hey, what's that?" said Uncle Bill. He spotted a car on its side just off the road.

"Looks like a wreck," Dad said, stepping on the brakes. "Wait here," he ordered, jumping out and running over to the car. Soon he returned, accompanied by a man who was limping. "This is Mr. Jackson," said Dad. "Thankfully, he's not seriously hurt, but his ankle needs attention. We'd better take him back to town to get help."

"I hate to put you to so much trouble," said Mr. Jackson. "Maybe I can catch a ride with someone going the other way."

"Don't worry about it," said Uncle Bill. "Besides, we're glad to help our neighbor."

Jack's heart sank as the truck turned and headed away from the lake. "Good-bye, Ol' Mossback," he whispered. But he felt better about the delay in their fishing trip as he listened to Dad explain to Mr. Jackson why Uncle Bill had called him their neighbor. "The Bible teaches that our neighbor isn't only the person living near us," Dad said. "It can be anyone we meet. God is pleased when we act like a good neighbor whenever we see someone in trouble."

By the time Mr. Jackson was taken care of, it was too late to go fishing. "I'm sorry about that," Dad told Jack. "But I think Ol' Mossback will wait for us, don't you?"

Jack nodded. He was disappointed, but he remembered how their "neighbor" had listened while Dad and Uncle Bill talked about the Lord. Mr. Jackson was more important than Ol' Mossback, anyway. *RSM*

HOW ABOUT YOU?

Have you been a good "neighbor" lately? Helping others isn't always easy, and it may cost you something. But when you do it for Jesus, you'll find that it's worth whatever it costs.

BE A GOOD NEIGHBOR

MEMORIZE:
"Love your neighbor as yourself."
Luke 10:27

August

6

MORE FOOD, PLEASE!

Read: John 6:28-37

"When are we going to eat?" asked Alex for the third time. "My stomach has been growling for an hour."

"Mine, too," agreed Dominick. "I hope we stop soon."

For weeks, Mr. Larson's Sunday school class of sixth-graders had been planning this overnight hike. They were backpacking in the mountains, and they were going to set up camp and sleep under the stars before hiking home in the morning.

After what seemed like a long time to the kids, Mr. Larson told them to stop and make camp for the night. "When do we eat?" Alex asked once again.

"As soon as we get a fire going," Mr. Larson answered.

Soon the kids were eating beef stew from their tin mugs. How good it tasted! Then they played games, told stories, and settled in for the evening around the fire. "I'm hungry again!" exclaimed Alex later. "Do we have any more food?"

The other kids agreed that food sounded like a good idea, but Mr. Larson got out his Bible. "Let's first have a time of devotions," he suggested, "and then we'll have a snack before we turn in. Who knows the Bible verses we studied in class the last few months?"

The kids began to recite the seven "I Am's" from the Gospel of John. They were doing fine till someone quoted, "I am the Bread of Life." Everyone moaned in hunger.

"Okay, okay!" Mr. Larson laughed as he instructed the kids to get out some fruit, cookies, and crackers. "We'll eat. But as you enjoy this food, I want you to think about how soon you'll get hungry again. The food we eat satisfies us for only a short time. When Jesus calls himself the Bread of Life, he means that he can satisfy our spiritual needs forever." *REP*

HOW ABOUT YOU?

When your body is hungry, you eat, right? Before long you're hungry again, so you eat again. How about your soul? Do you ever feel "hungry" deep down inside? Do you try to "fill up" with TV, friends, maybe even church—but you still feel empty? Depend on Jesus, the Bread of Life, to "fill" you and satisfy that empty feeling. Receive him as your Savior.

MEMORIZE:

"Jesus declared, 'I am the bread of life. He who comes to me will never go hungry.'" John 6:35, NIV

JESUS SATISFIES

WHY DID IT HAPPEN?

Read: Psalm 103:15-19

One Saturday, Alejandro was getting ready to go fishing with his friends, Tomas and Dillon. "This could be an important day," he told his dad. "I've had some good chances to tell the guys about Jesus lately. They seem interested, and they're asking questions."

Soon the boys were off for the lake. They were having a fine time together, when the weather changed suddenly. A wind came up, the sky turned cloudy, and the water became rough and choppy. They headed for shore, but before they could reach it, the boat overturned. Dillon and Tomas made it to safety and Alejandro . . . well, Alejandro was safe too—safe in the arms of Jesus. He died in the storm.

The church was packed on the day of Alejandro's memorial service, and Pastor Allen brought a comforting message from God's Word. "Why did Alejandro die?" he asked in conclusion. "I don't know. But I do know that Alejandro is in heaven. The question to ask is: 'Where will *I* spend eternity when *I* die?' "

A few weeks later, Dillon and Tomas went to see Alejandro's parents. "I have something to tell you," Tomas said shyly after they had visited a bit. "I'm going to see Alejandro again someday. After Alejandro's funeral, I thought of the pastor's question about where I would spend eternity, and I gave my life to Jesus."

With tears in her eyes, Alejandro's mother hugged Tomas close.

Dillon looked puzzled. "I still don't see why anyone as nice as Alejandro had to die," he said.

"Being nice doesn't make any difference," said Alejandro's father. "Because of sin, we all have to die sometime. The important thing is to be ready—like Alejandro was. How about it, Dillon. Do you want to know how to give your life to Jesus?"

Dillon looked thoughtful and nodded yes. *JLH*

HOW ABOUT YOU?

Do you find it hard to understand why a young person—or perhaps even an older person—dies? God uses circumstances in ways that we cannot understand. But we can trust that he is doing what he knows is best in the long run.

GOD KNOWS
WHY

August

8

"Wow!" exclaimed Paul as he scrambled aboard the helicopter. "I never thought I'd get a chance to ride in one of these!" Paul and his friend, José, were spending the weekend with José's Uncle Ted, a pilot for an emergency helicopter service.

Uncle Ted chuckled. "I always seem to have such eager passengers," he said. "Take my last one, for example. A couple of young fellows were mountain climbing near here when the rope that held them together broke. One of them fell over the edge of a cliff and landed on a ledge. He was trapped in an odd spot where no one could climb down to help him. So it was your old Uncle Ted to the rescue."

The boy's eyes were shining. "How did you get him out?" Paul asked. "Was there room to land?"

"No, indeed," replied Uncle Ted, "but you see this rope ladder? I lowered it to him, and since he wasn't hurt, he was able to climb up and into the helicopter. He was even more happy to be on board than you are."

The boys laughed as they examined the rope ladder. "It was the only thing that could save him, wasn't it?" asked Paul.

"Right," agreed Uncle Ted. A moment later, he added thoughtfully, "You know, boys, this ladder reminds me of the cross of Jesus. We're like the helpless mountain climber—unable to save ourselves. Christ's death on the cross is the ladder that leads to heaven." *HCT*

HOW ABOUT YOU?

Have you become a Christian? Jesus has provided the way for you. He died on the cross and paid the penalty for your sin. Come to God by way of the "ladder" he has provided. Accept what Jesus has done for you.

MEMORIZE:

"Everyone who believes in him may have eternal life." John 3:15, NIV

JESUS PROVIDES SALVATION

TRAPPED (PART 2)

Read: 1 Peter 5:8-11

"This sure is fun! I'm glad Uncle Ted let us use his boat," said José as he and Paul rowed down the river.

"Yeah," agreed Paul, "but I'm tired. Let's drift awhile."

"Okay," agreed José. "We have to go back soon, though. We're almost to those white trees—Uncle Ted warned us not to go that far. He said if we got beyond the trees, we'd be in a spot they call 'Devil's Trap.' He said it's a whirlpool and we'd never be able to get back out. We'd go right over the falls." Suddenly, he sat up. "Hey, look!" he said. "Look at that big fish!"

"Yeah—the water is so clear!" replied Paul. The fish held the boys' attention for several minutes. It was so pleasant resting and trailing their hands through the water and watching the fish, that they didn't notice how fast they were drifting. When they looked up again, they saw that they had gone beyond the trees. "Quick, José! Start rowing!" gasped Paul. He grabbed one oar and Jose grabbed the other. "Maybe we can still get back. Row! *Row!*"

The boys rowed and rowed, but it was no use. They only moved closer to the rapids and the falls. They feared that they were going to go over! Suddenly, they heard the sound of a helicopter overhead. "It's Uncle Ted!" shouted Jose. "He sees us. He's letting down the rope ladder!"

The boys clung to the ladder and reached the safety of the helicopter just as the boat went over the falls. "What happened?" asked Uncle Ted. "You boys promised me you'd stay closer to the dock."

"We didn't intend to go so far. Honest," said José with a sob. "We were just drifting along, having a good time, when all of a sudden we realized we'd crossed the danger line." *HCT*

HOW ABOUT YOU?

Are you aware that drifting along through life can be dangerous? Have you drifted away from God so you could drift along with the crowd? Ask God daily to help you resist the pull of the crowd.

DON'T DRIFT WITH THE CROWD

MEMORIZE:
"Resist the Devil, and he will flee from you." James 4:7

THE BURIED TREASURE

Read: Matthew 6:19-21

As Julie and Terry were digging in the sand at the edge of the river, Terry found something. "Hey, look!" he called. "Here's something gold. I bet it's buried treasure." He dug a little more, and a few minutes later he was holding a gold watch.

The children decided to take it to Mr. Poole's jewelry store to see if he knew how much it was worth. After Mr. Poole looked at the watch, he nodded. "Mrs. Jimenez bought this watch for her husband shortly before she died," he told them. "Here—let me clean it before you take it to him."

"We thought we had found some buried treasure," said Terry as he watched Mr. Poole.

"Mr. Jimenez will think you did, too," said Mr. Poole. "Tell him 'hello' for me. His wife was a Christian, and she attended our church. But he never came."

When Terry and Julie arrived at Mr. Jimenez's house, he was very surprised to see his watch, and he was pleased that Mr. Poole had cleaned it. "Hmmm. Fine man, Mr. Poole," he said. "He goes to the same church where my Sarah went."

"Oh, we go there, too!" the children exclaimed.

"Is that why you kids did an old man such a great favor?" Mr. Jimenez wanted to know.

Julie shrugged. "We're just doing what we know is right," she said.

When Mr. Jimenez offered the children a reward for the return of his watch, they glanced at one another, then shook their heads. "No, thanks," said Terry, "but I know what we would like—would you please be our visitor for church on Sunday?"

"Well . . . how can I say no?" said Mr. Jimenez with a smile.

As the children headed home, Julie sighed. "Wasn't that neat?" she said. "If Mr. Jimenez eventually becomes a Christian, *that* will be the real treasure." *DG*

HOW ABOUT YOU?

What do you think is the very best treasure you could find in this world? If you have Jesus, you have found the best treasure, a treasure that will last forever.

MEMORIZE:

"Store your treasures in heaven, where they will never become moth-eaten or rusty and where they will be safe from thieves." Matthew 6:20

STORE TREASURE
IN HEAVEN

DEAD MAN'S REEF

Read: Psalm 119:129-135

"Uncle Milo said I could take his boat out all by myself," said Steve. "Want to come for a ride?" His sister, Jody, nodded, and the children jumped into the boat. Steve started the engine. Minutes later, they were laughing as the wind blew through their hair.

"Aren't you supposed to use this map?" asked Jody, offering it to Steve. "We're pretty far away."

Steve shrugged. "Yeah . . . well, I'll just swing around and head back. I don't need the map."

Suddenly there was a jolt, followed by a crash! The engine sputtered and died. "We must be stuck on a reef," gasped Steve. "I didn't see it. Let me look at that map." He studied it a moment. "Oh," he groaned, "here's where we are—at Dead Man's Reef. Why do you suppose they call it that? Hey! This thing is leaking!"

The children looked at one another with despair in their eyes. "Oh, Steve," sobbed Jody. "What'll we do? We'll never be able to swim all the way to shore." But even as she spoke, they heard a sound—a motor! A Coast Guard launch was pulling up, and soon they were safely on board.

That evening, they sat in their uncle's cottage with heads bowed and faces downcast. "I'm so sorry, Uncle Milo," Steve said. "I've wrecked your boat. I don't know how I'll ever pay for it."

"My insurance will cover a lot of it," Uncle Milo told them, "and your father says you'll have to cut your visit short and return home now, so you can work to pay for the rest. I'm sorry about that. But more important, you might have lost your lives! Why didn't you look at the map?"

"I thought I could get along without it," admitted Steve. "Now I see how wrong I was." *HCT*

HOW ABOUT YOU?

Do you realize that you need a "map" to guide you through life? God's Word, the Bible, serves as a map, or guidebook. Are you using it? Do you read it each day? First of all, it will point you to Jesus, the only way to heaven. It will also teach you to be honest, pure, loving, patient, and much more, as it guides you in your Christian life.

READ THE
BIBLE DAILY

MEMORIZE:
"Guide my steps by your word, so
I will not be overcome by any evil."
Psalm 119:133

August

12

It had always been easy for Jimmy to give to missions—he just talked to his folks, and Mom or Dad gave him money for the offerings. But one Sunday, his Sunday school teacher suggested that the children give offerings of their own money.

Jimmy wasn't sure he liked the idea. "I don't know what difference it makes whether we give the money ourselves or whether our folks help us," he grumbled on the way home from Sunday school. "The missionaries get it just the same."

"The difference is that you don't get any real joy out of giving to the Lord when the gift doesn't cost you anything," said Dad.

"Maybe not . . . but I don't get very much money," protested Jimmy, "and I've got to keep saving for a new bike. I don't have anything I could give."

Dad smiled. "Sometimes we have to deny ourselves and go without things we want in order to give to God's work," he said. "But maybe you could find ways to earn extra money. Pray about this, Jimmy, and ask God what you could do."

Jimmy agreed, and over the next few weeks, he was surprised at all the extra jobs he was able to pick up—mowing lawns, delivering packages, cleaning basements. He was also surprised at how much he enjoyed earning money for the missionary offering. "It's a lot of work, but it's worth it," he said. "I pretend that I'm a missionary to Africa, and I'm doing the things I do so people can hear about Jesus. For the first time, I feel as though I really am a missionary myself." *BP*

HOW ABOUT YOU?

Do you truly give to God's work, or do you just pass along your parents' gifts? Pray about it and see if God will make it possible for you to earn money to give to him. Perhaps even at home you could do some extra chores to earn money. Giving gifts to Jesus that cost you something honor him, whether they're big or small.

MEMORIZE:

"I cannot present burnt offerings to the Lord my God that have cost me nothing." 2 Samuel 24:24

GIVE TO GOD

WHAT TO DO ABOUT DAD?

Read: Ephesians 6:1-3

Rolando, Misha, and their mother had recently given their hearts to Jesus. Now they were praying for Dad. Although Dad had noticed a difference in them, he wasn't ready to become a Christian.

"Say, kids," said Dad, "I borrowed Uncle Tomas's tent for the weekend. Let's get up early tomorrow, and head for Horn Lake campground. We can be there before noon!"

"But Rolando and I have special parts in our youth group meeting on Sunday, Daddy," said Misha. "Will we be back by then?"

Dad shook his head. "You can miss for once!" he said.

As far as Dad was concerned, the conversation was over. But later, Rolando and Misha talked to their mother about it. "Mom, Dad planned this trip and doesn't care if Misha and I miss Sunday activities," said Rolando. "Can we stay at Jian's and Carmela's instead of going on the campout?"

"I know your dad doesn't care about church, but he's eager for family activities," Mom told them. "I was thinking and praying about our family the other day, and I found eight places in the Bible where God says to honor and obey parents. If God said it that often, it must be important, don't you think?" Reluctantly the children agreed. "I know you want to go to church—and that's good—but I think it's more important to honor your dad," continued Mom. "Let's pray for him. And let's ask God to show us how to be patient as God works in his heart." *BJW*

HOW ABOUT YOU?

Are you obeying your parents? Even if they are not believers, try to be obedient unless they are asking you to do wrong things.

OBEY YOUR PARENTS

MEMORIZE:

"You children must always obey your parents, for this is what pleases the Lord." Colossians 3:20

GOOD IMPRESSION

Read: Philippians 3:4-9

Keshaun was not looking forward to the meeting with the church board. But he was one of the boys who had thrown the tomatoes at the building, so he had no choice in the matter. *I better wear my best clothes and make a good impression!* he decided. *Maybe when they see how nice I look, they'll forget about what happened.*

"It isn't Sunday," Keshaun's sister Paige called out when she saw how he was dressed.

"I know," Keshaun agreed. "I just thought I'd let those people see how good I can look."

Overhearing their conversation, Mom spoke up. "I think it's a little late for that," she said kindly. "No matter how good you look, the board already knows what you've done."

Keshaun shrugged. "I thought I might make them forget."

"Keshaun," said Paige emphatically, "it's not how a person looks on the outside that counts. It's what's inside."

"Hey!" protested Keshaun. "You're my sister. You're supposed to be on my side."

But as he left to walk to church, Keshaun thought seriously about what Paige had said. He had heard those same words from his mother, his father, his pastor, his Sunday school teacher, and now from his sister. He knew what he had to do—admit his guilt and ask for forgiveness. And he knew the place to start was with confessing his sin to God and asking him for help to live the right kind of life. *That's the only way,* he thought. *That's for sure! RIJ*

HOW ABOUT YOU?

Do you try to make people think you are a good person by dressing nicely, by going to church, or by giving money to God's work? You may be able to fool others, but you can't fool God. He sees what's on the inside of you—what you're really like. He's waiting for you to confess your sins and ask him for forgiveness.

MEMORIZE:

"The one who comes to Me I will certainly not cast out." John 6:37, NASB

BE CLEAN INSIDE

EASY—BUT WRONG

Read: Matthew 7:13-14, 21-23

Scott and his parents were going to spend a week vacationing at a friend's summer home. "I hope we can reach the place before dark," said Dad after several hours on the road. "I'm sure the route we're taking will be shorter than the one the Greys suggested, but the road may not be marked as well."

Mom smiled. "I still think we should have stuck with the route they showed you," she said, "but we're used to your shortcuts, dear."

The pavement ended as they neared the tiny village of Red Gap, and they wound their way along a twisting, dirt road. Soon they came to a fork in the road. To the left, it branched off into a narrow, rough road; to the right, the road was wide and newly paved. "Oops!" said Dad. "This doesn't show on the map. But the road to the right is in better shape—it must be the one we need."

After driving for several miles, Dad shook his head. "We should be getting there soon—in fact, we should have been there by now," he said. Suddenly, the road ended at a clearing. They saw a racetrack.

"Dad," asked Scott, "is the cabin near a racetrack?"

"I don't think so," replied his father. He turned the car around, drove back to the fork in the road, and took the other road. After a bumpy, but rather short ride, they reached their destination. Their friend's cottage was near a small country church.

As they unpacked the van, Dad said, "Remember that wrong turn I took? I was certain that the wide, smooth road was the right one. But when I saw the racetrack at the end of it, I realized that I had made a mistake."

Mom nodded. "It's a good illustration that the 'easy way' is not always right!" *SLK*

HOW ABOUT YOU?

Do you think that going to church and doing your best is the way to heaven—that everyone will be okay as long as they're nice? That's a popular idea, but don't be fooled. The Bible says you must believe on Jesus Christ and accept his sacrifice for your sins. It's the only way to heaven.

COME TO GOD THROUGH JESUS

MEMORIZE:

"But the gateway to life is small, and the road is narrow, and only a few ever find it." Matthew 7:14

August

16

Cliff was in trouble! Mr. Dunbar had called to say that he had caught Cliff and a friend shoplifting some candy bars from his store. Cliff's parents were talking it over when he came into the house. "Mr. Dunbar just called," Dad told him.

"Mr. Dunbar?" asked Cliff. "Oh, Mr. Dunbar! Aw, he gets excited about nothing. We'd have paid for the candy sooner or later."

Dad looked stern as he glanced at his watch. "We'll finish this discussion after we do chores," he decided. "It's late!"

But Cliff had failed to close the pasture gate that morning. The cows had gotten out and into the watermelon patch. They had ruined almost all of the growing melons. "Oh, I hate you, you old cows!" stormed Cliff.

"You're the one who left the gate open," reminded Dad. "You know, Son, this makes me think of a Bible verse—Proverbs 25:28. 'A person without self-control is as defenseless as a city with broken-down walls.'"

"What does that mean?" Cliff asked.

"In Bible days, cities were protected from their enemies by walls," explained Dad. "A city without a wall was open to attack from the enemy—sort of like the watermelon patch when the gate to the pasture was left open. This verse is saying that a person who cannot control his own feelings and actions is asking for trouble. You've never learned to control yourself, Cliff. You want something? You take it. You feel like fighting? You fight. You don't want to do something? You don't do it. And today you even tried to shoplift!"

Cliff was beginning to understand.

"You need God in your life—first of all for salvation, and then to help you develop self-control, Cliff," Dad replied. "He'll help you, if you'll let him." *BJW*

HOW ABOUT YOU?

Do you have a quick temper, a nasty tongue, and a "habit" of getting into trouble? First, make sure you are trusting Jesus to be your Savior. Then, when you are tempted to do wrong, pause and quietly ask God to keep you from doing it. He will help you.

MEMORIZE:

"A person without self-control is as defenseless as a city with broken-down walls." Proverbs 25:28

DEVELOP
SELF-CONTROL

WILLING SERVANT

Read: 1 Corinthians 9:16-19

As Grady ran into the house, he called for his mother. "What do you want, Grady?" asked Mom.

"Mrs. Batani just drove by and asked if I would mow her lawn," said Grady. "Can I? I'll have to hurry 'cause they're leaving in just a couple of hours, and Mrs. Batani has to show me around. I gotta go now, okay?"

"Okay," said Mom, as Grady ran out the door.

Mrs. Batani showed Grady the mower and instructed him to be careful around the trees. Grady nodded and started the mower. He carefully avoided the trees and finished the mowing in short order. Then he decided to pull the grass around the trees to make things look better. He pulled weeds out of the rock garden, too. He thought Mrs. Batani would give him more than the five dollars she had promised him for mowing the lawn.

When Grady finally finished, his back was sore from bending over. He knocked on the door, and Mrs. Batani opened it. "All finished?" she asked. "Here's your money." She handed him a five-dollar bill.

"I pulled the grass around the trees, too," Grady said hopefully.

"Great," said Mrs. Batani. "You've done a good job. Thank you, and have a good day."

When Grady arrived home, he was upset. "They're cheapskates!" he told his mother. "Five dollars for all that work! I even pulled grass around the trees, which they didn't tell me to do."

"That would have been nice, but they gave you the agreed-upon amount. I don't think you have any cause for complaint," observed Mom. "It's good that you did more than you had planned to do. You can consider that serving through love." *CSS*

HOW ABOUT YOU?

Do you expect special thanks when you wash the dishes, hang up the clothes, or clean your room? Think of doing those things as a way to serve Jesus. He wants you to have a servant attitude, just as he had a servant attitude.

BE A WILLING
SERVANT

MEMORIZE:
"By love, serve one another."
Galatians 5:13, KJV

THE BROKEN TRAIN

Read: Philippians 4:4-7

"My train is broken!" wailed Andrew.

"Oh, Andrew, don't cry," comforted Sheana, giving him a hug. "Maybe Grandpa can fix it."

They took the train to Grandpa, who assured them that he could make it good as new. "Honest?" exclaimed Andrew. Grandpa took the train to his workshop, and Andrew hopped onto the table to watch. "Don't do that!" protested Andrew as Grandpa started bending a wheel. "You'll break it for good."

"Don't be silly, Andrew!" scolded Sheana. "Grandpa's fixing your train, not breaking it. And he can't work properly when you get in his way."

Andrew pouted, but he wandered out into the yard. Soon he was back. "You're not doing it right," he informed Grandpa after watching for a few minutes. "That piece has to be fastened to the engine like this." He reached for the train.

"Andrew!" cried Sheana. "Stop trying to tell Grandpa what to do! Why don't you go play until Grandpa's done?"

"That's a good idea," said Grandpa. "This is going to take some time, Andrew."

"But I want my train now," complained Andrew. He suddenly grabbed the train and scooted out the door.

"Silly kid!" exclaimed Sheana scornfully. "He gave you his train to fix and then took it back without letting you fix it."

"We all do things like that sometimes," said Grandpa.

Sheana shook her head firmly. "Not me!" she said.

Grandpa smiled. "You told me you prayed about a problem you had with a friend and that you gave it to God, right?"

Sheana looked puzzled. "Yes . . . so?"

"But you were worrying about it again just this morning, Sheana," Grandpa reminded her, "so did you leave it with God, or did you take it back?"

"I—I guess I took it back," admitted Sheana. "I guess I'm as silly as Andrew!" *MTF*

HOW ABOUT YOU?

Do you bring your problems, worries, and needs to God in prayer? Having done that, do you start worrying all over again? Once you have given something to God, don't try to take it back. Handle the situation the way you believe he wants you to—without worrying. Trust him to work things out.

MEMORIZE:

"Be still in the presence of the Lord, and wait patiently for him to act."
Psalm 37:7

WAIT PATIENTLY FOR GOD TO ANSWER PRAYER

PASS THE SALT (PART 1)

Read: Matthew 5:13-16

"Can I help pack for our picnic?" asked Chad.

"I can always use another hand," replied Mom. "Put in some paper cups, paper plates, silverware, and don't forget the salt shaker. We'll need it for the fish we're going to catch."

Chad got busy, and soon everything was ready and they were off for the lake. To Chad's great delight, they did catch a lot of fish for their meal. They set the table and grilled the fish and the potatoes. "Mmmm . . . just look at those fish sizzle!" said Chad. "Makes me hungry!" In a few moments, they were ready to eat, and Dad thanked God for the food. "Boy, I'm starved," Chad stated, as he took a big bite of fish. "Oops! Kinda flat. Pass the salt, please."

"Salt!" Mom exclaimed. "Oh, dear! I don't remember seeing it in the picnic basket. Did you put it in, Chad?"

"Oh, no!" cried Chad. "I forgot the salt and these fish and potatoes sure could have used some!"

"You know," Mom said thoughtfully when they were on their way home, "some things taste rather flat without salt on them . . . and the lives of people can be sort of 'flat,' too, without the salt we, as Christians, can give them."

"What in the world are you talking about, Mom?" Chad asked.

Dad answered, "Ah-h-h . . . think of your friend Tim. Since his father died, his mom is pretty busy. Tim doesn't get to do very many special things. If we had invited him along on this picnic, it would have put a little 'flavor' in his life. Right, Mom?"

"You've got the idea—I wish we had done that," agreed Mom. "Let's all try to add 'salt' to the life of at least one person this week." *AU*

HOW ABOUT YOU?

What can you do to make someone's life better? Could you invite somebody to a party at your home? Adding "salt" to his life may open the door for you to talk about Jesus.

HELP OTHERS

MEMORIZE:

"You must have the qualities of salt among yourselves and live in peace with each other." Mark 9:50

PASS THE SALT (PART 2)

Read: Matthew 5:3-12

Chad's Sunday school lesson was from Matthew 5:13—"Ye are the salt of the earth." Chad felt he knew a little about that! So when his Sunday school teacher asked, "What does the salt do?" Chad's hand shot up. "It adds flavor," he said, and he shared with the class what he had learned at the saltless fish dinner they'd had a few weeks before.

"That's great," commented Mr. Adams. "Can you think of any other uses for salt?"

"Salt makes us thirsty," suggested Larry. "The more salt I put on my food, the more thirsty I get."

"Good." Mr. Adams nodded. "As Christians, we should be such an example of Christ's love that those around us will be thirsty—or eager—to know about Christ, too."

Tim, who had been coming to church with Chad, raised his hand. "That's true!" he exclaimed. "It really works! I think Chad has been 'pouring on the salt' in my life lately, and that's why I'm here."

"It doesn't always work like that, though, does it?" wondered Jim. "My mom's always doing nice things for the lady next door, but it seems like every time Mom tries to talk to her about Jesus, she gets mad and won't listen."

"Well, there's one more thing about salt that we should consider," said Mr. Adams. "In the days before modern medicine, salt was often used to clean a wound. When it's applied to the wound, it stings. People won't always appreciate your witness, because it will sting the wounds of their sin. Maybe that's what is happening with your neighbor, Jim, but don't give up on her yet." *AU*

HOW ABOUT YOU?

Have you made anyone thirsty for Jesus? Your witness, in action and words, is important. Don't be discouraged if it isn't accepted right away. Remember, salt has many jobs to do. Be faithful in applying the salt. Leave the results with God.

MEMORIZE:

"You are the salt of the earth."
Matthew 5:13

WITNESS
FAITHFULLY

THE QUIET TIMES

Read: 1 Samuel 3:1-10

Grandpa and Trent took their fishing gear and went to a nearby river. After sitting on the bank for a little while, Trent moved to another spot. Soon he got up and moved again. Before long, his excitement over fishing faded. "The fish aren't biting for me today," he said sadly. He looked at the fish his grandfather had caught. "Why are they biting for you?" asked Trent.

"Well, you keep pulling in your line to check your bait, and that's the fourth fishing spot you've tried, Trent," answered Grandpa. "If you want to catch fish, you can't keep moving. Try sitting still."

Trent sighed. "I don't like to sit still," he murmured.

"I know, Trent, but unless you do, you'll miss out on a lot," said Grandpa. "Here—today—you'll just miss a few fish, but if you don't learn to sit quietly, you'll sometimes miss more important things. For example, if you don't sit quietly and listen in school, you may fail. More importantly, if you don't take time to sit still and listen to God, you may fail to hear him."

Trent frowned. "You mean like Samuel heard him in the Bible?" he asked. "God doesn't talk to us like that anymore, does he?"

"Not like that," said Grandpa, "but if you set aside a special time to think about God, he may speak quietly to your heart. He may say he loves you, or he may make you aware of something he wants you to do."

"I pray every night," Trent told his grandfather.

"That's you talking again," Grandpa reminded him. "Let God talk to you." *BJW*

HOW ABOUT YOU?

Do you take time to quietly wait for God to speak to your heart? Before reading the Bible, ask God to teach you through it. Instead of rushing on to the next activity, it's good to pause and wait for him to bring to your mind the lessons he wants you to learn.

LISTEN TO GOD AND OBEY HIM

MEMORIZE:
"Be still, and know that I am God."
Psalm 46:10, KJV

UNDESERVED REWARD

Read: Psalm 103:8-14

Tim was frightened. A fire had started in the woods near his home, and the sawmill where his dad worked had been damaged. *It's my fault!* Tim thought to himself. *I shouldn't have made that little fire to roast my marshmallows.* He sighed. *I wonder if my eye operation will have to be postponed now that Dad will be out of a job for a while.* Tim felt awful!

Things got even worse when Mr. Simmons, the owner of the sawmill, stopped in. "A tramp was picked up in the woods, and he's in jail. Of course, he claims he didn't do it, but even if he doesn't confess, I think we have enough evidence to prove him guilty."

"But . . . but . . ." stammered Tim. *What should I do?* he wondered. *An innocent person is in jail for something I did.* "It . . . it's my fault." The words came tumbling out, and he told Mr. Simmons and his parents about his fire. "I thought I put it out, but it must have started up again," he confessed. Fearfully, he awaited the reaction. Mr. Simmons was staring. "Are you going to take me to jail?" Tim asked with a shaking voice.

After what seemed a very long time, Mr. Simmons shook his head. "No," he said, "you're going to go for that operation on your eyes instead. You get the reward money I offered for turning in the guilty party!" Tim and his parents couldn't believe it, but Mr. Simmons insisted. "The crime was against me, and I have the right to pardon the offender," he said.

"I bet this is the first time somebody ever pardoned and rewarded the person who wronged him," said Tim.

Mr. Simmons shook his head. "Not the first time," he said. "That's exactly what Jesus did for us." *HCT*

HOW ABOUT YOU?

Have you been pardoned and given eternal life? Have you come to God, confessing your sin and asking for his forgiveness? If not, do it today.

MEMORIZE:

"He does not treat us as our sins deserve or repay us according to our iniquities." Psalm 103:10, NIV

JESUS OFFERS
PARDON
FOR SIN

HERE, THERE, AND EVERYWHERE

Read: Psalm 33:13-15; Jeremiah 32:19

"Jeremy! Where are you?" Dad called.

Jeremy giggled. He loved to hide in the old apple tree. When he peeked through the leaves and branches, he could see to the ground. He could see all the way down the street. He could see Dad in the yard below. He could see Mrs. Underwood's cat, Tabby, creeping through the grass next door. He could see his friend Paula riding her bike down the sidewalk. But no one on the ground could see him.

"Jeremy!" called Dad. "Lunch will be ready soon—you have about five minutes left to play." He went back into the house.

Jeremy didn't feel like coming down just yet. He lay on a branch and stretched out flat on his stomach. He watched a blue jay land by the fence. He watched Mrs. Underwood come out on her back porch and call Tabby in. He watched a blue pickup truck drive down the street.

When Dad came out a little later, Jeremy was still in the tree. "Jeremy," he called. Jeremy didn't answer. "Jeremy, lunch is ready, so I want you to come in right now!" called Dad. Jeremy knew playtime was over. He swung down and dropped to the ground.

"Surprise, Dad!" said Jeremy as he entered the kitchen. "I could see you, but you couldn't see me. I could see everyone." He grinned. "Kind of like God watches us," he added.

"Kind of, I guess," said Dad, "but God doesn't just watch the people in one area for an hour or so. He watches everyone in the world all at once, all the time. He was watching you, even while you were hiding and watching me."

"I know." Jeremy smiled. "God always knows where we are." *KES*

HOW ABOUT YOU?

Do you like to hide from people? That can be fun, but remember that God always knows where you are and what you're doing. You can never hide from him. Thank him for watching over you every minute of every day.

GOD SEES EVERYTHING

August

24

Brandon jumped off the bottom rung of the ladder and stared in amazement at the scene before him. He whistled. "What a cave!"

His parents followed him down the ladder and the guide began to speak. "Hundreds of Native Americans, called cliff dwellers, lived here," he said. "In the summer, it was cooler in here than it was out in the open, and in the winter, it was warmer. The rocks protected them from the sun, wind, sleet, and snow."

Brandon and the rest of the group followed the guide around the ancient ruins, listening to his description of how the people lived there many years before.

"This is neat," Brandon said. "It is like an apartment complex carved out of rock."

Several hours later, the family was on the road, looking for a motel. "This is one of the best vacations we've ever had," said Brandon. "Let's find a motel with a pool—a swim sounds good." He became thoughtful. "I wish Kayla was with us. She always likes to swim." He scowled. "It was stupid of her to get involved in drugs. She said she was tired of all the rules in our family and in the church. She said she just wanted to do her own thing."

Mom sighed heavily. "Yes, and she did. Now she's paying for it."

Dad's eyes met Brandon's in the rearview mirror.

"Kayla thought our family and the church were like a prison," he said. "Actually, it was more like a cave built in a strong rock to protect her."

"Jesus is our Rock, isn't he?" asked Brandon. "And our church and family are like the caves?" He grinned as an idea struck him. "So we're cliff dwellers, too—spiritual cliff dwellers," he decided. *BJW*

HOW ABOUT YOU?

Do you realize that the rules in your family protect you from sin? Do you appreciate the shelter that your home and the church give you? Today would be a good time to thank God and your parents for all the help they provide for you.

MEMORIZE:

"My God is my rock, in whom I find protection." Psalm 18:2

GOD GIVES PROTECTION

GOD AT WORK

Read: James 1:2-4

"Why are we slowing down?" asked Trent, as they stopped behind a line of cars.

Melissa poked her head out the window. "It's construction," she announced. "I can see a digging machine and a sign lady."

"Oh, no!" exclaimed Trent. "We'll be late! It's bad enough being new in school. But being late and having everyone stare at me will be the worst!"

"I'm afraid I'll be late for my job interview, too," said Mom, looking at her watch.

"I wish Daddy hadn't left. Then we'd still be living in our old house," said Melissa, "and we'd have all our old friends and be close enough to walk to school."

"I wish that, too," said Mom, "but we have to carry on."

Just then the line of cars began moving and they followed the car in front of them onto a bumpy gravel path. They passed people working with loud jackhammers and a huge machine was digging up great chunks of asphalt.

"Why do they have to wreck a perfectly good road?" wondered Melissa.

"It reminds me of our family," said Trent glumly. "It was just fine. But then Dad left and now everything's broken and torn up."

"It does feel like that," agreed Mom, "but think about this . . . the people in charge at city hall have planned for this to be a better road, and that's why they're allowing it to be broken up and worked on. They know that after the construction is finished, it *will* be better. As for us, God has plans. He's with us during this very difficult time, and he knows that as we learn to trust him and rely on him, we become stronger and better people." *VEN*

HOW ABOUT YOU?

Is it hard to believe that anything good can come from disappointment or pain? Just like road construction leads to a better road, God can use hard times in your life to make you stronger, wiser, more patient, and more compassionate.

CONSTRUCTION— GOD AT WORK IN YOUR LIFE

MEMORIZE:

"No discipline is enjoyable while it is happening—it is painful! But afterward there will be a quiet harvest of right living for those who are trained in this way." Hebrews 12:11

A MIGHTY WEAPON

Read: Psalm 119:1-8

"That was Max," Sean told his sister as he hung up the phone. "He wants me to help him get even with Mr. Riley for chasing us off his property, but I said no. I keep remembering that verse Grandpa taught us—'Love does no harm to its neighbor.' "

Abby nodded. "Let's go tell Grandpa," she said, so they got out their bikes and rode to their grandfather's house.

When Grandpa finally opened the door, he didn't invite them in. "I can't visit with you today," said Grandpa slowly, "but I hope you've learned that verse—Psalm 22:11. Go on home and study it some more. That's Psalm 22:11. You can say it to me another day." He quickly closed the door.

"I wonder why Grandpa wants us to learn Psalm 22:11," said Sean as they started off on their bikes.

"Let's look it up," Abby said. "I still have my Bible in my bike bag." They stopped and quickly looked up the verse. After reading it, they gasped and hurried to get help.

Soon they were again at Grandpa's house, this time with their mother. A policeman was there, and he explained that two thieves had broken in. They had kept a gun pointed at Grandpa while he answered the door. They were hunting for any valuable things they could find when the police showed up. "How did you kids know there was trouble?" asked the policeman.

"Grandpa acted funny, and he sent us away with a Scripture reference," explained Abby. "When we looked it up, we knew he must be in trouble."

"The verse said, 'Be not far from me; for trouble is near; for there is none to help,' " said Sean.

Grandpa smiled. "The Bible is sharper than a two-edged sword. It's our weapon against sin—and a mighty weapon at that!" *JLH*

HOW ABOUT YOU?

Are you using your "weapon"—the Bible? Read it. Memorize it. Then, apply the lessons you learn from it to your daily life.

MEMORIZE:

"For the Word of God is quick, and powerful, and sharper than any two-edged sword." Hebrews 4:12, KJV

GOD'S WORD WILL HELP YOU DO RIGHT

CHRISTIAN CONSTRUCTION

Read: Proverbs 16:20-24

"Mike, listen to the verse," said Juan one day, "and then repeat it." Juan recited each word slowly. He was helping his friend learn their memory verse for Sunday school. Mike tried to repeat the verse, but he couldn't. After several attempts, Juan scowled. "You're hopeless, Mike," he said. Juan pushed a study book at Mike. "Take this and practice."

Mike held the study book close to his chest. "I'll do better next week," he whispered and left the room.

Juan rolled his eyes and muttered, "Yeah, right." As he stood up and turned to go outdoors, he saw his mom in the doorway. "How long have you been there?" asked Juan.

"Long enough," replied Mom. "You need to be more patient with Mike."

Later that day, Juan's parents were studying pictures they had spread across the table. Dad looked up when Juan came in. "These are pictures that were taken before, during, and after the hotel construction," said Dad. "I need to choose photos to use in my newspaper article."

Juan picked up a picture. "I like this one. You can see all of the old building and the crane." He pointed to dates stamped on some of the pictures. "They tore down the old building in one day," he said, "but it took over a year to build the new one. I guess it's easier to tear down than to build up."

Dad nodded. "That's true in any area of life, not just in building. We often find it easier to criticize people for what they do wrong rather than to praise them for what they do right." Mom looked at Juan, and he remembered how impatient he had been with Mike. He was sure that she was remembering, too.

Mom nodded. "God wants us to 'build up' others in the faith, not tear them down," she said. *RRZ*

HOW ABOUT YOU?

Do your words and your attitude encourage others? Be a builder. Criticize less and compliment more. Be patient with those who need extra help. Building others up in their faith also strengthens your own.

USE
ENCOURAGING
WORDS

August

28

Read: Romans 6:11-14; 1 Corinthians 10:13

The following story may not be appropriate for young children.

"I'm glad that you and I could go camping together, Dad," said William, as he and his father arranged wood for a campfire.

Dad smiled as he struck a match to the kindling. "Rumor has it that you're pretty fond of Mandy Mira."

"She's okay," mumbled William.

"Just okay?" asked Dad. "Your sister saw you in the hallway at school—and according to her, you were trying to 'plant a big kiss on her lips.' You're a little young for that, don't you think?"

William blushed. "I don't know what got into me." He stood looking at the ground. "Passion, I guess." Dad didn't act shocked or surprised as he turned away from the fire.

Suddenly William yelled, "Look, Dad! The fire has gotten into the dry grass."

Dad jumped up and began stomping on the nearest blaze. "Grab that pail of water," he called. "Quick!" In seconds, the wildfire was out. "Close call," said Dad. He put an arm around his son. "And I do know what you mean by passion. It's a strong force; everyone feels it. But like that fire, it can be controlled. It's a gift from God to be used carefully. If a fire gets out of control, it can cause a lot of damage. When passion is uncontrolled, it causes great problems, too."

William hesitated. "Oh, well, Mandy wouldn't go out with me now anyway," he said. "She got mad—she says I came on too strong. She just wants to do things in groups."

"Good for Mandy!" exclaimed Dad. "The Bible has lots to say about temptation and how God will provide a 'way of escape.' A good one is not to be in a position to be tempted. Mandy is right—young people getting together in groups is healthy." *RCW*

HOW ABOUT YOU?

Do you avoid situations where you might be tempted to sin? Feelings can be controlled. Ask God to help, but also do what you can to avoid places where you'll be tempted.

MEMORIZE:

"Do not let sin control the way you live; do not give in to its lustful desires."
Romans 6:12

THE WISE SQUIRREL

Read: Genesis 41:46-57

"Guess what Joseph is doing!" exclaimed Lemont as he burst into the kitchen. "He's burying nuts near the apple tree."

"Who's Joseph?" asked Mom. "The new boy next door?"

"Oh, Mom! Joseph is the squirrel who visits our garden," explained Lemont impatiently. "But why would he bury nuts instead of eating them?"

"He's storing them away to eat next winter," his brother Michael told him.

Mom nodded. "While it's warm, squirrels collect nuts and grains and hide them," she said. "Then, when winter comes and food is hard to find, they have their secret store to fall back on."

"That's like Joseph in the Bible," observed Michael. "He collected grain for seven years, so when the famine came, the people had plenty to eat. He was smart!"

"Hmmm," murmured Mom. "We can learn something from both Josephs."

"We need to store up food in case there's a famine here?" asked Lemont.

Mom smiled. "I was referring to a different kind of food—spiritual food," she explained. "I'm afraid that when things are going well for us—like now—we might be tempted to be lazy and neglect prayer, Bible reading, and meeting with other Christians. We seem to realize that we need God's help when difficult times come, but we don't always remember that we should use the good times to store up spiritual food and strengthen our relationship with the Lord."

"I get it," said Lemont. "If we store up that spiritual food, we can use it when hard times come. We can remember Bible verses and lessons we've learned in church."

Mom nodded. "Yes," she agreed. "We can draw spiritual strength from the many things we've previously learned from God's Word." *MTF*

HOW ABOUT YOU?

Is this time a "good time" in your life? Is God blessing you with happy times and pleasant circumstances? Then use this time to praise and thank him and to get to know him better. Is this a "hard time" in your life? Then draw upon the spiritual truth you've stored up.

STORE UP
SPIRITUAL
TRUTHS FOR
FUTURE NEEDS

MEMORIZE:
"I will delight in your principles and not forget your word." Psalm 119:16

TROUBLESOME MELON (PART 1)

Read: Psalm 32:1-5

Hearing his mother call, Jamal ran out to the backyard. Mom was standing behind the garage, looking at the ground. "Look at those melon plants," she said. There, almost hidden by tall grass. Jamal saw a cluster of green vines. "The funny thing is," continued Mom, "I didn't plant any watermelons this year."

"Maybe they got planted accidentally," suggested Jamal. "Maybe a squirrel dropped some seeds there."

"Think so?" asked Mom. "I was thinking of something else. Remember when someone stole a watermelon from the farm stand last summer?"

"Yeah." Jamal shifted uncomfortably. "It was one of those big green ones, with stripes, wasn't it?"

"You have a good memory," said Mom. "I don't remember what kind it was, but I was wondering if maybe the person who stole the melon came here, ate it, and then buried the rinds and the seeds so no one would find out." Jamal's face was red as Mom looked closely at him. "Is there something you need to tell me?" she asked. Jamal refused to look her in the eye. "It was you, wasn't it, Jamal?" added Mom softly. "I wondered about it last summer because of the way you reacted then."

"I . . . I . . . John and I did it," Jamal admitted, close to tears. "When we buried everything, I thought that would be the end of it. I didn't count on those little green plants coming up out of the ground to tell on me!"

"No matter how you try to hide sin, it always comes back to tell on you," said Mom. "The Bible says, 'Be sure your sin will find you out,' and, sooner or later, it always does." *HCT*

HOW ABOUT YOU?

Do you try to hide wrongdoings from others—and even from God? Trying to cover up sin causes more trouble in the end. Instead of trying to hide sin, confess it! Let God's forgiveness make you clean.

MEMORIZE:

"O God, you know how foolish I am;
my sins cannot be hidden from you."
Psalm 69:5

YOU CAN'T
HIDE SIN

TROUBLESOME MELON (PART 2)

Read: Luke 19:2-10

Jamal was horrified. He had confessed to his mother that he and a friend had stolen a melon from a farm stand the summer before, and now Mom said he had to go see Mr. Smolina, the owner, and tell him about it. "But, Mom, that happened a long time ago," he protested. "I'll bet Mr. Smolina doesn't even remember it. Why can't I just be punished and then forget about it?"

"It happened long ago, but you did *steal* from Mr. Smolina, and you'll have to repay that debt," replied Mom sternly.

"Well . . . well . . . can't we just buy another melon and leave it at his door after dark tonight?" asked Jamal hopefully. "Then he'll have been paid back. And . . . and I'll ask God to forgive me, too. Isn't that enough?"

"Asking God to forgive you would be enough if you had sinned against God only," replied Mom, "but when you lie or steal or hurt someone, you need to also apologize to the person you've wronged. You must show you're really sorry you did wrong, not just sorry you got caught. In this case, you not only owe Mr. Smolina a watermelon, but you owe him an apology, too."

Ten minutes later, Jamal and his mother arrived at Mr. Smolina's store, and Jamal haltingly confessed to the crime. Mr. Smolina agreed to forgive him and let him work off the debt.

"Well, Jamal, don't you feel better now that you've done the right thing?" asked Mom as they headed home.

Jamal nodded. "Yes," he said with a sigh, "but I never want to go through that again!" *HCT*

HOW ABOUT YOU?

Have you stolen, lied, disobeyed, or done some other thing that has hurt someone? Confess your sin to God, and be sure to also do what you can to make things right with the person you've hurt.

CONFESS SIN AND APOLOGIZE

CLOTHES TALK

1

Read: 1 John 2:15-17

Jon was excited. His parents had decided that he was old enough to have a clothing allowance and buy some of his own school clothes—"subject to our approval, of course," his mother had added. His older brother, Brent, offered to go shopping with him. Brent was a senior in high school and knew what kind of clothing to buy.

At the mall, Jon walked proudly beside his brother. "How are things at Westfield?" a clerk asked Brent while Jon tried on a jacket. At the shoe department, the clerk looked at Brent and asked, "What can I show you today—basketball or track shoes, maybe?"

Jon was puzzled. "How do all these people know you go to Westfield High and play sports?" he asked.

Brent grinned. "They noticed my letter jacket," he said. "It tells people something about me. Clothes say things about us just as sure as our words and actions do."

When Jon spied a rack of T-shirts, he pointed them out to Brent. "I could use a new T-shirt," he said. "What do you think of these?" They looked at the shirts, most of which had wild pictures of sports figures on them—all surrounding the name of a popular beer.

Brent frowned. "If you wear one of these, it will be saying you aren't very smart," he said.

"What do you mean?" said Jon. "Lots of kids wear these."

"Remember what we were just talking about—that what you wear can say something about you?" asked Brent. "These shirts would say you're not smart enough to know that you're doing free advertising for a product that's harmful to your body." He turned to go. "What you wear should say something good," he said, then added, "At the risk of sounding like a preacher, I'll also tell you to make sure it says something that pleases God." *DMG*

HOW ABOUT YOU?

Are you aware that you're a commercial for the things you wear? Did you know that people not only hear what you say, they also "see" what you say? Be sure the things your clothes say are things that won't offend a holy God and that they fit your Christian testimony.

MEMORIZE:

"And whatever you do or say, let it be as a representative of the Lord Jesus, all the while giving thanks through him to God the Father."

Colossians 3:17

CLOTHES SAY SOMETHING ABOUT YOU

2

KICK THE CAN'TS

Read: John 6:9-13

"My heart was full of sin . . ." *Clank!* "Until the Savior came in. . . ." *Clank!* "His precious blood I know . . ." *Clank!* "Has washed it white as snow." Zachary walked along, singing and kicking an empty soda-pop can.

"I used to play a game called 'Kick the Can,' " said Grandpa when Zachary reached the front porch where his family was sitting.

"And I remember singing that song," added Grandma.

"It's 'The Wordless Book' song. I wonder where the idea for a book without words came from," said Zachary.

"Let's search for the answer on the Internet," said Grandpa. Inside, he sat down at the computer and typed "wordless book." After clicking on one of the articles, he read it quickly, then summarized it for the others. "In 1866, a preacher, Charles Spurgeon, told of an old, unnamed minister who had put black, red, and white pages together to remind himself of his sinfulness and Christ's blood, which was shed for his cleansing. Today, the familiar black, red, white, gold, and green pages are used worldwide to explain that good news. When we depend only on Jesus to save us, we have an eternal home in heaven."

"Think of the thousands of people who have believed in Christ because of one unnamed man!" said Grandma. "God can take our small, feeble efforts to serve him and use them in a big way."

"I'm only nine years old," said Zachary. "I can't do much."

"That doesn't matter," said Grandma. "We say 'I can't' too often—like, 'I can't understand the hard words in the Bible . . . I can't give much in the offering . . . I can't explain salvation very well.' God only asks us to do what we can."

Grandpa grinned. "Instead of playing 'Kick the Can,' why not play 'Kick the Can'ts.' " *LJR*

HOW ABOUT YOU?

What "little thing" can you do? Pray for a friend to accept Jesus as Savior? Read your Bible every day and do what it says? Give a gospel tract to someone? Put a generous part of your allowance in the church offering? Don't grumble about being able to do only a "little." Get rid of the "I can'ts." Do the best you can and leave the results to God.

MEMORIZE:

"Whatever you eat or drink or whatever you do, you must do all for the glory of God." 1 Corinthians 10:31

YOUR WORK FOR GOD IS IMPORTANT

BEARING FRUIT

Read: John 15:1-5, 8

Susan and Nick had enjoyed picking apples at their grandmother's home. "What did Grandma Bergen mean when she said she had a bumper crop this year?" asked Susan, chomping into one of the apples.

"It means the trees have lots and lots of apples," Dad said.

"Grandma used a different kind of spray this year," Mom said. "And the new irrigation system helped water the trees. So the apples are bigger and better than ever."

"Picking fruit reminds me of some Bible verses about the fruit of the Spirit," said Dad. "Didn't you kids learn those in Sunday school a few weeks ago?"

"Yep," said Nick. "They're Galatians 5:22 and 23—and I still remember them." He quoted the verses.

"Good," said Dad. "Having the fruit of the Spirit should be natural for the Christian, just like it's natural for apple trees to have apples. It's not something they have to struggle to do."

"I don't think it's that easy to have the fruit of the Spirit," said Nick. "I think it's hard!"

Dad smiled. "Well, I'm afraid a lot of us would have to agree with you," he said. "But when Grandma's apple trees didn't produce many apples, she knew something was wrong, and when our lives don't show the fruit of the Spirit, perhaps there's something wrong, too. What do you think it might be?"

"Well . . . Grandma's apples had worms last year, so the fruit wasn't so good. Maybe our lives have sin in them when the fruit isn't so good," suggested Susan.

"Good thought!" said Dad. "Anything else?"

Nick spoke up. "Apple trees need water, and Christians need the Bible," he said.

Dad nodded. "Correct! God wants his children to live fruitful lives for him. Let's do all we can to make sure our lives show the fruit of the Spirit every day." *RB*

HOW ABOUT YOU?

Do you know what the "fruit of the Spirit" is? Think about the things listed in the verses below, and think about your own life—the things you do each day, your attitude and behavior. Is the fruit of the Spirit evident in your life? It should be if you know Jesus as your Savior. Read your Bible daily and confess to God any sin in your life. Let his fruit be seen in you.

MEMORIZE:

"But when the Holy Spirit controls our lives, he will produce this kind of fruit in us: love, joy, peace, patience, kindness, goodness, faithfulness, gentleness, and self-control." Galatians 5:22-23

SHOW THE FRUIT OF THE SPIRIT

LEFTOVERS

Read: Proverbs 3:9-12

"Grandma asked if you could clean her yard this week," Mom told Ben, "and Mr. Cohen wants you to sweep his shop."

Ben nodded. "I'll sweep Mr. Cohen's shop—he pays good," he said. "But I won't have time to do Grandma's yard."

All week Mom noticed that Ben had plenty of time for himself, but he was always "too busy" to help others—unless they paid him.

One afternoon, Ben was rollerblading on the driveway while his sister Erin was helping Mom prepare dinner. When it was ready, Mom quietly called Dad. "What about Ben?" Erin asked. "Isn't he eating?"

"Later," Mom replied. "He's busy now." When they finished eating, she called Ben. "You can eat now."

"About time," Ben answered as he took off his skates. "I'm starved!" When he walked into the dining room and saw three dirty plates and only one clean one, his forehead puckered. "Did you eat already? Why didn't you call me?"

"You're always giving everyone else leftovers," Mom answered, "so I didn't think you'd mind having some."

"What do you mean? Everything's cold, and the best pieces are gone and . . ." Ben's voice trailed off as he stared at the table. "There's not much left."

"Well, everyone was hungry tonight," responded Mom. "But like I said, all week you've been giving leftovers. You don't seem to have time for anyone but yourself, except maybe for a few leftover minutes when we have family devotions at the end of the day. I figured it was your turn to get leftovers."

"But I don't like leftovers," Ben wailed.

"Do you think God does?" asked Mom. "And what about your grandmother? You don't even have 'leftover' time for her. You only have time for jobs that pay."

Ben hung his head as he took a leftover chicken wing. "I'll clean her yard tomorrow," he promised. *BJW*

HOW ABOUT YOU?

Do you give God and others your leftovers? Do you give him an offering only after you've used what you want for yourself? Do you witness only if it's convenient? The Lord promises blessings if you give him the "firstfruits." Give God your best time and the first part of your money. You'll find there will be much more "left over" for you.

MEMORIZE:

"But seek first his kingdom and his righteousness, and all these things will be given to you as well."
Matthew 6:33, NIV

GIVE TO
GOD FIRST

NO DAD

Read: Psalm 10:12-18

Joshua walked slowly into the classroom. *I hate school,* he thought. *The guys will start telling what they did with their dads over the weekend, and I'll be left out.* Almost without warning, Dad had left home and moved to another state. Now Joshua hardly ever saw him anymore.

Sure enough, some of the boys started telling about going fishing or camping with their dads. Joshua pretended he didn't care.

That night as he got ready for bed, Joshua's heart was heavy. *All my life I've been taught that prayer can change things,* he thought. *Well, I prayed lots, but nothing changed. Dad's still gone. But I know I'm a Christian, so what else can I do?* Kneeling beside his bed, Joshua began to pray again, shyly at first, and then with more confidence. He prayed for his dad and mom and then for himself, telling God all about how he felt. For the first time, he didn't ask God to change only the circumstances. He also asked God to help him accept not having Dad home, and he meant it. He asked God to help him and his mom.

As Joshua climbed into bed, he was surprised to find that he felt better. *I guess I shouldn't be surprised,* he thought. *After all, Mom keeps telling me that God is a father to the fatherless. It's not like God is going to play baseball with me, but he does take care of me—and I can talk to him whenever I want.*

The next time Joshua heard boys talking about their dads, he still felt a little out of place. But he had something new—a peace in his heart as he realized that his heavenly Father was with him. He was even able to laugh at a joke one of the boys had played on his dad. *DS*

HOW ABOUT YOU?

Are you a member of a one-parent family? Do you feel an emptiness inside? If you're a Christian, pray about it. Tell the Lord exactly how you feel. Your heavenly Father cares, and he answers prayer. He's able and willing to meet each need of your life. Let him.

LEAN ON YOUR HEAVENLY FATHER

MEMORIZE:
"Father to the fatherless . . . this is God, whose dwelling is holy."
Psalm 68:5

WEEKEND PLANS

Read: 2 Timothy 1:6-12

Samuel raced into the house after school. "Mom! Where are you?" he called, running from room to room. When she answered from the basement, Samuel ran down the steps, two at a time. "Will asked me to go fishing with him and his dad this weekend. Can I go?" he asked. "Our plan is to leave after school on Friday and be back Sunday afternoon."

Mom looked up as she took clothes from the dryer. "Sounds like fun. But does Will know you go to church on Sunday?"

Samuel shrugged. "Can't I skip just once?" he asked. "The kids at school think anyone who goes to church is dumb."

"So you haven't told them you go, or that you're a Christian?" asked Mom. "Are you ashamed to tell them?"

Samuel looked embarrassed as Mom continued. "I remember hearing you tell our pastor that you thought God wanted you to be a missionary or preacher someday, but if you're ashamed to tell even your best friends about Christ, how will you be able to tell others?"

"But, Mom," protested Samuel again, "it's just that the kids won't be friends with me, and they'll make fun of me. It'll be different when I'm older."

Mom shook her head. "At your old school, your friend Jeffrey told you about Jesus, and that didn't harm your friendship," she reminded him. "What if he had been ashamed and too scared to tell anyone about Jesus? Perhaps you never would have been saved, and Jeff's mother never would have had an opportunity to lead me to the Lord." She paused. "Now, about your plans for this weekend . . ."

This time Samuel shook his head. "I've got a new plan," he said. "Tomorrow I'll tell Will I can't go with him—and then I'll invite him to come to church with us." *JK*

HOW ABOUT YOU?

What have you done for Christ lately? Have you told anyone about him? How many of your unsaved friends and neighbors know that you're saved? If you're ashamed of Christ now, he'll be ashamed of you when he comes.

MEMORIZE:

"So you must never be ashamed to tell others about our Lord."
2 Timothy 1:8

WITNESS FOR JESUS

Read: Ezekiel 33:7-11

"Class, I'd like to hear your opinions of last night's program," said Mr. Pike after calling the students in his social studies class to order. "Susan, what did you think?"

"I didn't sleep all night!" she exclaimed. There was a murmur of agreement.

Ron raised his hand. "Those terrorists are just trying to scare us. No one would be dumb enough to push the button that would destroy the world."

"Oh, yeah?" said Tony. "I think we should build more weapons so that other countries can't blow us to bits."

In the discussion that followed, there were various opinions about what should be done, but everyone agreed that it was a most frightening problem. A few students seemed quite alarmed. Near the end of class, Mr. Pike called on Mario. "You seem quite calm about all this," he said. "Tell us what you're thinking."

Mario cleared his throat. "It scares me, too," he said nervously, "but I'm a Christian, so I know that God is in charge. Even if I do die, I'll go to heaven because I asked Jesus to forgive my sins and be my Savior."

The class had become quiet. "Interesting," said Mr. Pike. "Well, I see it's time to go home. Tomorrow please turn in your reports on this TV special."

Brenda approached Mario after class. "Do you really believe what you said?" Brenda asked. "I mean, about going to heaven."

Mario nodded. "That's what the Bible says."

"Ever since I saw that program, I've been scared about dying," Brenda admitted. "And I don't know what to do."

"You need to trust Jesus as your Savior," said Mario. "Then you won't need to be scared anymore."

"Sounds good," Brenda said, "but how do you do that? Can you tell me more about it?" Happily, Mario nodded. *JLH*

HOW ABOUT YOU?

Do you use opportunities in school to share your faith? Could you tell someone else how to be saved by showing them appropriate verses in the Bible? God says it's your responsibility to warn the lost. Are you doing it?

WARN THE
UNSAVED

MEMORIZE:
"It is appointed for men to die once and after this comes judgment."
Hebrews 9:27, NASB

THE DEMONSTRATION

Read: Hebrews 13:16-21

"Our new principal has changed just about everything at school," grumbled Eduardo one day. "Mr. Peterman won't let us go out for our noon hour until quarter after twelve—we can't even line up until it's actually time to go, because he says we're too noisy. We can't eat any food on the playground, either, and there are lots of other things he's changed. It will be hard to get used to him and his rules!"

"I'm sure it will," agreed Dad. "There are bound to be differences of opinion when someone new takes over. But I'm sure the problems will be ironed out."

When Eduardo came home from school the next day, he was worried. "The kids are getting mad about the new rules," he told his folks at dinner. "Some of them are planning a demonstration. They're going to chant while they go through the halls."

"Eduardo," said Dad, "there's a principle in the Bible that you need to keep in mind. God says to obey our leaders and to respect them. I know you find it hard to understand all of Mr. Peterman's rules, and perhaps they aren't even the best rules, but your job is to obey them. So, make up your mind that things are going to be done his way. He is in charge at school. Once you get used to the rules, you'll probably find they aren't so bad after all."

"I hope not," said Eduardo with a sigh. "The kids want me to join the demonstration, but I told them the principal is the boss and I'm going to do what he says."

"Good for you," approved Dad. "The things we need to demonstrate are love, faith in God, and respect for others. We need demonstrations of this kind every day." *AGL*

HOW ABOUT YOU?

Does your principal make rules you don't like? Do your teachers have rules that seem unreasonable? They're the bosses in the classrooms. Do you disagree with your parents? They're the bosses at home. Obey God by showing respect and obedience to those who lead you.

MEMORIZE:

"Obey your spiritual leaders and do what they say." Hebrews 13:17

OBEY AUTHORITY

MAKING THE TEAM

Read: Proverbs 6:20-23

As Mr. Royko drove Kip Rogers home from Bible club, he noticed that Kip seemed discouraged. "How's your mother?" Mr. Royko asked.

"Oh, I don't know," answered Kip. "She worries about everything. Ever since Dad died, she hardly lets me go anywhere except to school or church. She says I'm all she has. I want to play football, but I don't know if she'll let me."

Mr. Royko nodded. "I see. Tell you what, Kip—we'll pray about this. Trust God to work it out. Meanwhile, remember that God says you should obey your mother. If you do, your actions will prove that she can trust you."

Kip did his best to build his mother's confidence in him. He hurried home from school each day; he promptly did his homework; and he often started supper. He tried hard to do everything his mother told him to do, but he wasn't sure she noticed. Then one night she surprised him by asking about the football team. "I told the coach not to count on me," he told her.

"I think you should play, Kip," said Mom. "I saw our neighbor, Mr. Royko, today. He stopped me to tell me how impressed he was with the way you always come straight home from school. He says you're always polite, and he's sure you're a hard worker. I felt so proud of you. I still wish football weren't so rough, but I think you deserve a chance to be on the team. You've earned it."

Kip's eyes were shining. "Thanks, Mom," he said. *AGL*

HOW ABOUT YOU?

When you want something, do you nag in order to get it? Why not try something new? Start by praying about your problem. Then instead of nagging, be pleasant and obedient. Do your work as well as you can. You may be surprised at the results.

EARN TRUST

September

10

A LOSING GAME

Read: 1 Peter 2:9-12

Jeff didn't bother to study for his history test; he just made a deal with his friend, George. George took the test at an earlier hour and supplied Jeff with test questions and answers.

Jeff's parents found out about it, and they grounded him and insisted that he tell his teacher. "I don't see what the fuss is all about," grumbled Jeff. "Everybody cheats a little."

Dad sighed. "We've been through this before," he said. "You're a Christian, Jeff, and God expects you to do what is right. Cheating is wrong. Besides, you'll always be the loser when you cheat. You lose your peace of mind and the respect of others."

A few days later, Jeff burst into the house waving a paper. "These are the rules for an essay contest we're having," he said. "The prize is a trip to New York City! I've just gotta win it." So Jeff worked hard, did a lot of research, and handed in a fine essay.

"Who won the contest?" Mom asked when he returned home the day the winners were to be announced.

"George Reemer," replied Jeff.

"George Reemer!" exclaimed Jeff's sister, Marge. "But he never got more than a C in English. Was his essay good?"

Jeff nodded. "Real good," he said slowly. "I remembered reading it in a book. An author named Noel Campbell wrote it. George just copied it."

"Copied!" said Marge. "Did you say anything about it?"

"Yes, when I saw George, I told him I'd read it before. He just winked and said, 'If George Reemer can help *you* with history, Noel Campbell can help *me* with English.' I didn't know what to say."

"That's terrible," said Mom. "I think your teacher needs to know about this."

"I told her," said Jeff. "But I sure felt rotten. After all, I had cheated just a few weeks ago." *AGL*

HOW ABOUT YOU?
Did you ever cheat and feel you got away with something? You didn't. Cheating is always a losing game. Do you think you can't stop cheating? You can. If you're willing to change, the Lord will give you the power you need to change.

MEMORIZE:
"We are careful to be honorable before the Lord, but we also want everyone else to know we are honorable."
2 Corinthians 8:21

CHEATERS ARE ALWAYS LOSERS

MINE TO SHARE

Read: Acts 4:32-35

"Give me that!" ordered Carlos when he saw his little brother, Antonio, reading a wildlife magazine. "It's mine!" Grabbing the magazine, Carlos took it to his room.

Mom sighed when Antonio complained to his parents about it. "Carlos never shares his stuff," he grumbled.

"Carlos does have a problem with being selfish about his stuff," agreed Mom, "but I have an idea. . . ." And she shared what she had in mind.

The next week was Carlos's birthday, and he eagerly opened his gifts. "Chess! Thanks, Juanita!" he exclaimed. "Will you play a game with me tonight?"

His sister shook her head. "I bought it for you, and I want you to have it all to yourself," she said.

"Look! A ball and glove!" shouted Carlos as he opened the next present. "Want to play catch, Antonio?"

"No, thanks," said Antonio. "I don't want to mess up your new ball."

And so it went. Everyone even insisted that the birthday cake and ice cream belonged to Carlos and he should eat it all himself. Carlos tried to look pleased, but he didn't enjoy it. "I like my birthday gifts," he said at last, "but what good are they when no one will enjoy them with me?"

"What good is anything," asked Mom, "if we keep it for ourselves?"

"I think you should know, Son, that we've all noticed your selfishness," added Dad, "and we wanted you to see how unhappy you would be when you kept lots of things for yourself. God wants us to have good things but he also wants us to be willing to share those things with others." *AGL*

HOW ABOUT YOU?

Are you willing to share your clothes, your food, and your time—even your money—with those who are in need? Do you complain if someone uses your things? Selfish people are not happy people. Freely share the good things God has given you.

SHARING BRINGS JOY

September

12

Read: Galatians 6:7-10

Barry was stretched out on the lawn, thinking about how his parents had been "bugging" him lately with questions like, "Have you had your devotions?" and "Have you sent your missions offering in yet?" He thought of other questions: "Are you going to help at Sunday school?" and "What about helping your grandmother with the yard work?" *Blah-blah-blah*, thought Barry. He yawned—it made him tired just to think of everything they wanted him to do. Why couldn't he just do what he wanted to do? It was his life, his money, and his time! Soon he dozed off and had an interesting dream. . . .

"Hello, Barry," came the voice of an ugly creature coming toward him. "My name is Mr. Self. My friends call me 'good old Self,' and my enemies call me 'Selfish.' And you? You're a guy after my own heart. You want to live life on your own terms and keep all your time and money to yourself. Don't make even one little sacrifice for anyone else."

"Sacrifice?" Barry asked. "Our minister said God asks us to give him a sacrifice of our time, talents, and money."

"Stop!" commanded Mr. Self. "Someone like you, Mr. Self, Jr., shouldn't be giving away time and money for free."

"Why not? I'm a Christian," declared Barry.

"You are?" asked Mr. Self, surprised. "I can't tell that by your attitude or your actions. Anyway, I'm just complimenting you. And besides, I *like* you."

"But . . . but . . . " sputtered Barry. Just then an acorn fell, striking him on the face. He awoke with a start. "Oh, my," he murmured, "what a horrible dream. Perhaps I'd better change my attitude. I don't want to be a Mr. Self, Jr." *BJW*

HOW ABOUT YOU?

How do you use your time, money, and other resources God has given you? Are you spending them wisely and generously or giving out as little as you possibly can to feel good about yourself? Making good use of your resources honors God.

MEMORIZE:

"A lazy person is as bad as someone who destroys things." Proverbs 18:9

USE TIME AND
RESOURCES
WISELY

IT'S JUST LIKE HIM

Read: 1 Peter 2:21-25

Juan was late for school. *Even if I run, I'll never make it in time,* he thought. *And if I'm late, I'll have to stay after school.* Juan didn't like that idea, so he headed for the river. There he met a boy he didn't know. "Hi! My name's Juan," he greeted the stranger. "Are you skipping school, too?"

"Hi! I'm Paulo," was the reply. "I've been sick with a heart problem, and my mom didn't want me to go back to school yet. But she said I could go for a walk."

Juan grinned. "I'm going to go wading," he said.

"You better not," advised Paulo. He pointed. "See all those 'No swimming' signs?"

But Juan just shrugged and waded into the water. Almost immediately he stepped into a deep hole. Paulo ran to help. "Here—grab this branch," he called. "I'll pull you out!" After a short struggle, Paulo managed to pull Juan back to shallow water.

Juan sank to the riverbank. "That's some drop-off," he said. "All of a sudden . . . Paulo? Paulo! What's the matter?" Juan knelt beside Paulo, who had dropped to the ground, moaning and clutching his chest.

Later, Juan was telling his mother about the frightening experience. "All that exercise caused his heart to act up, and I didn't know what to do," he said, "so I ran to the nearest house, and they called an ambulance. The whole thing is my fault. If only I had gone to school!"

"You can't undo the past, Juan," said Mom, "but you can do something about the future."

"I know, Mom," Juan agreed. "I talked with Paulo's mother, and she was so nice. I asked her why Paulo pulled me out of the water when he knew it could hurt him. She said he always tried to do whatever he believed Jesus would do." *AGL*

HOW ABOUT YOU?

Do you live your life the way you think Jesus would want you to live? Are you willing to follow his example in giving to others? It's the only way to be truly happy.

BE LIKE JESUS

MEMORIZE:
"Christ, who suffered for you, is your example. Follow in his steps."
1 Peter 2:21

Brianna desperately wanted to win the expensive camera being offered as a prize in a wildlife photo contest sponsored by a local photography shop. "But I haven't got a chance," she moaned. "My old camera has no adjustments for speed or distance, and I'll never get close enough to a wild animal to take a good picture."

"No problem!" said her brother, Tim. "Just snap a picture at the zoo."

"That would be cheating," protested Brianna, and though Tim urged her to do it, she refused. But when the contest was over, Brianna was notified that she had won! She was surprised and excited!

Tim went to the store with her to pick up her prize, but when she saw the winning picture, she knew there had been a mistake. It was a wonderful picture of a fox—a picture *she* had not taken. Tim nudged her. "I took it and entered it for you," he whispered. "I took it at the zoo."

Brianna's thoughts ran wild. *After all, I didn't do anything dishonest, and it isn't like the picture belongs to anyone else—and o-o-oh! That new camera is so beautiful! But, no! To keep it would be dishonest.*

Reluctantly, Brianna explained the situation to the man at the store, and the rightful winner was awarded the prize.

On the way home, Tim was very quiet. At last he told Brianna what he was thinking. "I wanted to help, and it didn't seem so terrible to me if I cheated just a little," he said. "But you've shown me something about myself today. Wanting to help you was a right thing, but I went about it in the wrong way. I guess I need to ask God to help me live in a way that will honor him." *BP*

HOW ABOUT YOU?

Are you kind? Helpful? Obedient? Slow to get angry? Honest? Happy? Today's Scripture lists "fruit," or characteristics, that should be seen in the life of a Christian. The things you do and the way you act can bring honor or dishonor to God. Point others to Jesus by your life.

MEMORIZE:

"Yes, the way to identify a tree or a person is by the kind of fruit that is produced." Matthew 7:20

YOUR LIFE IS A TESTIMONY

THE CHOICE

Read: 1 Corinthians 12:14, 20-22, 25

Elections for the church youth group were coming up, and Carl wanted to be president. "I'm sick of our dull meetings," he told his brother, Bobby. "If I were president, we'd have better meetings." So Carl did everything he could think of to make himself be noticed.

To Carl's dismay, the youth group did not elect him to be president. They chose Denny Sparks, and Carl was elected secretary. He was upset! *Why should Denny be president? He's so bashful he can hardly look at people,* thought Carl. He aired his views at home. "Now I won't get to try out any of my ideas," he grumbled. "Denny just doesn't have what it takes."

"But he must have some good qualities, or he wouldn't have been elected," Dad said gently.

Bobby spoke up for Denny, too. "He's so nice to everyone, and he's always willing for others to help him," he said.

"Oh, he's nice enough, but still . . ." Carl got up to answer the phone. It was Denny, and as Carl hung up, he looked ashamed. "Denny wants all the officers to bring ideas for programs and projects to the next meeting."

"That sounds like a good start," said Dad. "Apparently Denny wants you to have a part in planning the programs. He seems to recognize that all of you are important." Dad smiled. "It reminds me of what the apostle Paul wrote to the people of Corinth," he added. "Paul said that Christians are all members of the 'body of Christ.' Just as our eyes, ears, hands, and feet are important parts of our physical bodies, so every Christian is important to Christ. No one should be overlooked or looked down upon."

Carl nodded thoughtfully. "I'm glad now that Denny was elected president. If I were in charge, I'd have run everything my own way," he admitted. "It will be much better this way." *AGL*

HOW ABOUT YOU?

Do you always want everything your way, or are you willing to cooperate with others and let them develop their talents for God, too? God has a place for every Christian to serve him. Each one is important and needed.

EACH PERSON IS
IMPORTANT

September

16

Quon laughed as he saw his leg jump when Dr. Singh gently tapped his knee with a rubber hammer. This was his favorite part of the examination. Next, Dr. Singh placed the round metal part of the stethoscope against Quon's chest. It felt cold, and he shivered. Then the doctor looked in Quon's ears and throat with a little flashlight. At last he was finished.

A short time later, Quon and his mother left the medical building. "Why do I have to go to the doctor when I'm not even sick?" he asked.

"You know the answer to that—the school requires you to have an exam before you play on the team," replied Mom. "Besides, when you have an examination from time to time, Dr. Singh is better able to help keep you healthy."

"I felt like Dr. Singh was looking right inside me with that flashlight. And that one thing is cold—that thing he called a steth . . . steth . . ."

"The stethoscope," said Mom, "to listen to your heartbeat. It helps Dr. Singh know if your heart is healthy. God created us with bodies that are more complex than any machine, you know. Then in addition to our wonderful *physical* bodies, God gave each of us a *spiritual* nature that will live forever."

"But Dr. Singh can't see my spiritual nature," said Quon.

Mom smiled. "No, only God can see into that part of you," she said. "He gave you spiritual life when you received Jesus as your Savior. Just as it's important to care for your physical body and nourish it with food, it's also important to nourish, or feed, your spirit. Do you know how to do that?"

Quon nodded. "By praying and reading the Bible," he said, "and by practicing the things I learn." *BK*

HOW ABOUT YOU?

Do you keep your body healthy by eating nourishing food and getting plenty of exercise and rest? That's important. Do you also nourish your spirit? When did you last read from God's Word? Have you memorized any Scripture lately? How long is it since you've talked with God in prayer? Such things help keep your spiritual nature healthy.

MEMORIZE:

"Thank you for making me so wonderfully complex! Your workmanship is marvelous—and how well I know it." Psalm 139:14

NOURISH YOUR SPIRIT

ON GUARD

Read: Philippians 4:4-8

"Mom! Dad! I got the job! I'm a safety patrol this semester!" Jim burst into the house, all excited. "I start tomorrow!"

Jim's little brother, Shane, looked at his brother with pride. "I bet you'll be the best one," he said.

By dinnertime, Jim had begun to think about his new responsibilities. "We had a meeting after school to learn what safety patrols do," he said as they were eating. "I have to make sure the kids get safely across the street—but what if they won't wait when I hold out my arms? Or what if they won't listen to me?"

"You'll do fine," Mom encouraged him. "You do a good job when you take care of Shane."

But Jim continued to fret about all the things that might go wrong. "What if a car skids into the kids who are waiting to cross?" He pushed idly at his food.

"Now, Jim, this kind of thinking is taking all the pleasure out of getting the patrol job," his father said kindly. "It seems to me you need to call on Someone who can guard your mind and give you peace about it."

Jim thought he knew what his father was talking about. "You mean God?" he asked.

"That's right." Dad nodded and reached for his Bible. He turned several pages. "Look . . . here in Philippians God says to bring your worries to him, and he'll guard your mind against worry. Will you do that?" Slowly Jim nodded. "Good," said Dad, "and be sure to thank him for his love and care. We'll pray that God will help you, too." *CEY*

HOW ABOUT YOU?

Are you a worrier? Why not give your worries to God? Allow him to be "on guard" and keep your mind from worry.

LET GOD GUARD YOUR THOUGHTS

MEMORIZE:

"And the peace of God, which passeth all understanding, shall keep your hearts and minds through Christ Jesus."

Philippians 4:7, KJV

BAD APPLES

Read: 1 Corinthians 3:11-15

"Would you like to earn some money?" asked Keanu's Uncle Roy. "I'll pay you for each bushel of apples you pick. Just get apples from the trees. Don't pick up 'drops'—apples that have fallen to the ground."

Keanu eagerly went to work. To pick apples from high branches, he used a ladder or a long pole picker. At first that was fun, but he couldn't pick very fast that way. *This takes too long*, thought Keanu. *A lot of the apples on the ground look just as good as these. Why don't I just pick up some of them?* At first he was choosy about what he picked up. But the longer he worked, the less fussy he became.

Uncle Roy came back at lunchtime. "My! You surely are a fast worker!" he exclaimed. But when he began to load the apples onto his truck, he immediately noticed what Keanu had done. "I'm sorry. I can't pay you for picking up the drops," he told Keanu.

"But they're almost spotless!" protested Keanu.

Uncle Roy nodded. "Yes, but when they fell to the ground, they got bruised."

"And I thought I was making so much money," said Keanu with a sigh. "All that work for nothing!"

In church the next day, Keanu was surprised to hear an illustration the pastor gave. "Last year my wife and I went out to an apple orchard and picked up some good 'drops,' " said Pastor Grey. "And even though they didn't look bad, those drops didn't last. Many things in life are like that. People work so hard to gain many earthly things. They enjoy them for a while, but earthly things don't 'keep' well either. They last only a short time. God wants us to work for heavenly rewards—things that last for eternity." *LAP*

HOW ABOUT YOU?

Are you working for what the world says is good—nice clothes, money, popularity, a good career someday? Those things are nice, but they last only a short time. To earn lasting treasure, make sure you do the things that please God. His rewards are eternal.

MEMORIZE:

"Set your minds on things above, not on earthly things." Colossians 3:2, NIV

WORK FOR
ETERNAL
REWARDS

FOLLOW THE RULES

Read: Hebrews 12:5-11

Reno's friend, Nick, had a flat tire on his bike, so Reno ran home to see if he could use Dad's tire pump. He liked to use his father's tools, and usually Dad didn't mind. "Just follow my rules," Dad had told him. "Get permission before you use them, and put the tools away." But this time, Dad wasn't home to ask. Reno shrugged and took the pump anyway. The boys fixed the tire and then went for a ride.

As Reno and Nick were returning home, it began to rain. "Don't bother to stop for your pump. I'll bring it over in the morning," Nick promised.

Reno hesitated. "Well . . . all right," he agreed.

The next morning, Nick called Reno. "I can't find the pump anywhere," said Nick.

"Oh, no!" groaned Reno. "I have to get it back before Dad notices."

"Look . . . just don't let on that you know anything about it," urged Nick.

At first that seemed like a good idea, but as the morning passed, Reno found he was very uncomfortable about the whole thing. With a sigh, he went to his dad and told him the whole story.

Dad nodded. "Nick's dad called me just a few minutes ago," he said. "He found the pump last night and took it in out of the rain. He said he's sending Nick over with it now. As for you . . . consider yourself grounded."

"Aw, Dad . . . can't we just forget about it this one time?" pleaded Reno. "I did come and tell you about it."

"Yes, you did, and I appreciate that," said Dad. "Actually, I had intended to ground you for a week, but because you were honest about this, Reno, I'm going to ground you for only the rest of the day." *AGL*

HOW ABOUT YOU?

Do you follow the "rules" God gives in his Word? He expects you to obey them. If you disobey, confess your sin to him and experience his mercy. Then humbly accept any discipline he may allow, and learn from it.

FOLLOW GOD'S RULES

MEMORIZE:

"He who covers his sins will not prosper, but whoever confesses and forsakes them will have mercy."
Proverbs 28:13, NKJV

September
20

"I hate it here! I wish we were still in Hillsdale," said Austin, flinging his backpack to the kitchen floor. Since his family had moved from Hillsdale to Mapletown, Austin had been upset about leaving his old school.

Austin's mother handed him a snack. "I know it's hard for you, Austin," she said. "Adjusting takes time, but soon you'll be used to your new teacher, and you'll make new friends. Remember, too, that one of your old friends is always with you—Jesus is just as close to you here as he was in Hillsdale."

Austin sighed. "Well, the kids play different games," he complained.

"Oh, give your new school a chance!" said Mom. "You've been there only a couple of days." She opened the patio door. "How about coming out and helping me fill the planters?" she invited.

"Okay," agreed Austin. When the planting was finished, Austin stood and admired the bright petunias and geraniums. But when he came home from school the next day, he found the plants drooping. "Mom, what's wrong with the flowers we planted?" he asked.

"Their roots had a bit of a shock when we repotted them," said Mom, "but they'll be all right." She smiled at Austin. "How was your day?" she asked.

Austin plopped into a chair on the patio and thought about his day. When he had handed in a neat math paper, his teacher had said, "Good job." At recess time, two boys had asked him to play with them. *Maybe it won't be so bad here, after all,* he thought. He watched a geranium nod in the light breeze. "Hey," he said, "I'm something like those flowers we planted! Moving here shocked my roots, but I'm adjusting. Maybe I'll really like it here after a while." *CEY*

HOW ABOUT YOU?
Have you had to move recently or had some other "shock to your roots"? It's normal to be sad for a while, but be patient and learn to trust God to help you adjust to your new situation.

MEMORIZE:
"I will be with you, and I will protect you wherever you go." Genesis 28:15

TRUST GOD THROUGH CHANGES

STOP SIGNS AND CHRISTIANS

Read: Ephesians 4:25-32

"Look!" exclaimed Kemil as he pointed toward the ditch. "Someone knocked the stop sign down again."

Dad nodded and stopped the car. "I wish," he said as he got out, "that people would learn to slow down when they come around this corner."

Kemil and Jamiel got out of the car, too. "What are you going to do?" asked Kemil.

"We'll see if we can put the sign back where it belongs," replied Dad. "If drivers don't stop at this corner, there could be a serious accident." He walked down into the ditch. "Help me carry it back to the road."

"We're right behind you," said Jamiel.

Together the three of them lifted the sign and carried it to the corner. They tried to stand it up against the jagged pole still sticking out of the ground, but it kept falling over. Dad frowned. "We'll lay it down against the pole," he said. "That will have to do until it's fixed properly."

"Won't it be hard to read?" asked Kemil.

"Yes," said Dad, "but motorists can recognize it by its shape and color."

"That's like what Mr. Paul told us in church last week," said Jamiel. "He says there are ways people can recognize us as Christians—sort of like the way people will recognize this sign."

"They'll recognize us by our shape and color?" asked Kemil with a grin.

Jamiel laughed. "No, but people can recognize Christians by what they do as well as by what they say—or sometimes by what they don't do or say. Mr. Paul says we can't expect others to know we're Christians if we swear or lie or cheat."

"Mr. Paul is right," agreed Dad. "People should know we're Christians by our words—but more than that, our attitude and actions should show that we belong to God." *ECM*

HOW ABOUT YOU?

Can you be recognized as a Christian by the way you live? It's great to tell others that you belong to Jesus—but make sure they can also tell that you're a Christian by your attitude and by the way you act.

LET OTHERS SEE JESUS IN YOU

MEMORIZE:
"I will show you my faith through my good deeds." James 2:18

THE PROBLEM TONGUE

Read: James 3:5-10

"Ouch!" Kelly banged her foot hard against the floor. "I need new shoes! This one hurts my foot!"

"You probably have it on the wrong foot," said her brother William.

"I do not!" said Kelly. "This shoe really hurts!"

"You just don't know how to put shoes on right," insisted William.

Kelly frowned. "I know which shoe goes on which foot," she informed him.

"Let me see," said Dad, and Kelly lifted her foot for him to check. "It's the tongue of the shoe, Kelly," he said after untying it. "It's twisted and bunched up. Dad pulled hard on the tongue and retied the shoe. "How does it feel now?"

Kelly ran around the room and jumped. "Hey, that's a lot better! It's all fixed!"

"Did she have it on the wrong foot?" asked William.

"Be quiet!" said Kelly. "You don't know anything."

"At least I know how to put my shoe on!" said William. He grabbed the soccer ball and began bouncing it up with his knee.

"Show off!" shouted Kelly.

Dad caught the ball and held it up high. "It was the tongue in Kelly's shoe that was causing a problem," he said. "Tell me something else that causes trouble when it's not used correctly."

"Ah . . . that ball?" guessed William. "If it's used wrong—like if we throw it around in the house—we could break a lamp or something."

"I was thinking of something smaller," said Dad. He pointed to his tongue.

"Our tongues?" asked William. "I guess you mean we need to talk nicer to each other."

Dad nodded. "God's Word says the tongue is small but can do enormous damage," he said. "Our words can hurt people a lot more than shoes can hurt our feet." *MFW*

HOW ABOUT YOU?

Have you listened to the words you say? Do you say encouraging things to others, or do your words hurt others? Ask God to help you use your tongue to help people, not hurt them!

MEMORIZE:

"I said to myself, 'I will watch what I do and not sin in what I say.'" Psalm 39:1

USE YOUR
TONGUE WISELY

LOCKED OUT

Read: Psalm 119:57-64

Arturo and Mario were locked out on the school roof because of their foolishness. Arturo had known it was wrong to go through that window, but he was so tired of being called a "goody-goody." He wanted to be popular, but being stuck on this roof just wasn't what he'd planned.

The boys had gone to the school swim meet. About halfway through, Mario had nudged Arturo. "Let's do something exciting," said Mario. He led Arturo up to the third floor where the balcony running track was located. At one side, a hinged window opened to the roof. Mario crawled through and dared Arturo to follow. Too scared to refuse, Arturo climbed out, too, but when the wind blew the window shut, he wished that he hadn't come.

Cautiously, they felt their way over the dark gravelly surface hoping to find another entrance into the building, but there was none. Arturo shivered in his thin red jacket. He prayed silently, *Dear God, I'm sorry. I shouldn't have listened to Mario. Forgive me and please help us find a way down.*

Just then he heard a whisper. "Hey, Arturo! Over here! We can slide down this pole." Arturo stumbled across the roof, dangerously close to the edge. He finally reached the corner where his friend was clinging to the downspout anchored there.

Mario first, and then Arturo, slid slowly to the ground—right into the waiting grasp of Mr. Cooper, the custodian. He had caught a glimpse of them from the parking lot. *Thank you, Lord*, breathed Arturo.

"I'm going to stop worrying about being friends with the popular kids—and trying to be part of the 'in' crowd," Arturo told his parents when he got home. "I'm going to look for the kind of friends that encourage me to do what's right." *PIK*

HOW ABOUT YOU?

Do you do things you know are wrong just so the popular kids at school will accept you? As a Christian, Jesus wants you to stand true for him. As the Psalmist said, "Be a friend with those who love God." Having his approval is more important than having the approval of anyone else.

LIVE TO PLEASE GOD, NOT OTHERS

MEMORIZE:

"Be on guard. Stand true to what you believe. Be courageous. Be strong."

1 Corinthians 16:13

BORN TO BE ME

Read: Psalm 139:13-17

Chen and his younger brother, Lee, were walking home from school. Chen was especially excited. "I'm so glad I made the football team this year, Lee-lee!" he said.

"Don't call me Lee-lee!" said Lee grumpily. "I knew you'd make the team. You're big enough!"

"It doesn't matter how big you are," answered Chen. "It's how well you can play."

"Well, I'm a good player, but they'll never put me on the team 'cause I'm too small," complained Lee. "How come God made you the family giant and me the runt?"

"How would I know what God had in mind!" answered Chen. "Let's hurry. I've got a practice game tonight."

When it was time for family devotions that evening, Lee was still hurting inside. "Why did God have to make me such a shrimp?" he asked.

"Are you angry with God?" asked Dad.

Lee shrugged. "I guess so," he admitted.

Dad was sympathetic. "I can only imagine how you feel," he said, "but I hope you'll remember that God doesn't measure your worth by how big you are. He didn't make a mistake when he made you, Lee. He has a reason for making you just the size you are."

About a week later, Lee arrived home all excited. "The soccer coach was looking for someone who could run fast, handle a soccer ball, and stop quickly," he told his dad, "so I tried out, and I made the soccer team!" Lee grinned as he added, "My size actually helped me!"

"Great!" exclaimed Dad. "I hope, Son, that you've learned a very important lesson—that everything God made is good." *MM*

HOW ABOUT YOU?

Do you like the color of your eyes? Is your nose too big for your face? How about your hair? Too stringy? Too straight? Too curly? Are you too tall? Not tall enough? Too chubby? Are you blaming God for what you consider to be your imperfections? Remember, God didn't make a mistake when he made you.

MEMORIZE:

"You formed me with your hands; you made me." Job 10:8

GOD MADE
YOU SPECIAL

FROM BAD TO WORSE

Read: Jonah 1:1-4, 15-17; 2:1, 7-10

I don't have my book report ready, thought Andy, *and I didn't study for my test!* He paused. *I know what I'll do—I'll skip school and go exploring at the old Quigley farm!*

So Andy hiked into the country and slipped under a "No Trespassing" sign. He went wading in the creek until he heard a dog growling—and coming closer! Andy grabbed his shoes and took off running, until he fell right into a briar patch. At least the dog didn't follow him.

Andy decided to poke around in the dusty old farm buildings. Suddenly, he let out a cry. "Oh, no! Wasps! I've got to get out of here!"

Back home that afternoon, Andy avoided talking about school. Just before bedtime, Dad said, "Tomorrow's Saturday, so let's go fishing, Andy. What do you say?" Andy agreed, and Dad announced they would go fishing at—of all places—the Quigley farm!

They were about to leave on their fishing trip the next morning when Mom spoke up. "Andy, what are those spots on your arm?" she asked. "Have you been around poison ivy lately?"

Andy spoke guiltily. "W-w-where would I have gotten p-poison ivy?"

Mom looked again. "Andy, where have you been?" she asked sternly. And so the story came out—the dog, the briars, the wasps! "All day I had nothing but trouble!" Andy sobbed. "Things just got worse and worse."

"You know," said Dad, "you remind me of Jonah. He was very unhappy about the job God gave him to do, and he was unwilling to do it. God has given you a job to do, too; he wants you to be the best student you can possibly be. Like Jonah, you neglected your job. You ran away from it—into worse trouble. Like Jonah, you need to ask God to forgive and help you." *BJW*

HOW ABOUT YOU?

Are you trying to run away from your school work or home duties? Ask God to help you do your very best in the place where he has put you right now.

STUDY AND WORK WILLINGLY

MEMORIZE:
"Be strong and steady, always enthusiastic about the Lord's work."
1 Corinthians 15:58

THE "FIX-IT" KID

Read: Proverbs 16:21-24

Red lights flashed as Kyle made his remote control jeep race into the living room where his brother, Pete, was sitting on the couch. The jeep ran over Pete's foot and crashed, causing a piece of the motor to fall off. Kyle tried to fix it—but it was no use. "Pete, can you fix my jeep?" he asked.

"Not again!" exclaimed Pete. But he took it and fixed it so that it was as good as new.

"Thanks," said Kyle. "I sure wish I could fix things." Kyle raced the jeep into his bedroom, then he sat on his bed. *I can't fix anything,* he thought. *Yesterday when the chain flew off my bike, Kaitlyn had to fix it. When my bird feeder fell apart, Dad fixed it.*

Kyle noticed his Sunday school paper on his night stand. It had a picture of Jesus healing a blind man. *Jesus fixed blind and lame people,* thought Kyle. *Best of all, he "fixed" me so I can go to heaven.* Kyle sat up straight. *Jesus can help me learn to fix things!* So Kyle prayed, asking God to help him fix something.

Kyle went to the kitchen where Dad was making dinner. He looked sad, and Kyle heard him sigh. "What's the matter, Dad?" he asked.

"Oh, Kyle," said Dad, "it's nothing for you to worry about. I've just had a difficult day, that's all."

Kyle wrapped his arms around his father and gave him a big hug. "Don't be sad, Dad," he said. "I love you. You're the best dad a kid could ever have!"

Dad broke into a smile.

"Thank you, Kyle," he said. "You've just made me the happiest dad in the whole world."

Kyle smiled, too. God had answered his prayer and helped him fix something—Dad's sad heart. *SRS*

HOW ABOUT YOU?

Are you a Christian? Then you're a special person with a special purpose. God has given you the power to "fix" broken people with kind words and deeds. Encourage someone today—do it for Jesus.

MEMORIZE:

"Kind words are like honey—sweet to the soul and healthy for the body."
Proverbs 16:24

ENCOURAGE
SOMEONE TODAY

WWJS

Read: James 3:2, 7-8

"Mom said I could water her plant," said Bobby. As he headed for the sunroom with a cup of water, he stumbled. The cup slipped, spilling water on Jason, who was doing homework.

"Just look at what you've done! Clumsy!" snarled Jason. "There's water on my homework paper, too, you idiot."

"I'm sorry," said Bobby, but Jason continued to call his brother ugly names.

"Jason, that was an accident, and Bobby said he was sorry," scolded Mom. "Stop using those names. A few weeks ago, we wrote WWJD on your hand, remember? Now I think we need to write WWJS—what would Jesus *say*." Jason frowned, but Mom went and got the marking pen.

As Jason and his friend Aaron played outdoors that afternoon, Bobby came out. Bobby started down the driveway on his bike and almost bumped into Jason. Jason was about to call Bobby a few names when he noticed the WWJS on his hand, and when Bobby apologized, Jason managed to say, "Oh, that's all right."

Just then, Mrs. Woo, who lived in the house behind theirs, strode out the door. "Look what your dog did to my flowers," she scolded. "Can't you keep that animal in your own yard?"

With WWJS still on his mind, Jason muttered, "Sorry."

After Mrs. Woo left, Aaron looked at Jason with a puzzled expression. "What do you have written on your hand?" asked Aaron.

"Something my mom put there to remind me not to call people names," muttered Jason. He was embarrassed, but he showed Aaron the letters and explained what they meant.

"Hey, that's neat!" exclaimed Aaron. "Let's get a pen so I can write it on my hand, too." *VMH*

HOW ABOUT YOU?

Do you remember to say kind things? Perhaps you'd like to write WWJS on your hand, or you could write it in large letters on a poster and hang it in your room.

MEMORIZE:

"May the words of my mouth and the thoughts of my heart be pleasing to you, O Lord, my rock and my redeemer." Psalm 19:14

GUARD YOUR LIPS

ALL BUT ONE

Read: James 2:8-10

Josh sat at the table surrounded by art supplies. "Tomorrow is the deadline for the ecology poster contest," he told his mother. "First prize is 25 dollars."

Mom looked over his shoulder. "Looks good."

Three-year-old Kendra tugged at Josh's arm. "I wanna color, too," she said. Josh grinned and gave her paper and markers.

After dinner, Josh and his parents were in the living room when Kendra bounded in. She shoved a magazine into Dad's hand. "Read me a 'tory, Daddy."

Dad raised his eyebrows. "Where did you get this?"

"Under Josh's bed," the little girl answered.

"I told you to stay out of my room!" Josh exploded.

Dad frowned. "Where did you get this magazine, Josh?" he asked.

Josh glared at Kendra. "Mike gave them to me," he answered sullenly. "What's wrong with them?"

"Did you say 'them'?" asked Dad. Too late, Josh realized his mistake. "Throw this and any other magazines of this kind into the dumpster right now," ordered Dad. "We will not have them in our home."

Josh reluctantly pulled the magazines from under his bed. He quickly stuck one under his pillow and then carried the others to the dumpster.

A short time later, Josh returned to the living room, waving his poster and shouting, "Look what Kendra did! She ruined my poster!"

"I just colored it," explained the little girl.

"Yeah, with a purple marker," moaned Josh.

"I thought you returned Josh's markers," said Mom.

Tears filled the little girl's eyes. "I kept only one."

"It took only one to ruin my poster!" Josh stormed. "It took only . . ." A thoughtful look crossed his face. Slowly, he repeated, "It took only one." Without another word, he went to his room, got the magazine from under his pillow, and threw it in the dumpster. *BJW*

HOW ABOUT YOU?

Are you tempted to hold on to "one little sin"? When God makes you aware of sin in your life confess your sin to him and ask him to forgive and help you leave all of it.

MEMORIZE:

"The person who keeps all of the laws except one is as guilty as the person who has broken all of God's laws."
James 2:10

BLOW IT AWAY

Read: Proverbs 16:20-32

Cody punched his pillow and looked at his clock. It was almost midnight. He sighed. *How can I face the kids tomorrow?* he thought. The whole class had roared when Cody's tongue had gotten tangled up while he was giving a book report. Then he said some hurtful things to his classmates. *Why can't I control my temper?* he thought.

Buzzzzzzz! A mosquito dive-bombed Cody's ear. He slapped at the air. *Buzzzzzz!* Missed! He waved his hand again, and the clock hit the floor with a loud crash. As he groped in the dark for the clock, Dad appeared in the doorway. "What's going on?" asked Dad.

"There's a mosquito bugging me. When I tried to get him, I knocked the clock off the night stand," he said.

"Did the mosquito wake you?" asked Dad.

"No," replied Cody. "I haven't been asleep."

Dad sat down on the edge of the bed. "What's wrong?" he asked.

Tears filled Cody's eyes. "I can't go to school tomorrow."

"Are you sick?" asked Dad.

"Yes. I'm sick of being teased," answered Cody. "The kids know it will make me mad so they torment me—just for fun."

Dad jumped up. "I just heard that mosquito," he said, turning on the light, then reaching to turn the ceiling fan on. "The air from this fan should blow him away," said Dad. He sat down again. "Cody, maybe you could try to 'blow off' the kids' teasing."

"Blow it off?" Cody repeated. "How?"

"Hang close to your friends and ignore the taunting," Dad replied, as he got up and turned off the light.

Maybe Dad's right, thought Cody. *I think I'll try that.* He turned over. "Please help me, God," he whispered. "I know you care about my feelings being hurt, and I know you can help me keep my temper. Please help me." *BJW*

HOW ABOUT YOU?

Do you have trouble controlling your temper? Do you let little things bug you? Ask God to help you simply blow them away. Ask him to help you control your temper.

DON'T LET LITTLE THINGS BUG YOU

WRINKLE FREE

Read: 2 Corinthians 1:3-8

Jay dropped his books on the table in the entry and went down the hall to the utility room.

"How was your day?" Mom asked as she looked up from ironing.

"Terrible!" grumbled Jay angrily. "I failed a math test. I'm up to my neck in homework. Tony, my best friend, is moving. And to top it off, I ran into the principal's daughter in the hall and knocked her down."

"Wow!" Mom said. "Sounds like quite a day."

"Why did it have to be her?" moaned Jay.

Mom shook her head. "I don't know, but I wouldn't worry about it. I'm sure she knows you didn't do it on purpose."

"Is that my club shirt you're ironing?" Jay asked. "I need it *now*. I'm in a hurry."

Mom frowned and offered him the half-ironed shirt.

Jay shook his head. "I'm not in that big a hurry," he said. "I'll wait."

Just then the phone rang. "You can finish ironing it," suggested Mom as she headed for the phone. She grinned. "It will be good practice for when you grow up," she teased.

When Mom returned, Jay proudly held up his just-ironed shirt. "Look at this—wrinkle-free," he said with a grin.

Mom smiled. "The heat and pressure of the iron took the wrinkles out of the shirt," she said, "and God uses the heat of trials and trouble to get the wrinkles out of us, Jay."

"Wrinkles?" Jay repeated as he pulled off his T-shirt. He rubbed his forehead. "I don't have wrinkles yet."

"I'm thinking of wrinkles in our personalities—things like impatience, anger, and self-pity, just to name a few," Mom said. "They need to be 'ironed' out, and God knows just how much 'heat' and pressure is needed to take care of them." *BJW*

HOW ABOUT YOU?

Do you ever feel like you are being pressured on all sides? Remember the iron and the shirt. Be patient as God presses the wrinkles out of you. It may be uncomfortable for a little while, but it will make you a better person.

MEMORIZE:

"But you should keep a clear mind in every situation." 2 Timothy 4:5

ENDURE
DIFFICULTIES
PATIENTLY

THORNY HEDGE (PART 1)

Read: Hebrews 6:7-12

Thad tucked the pink slip of paper into his pocket, ran out the school door, and headed for home. As he walked up his driveway, he noticed that Dad was home early. "Hi, Dad! Let's go toss the football around," Thad called out.

"Well, hello! Okay," agreed Dad with a smile.

A little later, one of Thad's wild throws ended up in the barberry thorn hedge at the back of their yard. Thad went after the ball. "Ouch!" he exclaimed with a frown as a long thorn pricked him. "Dad, you're gonna have to help me get that ball."

Just then Mom appeared at the door. "Thad," she called, "I just got a phone call from your school librarian. She was checking to see if you gave me a note from her today. She said it was the third one she had sent to ask us to help you look for an overdue book. Why haven't I seen any of those notes?"

"Oh, I forgot," Thad said with a shrug. "The note is in my tan jacket. I'll get it later."

"Thad!" exclaimed Mom. "Lately you've become pretty careless about a number of things you know you should do. What's going on?" Thad just shrugged.

Dad frowned. "You'd better straighten up, Son," he said. "Proverbs 15:19 says that the way of the lazy man is like a hedge of thorns." He pointed to the football stuck in the barberry hedge. "That hedge is making it very difficult for us to use your football. And the life of a slothful person makes it difficult for God to use him."

Thad eyed his ball silently. "Yeah . . . okay," he said finally. "Will you help me get the football? Then I better start looking for that book right away." *JAG*

HOW ABOUT YOU?

Are you careless about doing projects or school work? Do you feel it doesn't matter what your room looks like? Is Bible reading and prayer something you plan to do "later," and then you never get to it? Ask God to help you break slothful habits before your way becomes a "hedge of thorns."

STOP LAZY HABITS

2

THORNY HEDGE (PART 2)

Read: Matthew 13:3-9

Thad's dad decided to remove the barberry thorn hedge from their backyard. "All it seems to do is make problems for me, especially when I cut the grass near it," he said. "I'm going to get rid of it."

"I'll help," volunteered Thad.

"Better wear something to protect yourself from the thorns," Dad suggested.

Thad and his dad worked all afternoon removing the large hedge. Before they finished, they both had scratches where their faces and necks had not been covered. "What did God make thorns for?" asked Thad when Mom commented on all their scratches. "What are they good for anyway?"

"Well, actually, they're a result of sin," said Dad. "After Adam and Eve sinned, God told Adam that the ground was cursed and would bring forth thorns and thistles."

Mom nodded. "The Bible speaks of thorns quite often," she said. "The book of Matthew tells how Jesus used them to help explain the gospel message."

"I remember that story," said Thad. "Jesus talked about a man who sowed some seed, and some of it fell in good ground and some fell among the thorns.

"Do you remember what happened to the seed that fell among thorns?" Dad asked.

"Yeah—it never had a chance to really grow."

"That's right, Thad," Dad said. "As Christians, we can compare sin to thorns, because if we let sinful thoughts and habits crowd our minds and our lives, we cannot grow in our Christian lives."

"I don't think I'll ever forget about thorns," said Thad as he looked in the mirror at his stinging scratches. *JAG*

HOW ABOUT YOU?

Did you ever prick yourself with a thorn? That hurt, didn't it? Sins such as lying, stealing, complaining, and quarreling hurt, too. They hurt both God and you. Get rid of "thorns"— sins in your life. They only choke out God's blessings and keep you from growing spiritually.

MEMORIZE:

"The good soil represents the hearts of those who truly accept God's message and produce a huge harvest."
Matthew 13:23

SIN PREVENTS GROWTH

THE LOST JOB

Read: Daniel 3:14-18

Brian knew that his job as a paperboy was on "shaky" ground. It was not that he was bad at the job, but he was the newest carrier. "We might have to cut back one route," his boss explained. "If we do, we'll have to let you go because the others have been working longer."

Brian hoped and prayed that he wouldn't lose his job, but one Friday, it happened. Mr. Powell called him into the office and explained that due to the cutback in circulation, his route was being eliminated.

On Saturday night Brian said, "Dad, I don't see much point in going to church tomorrow. Do I have to go?"

Dad was surprised. "Why don't you want to go, Brian?"

"Oh, I just don't have much faith in God anymore," said Brian. "I've tried to be a good Christian and do things that would please him, but he still let me lose my job. I don't think it's fair!"

Dad reached for his Bible and asked Brian to sit down with him. Turning to the book of Daniel, Dad asked Brian to read chapter three.

"Oh, Dad, I know this story," Brian said after reading just a few verses. "It's about the Hebrews who were put in the fiery furnace. But God didn't let them burn up like he let me lose my job! So it was easy for them to keep their faith."

"I think you should read verses 17 and 18, Brian," said Dad. "Their faith was in God, not in their circumstances. They said that even if God chose to not deliver them, they would not worship the idol. That means they still would worship God."

Brian thought it over, then headed for his room. He turned back with a grin. "Get me up for Sunday school the same as always, okay?" *REP*

HOW ABOUT YOU?

Does your faith in God remain firm in spite of circumstances? If you don't get exactly what you want when you pray, don't let it get you down. God always works for your good, even though sometimes you can't see what good could possibly come from something. Have faith in him no matter what happens.

MEMORIZE:

"The God we serve is able to save us. . . . But even if he does not, we want you to know, O king, that we will not serve your gods."

Daniel 3:17-18, NIV

GOD WORKS FOR YOUR GOOD

4

FLASH KNOWS THE WAY

Ben felt happy and carefree as he and his uncle took off on horseback for a day's hunting trip on Uncle Alan's ranch. But late that afternoon, things changed. Uncle Alan's horse suddenly reared as a pheasant whirled up right under his feet! Experienced though he was, Uncle Alan fell from the horse and broke his leg. "I'll be all right," he assured Ben, "but I can't move. You'll have to ride for help."

"Ride for help!" exclaimed Ben. "It'll be dark soon, and I'll never find my way back to the ranch."

"Flash knows the way," Uncle Alan told him. "Just lay the reins over the saddle horn and don't try to guide him. Even in the darkness, he'll find his way. Just trust the horse. Tell the boys I'm in Coyote Canyon—they'll know where to find me."

Ben started off. It seemed to take a long, long time, and he shivered when he heard coyotes howl. Sometimes he thought Flash was surely going the wrong direction, but even then he didn't touch the reins. He let Flash choose the way. Finally he saw lights in the distance. Soon he was telling his story to Aunt Jenny, and it wasn't long before some of the cowboys were riding off in the night to help Uncle Alan.

"Flash is a great horse," declared Ben after his uncle was safely home. "I just trusted him to bring me home, and he did."

Uncle Alan nodded. "You know, that's a good example of how we all need to trust the Lord," he said. "You couldn't have found the way home by yourself—you had to trust Flash. And none of us can find the way to heaven by ourselves—we need to trust Jesus. He's the only One who can guide us safely there." *HCT*

HOW ABOUT YOU?

There's nothing you can do to find your own way to heaven. The Pharisee (in today's Scripture reading) mentioned all the "good" things he did. But it was the simple prayer of the other man that God heard. If you're not a Christian, make that prayer yours.

MEMORIZE:

"O God, be merciful to me, for I am a sinner." Luke 18:13

TRUST JESUS

THE UNLOVABLE

Read: Matthew 9:10-13

"Dad, I've been thinking about TJ," said Rehman one day. "He doesn't have a single friend. Do you think I should be a friend to him and invite him over? We could . . ."

"Not TJ!" interrupted Rehman's sister, Nena. "He's dirty, and he smells bad. Doesn't his mother ever wash his clothes? If any of my friends found out that he came to our house, I'd die! What would they think of me?"

"Well, Jesus wants us to love everyone," Rehman told her.

"You can be his friend at school," protested Nena. "Just don't invite him here!"

Dad broke into the conversation. "I think Rehman is right, Nena," he said. "Jesus would be friends with TJ, and he'd want Rehman and you to be friendly to him, too."

So the next day Rehman invited TJ over to play. At first TJ couldn't believe Rehman meant it. "Aw, I've always gotten along without friends," he said. "You don't really want me for a friend."

"Sure I do," insisted Rehman. "Come on over."

"You really mean it?" TJ looked at him questioningly.

"Sure." Rehman nodded. "I invited you!"

"Wow! Okay, I'll come," said TJ eagerly. "I just gotta stop home a minute and get my mitt." And he dashed off.

That evening Nena said thoughtfully, "You know, TJ doesn't seem like such a bad guy. I wonder why he usually acts so tough, though."

"I have an idea that he thinks no one's going to like him anyway," suggested Dad, "so he gives them a reason not to like him."

Nena nodded. "I guess I just didn't understand," she said. "You know, I think that's what Jesus did—he took time to understand people." *DKL*

HOW ABOUT YOU?

Do you have a classmate whom nobody seems to like—someone who needs a friend? Will you share a smile and a bit of your time to be friendly?

SHOW GOD'S LOVE

UP, UP, AND AWAY

Read: Philippians 4:6-9

Michael and his father stood in the crowd, waiting to see a group of hot air balloons lift off the ground. "How many balloons are there?" asked Michael.

"I don't know," replied Dad, "but people come from all over to take part in this balloon rally."

Before long, most of the colorful balloons were inflated and had ascended into the sky. As Michael watched, he remembered the day when he and a few friends had gone up in a hot air balloon. The owner, a friend of his father, had kept the balloon anchored to the ground with a long rope because the wind had become gusty, but Michael remembered how it had felt to be floating up towards the clouds.

Dad looked up at the balloons. "Michael, do you know what this event reminds me of?"

"A bird?" said Michael, looking up. "Birds can fly, and so can hot air balloons."

Dad smiled. "Actually, I was thinking of something quite different," he said. "I'm reminded that if we truly give our problems to the Lord, he will lift them from us and carry them away."

"I've heard preachers say something like that," said Michael, "but I don't really see how we give problems to God."

"We allow him to lift our burdens by praying and then trusting him," explained Dad. "Sometimes we pray but fail to trust. We don't let go of our problems but stay attached to them."

"Like when I went up in the hot air balloon that was attached to the ground with a rope?" asked Michael. "I couldn't really float away."

Dad nodded. "We need to remember that the Lord doesn't want us to worry or fret. He cares for us very much, and he can handle our problems. We need to release our fears and trust him to work everything out in the best possible way." *ASB*

HOW ABOUT YOU?

Do you have problems that seem too big to handle? Do you wish they would float away? God wants you to give those problems to him. He knows just how to take care of them. Trust him, and let him lift your burdens and carry them for you.

MEMORIZE:

"Give all your worries and cares to God, for he cares about what happens to you." 1 Peter 5:7

TRUST GOD AND LET HIM LIFT YOUR BURDENS

WARNING SIGNALS

Read: Hebrews 2:1-4

The Miller family was driving to Grandma's house in the country when, suddenly, a red light appeared on the dash. "Oh, no!" moaned Dad, pulling to the side of the road. "We've got a temperature light, and here we are miles from anywhere!"

"A temperature light?" asked Brandon. "Can't you just turn it off? The car seems to be running fine."

"This light doesn't operate on a switch. It's a signal that the car needs something—probably water," said Dad, getting out and opening the hood.

Dad was right. The car did need water, and he was able to get some from a nearby farmhouse. "I'll still have to take it in to see if there's something more wrong with it," he said, "but this will take care of the problem for now."

The next day, the children listened to a program on a Christian radio station. Mom noticed that Brandon listened carefully to the story but squirmed uncomfortably when the application was made. When she questioned him about it, he shrugged, grabbed his coat, and headed outdoors to play.

"Don't ignore warning lights, Brandon," said Mom. He stopped and looked at her. "Remember the red warning light in the car?" Mom asked. "The car needed something, and if Dad had ignored the warning, the engine might have been ruined." She paused. "You have a need in your life too. That's why the stories you hear about Jesus bother you. Running outside to play is like knocking out the temperature light. The need is still there. When that 'red light' goes on in your mind, you need to deal with it, not just ignore it or try to turn it off."

"I guess you're right," Brandon said slowly. "I guess the red light comes on in my mind because I need Jesus in my life." *PMR*

HOW ABOUT YOU?

When you hear an invitation to accept Jesus, do you feel uncomfortable? Could it be a red light going on in your mind telling you that here is something you really need? Accept Jesus.

ACCEPT JESUS

MEMORIZE:
"What makes us think that we can escape if we are indifferent to this great salvation?" Hebrews 2:3

LIVER OF THE TEAM

Read: 1 Corinthians 12:20-27

The moment Tim put on his shoulder pads, he knew the team manager had goofed again. As quarterback, his shoulder pads weren't supposed to flop down to his elbows. A bellow from the other side of the locker room confirmed it. "Where's the manager?" shouted Boomer, the team's biggest lineman. "He's given me the quarterback's teacup pads instead of my own."

Tim laughed as he took off Boomer's pads and threw them to him. "There's only one thing worse than a team manager," growled Boomer as he caught them. "That's a new team manager."

Just then, Barry, the team manager, came over. "Sorry about the mix-up," he said. From the flush on his face, Tim could see Barry was embarrassed.

"Mess up one more time," threatened Boomer, "and I'll throw you in the shower."

Barry's face turned even redder. "Try it," he shot back.

"Quit fighting," said Tim. "A team should be like . . . like . . ." He puckered his forehead, trying to think of a good comparison. "Like a human body," he finished. "When one part fails, the others pitch in."

Barry remarked, "A team manager like me must be the liver of the team then," he said. "I mean, who likes liver?"

"Well, a person can live without an arm or leg," retorted Tim, "but he can't live without a liver!"

A loud groan came from Boomer. He was holding up a torn, dirty jersey. "I forgot to hand this in to be washed," he said. "Coach'll be furious!"

Barry grinned and reached into his equipment bag. He plucked out a clean jersey with Boomer's number on it. Boomer grabbed the shirt gratefully and pulled it on. "Let's go, men," he said, with a grin in Barry's direction. With a whoop, the boys dashed out of the locker room and onto the playing field. *LLZ*

HOW ABOUT YOU?

Do you ever feel unappreciated? Like people don't really notice the good things you do? Don't be discouraged. Even the most hidden parts of the human body are as important as the more "showy" ones. That's especially true in the "body of Christ"—that's another name for Christians.

MEMORIZE:

"Since we are all one body in Christ, we belong to each other, and each of us needs all the others." Romans 12:5

YOU ARE NEEDED

STORY OF A PRETZEL

Read: Philippians 4:4-9

Kyle took out a small bag of pretzels at recess. He offered one to his teacher. "Why, thank you," said Miss Gates. "Do you know why pretzels were invented? I read about it just the other day. I'm not sure how accurate the story is, but it was interesting. I'll share it with the class when recess is over."

When the bell rang, Miss Gates gathered the children and told the story. "Many years ago," she began, "the children in a church in Italy had to memorize certain prayers. They were being rather slow about it, so the monk (who is like a pastor) of that church decided that maybe if he rewarded them for learning, they would work harder at it. Guess what he gave them?"

"Candy," guessed one of his classmates.

"That's what we'd probably give today," said Miss Gates, "but this monk gave them a small biscuit shaped like a pair of praying hands. It was called a 'pretiola,' which really means 'little gift.' These little biscuits fascinated people traveling through the area, and soon they started making them in Germany, too. There the people glazed and salted them, and they became very popular. They were introduced to the United States by the German people, and guess what we call them today?"

Kyle raised his hand. "Pretzels!" he said.

Miss Gates smiled. "Right," she said, "and now they're popular in America, too." She paused, then added, "Whenever we see a pretzel, I think we should be reminded of something very important. What do you suppose it is?" She waited, but no hands were raised. "Think of how they were originally used," prompted Miss Gates.

"They should remind us to pray?" timidly ventured one of the girls.

Miss Gates smiled. "That's right," she said. "The privilege of prayer is a wonderful blessing." *HWM*

HOW ABOUT YOU?

Do you pray throughout the day? You don't have to be in church. You can talk to God at your desk, on your bike, or anywhere. You can tell him anything. He hears and he cares.

PRAY ANYWHERE

RIGHT SIDE UP

Read: Matthew 6:25-34

Lee took a bite of chicken. "How come there are so many sour Christians?" he asked. "You should have seen the scowl Mrs. Chang gave me today."

"It's too bad Christians get so caught up in what's going on in the world that they forget to enjoy the peace and joy available to them," agreed Dad.

"It's not just the adults either," added Mom.

"Wadah!" demanded two-year-old Davy. He wasn't at all interested in this discussion. "Wadah! Wadah!" he said, pounding his glass.

"Be patient," said Lee, picking up the water pitcher to pour water into the glass Davy was holding. Just as the water spilled out of the pitcher, Davy heard a fire truck outside. As he turned to look out the window, he moved his glass. Instead of going into the glass, the water poured onto the floor. "Davy!" exclaimed Lee. "Look what you've done!"

As Mom mopped up the water, Dad turned to Lee. "When Davy was interested in something else, he turned his glass away from the pitcher," he said. "And when Christians get too interested in the things of this world, they tend to turn away from God. Then they aren't in a position to receive his blessings."

Lee was thoughtful. "But we can't sit around just thinking about God all day," he protested. "We need to go to school, for example. And is there anything wrong with playing with friends or reading a book?"

"No," said Dad, "but when we spend time with God, try to live as he wants us to, and think of him often throughout the day, we're turned toward him. Then we can be filled with his joy and peace, no matter what our circumstances." *HWM*

HOW ABOUT YOU?

Are you "turned" toward God? There's nothing wrong with riding your bike or enjoying your toys. It's okay to wear nice clothes and live in a nice home. But none of the "things" you have are as important as your relationship with the Lord.

MEMORIZE:

"Seek first the kingdom of God and His righteousness." Matthew 6:33, NKJV

PUT GOD FIRST

BETTER THAN CHOCOLATE CAKE

Read: Psalm 33:12-22

"Jameel and Blake, how about coming in for some dessert?"

"Sounds great, Mom!" said Jameel as they came in. "We were having fun playing Civil War, and Blake was a Redcoat!"

"You have your wars mixed up," Mom told him. "It was the Revolutionary War that our country fought against the British Redcoats for independence. We're thankful for those who were willing to fight or die so we can live in this free nation! Now come have a snack."

Dad joined the boys as Mom served chocolate cake and tall glasses of cold milk. "Did you ever go to war, Mr. Hopkins?" asked Blake.

Dad nodded. "I sure did, and it's an experience I hope you boys will never have to face," he answered. "The war did teach me a couple of things, though. Can you guess what they are?"

"How to march?" asked Blake. Dad shook his head.

"I know," grinned Jameel. "You learned what a good cook Mom is—you missed her chocolate cake."

Dad laughed out loud. "That's true," he agreed, "but a more important thing I learned was how much my family means to me—and how much my country means to me. Even with all its problems, there's no place quite like our home country. We have been blessed with food, clothes, cars, houses, and . . ."

"And chocolate cake," interrupted Jameel.

Dad nodded as they all laughed. "Even better than chocolate cake is the freedom we have to go where we want, to be what we want—and especially the freedom to worship God as we choose," he said. *HWM*

HOW ABOUT YOU?

Have you thanked God for your country? Have you prayed for your president and other leaders? Thank God for freedom, and pray that America will turn anew to God and continue to be blessed.

PRAY FOR YOUR
COUNTRY

CRAB FISHING

Read: 2 Timothy 2:19-26

Mike and his friend Emma were standing in water up to their knees as Mike's dad gave instructions for crab fishing. "Here, Mike," said Dad, "tie a chicken neck to one end of your string, and tie the other end around your ankle."

"Why would those crabs want to eat a raw chicken neck?" asked Emma.

"I don't know, but they'll go for it," replied Dad. "Now, Mike, throw the chicken neck out as far as you can. Wait a few minutes. Then start pulling in the line real slowly so the crabs don't get scared off." Dad turned to Emma. "Wait till the crabs come close, then scoop them up with this net."

Sure enough, Mike soon felt something tugging on the line as he pulled. "I see them!" yelled Emma.

"Wait till you can reach them with your net," cautioned Dad. "Then drop it right behind them. They'll see you and run backwards right into the net." And that's exactly what happened.

"Wow!" the kids yelled. "Three at once!" They put the crabs in a bucket, then started fishing for more.

On the way home, the kids talked about school. "Whoever wrote on the restroom walls is going to be in big trouble," said Mike.

"Yeah," agreed Emma. "And those students who got caught smoking are in big trouble already."

"Sounds like Satan is fishing in your school like we've been doing in the ocean today," said Dad.

Emma laughed. "I didn't see any chicken necks there."

"No," replied Dad, "but Satan is using things to lead kids into trouble. Remember the crabs? When they were being pulled in with the chicken lure, they missed the danger because they were too intent on having what they wanted. By the time they sensed danger and began to run, it was too late. And if you play around with temptation and sin, you can end up in Satan's trap." *SKV*

HOW ABOUT YOU?

Do you find that sinful things often look like innocent fun? That's what Satan wants you to believe. Don't be fooled into thinking there's no danger ahead. Get your eyes off the temptation; walk away before Satan lowers the net.

MEMORIZE:

"Then they will come to their senses and escape from the Devil's trap. For they have been held captive by him to do whatever he wants." 2 Timothy 2:26

DON'T "PLAY AROUND" WITH TEMPTATION

IT PAYS TO ADVERTISE

Read: 2 Corinthians 3:2-6

Darrin's father slammed on the brakes, barely missing the van that passed him and then cut in front of him. "That man almost got my front fender!" Dad exclaimed. "I've been watching him in the mirror—he's been darting in and out of traffic like a maniac."

"Pipes-A-Plenty Plumbing," Darrin read, gathering his scattered books. "For fast, courteous service, call now."

"His driving isn't helping his business," Dad said.

At the dinner table that evening, the family discussed the day's events. Dad told about the van. "If that fellow keeps driving like that, he'll soon lose all his business," he concluded.

"I guess so!" agreed Mom. "He's a bad advertisement for his business by driving that way."

Dad nodded. "You know, I've often thought how we, as Christians, are advertising everywhere we go. We advertise by all the things we do or say," he said. "If we're kind and Christlike, it's a good advertisement for Jesus. If we're hurtful and dishonest, it's a bad advertisement."

Mom turned to Darrin. "How was your day?" she asked.

"We had a hard test at school, and I think everyone cheated except Heather and Omar and me. So now we'll get the lowest grades," complained Darrin.

"Well, we're proud of you, anyway," said Mom. "It's more important to do what's right."

Dad nodded. "By refusing to cheat today, Darrin, you and Heather and Omar advertised in a good way," he said.

The next afternoon Darrin came home beaming. "Guess what?" he said. "They say it pays to advertise, and it's true! Everyone who cheated got an F— Mr. Phillips knew what was happening. After class, he asked Heather, Omar, and me why we didn't cheat. We told him we're Christians." *AU*

HOW ABOUT YOU?

What kind of advertisement for God are you? The way you treat others could make them want to know more about your faith. Be careful how you advertise.

ADVERTISE FOR
JESUS

MEMORIZE:
"Clearly, you are a letter from Christ prepared by us." 2 Corinthians 3:3

October

14

THE GANG (PART 1)

Read: Matthew 9:10-13

"You know what's happening at school?" Alishuwan asked in Sunday school one day. "A new boy, Jerry Stone, is trying to form a gang. He's always causing trouble." Mr. Carrilli, the Sunday school teacher, looked thoughtful as some of the other boys made comments about the new gang Jerry was trying to get together. "What can we do about it?" the boys wanted to know.

"Well, let's talk this over a bit more," suggested Mr. Carrilli. "Give me your ideas—what do you think you can do to keep this gang from causing trouble? Any ideas, Brad?"

"Well, there wouldn't be a gang if nobody would hang around with Jerry," suggested Brad.

Mr. Carrilli smiled. "True," he agreed, "but even if all the boys in this class refuse to hang around with him, there are others who would. Any more suggestions?"

Sarah raised her hand. "Couldn't we get Jerry sent to another school?" she asked.

Mr. Carrilli shook his head. "No," he said, "but even if you could, would it really help to send your problem to another school? No, I believe you can lick this problem here."

Will spoke up. "Since the kids who join this gang are those who need friends, maybe we could include them more in our friendships," he suggested. "We could walk along to class with them and even invite them to parties and stuff. We could do that with Jerry, too. I guess he's just so different that we're afraid of him. Maybe he's forming this gang in self-defense."

That was the kind of answer Mr. Carrilli was looking for. "You have the right idea, Will," he said. "I'm not suggesting that you become best friends with them, but it is important to make others feel needed and wanted." *AU*

HOW ABOUT YOU?

Has it occurred to you that the kids you would normally avoid may be just the ones Jesus wants you to befriend? The Bible says Jesus ate with sinners, but he did not participate in any of the sinful things they did. Perhaps you, too, should be friendly to them. But make sure you don't join them in sinful activities. Pray about it and see what God would have you do.

MEMORIZE:

"I have come to call sinners, not those who think they are already good enough." Matthew 9:13

THE GANG (PART 2)

Read: 1 Corinthians 9:19-23

"Our Sunday school class is going to try to befriend the kids in the new gang at school," Will told his father. "I'm going to see if I can get Jerry to come—he's the gang leader."

"Good." Dad nodded. "I'll be praying with you, Son. It may not be easy. Jerry may laugh at you."

Dad was right—Jerry was hostile. Will began by offering to study with Jerry for an upcoming history test. Jerry eyed him suspiciously and snarled, "When I want your help, I'll ask for it!" Next, Will walked to class with Jerry a few times. He thought Jerry was beginning to act more friendly, so Will invited him to church. "Go to church? Oh, sure. That's just what I was hoping to do," mocked Jerry. "Tell you what, Will—I'll go with you on Sunday morning if you'll join our gang on Sunday night. Fair enough?"

"N-n-no," stammered Will. "I'm sorry, but I can't join your gang." Will was getting discouraged.

One day when Dad came home from work, he found Will waiting impatiently. "Can you teach me about your stamp collection right away, Dad?" he asked.

"Well, now, hold on a minute," said Dad in surprise. "I'll be glad to get it out right after supper, but why this sudden interest?"

"Well, see . . . I was trying to think how I could make friends with Jerry," explained Will, "and I remembered a sermon that told how the apostle Paul became 'all things to all men' in order to bring them to Jesus. I heard Jerry mention his stamp collection, and I figure if learning about stamps will help win Jerry to Jesus, that's the least I can do. I told him about your collection, and he wants to see it. I'll study up on it a little and then ask him over . . . if that's okay with you, Dad."

Dad smiled. "It's 'A-OK,' " he agreed. *AU*

HOW ABOUT YOU?

Are you having trouble making friends with someone? Is there something that person especially enjoys, such as a collection or a certain game or activity? Even if that's not your special interest, would you be willing to spend time at it, and do it cheerfully?

WITNESS
THROUGH
FRIENDSHIP

October

16

Read: James 1:2-4; 1 Peter 1:6-7

"No job yet, Dad?" asked Colin when he got home from school. Dad looked up from working on his car and shook his head. Colin sighed. Ever since he and his dad became Christians, things had seemed to go from bad to worse. His father had been laid off. But he hadn't been able to find another job, and it was almost a month since they'd had a regular income. Colin was worried and he was sure Dad must be, too.

One day Colin's Sunday school teacher gave him a part-time job helping in his carpenter shop after school. Colin was delighted. As he worked one day, he noticed a big difference in the wood used for the various cabinets Mr. Warter was making. "Mr. Warter, why is the grain in some of the wood so smooth and straight, and other wood has circles and twists in it?" Colin asked.

"Which do you like best?" Mr. Warter wanted to know.

"I like the grain that has variations in it—the one with the circles and twists. But what makes the difference in the grain?" Colin asked again.

"The part you think is pretty is called a burl, or knot," Mr. Warter replied. "It's caused by a problem in the life of the tree. Sometimes insects invade a certain section of the tree, causing a burl. Other times, it's caused by a disease the tree had." He smiled. "Isn't it interesting, Colin, that God takes the problems a tree has and turns them into beautiful burls in the wood?" he asked. "And even more wonderful—God takes the problems in our lives and turns them into something beautiful, too." One of the beautiful "burls" developing in Colin's and his father's lives was that of patience. *AU*

HOW ABOUT YOU?

Do you find it hard to understand why problems come into your life? When your dog dies, your best friend moves, or when you can't afford the things you want, trust God. He is doing something wonderful in your life.

MEMORIZE:

"For when your faith is tested, your endurance has a chance to grow."
James 1:3

PROBLEMS TEACH
PATIENCE

OUT TO WIN

Read: 2 Timothy 2:1-5

"I'm going to win!" Darien told himself as he studied the checkerboard on the table. Jumping three of his grandmother's red checkers, he flashed her a smile of victory.

But Darien's smile faded when his grandmother jumped two of his black checkers and landed in King's Row. "Crown me!" she said with a gleam of triumph.

"I quit!" Darien muttered. He shoved back his chair and jumped up to leave.

"Young man, don't be a quitter!" his mother ordered. "Sit back down and finish your game."

Darien frowned and slumped back down in his chair. With a sullen look, he made his next move. After a few more moves, Darien's face lit up as he saw a way to take out all his grandmother's checkers.

"Crown me, Grandma! I won!" he crowed.

Grandma smiled. "Darien," she said later while they waited for a pizza to bake, "it's a good thing you didn't quit when things weren't going your way, because you won in the end. That reminds me of my life as a Christian. If I hang in there, loving and serving God, King Jesus will crown me with a crown of righteousness. We have to continue doing God's will, even when life seems to be unfair or unpleasant. We may feel at times that we're losing the battle, but the Bible tells us we will win in the end." *NIM*

HOW ABOUT YOU?

Do you sometimes feel left out because you don't do some of the things other kids do—like laughing at dirty jokes, ignoring your parents, or going to unsupervised parties? Hang in there for what you know is right.

DON'T EVER GIVE UP

A LESSON FROM THE LAWN

Read: Psalm 119:129-136

"Mark, I have a little work you can do for me," said Mom. She handed him the smallest of the two rakes she was carrying. "I'd like you to help me rake the lawn."

Mark dropped the head of his rake onto the lawn and began raking. As the grass tangled around the tines, it was hard to pull. He tugged harder, and the rake moved a few inches. "Why do we have to do this?" he asked.

Mom put her rake down. "I'll show you why," she said, kneeling on a spot she had already raked. Mark knelt beside her. "See how much cleaner the area is after the rubbish is gone."

Mark nodded. "The grass looks like it's reaching for the sun."

"It is," Mom agreed, "and since the sun no longer needs to find a way around the rubbish, the grass will grow stronger and thicker." Thought wrinkles appeared on Mom's forehead. "You know," she said at last, "this lawn is a lot like our lives as Christians."

Mark looked puzzled. "How?"

"Dead leaves from last fall and other winter trash in the lawn are like the sins we allow in our lives," explained Mom. "The rubbish keeps the new grass from getting the sunshine it needs, and sin in our lives keeps us from receiving the light of God's Word."

"When you say 'God's light,' do you mean the Bible?" asked Mark.

"I do," replied Mom. "The 'light' we get from the Bible gives us wisdom in knowing how to live for God. When we allow the rubbish of sin in our lives, we're not as ready to hear and do what God tells us. God's Word makes us aware of sin, and a prayer of confession starts the 'raking' process. If we're sincere, we'll not only confess our sin, but 'forsake' it." *ECM*

HOW ABOUT YOU?

Do you allow the clutter of sin in your life? Is the Word of God shining into your heart and life—perhaps convicting you of sin? If so, confess it. Then you will be able to grow spiritually.

MEMORIZE:

"As your words are taught, they give light." Psalm 119:130

OPEN YOUR HEART TO GOD'S WORD

WARNING! WINDOW HERE!

Read: Psalm 19:7-13

"Oh, no! That bird flew into the glass!" exclaimed Zachary after hearing a thud at the window. He turned to his father. "I hope he's okay!"

Dad and Zachary got up from the table and went over to the large plateglass window. "I don't see him," said Dad as they looked down at the ground. "I guess he must be okay—apparently okay enough to fly away, anyhow."

"Well, I think we should put up a poster or something to warn the birds that there's a window here," said Zachary. "They can't see the clear glass."

Dad smiled. "What should it say?" he asked.

"Dad! You know they can't read," protested Zachary. "It would just have to be something big and bright."

"Yes. Well, I'm afraid your mother would object to that kind of sign on her front window," said Dad.

Zachary nodded. "I guess so," he agreed.

"You know, we're like that bird sometimes," said Dad thoughtfully.

"We are?" asked Zachary. "How?"

"There are dangerous things in life that we don't see, either," replied Dad. "There's a difference, though—we don't know quite how to warn those birds, but someone does warn us of many dangers. God often warns us." Dad smiled at Zachary. "Do you know how he does that?"

"Well . . . ah . . . my Sunday school teacher warned us about some bad shows on TV," said Zachary. "Is that how God warns us? Through our teachers?"

"That's one way," Dad replied. "God often uses people to warn us, but he also speaks to us through his Word—the Bible. He quietly impresses something upon our hearts and minds as we think about what he has said. Always remember that when God warns you, you need to pay attention!" *KRL*

HOW ABOUT YOU?

Do you pay attention when God uses parents, teachers, or his Word to warn you about something? God sees dangers that you can't see. Avoid hurt and heartache by listening to his warnings and obeying him.

PAY ATTENTION
TO GOD'S
WARNINGS

MEMORIZE:

"[God's laws] are a warning to those who hear them; there is great reward for those who obey them."

Psalm 19:11

OUT OF BALANCE

Read: Luke 2:42-62

"And Jesus increased in wisdom and stature, and in favor with God and man," read Dad during family devotions one evening. He closed the Bible.

"Jesus was well-balanced," observed Mom.

Patrick laughed. "I think you have balance on the brain," he teased. Due to an inner ear problem, Mom had been very dizzy and unable to keep her balance the day before.

Mom grinned. "I sure found out how important balance is," she agreed.

"And you think Jesus could walk without almost falling over?" asked Elena, but she knew that wasn't really what Mom meant.

Dad smiled. "Jesus was well-balanced in the way he was growing and developing," he said. "He 'increased in wisdom'—that's growing mentally."

"Brain power," said Patrick with a grin. "And growing 'in stature' means he grew physically, right?"

Dad nodded. "He was 'in favor with God,' and that tells of his good relationship with God. His growth 'in favor with man' shows that he developed socially and got along well with others."

"Right. He lived a well-balanced life. He's our perfect example," said Mom. "Too much of one thing and not enough of another will throw you off-balance and cause you to fail. For example, people may be very smart, but it will not make them happy if they can't get along with other people."

"Yeah—like you, Elena," said Patrick. Elena did very well in school, but she recently seemed to have problems with the other kids in her class.

"Look who's talking!" grumbled Elena. "All you ever do is work at your bodybuilding stuff. You have strong muscles but a weak brain."

"That will do," said Dad sternly. "Instead of criticizing one another, each of you should be thinking about how you can develop balance in your own life. And don't forget the spiritual side." *BJW*

HOW ABOUT YOU?

Are you well-balanced? Do you eat well, get enough rest and exercise, enjoy and help people, and learn about and serve God? Check to see what you need to do to achieve a good balance to grow physically, socially, mentally, and spiritually.

MEMORIZE:

"So Jesus grew both in height and in wisdom, and he was loved by God and by all who knew him." Luke 2:52

BE WELL-BALANCED

ON BECOMING FOSSILS

Read: 2 Corinthians 4:7-16

Randy rushed into the house and dropped his books. "Look at this!" he said, holding out a fossilized bone. "My teacher said I could borrow it to show Great-Grandpa Parks. Can I show it to him today?"

Mom smiled. "We'll go over there right after supper."

"Mrs. Patterson says only one out of millions of bones becomes a fossil," Randy told his mother. "They have to be buried in just the right minerals. As the bones decay, the minerals seep into the pores, and bit by bit they replace the bone until there's no bone left, just hard, strong rock mineral."

"Really? Grandpa will love to hear about that," Mom said. "I bet his neighbor, Mr. Wyatt, would like to see that fossil and hear about it, too."

"I doubt it," mumbled Randy. "He doesn't like anything—or anybody." Randy frowned. "He's too grumpy!" he added. "I know he's old, but Grandpa Parks isn't grumpy like that, and he's even older than Mr. Wyatt."

Mom thought for a moment. "Grandpa is a lot like that fossil," she said. "All through his life, Grandpa let God's Word and God's love seep into his heart. Like minerals filled and replaced the materials of the bones, God's goodness filled Grandpa with love, joy, and peace. Now he's growing weak and tired and is starting to forget things, but God's Spirit is evident in him."

"And it isn't in Mr. Wyatt, right?" asked Randy.

"It doesn't seem to be," said Mom. "As far as we know, Mr. Wyatt never let God into his life. He never let God's goodness replace his old self."

Randy looked at the fossil. "Maybe I should show this to Mr. Wyatt," he decided. He looked at Mom anxiously. "But will you tell him how God changes us like minerals change bones?"

"Sure," Mom agreed, smiling. *HMT*

HOW ABOUT YOU?

What things are seeping into you? Is God's goodness replacing your old self? Don't become like an old bone—become like a strong fossil by being buried in the right "minerals" as you read your Bible, pray, enjoy Christian fellowship, and obey God.

LET GOD FILL
YOUR LIFE

MEMORIZE:
"Though our bodies are dying, our spirits are being renewed every day."
2 Corinthians 4:16

A GOOD RULE

Read: Luke 6:27-31

"A deal's a deal," insisted William, laughing—but Grant didn't laugh. After buying a computer from William the day before, Grant had discovered that it didn't work. William refused to return his money, and Grant was angry.

Several days later, William went with his father to the store. As he was looking over some movies, he saw that Grant was there, too. William joined his dad at the counter, hoping Grant wouldn't see him. Grant spotted them and walked over to where William stood with his dad. "Hey, William," said Grant with a scowl, "got another busted computer?"

As Grant angrily strode away, Dad asked, "What was that about?"

"I sold Grant my old computer," said William. "He wants his money back, but after all, a deal's a deal."

"You didn't tell him it didn't work?" asked Dad.

"He didn't ask," mumbled William.

Dad frowned. "How would you feel if someone did that to you?" he asked.

"It would never happen," said William.

"Don't be so sure," warned Dad. "You said you and Tad Cates are trading baseball cards, right? You already gave him a couple of yours, and he's going to bring his to school on Monday?"

"Yeah . . . so?" asked William suspiciously.

"I saw Mr. Cates a few minutes ago," said Dad. "He mentioned that the dog got hold of Tad's cards."

"If they're the ones he's promised to give me, he's going to have to give mine back!" exclaimed William.

"Isn't a deal a deal?" asked Dad. William looked at the floor. "I think you can see that you need to start practicing a principle Jesus gave us," said Dad. "He said, 'Do for others what you would like them to do for you,' " said Dad. "And, by the way, it was football cards the dog chewed!" *WAW*

HOW ABOUT YOU?

Do you follow the "Golden Rule"? When someone needs help, looks lonely, or attempts to join a game or conversation, do you think about how you'd like to be treated if you were the "new" person?

MEMORIZE:

"Do for others what you would like them to do for you." Matthew 7:12

CHANGE NEEDED

Read: Psalm 19:12-14

"I'm glad you're letting me help repair this horse stall," said Eric as he joined his father in their small barn. "I love to pound nails." Just then a large striped cat jumped from the hayloft to Eric's shoulder. "Hey, cat," exclaimed Eric, "do you want to help us fix this stall?" Laughing, he picked up his hammer. "Tell me what to do, Dad," he said.

After getting his instructions and working several minutes, Eric missed the nail he was using and hit his thumb instead. Without thinking, he muttered a swear word—one often used by kids at school.

"Eric!" exclaimed Dad sternly.

"Uh . . . Dad . . . I . . . I don't usually say those words," Eric muttered. "You've never heard me say them before!"

"*I* may not have heard them," admitted Dad, "but how about the kids you play with at school? Have they heard you use words like that?"

Eric looked down without speaking. He knew he sometimes used the same kind of language he often heard other kids use. "I'll do better," he mumbled.

"Good," said Dad, "but think about the cat we saw a little while ago. It has stripes, right? And it can't change that. There's a Bible verse that reminds us that just like we can't change the color of our skin, and an animal—a leopard, in the verse—can't change its markings, we can't do good when we're doing evil. I think that principle applies to the language we use. When you're in the habit of using bad words, they sometimes slip out when you don't intend for them to do so. I'm glad you want to repair that bad habit, but you need God's help with that. Ask him to help you control your language." *AJS*

HOW ABOUT YOU?

What words do you use? Be honest! If you swear or use bad language, confess it to God. Ask him to help you change that bad habit. You can't change yourself, but he can change you.

NEVER USE
SWEAR WORDS

MEMORIZE:

"Can an Ethiopian change the color of his skin? Can a leopard take away its spots? Neither can you start doing good, for you always do evil."

Jeremiah 13:23

24

LOST INHERITANCE (PART 1)

Read: Luke 17:26-30

Henri came into the family room where his parents were watching the news. Together they listened to the report of a man trying to collect a large inheritance. "If that man's parents are dead, why can't he get the money that was left?" asked Henri.

"He ran away from home when he was 16 years old," Dad explained. "That was 30 years ago, and he never contacted his family again. Apparently his parents did discover what area of the country he had gone to, and they made repeated efforts throughout the years to contact him, but he wouldn't respond."

"But now that he's back, won't he get at least some of the money?" asked Henri.

Dad shook his head. "It doesn't sound like it. I guess his parents gave up and decided not to leave him anything. They didn't put him in their wills. Now, after they've both died, he has finally shown up. He thinks he should have the inheritance, but now it's too late. He contested the will, but the courts upheld it. They said he wasn't entitled to anything."

"Wow!" exclaimed Henri. "According to that news report, he claims that he always intended to come back sometime. I bet he's sorry now that he didn't come sooner."

"He's learned a hard lesson," said Dad. "Do you realize that something similar happens every day?"

"You mean there are lots of people who leave home and ignore their parents and aren't left any money?" asked Henri.

"That happens often enough," said Dad, "but what I really meant is that God calls people to believe in him, yet many ignore him." *HMT*

HOW ABOUT YOU?

Will you be able to claim the great inheritance God offers to all who trust in Jesus? He's offering something far better than money—salvation and a home in heaven for all eternity. Receive Jesus as Savior. Then he'll be able to say, "I know you! Welcome home!"

MEMORIZE:

"The Lord knows those who are his."
2 Timothy 2:19

LOST INHERITANCE (PART 2)

Read: Romans 10:13-15

When Henri came home from school, he had some exciting news. "Guess what happened at school today!" he said. "We got a new kid in our class, and you'll never guess where he came from!" Henri paused and waited to see what his mother would say.

"Well, where?" asked Mom after a moment. "You said I'd never guess, and I believe you, so tell me."

"From Melville, Texas," said Henri. "That's the city that guy lived in—the one who came back hoping to get an inheritance, but his parents had left him out of their wills, and he . . . "

"Whoa! Slow down," said Mom. "I remember! Did the boy in your class know that man personally?"

Henri shook his head. "No, but I thought it was interesting that he came from the same town."

Mom nodded. "If you had known the man we heard about in the news, and if you also had known his parents when they were alive, what would you have done?"

"What would I have done?" repeated Henri. "Well . . . I would have told him his parents were looking for him and that he'd better contact them."

"Good," said Mom. "Then it would have been up to him to decide what to do. Now, Henri, I'd like you to tell me something else. Do you think there's anybody you know that your heavenly Father would like to have contact him?"

"Lots of people," admitted Henri. "I guess I should do the same thing for them, shouldn't I? I should let them know that God wants them to trust in Jesus."

"It's something we all should do," agreed Mom. "In a way, they're runaways from God, and we should warn them to contact their Father." *HMT*

HOW ABOUT YOU?

Do you have friends who aren't Christians? Do you think of them as runaways from God? He wants them to come to him, and he may want you to be the one to tell them. Will you help point the runaways toward home?

TELL OTHERS ABOUT JESUS

LIKE A BADGER (PART 1)

Read: Romans 12:9-18

"Hey, this animal is cool!" said Caleb, looking up from his magazine.

Kate peered over his shoulder. "Oooh! A badger! Isn't he cute?"

"You say 'cute' for everything!" protested Caleb. "When I say cool, I mean it's interesting, not cute!"

Kate sniffed. "Well, I think that badger is cute," she insisted, "but what do you find so interesting about it?"

"Well, according to this article, badgers' homes are underground, and they're interconnected by a whole maze of burrows and passages," said Caleb.

"Hey, that is cool," agreed Kate. "That means they can visit each other."

Caleb nodded. "This says that badgers are nocturnal animals." He grinned. "That means . . ."

"I know what that means," said Kate. "It means they are awake at night and sleep during the day."

"You got it!" said Caleb. "Listen to this: 'If a badger is away from home when day breaks, he may stay and rest with another badger family for a while before heading for his own home.'"

Kate laughed. "Maybe the ones traveling are missionary badgers, and the ones they stay with are like our family," she joked. "Remember when those missionaries stayed with us?"

Caleb grinned. "There's more," he said. "It says here that sometimes the badgers even allow a fox to stay over! I haven't seen you entertain any foxes lately."

"Oh, I don't know," said Kate. "That's like . . . that's like . . . I can't think of anything that it's like."

"I can," said Caleb. "That might be like inviting someone you don't know very well—like those new kids who have started coming to Bible club—to come over and play."

"Better not let them hear you comparing them to foxes," said Kate, "but you're probably right. We'd be practicing hospitality." *MTF*

HOW ABOUT YOU?

Do you practice hospitality both with friends and with kids you don't know well? Make each one feel welcome and wanted.

MEMORIZE:

"Get into the habit of inviting guests home for dinner or, if they need lodging, for the night." Romans 12:13

PRACTICE HOSPITALITY

LIKE A BADGER (PART 2)

Read: Romans 12:4-8

"I found out more about badgers," announced Kate as the family sat down to dinner. "I checked out the encyclopedia."

"I can't imagine you bothering with heavy stuff like research," teased Caleb.

"I know I'm not as good as you at intellectual stuff, but I'm better at sports than you are," said Kate. "Anyway, have you ever heard of a ratel?" Caleb, Mom, and Dad all shook their heads. "It's a small animal, like a badger, and it's sometimes called the 'honey badger,' " Kate told them.

"Because it likes honey?" guessed Caleb.

"Right!" said Kate. "The honey badger has a bird-friend called the 'honey guide.' When the honey guide discovers a beehive full of honey, it calls the honey badger and leads the way to the hive. Then the honey badger uses its claws to break open the hive, and it enjoys a treat of lovely, sticky honey while the honey guide patiently waits."

"Doesn't the honey guide get to eat some of the honey, too?" asked Caleb. Kate shook her head. "Well, eating up all the honey isn't a friendly thing to do!" declared Caleb. "I don't think the honey badgers are very hospitable."

"The honey guide doesn't want the honey," said Kate. "It likes the beeswax and larvae, and that's what the honey badger leaves behind."

"Interesting," said Mom. "Each one helps the other."

Dad nodded. "It's another example of how the Lord has blessed each one with different gifts and talents," he said. "That seems to be true both in the animal kingdom and among humans. Some people are blessed with musical ability. Some are good at sports. Some have the gift of helping others. God wants us to use our gifts, not just for our own benefit, but also to serve one another." *MTF*

HOW ABOUT YOU?

What special talent, skill, or ability has God given you? Think about it. There is something you do well. Use that ability to help someone. Can you visit, share your things, give money, listen, pray, or lend a helping hand?

USE THE TALENT GOD GAVE YOU

MEMORIZE:
"Do not neglect the spiritual gift within you." 1 Timothy 4:14, NASB

"I wonder why geese always fly in a V-formation," said Sam as he and his father trudged through the tall grass around Grandpa's pond. Overhead, a flock of geese honked their way southward.

"When I was a boy out here on the farm, I used to wonder about that, too," replied Dad. "Do you see how closely they fly together? I've read that as each bird flaps its wings, it creates an uplift for the bird following it, and that by flying in this V-formation, the whole flock has about a 70 percent greater flying range than if each one flew alone."

"Hey, that's cool!" exclaimed Sam. "Smart birds!"

The next evening, there was a special meeting at church for the young people in Sam's age group. "Are you ready to go?" asked Mom.

"Oh, no! I forgot all about it," said Sam. "Joe and I planned to work with his new chemistry set tonight."

"I think," said Mom, "that you'll have to call Joe and tell him you can't come."

Sam groaned. "Do I have to?" he asked. "Our church group is going to finish plans for our next service project, and I already know what I'm supposed to do for that."

Dad put down the newspaper. "Sam, remember the geese we saw yesterday—and how they cooperated with one another by flying in formation?" Sam nodded. "Their cooperation helped all of them," continued Dad. "We need that kind of cooperation in Christian circles, too. You're one of the 'flock' that makes up your youth group, so even if you don't need the group tonight, they need you." He paused, then added, "But actually, you need each other."

"Well, I suppose I better go then," said Sam with a sigh. A moment later, he grinned as he added, "Each of us birds has to do his part." *RCW*

HOW ABOUT YOU?
Do you realize that regular attendance at church activities is important? Your commitment to "the flock" could very well inspire others.

MEMORIZE:
"Two are better than one because they have a good return for their labor."
Ecclesiastes 4:9, NASB

COOPERATE WITH OTHER CHRISTIANS

MYSTERIOUS NOISES

Read: Psalm 118:5-9

It was later than usual as Dave and Jordan walked home from their youth meeting at church. Their country home wasn't far from the church, but the last several yards were rather lonely since there was only one other house besides theirs. "Boy, it's sure getting dark," said Jordan nervously. "Let's run!" As the boys ran toward home, they heard a loud rustling in the underbrush at the edge of their driveway. "Run faster!" yelled Jordan.

The boys raced into the house, slammed the door, and locked it. "Whoa, boys!" said Dad. "What's the problem?"

"You know those bushes at the edge of our driveway?" asked Jordan excitedly. "We heard something coming after us."

"Some of the neighbors' chickens got loose earlier. Maybe I'd better go investigate." Dad headed out the door with his flashlight, the two scared boys cowering behind him. Reaching the bushes, they stopped and listened. Soon they heard the same noise the boys had heard. Dad turned the light toward a bush in time to see two rabbits scampering away. "Well, boys, that's probably what was after you," said Dad.

"I wouldn't have been so scared if you'd been walking home from church with us," said Dave as the trio headed home.

Dad put an arm around each boy as they headed back indoors. "I'll do everything I can to protect you, boys," he said, "but I want you to remember that only God can keep you truly safe. A Christian doesn't need to have that terrible fear some people experience. We should always be careful, of course, but as Christians, we don't need to be fearful! Even if something we would call 'bad' does happen to us, we can still trust the Lord, because he knows what's best for us." *PMR*

HOW ABOUT YOU?

Are there times when you're afraid? Maybe it's dogs, the dark, strange sounds, or bullies in the neighborhood that frighten you. God is greater than anyone or anything. He can help you to be "careful but not fearful."

BE CAREFUL— NOT FEARFUL

October

30

"Look out!" yelled Cody as his sister stumbled over a chair. "You're as blind as a bat, Mara!"

Mara tossed her head. "Bats aren't blind," she said.

Cody started to argue, but Dad interrupted him. "Mara's right," said Dad. " 'Blind as a bat' is an expression people use, but bats really aren't blind."

"They don't see very well, though, do they?" asked Cody. "In science class we learned that they find their way around by listening to sound waves instead of by seeing things with their eyes."

"That's true," agreed Mara. "We studied bats last year, and I remember that my teacher said they fly at night and make squeaky, high-pitched sounds and then listen for the echoes. When sound waves bounce off something and the echo comes back quickly, the bat knows there's something close by. If the echo takes a long time, he knows the thing is far away."

"Very good!" applauded Dad. After a moment, he asked, "Did you know that, like the bats, you should depend on something other than just the things you can see and understand?"

"We should?" asked Mara. "Like . . . ah . . . like what?"

"I know," said Cody. "The bats use their ears, and we should use our ears, too. A train whistle warns us that we'd better stop because a train is nearby. Traffic sounds warn us to be careful crossing the street. Right?"

"That's right," agreed Dad, "but there's something even more important than either eyes or ears. What you need is faith in Jesus and in what the Bible says. The bat's wonderful sense of hearing helps him get around safely at night. A strong faith helps you to walk safely through life. It helps to keep you from stumbling into sin in times of difficulty and temptation." *MTF*

HOW ABOUT YOU?

When bad things happen, do you continue to trust God? For example, if you're treated unfairly, a loved one is sick, or you're having trouble with schoolwork, do you see beyond the problems and remember that God cares about you and is in control? Christians must walk by faith in Jesus—not just by sight.

MEMORIZE:

"We live by believing and not by seeing." 2 Corinthians 5:7

LIVE BY FAITH

THE BAT (PART 2)

Read: 1 Peter 5:8-11

"At school today, we learned more about bats," announced Cody. "We learned that there are different kinds, and one kind is the fruit bat. Fruit bats are . . . "

"That's easy!" Mara interrupted him. "They're bats that eat fruit—that's why they're called fruit bats. Even I knew that, Mr. Smarty!" She grinned at her brother.

Cody grinned back. "Right," he agreed, "so farmers who grow fruit have to find ways to protect it."

"How about putting up a notice that says, 'Bats that eat this fruit will be prosecuted'?" suggested Mara, giggling.

"Genius!" said Cody. "Got any other good ideas?"

"What do the farmers really do?" asked Mara.

"They harvest their crops early, before the fruit bats attack," replied Cody, "or they use nets to protect their crops."

Dad, who was listening to the conversation, smiled. "We learned a lesson from the bats yesterday," he said, "and today the fruit farmers have something to teach us. From them, we learn that we need to protect our fruit."

Cody and Mara stared at him. "What fruit?" asked Mara. "We don't grow any fruit."

"I'm thinking of a different kind of fruit," replied Dad. "The Bible says the fruit of the Spirit is . . ."

"Love, joy, peace, patience, kindness, goodness, . . ." chanted Mara.

"Faithfulness, gentleness, and self-control," finished Cody.

"I'm glad you know your fruit," said Dad, "but don't forget—just like the hungry fruit bat is waiting to gobble up that freshly-ripened fruit, Satan is on the lookout for ways to attack your fruit. Use a net of prayer and obedience to God to protect your fruit." *MTF*

HOW ABOUT YOU?

Is Satan trying to destroy the fruit of the Spirit in your life by tempting you to do wrong? Ask God to help you.

GUARD AGAINST SIN

SAVED FROM THE FIRE

Read: 1 Corinthians 3:10-15

Ryan awoke to the sound of the smoke detector in the hall. "Fire!" he shouted, throwing off the covers. The smell of smoke made him cough, and his eyes smarted. Quickly he grabbed a T-shirt and held it over his face as he crept to his bedroom door. "Oh, no! The doorknob's hot!" Ryan exclaimed. "That means there's probably fire right in the hall!" He stuffed a blanket in the crack under the door. Then he heard the sound of sirens outside. Opening his window, he saw several fire trucks approaching the house.

"There he is! My boy's up there!" shouted Dad. Quickly the firefighters raised the ladder, and soon Ryan was safe on the ground with his father and mother.

The next day, Ryan and his parents picked through the charred remains of their home. "Just think," said Mom with a sigh, "we lost all of our clothes, our furniture, our important papers—everything!"

"No, not everything," corrected Dad. "We have our lives, and we still have the Lord. We have wonderful friends and family, too. We have much to be thankful for." Ryan knew it was true, but he still felt bad about all they had lost.

That night they all stayed at his grandparents' home and talked. "I hate fire!" said Ryan angrily.

Grandpa looked at him thoughtfully. "You know, the Bible speaks of another fire—the fire that will judge the works of Christians," he said. "Everything we've done for Christ will stand, but all our other works will be 'burned up.' We'll still be saved, but we'll miss much of our reward if we've lived for ourselves and not for Christ."

Dad nodded. "This fire should remind us to do all we can for God. Then we'll not only have a home in heaven—we'll have rewards that no fire can ever touch." *SLK*

HOW ABOUT YOU?

Are you a Christian? Do you feel that because you're going to heaven, you don't need to worry about sin in your life? Stop and think! It would be terrible to lose everything you have in a house fire. It would be much worse to arrive in heaven and see all you've done on earth go up in smoke. Don't live for things that won't last.

GOD WILL JUDGE

MEMORIZE:
"Everyone's work will be put through the fire to see whether or not it keeps its value." 1 Corinthians 3:13

POLITICS AND PRAYER

Read: Romans 13:1-4

"The people who work for our government sure have a lot of responsibilities," said Jason as he watched the news with his dad one evening. "They look like they're under a lot of pressure."

"That's a very good observation, Jason," replied Dad. "Those men and women do work hard, and not everyone agrees with the decisions they make. That's probably one of the reasons God tells us to pray for our leaders." Dad picked up his Bible and opened it. "Look here. Read what it says in 1 Timothy 2, verses 1 and 2." Dad handed the Bible to Jason.

" 'I urge you, first of all, to pray for all people. As you make your requests, plead for God's mercy upon them, and give thanks. Pray this way for kings and all others who are in authority.' " read Jason. "But how should we pray for them, Dad?"

"Well, let's make a list," suggested Dad. "I think we should first thank God for our leaders—especially those who are Christians."

"Yeah," agreed Jason, "and we should pray that they'll have wisdom to make decisions—and good health so they can do their jobs. And that they'll be honest," he added.

"Good," nodded Dad, "and let's be very specific whenever we can. For example, this Tuesday our city mayor and town council will be deciding whether a bike path should be put in along River Road. Let's pray that they'll make the right decision on that."

When the list was finished, Dad and Jason looked it over. "Let's go show our list to Mom," said Jason. "I bet she'd like to see it, and maybe she'll have more ideas of things to pray for." *DLR*

HOW ABOUT YOU?

Do you find it difficult to pray for your leaders? You should not only pray for your President and congresspeople, but also for your governor, mayor, and other local officials. Be specific. Maybe it would help for you to make a list of things to pray about in regard to your leaders.

MEMORIZE:

"I urge you, first of all, to pray for all people. As you make your requests, plead for God's mercy upon them, and give thanks. Pray this way for kings and all others who are in authority."
1 Timothy 2:1-2

PRAY FOR YOUR COUNTRY'S LEADERS

BRAD CONQUERS FEAR (PART 1)

3

Read: Deuteronomy 31:6-8

Brad's heart beat rapidly as he neared the house where a fierce dog lived. If only he could walk on the other side of the street! But Mom insisted that he cross the busy street only where there were crossing guards, and that meant he had to pass the dog first. Sure enough! There was the dog—snarling and growling at him as usual.

Why am I so afraid? Brad wondered. *I know that dog is tied, and it can't reach me. Besides, there's a fence between us.* But as the dog snarled and strained at his chain, Brad hurried on. He was afraid the dog would break loose and attack him!

That evening, Dad read Deuteronomy 31:6-8, then commented on the words. "In these three verses God tells us many times to be brave," said Dad. "He tells us two times to be strong and have courage; he says two times that he won't fail or forsake us; twice he tells us to 'fear not'; three times he says he goes with or before us. I'd say that's pretty good."

"That's talking about things like earthquakes or storms or being healed from a terrible disease . . . or something like that, isn't it?" Brad asked.

"Yes, it's talking about that type of situation—but also about any other time we're filled with fear," said Dad. "God says he's with us at such times, and we can show that we believe he's with us by acting as if we believe it."

"Those would be good verses for me to memorize," decided Brad. He studied them before he went to bed, and soon he knew the first one. Then he asked God to help him be brave when he passed by the mean dog the next day. With a contented sigh he went to sleep. *CEY*

HOW ABOUT YOU?

Are you afraid of dogs? Of the dark? Of being alone? God wants you to talk with him about your fears. Then when fear comes, remember that he is always with you and can help you. Trust him and don't be afraid.

MEMORIZE:

"Be strong and courageous! Do not be afraid of them! The Lord your God will go ahead of you." Deuteronomy 31:6

HAVE COURAGE

4   BRAD CONQUERS FEAR (PART 2)

Read: Mark 9:17-27

Be strong and courageous. The words of the verse Brad had learned were repeated over and over in his mind as he started home from school. He pictured himself bravely walking past the dog, remembering that God was with him. When he saw the dog waiting, he paid no attention. He kept saying the verse to himself as the dog snarled at him. Brad seemed calm as he walked on, still repeating the verse to himself—but the palms of his hands were wet from nervousness. Then he was past the dog. *I still was scared, but it was a little better,* Brad thought. *I'll try that again tomorrow.*

That evening, Brad listened carefully as Dad read a Bible passage. (See today's Scripture.) Just before healing a boy, Jesus told the boy's father, "All things are possible to him who believes." Brad noticed Jesus had said *all* things. To him it meant that even conquering fear of a dog was possible.

At bedtime, Brad thanked God for helping him get past the dog. He also thanked the Lord that all things were possible if he believed, and he asked for strength and courage for the next time he would have to pass the dog. Then he fell asleep.

For several days, the dog glared and growled. But when Brad walked past again and again without showing fear, the dog seemed to lose interest in him. Brad noticed that his heart wasn't beating as fast as before, and his palms were nearly dry.

Before long, Brad hardly noticed the dog anymore. *It's true,* he thought. *All things are possible—even getting over fear of dogs. When I started showing God that I really believed he'd help me, I felt less afraid. And the more I believed—and showed God I believed—the braver I became. Now I'm not even scared anymore.* CEY

HOW ABOUT YOU?
Do you ask God for help, and then act as though you have to handle your problems all alone? Decide that you do believe God will help you, and then act as if you believe it. That's faith!

MEMORIZE:
"I do believe, but help me not to doubt!" Mark 9:24

SHOW THAT YOU BELIEVE

REMEMBER ME

Read: Mark 14:3-9

The essay contest on great Americans was over. The winner had been chosen, and some of the boys were discussing it with their teacher, Mr. Nelson. "Boy, to think that Solomon wrote the best essay—and about a woman, too!" Herb whistled. "Who else would think of an author as a great American?"

Mr. Nelson smiled. "You must admit that when Harriet Beecher Stowe wrote *Uncle Tom's Cabin,* her pen was a very effective weapon against slavery."

"Yeah," agreed Chris. "She was a Christian who helped people see we're all created equal. But I wrote about George Washington Carver."

"You would think of him," teased Alberto, "considering how much you like peanut butter. Imagine making 300 products from peanuts! But who was really the greatest American, Mr. Nelson?"

Mr. Nelson smiled. "The person who is truly greatest might be someone we've never heard of. It could be a doctor, a missionary, a scientist, or even one of our neighbors. God keeps the records, and only he knows." The boys considered this new idea silently for a few minutes.

Finally, Alberto got up and stretched. "Well, I gotta go home and mow the lawn and hit the books," he said. He grinned. "Tell you what—I'll work hard, and a hundred years from now, your great-grandkids can write a 'Great American' essay about me."

The others laughed. "Do you think any of us will ever make the history books?" wondered Chris.

"It's possible," said Mr. Nelson, "but whether you make history or not, remember that everybody is remembered by someone for something. It's up to you what it will be." *AGL*

HOW ABOUT YOU?

How will you be remembered? Will people say you were a generous person? An honest one? A hard worker? A Christian? Or will they say the opposite? Being remembered as a true Christian who has done his best is more important than any other fame you might achieve. Live by the instructions of today's verse.

LIVE FOR GOD

November

6

"Kent," said Mom as she listened to her son tell about a fight at school, "are you sure the principal said Dane could never come to school again?"

"We-e-ell, maybe he didn't say 'never,' " Kent admitted, "but he was awful mad."

Mom sighed. "Your habit of adding to a story to make it more exciting will cause trouble someday," she warned.

Remembering Mom's words, Kent tried hard to stick to the facts, but soon he was back to his old habit of exaggerating. One day, when some boys bragged about the way their dads drove, and how they managed to break the law now and then without getting caught, Kent burst out, "My dad drove a hundred miles an hour one time!"

Dane Edwards was surprised. "Wow!" he exclaimed. "And my dad thinks your dad is such a great Christian!"

A few nights later, Kent was doing his homework when he heard his dad say, "I've been witnessing to Mr. Edwards, and I felt he was almost ready to become a Christian. But now, he hardly speaks to me, unless it's to make some snide comment about Christians." Dad glanced at Kent and was surprised to see a startled expression on his face. "What's wrong?" asked Dad.

"N-nothing," stammered Kent. But his parents knew something was bothering him, and before long the story came out. Kent told them of his boast about Dad's driving and of Dane's comment. "But I didn't exaggerate much," he insisted. "Dad was driving fast."

"But did you tell them Dad was driving an ambulance and rushing a little girl to the hospital?" asked Mom.

"No," Kent admitted. "I'm sorry. I'll tell the guys how it really happened. And I'll try harder to quit exaggerating." He sighed as he added, "But I've tried before."

"Have you prayed for the Lord's help?" asked Dad. *BJW*

HOW ABOUT YOU?

Do you stick to the truth of a story without adding a little here or taking away a little there? Exaggerating is really lying. The Lord can help you to overcome this bad habit.

MEMORIZE:

"He whose tongue is deceitful falls into trouble." Proverbs 17:20, NIV

DON'T
EXAGGERATE

JOE AND THE YO-YO

Read: Matthew 25:14-23

"This is dumb," Joe said as he put on his coat. "All the boys are doing cool things for the Bible club talent show tonight except me! I can't sing, I can't draw, and I can't play an instrument. All I can do is yo-yo tricks."

"I don't know anyone who can do them as well as you can," said his mother encouragingly.

"Maybe not, but after the talent show, our leader is having a devotional about using our talents for the Lord. How can you use a yo-yo for the Lord?" asked Joe.

Mom smiled. "Well, there must be some way, Joe," she said. "Let's think about it. But right now we'd better get going. It's ten minutes to seven."

The talent night went well. Joe did his yo-yo tricks, and all the boys clapped loudly.

As Joe waited in the lobby for his mother after the meeting, the pastor walked up with a lady and her small son. "Joe," said Pastor Schaeffer, "would you mind watching Stephen for a few minutes while I talk to his mother?"

Joe looked at the little boy. He didn't know much about taking care of preschoolers, but then he remembered his yo-yo. So for several minutes, Joe entertained Stephen with his tricks.

"Thank you so much," said Stephen's mother as she came out of the pastor's study. "I don't remember the last time he was so quiet for so long."

And after the others had left, Pastor Schaeffer said, "I thank you, too. That lady has been coming to our church for a while and today she prayed to become a Christian. You were part of that decision, Joe, because you were helping with Stephen."

Joe smiled, then prayed silently, "Thank you for letting me use my talent for you, Lord." *LMW*

HOW ABOUT YOU?

Do you have a special talent you can use for the Lord? Maybe you can memorize quickly and could do a good job reciting Scripture at a church program. Maybe you're a good cook and could bake cookies for shut-ins. Maybe you're quick with numbers and would be an efficient treasurer for your church kids' club. If you're willing, God can use any talent you possess for his honor.

**GOD CAN
USE YOU**

MEMORIZE:

"Whatever you do or say, let it be as a representative of the Lord Jesus, all the while giving thanks through him to God the Father." Colossians 3:17

November

8

There was excitement in the courtroom as one witness after another told of his or her relationship with the defendant. All agreed that he often was fun to be with; he amused and entertained them; he told them of his travels; he taught them many things. But after he had established himself in their houses, many parents noticed that he often used very bad language; that he told dirty stories; that he displayed anger and violence; and that he taught their children evil ways.

"He taught me that it's cool to drink," said Josh.

"Because of a story he told, I ran away from home," testified fifteen-year-old Salena.

Salena's brother, Roberto, stared at the floor. "He told me and my friend, Cory, that he had a foolproof plan for robbing a store," said Roberto. "We tried it, but the store owner had a gun. Cory was killed."

"He told me that whatever I want to do is okay, as long as it makes me feel good," stated another girl.

And so it went all morning. Finally the defendant himself was called to the stand and asked to state his name. "I am Mr. T. V.," he said. He went on to point out that the government allowed freedom of speech. "I was only exercising my rights," he stated. "Besides, I was invited into each home by parents and children alike. They could have asked me to leave, but they never did."

When all testimony had been heard, the judge spoke. "Although I believe Mr. T. V. is guilty of the charges brought against him, I cannot convict him," stated Judge Smith. "He was an invited guest in each home, and the law does allow free exchange of ideas. It was the responsibility of those in the home to ask him to go. Since they did not, they are as guilty as he is! Case dismissed!" *HCT*

HOW ABOUT YOU?

Is your TV on too much? Do you listen to the dirty jokes? Immoral stories? Watch the violence? These things will influence you whether you believe they do or not. Turn off the TV set when this kind of programming is on. You're responsible for what you see and hear.

MEMORIZE:

"Take no part in the worthless deeds of evil and darkness; instead, rebuke and expose them." Ephesians 5:11

QUESTIONS

Read: James 4:13-17

As Mr. Shah prepared to close his Sunday school class with prayer, he paused for a moment. "Before I pray," he said, "I wonder if any of you boys would like to give your life to Jesus and be saved today. If so, would you let me know by raising your hand?" Ned squirmed in his seat for a few moments and then sat still. Mr. Shah prayed, and the class was dismissed.

"I thought about giving my life to Jesus today," Ned said, approaching Mr. Shah after class. "But I have so many questions. How can you know that you really are a Christian? Will God ask me to do really hard things if I become a Christian? Why do Christians continue to do wrong things if they are Christians?"

"Your questions are good ones," Mr. Shah said, nodding. "I used to have some of the same questions."

"You did?"

"Yes—and the Bible has the answers," said Mr. Shah. "Perhaps I could drop by your home this week for a visit, so we can talk more."

"That would be great," said Ned. "I'll check with my parents to see when they're free."

"That's a good idea," replied Mr. Shah. "Maybe all of us can sit down together. Who knows? Maybe your parents have questions, too. You know, Ned, becoming a Christian doesn't mean that all your questions will be answered. But it does mean that you will know where to go to find answers for your questions. And for those questions that don't have clear answers, we trust that God knows what he is doing even when we don't understand." *HCT*

HOW ABOUT YOU?

What questions do you have about becoming a Christian? Talk to your parents, your pastor, or a trusted Christian friend.

MEMORIZE:

"For God says, 'At just the right time, I heard you. On the day of salvation, I helped you.' Indeed, God is ready to help you right now. Today is the day of salvation." 2 Corinthians 6:2

BE SAVED

THE TURNABOUT (PART 1)

Read: 1 Corinthians 3:5-11

"But, Daddy, why must we leave?" asked Sean. "We like it here."

Dad nodded understandingly. "I know," he said sadly, "but the government has ordered all missionaries out of the country in eight months. That includes us. We'll have to return to the States."

"I don't see why," snapped Sean. "The people here need us."

"I don't understand why, either," replied Dad.

"But our friends are here," protested Ben. "Besides, what about the Bible translation? The New Testament is almost finished!"

"I know," said Dad, "but this is God's work. We'll trust it to his care. He wants his work to go on even more than we do! We may have only eight months, but we can make each day count. We'll cancel all furloughs, and everyone will be assigned extra duties. We'll work around the clock to get the translation completed. The government may force us to leave the country, but it can't stop us from leaving God's Word behind when we go."

Sean started to smile. "What can Ben and I do?" he asked eagerly.

Mom smiled. "You children can work on the prayer letters I'll be sending all over the world," she said. "You can also help more at home, so I'll be free to help Dad."

Ben jumped up. "Let's get started," he urged. "We won't give up!" He grinned. "I'm glad they can't make God leave!" *JLH*

HOW ABOUT YOU?

Do you give up when things get tough? Jesus wants dependable workers—people who will trust him, keep at the job, and leave the results to him. Can he count on you to keep working with him?

MEMORIZE:

"We work together as partners who belong to God." 1 Corinthians 3:9

KEEP WORKING WITH JESUS

THE TURNABOUT (PART 2)

Read: Philippians 1:12-18

The Watson family and the other missionaries worked hard to preach and publish the gospel before they had to leave the country. They trained national people to take over the work when they left. They were encouraged as people all over the world prayed about the situation and sent extra gifts of money to buy more equipment and paper to speed up the publishing of the newly translated Bible.

Election time brought a wonderful surprise as several new leaders took office. "I've heard that the new government officials are going to investigate our work again," said Dad one day. "I think they'll be surprised and pleased at the great amount of good the mission does by building hospitals and schools throughout the country."

Dad was right. The new officials decided they couldn't let the missionaries leave! How Ben and Sean and their parents praised God when they learned that their visas were extended! "Our enemy became our friend," Dad said. "Those who tried to stop our work made it grow."

"They did?" asked Ben. "How?"

"The possibility of having to leave made us work harder, pray more, and train others to get involved," explained Dad. "The news reports made more people aware of our work. Christians prayed and gave."

Ben was beginning to understand. "And so more Scriptures are being printed and passed out than would have been otherwise," he said thoughtfully.

"Yes." Dad nodded. "God took the problem and turned it about. He had everything under control." *JLH*

HOW ABOUT YOU?

Do things sometimes seem to get out of control in your life? Do you wonder where God is, or what he is doing? Don't be discouraged. God is greater than anything or anybody. Nothing comes as a surprise to him. In his time he will work out all things for good.

GOD IS IN
CONTROL

MEMORIZE:

"When a man's ways are pleasing to the Lord, he makes even his enemies live at peace with him."
Proverbs 16:7, NIV

TEACHER CONFERENCE

Read: Ephesians 6:5-8

Peter dreaded parent-teacher conferences! Every year, the report was the same. "Peter is a good student, and he gets along well with the other kids," his teacher would say. Peter wished she would stop with that, but she didn't. "He could be an excellent student," she'd tell his parents, "except that he's careless."

Peter knew it was true. Ever since first grade, he would start the year with almost all A's. Then his grades would slide steadily downhill until he was getting C's or even lower grades. Peter didn't understand this himself. *Schoolwork is easy,* he thought, *but it gets awfully boring. Why waste time making sure every problem or spelling word is correct?* He knew he could do it, but he just did not care!

This year was no different, and Peter knew what he could expect to hear when his parents returned from the conference. But Mom looked more serious than usual as she said, "Miss Dickman told us that you could do better. Then she looked at us and said, 'Do you know what I don't understand about Peter? I've heard him tell other kids that he goes to church and that he's a Christian. Well—I don't know too much about the Bible, but I remember hearing once that God expects Christians to do their best!' "

Peter felt terrible. It had never occurred to him that his schoolwork could be a reflection of his love for Jesus.

As Peter and his parents talked about the problem, Dad suggested that he read Ephesians 6:5-8 each morning to remind himself to do his best at school. "Substitute the word *students* for *servants* in the first verse," suggested Dad.

"Okay," agreed Peter. After reading the passage, Peter decided to memorize the seventh verse. He smiled slightly. *If I follow this, maybe next time I can look forward to parent-teacher conferences!* he thought. *REP*

HOW ABOUT YOU?

Do you try to do your best at whatever you do? God expects you to work as if you were working for him! Maybe you, too, can witness in this way.

MEMORIZE:

"Work with enthusiasm, as though you were working for the Lord rather than for people." Ephesians 6:7

DO YOUR BEST

A BORED FRIEND

Read: 1 Samuel 18:1-5

"Mom," yelled Carrie, "tell Kevin and Sean to get out of my room. I'm trying to do my homework, and they're throwing paper at me." Mom went upstairs and again reminded Kevin and his friend to stay away from Carrie. So they decided to play outside.

"Kevin, whenever Sean is around, you two seem to get into trouble," Mom said that night. "You don't have that problem when Thomas or Gar are playing here."

"That's because Sean never wants to do anything I want to do," answered Kevin. "He doesn't like to play with my trucks or with my electronic set. Actually, there's nothing he likes to do."

"I think I know why the two of you often find yourself in trouble," Kevin's father said. "It's because you're bored, and when you are bored, it's easy to get into mischief. You know, Kevin, the Bible has a solution to the problem of boredom."

"It does?" Kevin was surprised.

"It sure does," nodded Dad. "Verse 17 of Proverbs 27 reads, 'As iron sharpens iron, a friend sharpens a friend.' That means that friends should help each other and encourage each other to become better people."

"A good example of doing what that verse says is the time you taught Thomas to play Ping-Pong," added Mom. "As a friend, you helped him."

"I guess the only thing Sean and I help each other do is to get into trouble," Kevin admitted. "I don't think we ever encourage each other. Usually we're cutting each other down." Kevin paused, then added thoughtfully, "Sean is a Christian, you know. I'm going to show that verse to him, and maybe together we can figure out an answer to our problem."

Dad smiled. "I think that would be a good idea, Kevin." *LMW*

HOW ABOUT YOU?

Do you sometimes get bored when a friend comes over to your house? Do you waste time watching TV or wondering what to do? Why not think of projects you can do together? Maybe your friend has a skill which he or she can teach you. Maybe you have a skill you can teach your friend. Work at making your friendships interesting.

WORK AT FRIENDSHIPS

MEMORIZE:
"As iron sharpens iron, a friend sharpens a friend." Proverbs 27:17

14

WOULD YOU STEAL?

Read: 1 Thessalonians 4:1-2, 11-12

One day Bud arrived home from school and proudly showed his mother his history test—all questions were answered correctly! "Hmmmm," murmured Mom, for she knew he had not studied. "This is interesting. Let's play a game. I'll ask you some questions, and then you can ask me some. We'll see who can do best."

"Aw, Mom," objected Bud, "I want to go play." But Mom insisted, and it was soon apparent that Bud knew little or nothing about the material covered on the test.

"Bud, have you been cheating?" Mom asked.

"Well, not exactly," stammered Bud. "Lots of kids share answers."

"Perhaps they do, but that doesn't make it right," Mom answered. "Besides, you're a Christian, and that makes you different from 'lots of kids.' "

"Yeah . . . well, I suppose. But I am human," Bud defended himself, "and it's like getting a little help, that's all."

"Bud, would you steal from someone?" Mom asked.

"Of course not!" Bud replied. "It's wrong to steal."

"Exactly," agreed Mom. "And what is stealing?"

"It's taking something that doesn't belong to you," Bud answered.

"Correct again." Mom nodded as she held up his paper. "And you stole these answers, Bud."

Bud looked at her solemnly. "I . . . I . . ." He didn't know what to say. "I didn't mean to steal," he said finally.

Mom shook her head. "No," she said, "perhaps not. But you did, so you'll have to take this paper to your teacher tomorrow and tell her about it and about any other times you've cheated. She'll decide what you must do about it. Right now, you might want to confess it to the Lord and ask his forgiveness. And then, instead of playing after school, you'll have to stay in and study until you know this material." *AU*

HOW ABOUT YOU?

Do you see cheating as a wrong thing to do? Or do you think of it as just getting a little help? It is actually stealing. It is sin. It must be confessed to God and perhaps to others as well.

MEMORIZE:

"Thou shalt not steal."
Exodus 20:15, KJV

CHEATING IS STEALING

A FORGIVING JUDGE

Read: 1 John 1:6-10; 2:1

"F-R-I-E-G-H-T," Riley spelled.

"Sorry," said the spelling bee judge. "That is incorrect. The word goes to Nathan Hall. Nathan, spell freight."

"F-R-E-I-G-H-T," Nathan spelled.

"Correct!" the judge exclaimed. "Nathan Hall is our winner today!"

Riley stood in shock as the crowd cheered and the judge placed the winner's ribbon around Nathan's neck. He couldn't believe he had misspelled that word.

"What happened, Riley?" Mom asked on the drive home. "You spelled *freight* correctly last night."

"I don't know, Mom," Riley grumbled. "But I should have won. I knew how to spell the word. I just got nervous and made a mistake."

"Well, Riley you only get one chance in a spelling bee," said Mom, "and that mistake cost you the championship. I'm so glad it's not that way in being a Christian."

"What do you mean, Mom?" asked Riley.

"You made a mistake in spelling, and the judge had to disqualify you," said Mom. "That was his responsibility as a judge. But God is a forgiving judge. If you sin and you're really sorry, you can go to him in prayer and he'll forgive you. You don't lose your salvation. You're still a winner with him."

"Yeah!" Riley said with a sigh. "I try to do what's right, but sometimes I don't realize what I'm doing, and I mess up. I'm glad God is a forgiving judge." *NIM*

HOW ABOUT YOU?

When you do something you know is wrong, do you ask God for forgiveness, or do you get upset with yourself and think about giving up? God knows your heart. Trust him to forgive when you try and fail.

MEMORIZE:

"If we confess our sins to him, he is faithful and just to forgive us and to cleanse us from every wrong."

1 John 1:9

GOD FORGIVES CONFESSED SIN

PRAYER IN A PUBLIC PLACE

Read: Daniel 6:6-11, 16-23

Roberto glanced around, then bowed his head as his dad led the family in prayer before their meal. "Why do we pray when we're at a restaurant?" he asked after Dad finished. "Most people don't."

"No, they don't," said Dad, "but we're thankful for what God does for us, and we want to tell him so, no matter where we are."

At a nearby table, a middle-aged couple—Mr. and Mrs. Brown—noticed them. The Browns had not been getting along very well, and they had decided that they just couldn't live together anymore. They knew their children, Tommy and Bree, would be hurt, but they felt they must get a divorce. They had decided to go to a restaurant and discuss it over dinner. "Look," said Mr. Brown softly. "Did you see that family pray before they started eating?"

"Yes," murmured Mrs. Brown. "You know, Bill, I just remembered a little saying—'The family that prays together stays together.' Do you believe that?"

"I don't know," replied Mr. Brown, "but by the looks of that family over there, I'd say there might be something to it. Look at them now—laughing and having a good time." He hesitated, then continued, "You know, I think we've both tried hard to settle our differences, but before we go ahead with the divorce, maybe there's one more thing we should try. We were married in church—that's where we started our life together—but we've hardly been there since then. Maybe we should go back now and renew our vows to each other and to God. Maybe we should pray and ask for his help in getting along."

"I've been thinking the same thing," Mrs. Brown replied, "but I've wondered if it's too late."

"It can't hurt," replied her husband. *HCT*

HOW ABOUT YOU?

Roberto knew he was being watched, but he was not afraid to pray. Do you have the courage to pray when others are watching? Do you thank God in public—even in the school lunch-room? Praying in public can be a testimony to others. It can be a good influence in their lives.

MEMORIZE:

"Evening and morning and at noon I will pray." Psalm 55:17, NKJV

DARE TO PRAY IN PUBLIC

READY ON TIME

Read: Mark 13:32-37

Dad walked into the kitchen and poured himself a glass of milk. "Jameesh, have you eaten breakfast?" he asked.

"No." Jameesh shook his head and turned a page in the book he was reading.

"You'd better get a move on if you want me to give you a ride to school," said Dad as he left the kitchen. Jameesh glanced at the clock. *I have time to finish this chapter*, he thought.

Just as Jameesh finished the chapter and closed the book, Dad poked his head into the room. "Let's go," said Dad.

"Already?" asked Jameesh. "It's awfully early."

"I told you last night that I can't run late today," said Dad. "I have an early meeting."

Dad waited at the door as Jameesh quickly dropped the book into his backpack, grabbed a juice box from the refrigerator, and picked up a cereal bar from the cupboard. Dad shook his head as Jameesh held his breakfast in one hand and tried to zip the backpack with the other. "In the morning, you need to spend your time getting ready for school—not as recreation time," said Dad as they went to the car.

"Yeah, I guess so," replied Jameesh. "I didn't think it was time to go yet."

"At an hour when you think not . . ." murmured Dad.

"What are you talking about, Dad?" asked Jameesh.

Dad smiled. "Your comment made me think of something Jesus said. He's coming back, you know, and we need to be ready. Unfortunately, a lot of Christians are more interested in having a good time than they are in preparing for Christ's return. It's easy to skip church and Bible reading in order to do other things. It's easy to think we have plenty of time to tell our friends about Jesus, but no one knows exactly when he will return." *RRZ*

HOW ABOUT YOU?

If Jesus came back to earth today, would you be ready—or would you be caught off guard? Prepare to meet Jesus. Make sure you know him as Savior. Then spend time with God and his Word, and take advantage of opportunities to serve him.

BE READY TO MEET JESUS

MEMORIZE:

"You must be ready all the time, for the Son of Man will come when least expected." Luke 12:40

November

18

The school bell rang, and the fourth graders sprang from their seats and headed toward the door. "Ryan, would you stay for a minute? I need to talk to you," said Mr. Clark.

"Yeah? What did I do now?" Ryan asked as he frowned.

"I've noticed that your grades dropped lately—but I'm even more concerned about something else," said Mr. Clark. "I'm afraid the guys I've seen you hanging around with after school will get you into trouble."

"You mean J.J. and the guys?" asked Ryan.

"I believe those boys belong to a gang, Ryan," said Mr. Clark. "They're not a good influence for you."

"But they like me," answered Ryan. "I feel like I'm a part of a family when I'm with them."

"Do you remember how we watched mold grow on a piece of bread in science class?" asked Mr. Clark.

"Yeah, I remember," replied Ryan.

"The mold started off small, didn't it?" continued Mr. Clark. "It was a tiny spot—but within a week it covered the whole slice of bread. The influence of the guys you hang out with is like that mold. It is starting out small but as you spend more time with them their influence will grow and grow until your whole life may be affected."

Ryan shrugged. "Like I told you, I feel like I belong when I'm with them," he said.

Mr. Clark nodded. "I know, but they're not a good gang to belong to. Look—this Friday the Kids' Klub at my church is having a basketball tournament. Why don't you come with us? They aren't perfect kids, but I think you'll find they'd be good friends." Mr. Clark smiled. "God's got his own gang," he added. "They're called Christians. Why don't you come and see what it's all about?" *MRC*

HOW ABOUT YOU?

Have you been spending time with people who may get you into trouble? If you want to have fun and be accepted, hang around kids who love the Lord. They're often the best kind of friends to have.

MEMORIZE:

"Since we are all one body in Christ, we belong to each other, and each of us needs all the others." Romans 12:5

"HANG OUT" WITH OTHER CHRISTIANS

JESUS, MY FRIEND

Read: John 15:12-15

"Bryce spends more time with other kids than with me," complained Tim one afternoon. "Those guys want to play basketball all the time. I like to play for a while, but then I get bored."

"I see," said Mom. "Maybe you should look for friends who enjoy the same things you do."

"I guess so," agreed Tim. Grinning, he reached into his book bag. "I got an A on my math test! Since I did so well, can I have an extra half-hour of TV tonight?"

"Well . . . okay," agreed Mom, "but no TV until your homework is finished—and until you've finished your Bible reading, too. We've all agreed to read and think about a few verses each day, remember?"

"Okay! Thanks, Mom," said Tim as he hurried off. It wasn't long before he returned to the family room and turned on the TV.

"Is your work done already?" asked Mom. "Bible reading, too?"

Tim frowned. "Well . . . um . . . " he stuttered. "I'll do that later."

Mom turned the TV off. "That wasn't the agreement."

"But, Mom," wailed Tim, "Bible reading is boring."

Mom sat on the couch beside Tim. "Were you happy when Bryce went off to play with others instead of spending time with you?" she asked.

"No," muttered Tim. "Of course not."

"Friends want to spend time together—they enjoy *fellowship* with one another," said Mom. "The Bible says we should have fellowship with Jesus, too."

"I guess so," Tim replied slowly as he stood up and moved toward the door. "But won't Jesus know I'm bored?"

Mom smiled. "If Jesus were standing here and wanted to tell you something, would you want to hear it?" she asked. Tim nodded. "Well, he does have something to say to you, and he speaks through his Word," said Mom. *JD*

HOW ABOUT YOU?

Do you have time for TV, video games, playing with friends, and talking on the phone? Do you have time for Jesus? Give him time each day.

TREAT JESUS AS A FRIEND

DO UNTO OTHERS

Read: Luke 8:27-36

Dad surveyed the living room with dismay. Jai's toy cars were parked under the couch; a toy airplane had landed on the television; toy soldiers surrounded the lamp and held it under siege; a Lego collection was on the bookcase.

Dad sighed. Then he grinned. He had an idea. He scooped up some army figures, cars, and Lego pieces. As he lifted the aquarium lid, his apology to the fish went unnoticed. A guppy swished to one side, and a bright, colorful fish darted to the other as the handful of toys sank to the bottom.

An explosion erupted when Jai went to feed his fish after school. "What's all this junk doing in my fish tank?" he yelled. "I just cleaned it Saturday afternoon!" He stormed into the kitchen where Dad was fixing supper. After dumping the dripping toys on the table, Jai put his hands on his hips. "What's going on?" he demanded.

"Isn't a tankful of toys mixed with fish what you want?" asked Dad calmly.

"Of course not!" exclaimed Jai.

Pointing to Jai's Bible, Dad said, "Well, when you were studying your verse for church last night, you said you wished people would live the way the verse said they should. Recite the verse for me, please."

Jai hesitated a moment, then he slowly quoted Matthew 7:12. " 'Do for others what you would like them to do for you.' "

"I spent Saturday cleaning the living room, while you cleaned your aquarium," said Dad. "Then last night you left your things all over the living room. If you were treating me like you want to be treated, it must mean that you would like me to clutter up your aquarium."

Jai felt foolish. He knew he'd been pretty vocal about people not living up to the verse. "I'm sorry," he apologized. *TBC*

HOW ABOUT YOU?

Do you expect as much of yourself as you expect of other people? Are you careful and considerate of your family and friends? Think about it. Take a good look at yourself. Then follow God's advice about how you should treat others.

MEMORIZE:

"Do for others what you would like them to do for you." Matthew 7:12

BE CONSIDERATE

SOMEONE TO TRUST

Read: Psalm 37:3-9

"Look, Daddy!" exclaimed four-year-old Emil as he peered out the airplane window. "Look! There's snow down there!"

His older brother Mason chuckled. "That's not snow," said Mason. "Those are clouds."

Dad smiled and nodded. "The clouds look like snow, don't they?" he asked. "They look solid—as though you could walk right out on them."

Mason grinned. "But they won't hold you up," he warned. "If you stepped out on them, it would be a giant first step down to earth."

"Maybe they're clouds of snow," suggested Emil.

Mason shook his head. "No. Clouds are only water vapor," he said in his best big-brother tone. "I learned that in science class. They can't hold anything up."

"Oh-h-h-h," murmured Emil. Then he had another question. "Why does the plane stay up in the air?"

"The plane is built just right for flying," answered Dad, "and the pilot goes to school to learn how to make it stay up." Emil seemed satisfied with that explanation and turned back toward the window.

"Emil believes everything we tell him," observed Mason, speaking softly.

"That's because he has faith in us and trusts us to tell him the truth," said Dad. "As we grow older, we find that there are some things and some people we can't trust, while many others are trustworthy—such as most doctors, firefighters, police officers, preachers, and teachers. But even people we trust may sometimes disappoint us."

Mason looked thoughtful. "Last week Pastor Mike said there was someone who would never fail us," he said. "He was talking about Jesus."

Dad smiled. "I'm glad you were listening," he said. "It's important to remember that God keeps every promise he makes. You can put your faith in him and trust him. He always does what he promises." *RA*

HOW ABOUT YOU?

Has someone you trusted let you down? If that happens, let it remind you to be a trustworthy person yourself—one who doesn't let others down. Most of all, let it remind you to put your faith and trust in God. He loves you and will never fail you.

TRUST GOD—
HE NEVER FAILS

MEMORIZE:
"O Lord my God, in You I put my trust."
Psalm 7:1, NKJV

A DISASTER ZONE

Read: Colossians 3:12-17

"We are going to clean your room, Christopher," Mom announced one afternoon.

"Oh, Mom," Christopher protested. "Do we have to?"

"Yes, we do." Mom took cleaning supplies from the closet. In Christopher's bedroom she handed him a large black garbage bag. "Start with the things under the bed. Throw away everything you do not absolutely have to have," she ordered.

Mom quickly filled a basket with clothes Christopher had outgrown. Christopher put a few things from under the bed in the garbage bag, but piled most of them beside him. He pulled out a few tattered game cards and looked at them. "The last time we played this game, Jason cheated," he said. "I won't be playing with him anymore."

"He said he was sorry, Christopher," Mom reminded. "You need to learn to throw away the bad memories and keep the good ones. You—"

The phone interrupted her, and she went to answer it.

"Grandma wants to know if we're going to be at Aunt Jennifer's for Thanksgiving," said Mom when she returned. "She failed to remember that we haven't been there since Uncle Phil lost his temper and ruined the last holiday for everyone." Mom knelt beside Christopher's "keep" pile. "Christopher, you've got to learn what to keep and what to throw away!" exclaimed Mom. "This junk is making a disaster zone of your room."

Christopher grinned. "Mom, you have to learn to throw some things away, too—like bad memories. They make life a disaster zone. After all, Uncle Phil did apologize. If you'll get rid of your clutter, Mom, I'll get rid of mine." *BJW*

HOW ABOUT YOU?

Do you hang on to bad memories? Don't do that. Learn to get rid of the mental clutter—throw bad memories away as you practice God's directions to forgive one another.

MEMORIZE:

"You must make allowance for each other's faults and forgive the person who offends you." Colossians 3:13

TOSS BAD
MEMORIES
AND FORGIVE

SHOES AND SALVATION

Read: Acts 4:8-12; John 14:6

"Mom, I've got a question," said Mario as he climbed into the car. "Some of the kids in my class say it doesn't make any difference who you believe in to get to heaven—Muhammad or Buddha or . . . or whoever." Mario sighed. "How can anybody ever convince them that they're wrong?" he asked.

"That's something only the Holy Spirit can do," said Mom. "We can gently point out the truth to people and pray for them, but only God can change their hearts."

Mario nodded, then changed the subject, "We're going to look for new gym shoes, aren't we?"

"Yes," Mom assured him.

When they arrived at the shoe store, Mario headed toward the display of the most expensive shoes, while his mother went to the discount brands. "How about these, Mom?" Mario held up a pair of brand-name shoes.

"Those are too expensive," objected Mom. She held up another, cheaper pair. "These are almost the same." Mario frowned, but when they left the store, he was carrying the cheaper shoes.

On the way home, he sighed. "I still wish I could have gotten those other shoes," he said. "That brand name would have impressed my friends."

"You need to impress your feet," said Mom with a grin, "not your friends." After a moment, she added. "I know what you can tell the kids when you wear those shoes tomorrow. Tell them that since they're impressed only when kids wear a certain brand-name shoe, they should be able to understand that when it comes to getting into heaven, God is impressed only with a certain name."

"Yeah, that's right," said Michael. "The name that will impress God is the name of Jesus."

Mom nodded. "The Bible says Jesus is the only name that we can call on to save us." *JCP*

HOW ABOUT YOU?

Have you trusted in the only name that will get you to heaven—the name of Jesus? If not, talk to a trusted friend or adult.

JESUS IS THE ONLY WAY TO HEAVEN

MEMORIZE:

"There is salvation in no one else! There is no other name in all of heaven for people to call on to save them."

Acts 4:12

MARVELOUS MARVIN

Read: Romans 6:16-23

Michael popped a handful of caramel corn into his mouth. The lights in the circus tent dimmed, and Michael looked down from his seat. The ringmaster called out, "Introducing . . . Marvelous Marvin!" There was a drum roll and a man leaped onto the stage. The crowd applauded.

"Watch as Marvelous Marvin is tied with ropes, weighted down, and submerged underwater," shouted the ringmaster. "Can he loosen the ropes, get rid of the weights, and swim back up?"

After the ropes and weights were attached to him, Marvelous Marvin plunged into the pool. The rustling of the crowd hushed as everyone watched. The ringmaster held a stopwatch and frequently announced the amount of time left. "Only ten seconds left," he finally called out. "Now five . . . four . . . three . . . two . . ."

Suddenly, Marvelous Marvin rose to the top of the water! He leaped out of the pool and took a bow. The crowd rose and cheered, and Michael jumped to his feet, too.

At dinner that evening, Dad mentioned that he had run into an old school friend. "We need to pray for Russ," said Dad. "He's a Christian, but he told me that he feels like he's drowning in some habits he's developed."

"Speaking of drowning, I was afraid Marvelous Marvin might drown this afternoon!" exclaimed Michael. "I don't know how he was able to break free from those ropes!"

Dad nodded. "When we have habits that aren't healthy, or attitudes that aren't pleasing to God, we're bound up, too," he said. "Marvelous Marvin had to free himself, but we can't do that."

"I guess you mean that God has to free us, right?" asked Michael.

"Right," agreed Dad. *ASB*

HOW ABOUT YOU?

Do bad habits, improper thoughts and attitudes, or sinful actions bind you? Is it hard to change? God wants to free you from those things. Ask him to help you study his Word, and then obey his leading in making choices. Determine to serve God, not sin.

MEMORIZE:

"Now make sure that you stay free, and don't get tied up again in slavery to the law." Galatians 5:1

JESUS CAN SET YOU FREE FROM SIN

A BAD SICKNESS

Read: Psalm 78:10-22

"Come and wipe these dishes please, Dylan," called Mom.

"I'm sick of wiping dishes!" Dylan grumbled.

Dad spoke up. "We seem to get the 'sick-of-something illness' too often around here," he said. "We're as bad as the Israelites, who complained in spite of all the good things God had done for them. Hey, why don't we play the 'stop grumbling game'?"

"What's that?" asked Dana.

"When one of us is caught saying that we're sick of something, we'll also have to tell something we're thankful for about that same thing," said Dad.

"Okay," everyone agreed. From then on, they were all more careful about what they said. Dana and Dylan also hoped to catch each other using the forbidden phrase.

One day, Dana walked in from school with a bulging backpack. "I'm so sick of all this homework!" she said.

Dylan was listening. "What is it about your homework that you're thankful for, sister dear?" he asked with a grin.

"Oh, no!" exclaimed Dana. Then she smiled and said, "I guess I'm thankful I have the brains to do it."

A couple days later Dana caught her brother using the phrase, too. As he was coming around a corner with a glass of milk, Dana was coming the other way and bumped into him—and the milk spilled on his clean pants. "Now look what you've made me do!" he exclaimed in disgust. "You make me sick!"

A mischievous glint came into Dana's eyes. "I'm sorry, Dylan," she said sweetly, "but what is it about your sister for which you're thankful?"

Dylan looked startled for a moment. Then he solemnly said, "Well, I'm thankful she isn't twins."

"Oh, you!" sputtered Dana, starting after him.

Mom and Dad laughed as they watched. "I think this game is doing our family good," said Dad. "I think we're all happier when we're careful not to grumble." *VMH*

HOW ABOUT YOU?

Do you have a habit of grumbling and complaining? God was not pleased when the Israelites grumbled, and he is not pleased when his children grumble today. When you catch yourself grumbling, stop! Pause what you're doing until you think of a reason to thank God for the very thing that made you complain.

TURN GRUMBLING INTO THANKFULNESS

MEMORIZE:

"In everything you do, stay away from complaining and arguing."

Philippians 2:14

November
26

THE HUMAN RACE

Read: Genesis 2:7, 21-23

"Our science teacher says God didn't create the world but that all life began in the water that used to cover the earth," Joe told his parents one evening. "He says that when dry land began to appear, some of the creatures grew legs and lungs so they could live on land. They kept on changing, and finally they became half animal and half human. Then they slowly developed into humans, and that was the start of the human race."

"Mr. Broom called it evolution," added Chloe.

"Do you believe all that?" asked Dad.

"Not me," Joe declared. "It sounds dumb! We asked Mr. Broom about creation in the Bible, and he says it's a myth."

"Joe asked the teacher if he really believed in evolution," interrupted Chloe, "and he said yes. Then Dan said, 'I guess it's all right for you to believe your way as long as it's all right for us to believe the right way.' The whole class howled!"

Joe and Chloe laughed, but their parents didn't laugh. "It's never right to show disrespect for a teacher," said Dad, "even if you know he's wrong."

"But we can't learn stuff we don't believe!" said Chloe.

"Mr. Broom says we'll fail the subject if we don't answer the test questions correctly," added Joe.

"Learn the material well, and when you write test answers with which you don't agree, you can add that the answer is according to the science book," suggested Dad. "At the end of the year, you can both go to Mr. Broom and tell him you still believe the Bible and that the human race began when God created Adam."

"Okay," said Joe. "Let's try to get the best marks in class, and then we'll let Mr. Broom know that we still don't agree with everything in the science book."

"All right!" said Dad. "Mom and I will pray for you—and for him." *HCT*

HOW ABOUT YOU?

Do your teachers tell you that humans evolved from animals? The Bible says God made you. Be faithful to God. Let your teachers and classmates know you believe what the Bible says, but be sure to show respect to your teachers so you can be a good testimony to them.

MEMORIZE:

"So God created man in his own image." Genesis 1:27, NIV

GOD CREATED HUMANS

SILENT FRIEND

Read: Philippians 2:1-4

Nate plopped down on the couch. "Why so gloomy?" asked Dad.

"I tried to be friendly to Paul, a new boy in my class, but he didn't seem to care," said Nate. "When I asked if he wanted to sit with me at lunch, he said no."

"Any idea why he acted that way?" asked Dad.

"Mike said Paul had to change schools because his dad is in jail."

"Sounds like Paul has a lot on his mind," said Dad.

"Yeah, but doesn't he need a friend?" asked Nate.

"Remember the day you broke your leg?" he asked. "Your friends came over with some games to cheer you up, but you weren't interested in them that day. You were sleepy from the pain medicine, so Mom asked the kids to come back when you were feeling better. Remember?"

Nate nodded. "That was a bad day."

"With all the difficult things that have happened in Paul's life recently, he must be hurting. Maybe he doesn't have energy to put toward making friends right now."

"Maybe not," agreed Nate. As he went to his room and got ready to study, he had an idea. He took a piece of paper and wrote this note: "To Paul—I'm sorry if I bugged you at school. How about if I be your silent friend? If you ever want to hang out with me, just let me know, okay? Nate."

The next morning, Nate saw Paul standing alone on the school playground. Nate walked over and handed him the note. "What's this?" asked Paul.

Nate decided to remain a silent friend, so he just smiled. As he left, he glanced back over his shoulder. Paul was reading the note, and Nate thought he saw a small grin appear on Paul's face. *JMJ*

HOW ABOUT YOU?

Are you glad when other kids do well—and sorry if they're hurting? God wants you to be sensitive to the feelings of others. Be friendly, but don't be upset if someone seems to prefer being left alone. Don't try to force anyone to do things with you. Pray about the situation, and help whenever you can.

BE SENSITIVE TO OTHER KIDS' FEELINGS

MEMORIZE:
"When others are happy, be happy with them. If they are sad, share their sorrow." Romans 12:15

SORRY—BUT, NO

Read: Ephesians 3:1-3

John was helping his mother prepare snacks for company. "How about slicing this cheese?" suggested Mom.

"Sure," agreed John.

As John began slicing cheese, two-year-old Mark ran into the kitchen. "Some!" said Mark, holding up his hand.

Mom shook her head. "Sorry, Mark," she said firmly. "No cheese. It makes you sick."

Mark frowned and ignored her. "Some pwease!" he begged, tugging on John's arm.

"I can't give you any, Markie," John told him. Mark pouted as he walked away. "Too bad Mark doesn't understand that cheese will make him sick," said John.

"Parents often have to make decisions their kids can't understand," said Mom, giving John a knowing look.

"You're talking about the party last night, aren't you?" asked John.

Mom nodded. "When you asked if you could go, Dad and I didn't say 'no' to be mean. Like we told you—based on our experience and knowledge—we said 'no' because it wasn't the kind of party you should be going to. We're sorry you can't understand that."

"I do understand better now," said John. "Actually, I'm glad you didn't let me go. I talked to Pete this afternoon, and he told me he left halfway through because they were starting to show a really bad movie."

"I'm proud of Pete for getting out of there—he did the right thing," said Mom. "I'm glad you have a little better understanding about the reasons we make the rules we do. We're doing our best to teach you about God and how to live for him. Someday, we won't be able to make decisions for you. You'll have to choose to do right by yourself." Mom gave John a quick hug and handed him a small bowl of grapes. "Here, take these grapes to Mark. I'll take the snacks to the living room." *HLA*

HOW ABOUT YOU?

Do you ever think your parents make rules just to keep you from having fun? They have greater knowledge and experience than you do. Rules are actually a sign of their love for you as they follow God's directions to bring you up in the way you should go.

MEMORIZE:

"You children must always obey your parents, for this is what pleases the Lord." Colossians 3:20

THANK GOD FOR PARENTS AND OBEY THEM

MEMORY PROBLEMS

Read: Philippians 4:5-9

"Dad! The computer's not working!" Ramon hollered from the office to his dad.

Dad looked up from his newspaper. "Son, please come in here and explain the situation without yelling through the house."

Ramon came to stand before his dad. "I just finished typing my report for school," he said. "I tried to save it, and it won't let me. It just says, 'not enough memory.'"

"All right," said Dad. "Let's go take a look."

Ramon and his father went to the office, and Dad sat down to see if he could fix the problem. "It seems like we have a lot of files I don't recognize," said Dad as he brought up the file directory. "Do you know what these are?"

Ramon studied the list. "Well, one is the picture I made with the art program, and that one is the list I made for my birthday," he said.

"We'll have to clean out some unnecessary files to free up some of the computer's memory," said Dad. So together, Dad and Ramon went through the list of files and deleted any that weren't important.

When they were done, Ramon grinned at his dad. "My teacher says our minds are like computers," he said.

Dad smiled. "Yes, and like the computer, our minds sometimes get filled with stuff that isn't important, too. Then we don't have enough 'memory' for the important things that God wants us to think about. We have to be careful to fill our minds with good, honest, and worthy thoughts—after all, our minds don't come with a delete button." *BT*

HOW ABOUT YOU?

Are you filling your mind with thoughts that will honor God? Make sure TV programs you watch, music you listen to, and games you play help to fill your mind with good things.

STORE GOOD THOUGHTS IN YOUR MIND

MEMORIZE:

"We take captive every thought to make it obedient to Christ."

2 Corinthians 10:5, NIV

THE VERY BEST NEWS

Read: Romans 1:15-17

Nate jumped off the bus and burst into the kitchen. "Mom! Mom! Guess what!" Nate ran through the house yelling. "I won!" His eyes shone as he held out a trophy for her to see. "I got a gift certificate to Ice Cream Palace, too," he added.

"That's wonderful, hon . . ." Mom began, but Nate wasn't listening.

"I've got to call Gary and tell him," he said as he picked up the phone.

Mom smiled and waited patiently for Nate to finish his call. She admired his trophy, and they discussed a trip to Ice Cream Palace. "By the way, what did Gary say?" asked Mom.

"Oh, he thought it was great. He's still my best friend, you know," Nate answered. "I wish he hadn't moved away."

"That would be nice," agreed Mom. "A lot has happened since he moved a year ago. We weren't even going to church back then, but now we've all come to know Jesus." Nate nodded. "I can understand why you wanted to call Gary right away and tell him that you won the trophy," continued Mom. "That's certainly good news, but you know even better news than that." She smiled at the bewildered look on Nate's face.

Suddenly it occurred to Nate what Mom was talking about. Nate and his parents had been talking about ways that Nate could share the good news of Jesus Christ with Gary. For a moment, Nate ducked his head sheepishly, but then he smiled. "I'm a little afraid to come right out and tell Gary about Jesus," he admitted, "but I do want Gary to know him, too. Can I invite him to come and stay with us this weekend? I think his mom will let him. He could come to church with us and learn more about Jesus." Smiling, Mom agreed. *BT*

HOW ABOUT YOU?

Have you shared the good news of your salvation with those around you? It's the very best news there is, and you have the privilege of telling other kids about it.

MEMORIZE:

"For I am not ashamed of this Good News about Christ. It is the power of God at work, saving everyone who believes." Romans 1:16

SHARE THE "GOOD NEWS"

December

UP THE DOWN ESCALATOR

1

Read: Titus 3:3-7

While Mom shopped for a bike on the first floor of a department store, Tim and his sister Kate rode the escalator up to the top floor and down again. Mom had said they could do it one time—as long as they didn't push, or run up and down, or bother the other shoppers.

"Let's try going up the 'down' escalator," said Tim when they got back to the first floor. "Let's see if we can make it to the top."

Kate didn't think Mom would want them to do that, but Tim was determined to try it. Soon he was headed up the "down" escalator. He was really working hard. His face got all red. Some of the people riding down the escalator were annoyed with Tim. But Tim didn't care—until he bumped into the store manager.

With a few scolding words, the manager took Tim's arm and accompanied him back down. Tim knew he was in real trouble when he spotted his mother waiting at the foot of the escalator. Mom scolded him too, and he had to apologize to the store manager.

On the way home, they talked about what happened.

"I guess I worked pretty hard to go up the 'down' escalator, but I ended up right back where I started," admitted Tim.

Mom nodded. "That's like people who think they can 'ride to heaven' on their own good works," she said. "They try so hard to be good, but before they know it, they're right back where they started! And all that's waiting for them is eternal punishment. That isn't the way God meant it to be." She paused, then added, "No amount of effort will ever gain heaven for anybody. You'll get there only by trusting Jesus. You can never make it on your own." *CVM*

HOW ABOUT YOU?

Have you been trying to earn God's favor and get to heaven by doing good works? Good works are important, but they will never get you to heaven. God wants you to trust his Son, the Lord Jesus Christ, as your Savior! Only Jesus lived perfectly. He is the only way to heaven.

STOP TRYING; TRUST CHRIST

MEMORIZE:
"He saved us, not because of the good things we did, but because of his mercy." Titus 3:5

December

2

Brad's father had been out of work, and he was discouraged. "Don't worry, Dad," said Brad. "Lots of people are praying for you. God will take care of us."

"You not only look like your grandpa," grunted Dad, "you sound like him, too! All he ever talked about was God and his Bible."

"Grandpa's Bible is up there on the shelf," said Brad. "Pastor Sims says the Bible has answers to our problems, so maybe we should get it down and read it now. Should we do that, Dad?"

To Brad's surprise, Dad agreed! He pulled the Bible from the high shelf, dusted it off, and opened it. As Dad was leafing through it, suddenly he stopped. A strange look was on his face. "There's an envelope here with my name on it!" exclaimed Dad. He took the envelope and opened it. "I must be dreaming. Brad, look! It's a saving bond! We can cash it in for money."

Brad's eyes were wide. "Wow!" he exclaimed. Then he noticed another paper. "Dad! That looks like a letter. What does it say?" he asked.

"Let's see," said Dad. "It's my father's handwriting." He read the paper silently. "Well, what do you know?" he murmured. "It says, 'My dear son, Surprised, aren't you? You may be wondering why I didn't just give the bond to you or leave it in a will. Well, guess I always hoped that you would eventually read this Bible. My boy, this bond is only a token of all the wealth stored up in the pages of God's Word. Read it. Come to know your Savior, and find life. With all my love and prayers, Your father.' "

Dad looked up. "This money will be a big help to us," he said slowly, "but I guess the best inheritance he left us is in this Book." *HCT*

HOW ABOUT YOU?

Do you believe that God's Word is more valuable than money? It may not seem that way in this world, but it is true.

MEMORIZE:

"Your law is more valuable to me than millions in gold and silver!"
Psalm 119:72

A HORRIBLE PIT!

Read: Psalm 40:1-5

Jordan and his friend Carlos had planned to go exploring in a wooded area near their town one Saturday afternoon, but when Jordan found out Carlos couldn't make it, he decided to go alone.

The ground was covered with a thick matting of leaves, and in some places the leaves were covered with a fresh blanket of newly fallen snow. *This is really neat,* thought Jordan when he got to the woods. *Hey! I'm gonna follow those animal tracks.* Jordan followed the tracks deep into the woods. *I guess I better go back,* he decided after a while. *I don't think I've ever been this far in the woods before.* He was enjoying himself as he headed back home, when suddenly . . . *CRASH!* His feet went right through a snow-covered hole and he found himself at the bottom of a deep pit!

Jordan tried to climb up the steep sides of the pit, but he fell back to the bottom again and again. *These sides are so steep, I might as well quit,* he thought. *But it's gonna get awful cold before anybody finds me!* So he kept trying, but he could not get out—and it was getting dark. Frightened, he desperately renewed his efforts. *It's hopeless,* he thought in despair. Just then he heard voices! "Help!" he called at the top of his lungs. "Help!" Soon a face appeared over the edge of the pit. He was rescued because his parents had begun looking for him when he didn't come home.

Several days later, Jordan read a verse in the Psalms about being taken up out of a pit. "Hey, I can understand this verse," he said. "It sounds like me!"

Dad nodded. "You tried to save yourself from that pit, just like people try to save themselves from their sin. Only Jesus can do that!" *CVM*

HOW ABOUT YOU?

Are you trying hard to get out of "the pit of sin" by being good, going to church, or giving your money? The Bible says you must be saved by faith in Christ, not by your own good works. Stop trying to save yourself . . . and start trusting!

TRUST CHRIST, NOT WORKS

JASON'S TREASURE

Read: Matthew 6:19-24

Jason was proud of his stamp collection. He was sure it would be worth a lot of money someday. But one day while Jason was at school, a neighbor stopped in with her little boy, Robby. As the ladies were visiting, Robby came out of Jason's room. "See, Mommy. Pretty pi'chers," he said. Clutched in his small fist were some of Jason's stamps! Robby had climbed onto Jason's bed and reached the collection on the dresser. He had picked up loose stamps and had torn some pages in the stamp book.

When Jason came home, Mom told him what had happened. Jason rushed to his room. "That little brat! My collection is ruined!" he yelled. "I might as well throw it out!"

"No, it's not ruined, Jason. You can smooth out the rumpled pages, and we'll tape those that got torn," comforted Mom. "It may not look as nice as before, but you do still have your collection."

"I don't even want it now," said Jason angrily. "It won't be worth anything anymore!"

Mom frowned. "That's not true, but it sounds to me like your collection is a little too important to you," she said. "You need to remember that it's just an earthly treasure—and God says we're to store treasures in heaven."

"What does that mean?" growled Jason.

"It means we need to be more concerned about the things that are important to the Lord than we are about things on this earth—things like your collection. We need to read God's Word, work for him, and tell others about Jesus."

"Is it wrong to have a collection then?" asked Jason.

"No," Mom replied. "And I am sorry that some of your stamps are ruined. But it's wrong to make it, or anything else, so important to you that it comes before your love for God—or for people." *BR*

HOW ABOUT YOU?

Are you so interested in your earthly "stuff" that you've forgotten about storing treasure in heaven? Begin now to learn about the Lord. Work for him, and you will be "laying up" treasures in heaven.

MEMORIZE:

"Wherever your treasure is, there your heart and thoughts will also be." Matthew 6:21

STORE TREASURE IN HEAVEN

TRIED AND TRUE

Read: James 1:1-4

BANG! BANG! BANG! The quiet of early morning was broken by the sound of a hammer being used with great force. Justin's Mom woke with a start. What was going on? There it was again—*Bang! Bang! Bang!* She got up hurriedly and went downstairs to see what was happening. She found her small son pounding nails into a square board laid across four upright pieces of wood.

"Justin, why are you making all this noise so early in the morning?" Mom demanded.

Justin looked at her, a little bit embarrassed. "I'm just trying to make a footstool for you, so you can reach things up high," he said.

Mom smiled. "How nice of you to do that, Justin, but people are still sleeping. Maybe you should wait until a little later," she suggested.

"Okay." Justin put down the hammer. "Can we eat?"

"Right away." Mom nodded. As she went to start breakfast, Dad and Justin's older sister, Rosa, poked their heads in at the door. "You may as well join us for breakfast," Mom said, laughing at their sleepy appearance.

After breakfast, Mom took her Bible and read from the book of James (see today's Scripture). "The early Christians were persecuted because of their faith," she said. "James said they should be joyful when their faith was tried—or tested—because it taught them patience. Today, most of us are not really persecuted in this country, but sometimes our faith is tried in other ways. For example . . . uh . . . ."

"Like when we wake up too early because somebody is banging away with a hammer," interrupted Rosa, glancing at her brother. "That teaches us patience."

"Right!" Dad chuckled. "We should all develop patience as we experience the difficult things we have to deal with in life, whether they're big or small." *HMP*

HOW ABOUT YOU?

Are there big things in your life that "try your faith"—a death or divorce in the family, unkind people, difficult classes? Are there little things that "bug" you, such as a friend who is always late or a nickname you don't like? If your faith is real, these things will help you to develop patience.

DEVELOP PATIENCE

December

6

Read: Exodus 16:2, 8, 11-12

When four-year-old Mark was finished at the dentist, the office nurse gave him a big, yellow balloon. With a wide smile, he carried it to the waiting room where he met his mom and older brother, Alan. Alan was delighted when the nurse gave him a balloon, too—an orange one.

Now there should have been two happy boys as they headed home. But Mark decided he wanted the orange balloon, and he tried to trade with his big brother. "I don't want this yellow balloon," Mark grumbled. "I like your orange one!"

"Play with your own balloon," said Alan. Mark continued to grumble and complain all the way home. Finally, in frustration, Alan handed Mark the orange balloon, and the trade was made.

As they entered the house, Mark's face wore a smug, self-satisfied look. He moved the orange balloon up and down. Suddenly, for no apparent reason, the balloon popped! Mark's face screwed up, and he began to cry as he watched Alan play with the yellow balloon.

Mom sat down and put Mark on her lap. "Mark," she said, "I'm afraid you've forgotten the verse you memorized for Sunday school last week. It said to be content with what you have. If you had done that, you'd still have a balloon." *BMC*

HOW ABOUT YOU?

Are you thankful when someone gives you a gift? Or do you complain if it isn't just what you want? Maybe you'll get a gift for Christmas that isn't exactly what you would have chosen. Be nice about it. Ask God to give you a thankful and contented heart.

MEMORIZE:

"Be content with what you have."
Hebrews 13:5, NIV

APPRECIATE GIFTS

THE RIGHT CLOTHES

Read: Isaiah 61:10-11; Ephesians 2:8-9

Mr. Brown, who lived next door to Dan, had said that he was hiring helpers during the Christmas season. So the next day, Dan hurried toward Brown's Garden Store. He and several other boys got instructions from a man in brown coveralls. "See those trucks?" said the man. "We'll take them to the field, then you load the trees."

As they headed for the trucks, Dan noticed that the others were wearing old clothes. *Oh, no!* he thought. *I forgot to wear my old stuff!* "Mister," Dan yelled to the man in brown coveralls, "I forgot about old clothes, but I can hurry home and change!"

"We can't wait," the man replied gruffly. "Go inside and tell Mr. Brown."

After hearing Dan's explanation, Mr. Brown spoke kindly to him. "I'm so sorry, Dan. If they don't get everything done today, we can use you tomorrow— but be sure to wear the right clothes." Mr. Brown paused, then said, "Do you remember our talk about heaven?"

"What about it?" replied Dan.

"Well, you've told me that you want to go to heaven," said Mr. Brown, "but you've never accepted Jesus as your Savior, have you?"

"No," said Dan. "Like I've told you, I'm a pretty good kid."

"Instead of being 'good,' you need to be 'right,'" said Mr. Brown. "You came to work today with 'good' clothes, but they weren't the 'right' clothes. The Bible tells us that we need God's righteousness—the 'right clothes'—to enter heaven. The prophet Isaiah wrote, 'He (God) has clothed me with the garments of salvation.'"

"Garments of salvation," echoed Dan. "What does that mean?"

"Salvation refers to God's righteousness," replied Mr. Brown. "By putting our faith and trust in Jesus and accepting him as Savior, we receive his righteousness," said Mr. Brown, "and that means we're free from the guilt of sin." *PIK*

HOW ABOUT YOU?

Are you "clothed" in salvation? Have you accepted Jesus as Savior? Salvation through Jesus is the only way to heaven.

BE CLOTHED
IN GOD'S
RIGHTEOUSNESS

December

8

"Guess what, Mom!" Max exclaimed, as he dropped his books on the table. "We're having a poster contest. The winner gets five dollars, and I'm going to use it to buy . . ."

Mom laughed. "Better not spend it until you win it," she warned. "What kind of poster do you have to make?"

"It's to be about conservation—saving our natural resources such as water, trees, and wildlife. I got an idea before Mrs. Lawson even finished reading the rules. My slogan is, 'Here today—Gone tomorrow.' On half of the poster I'll put some blackened tree stumps. In the middle I'll draw a lighted match."

"Not bad," Mom agreed. "You just might have a winner."

"Sure I do!" exclaimed Max. "Now can I have some money to buy poster board?"

"What size does it have to be?" Mom asked as she handed him some money.

"Uhhhhh . . . " Max scratched his head. "I think it has to be half of a regular poster board."

For the next two weeks, Max worked untiringly on his poster. On the last day, just before the final bell, he handed it in. "Very neat, and a good idea, too," said Mrs. Lawson with a smile. But she frowned as she studied it. "Max, didn't you read the rules?" she asked.

"Well . . . well . . . ah, you read them to us," stammered Max.

"Rule number four says there must be a one inch margin on all sides," reminded Mrs. Lawson. "The branches of your trees go all the way to the edge." Max could have cried! "I'll give this to the judges, but I'm afraid it isn't eligible to win," Mrs. Lawson continued. "Too bad, Max. It might have been a winner." *BJW*

HOW ABOUT YOU?

Have you been reading God's rule book—the Bible? It's important to know and obey the rules God has given for your life.

MEMORIZE:

"Yes, I obey your commandments and decrees, because you know everything I do." Psalm 119:168

KEEP GOD'S RULES

THE BIRTHDAY PRESENTS

Read: Matthew 2:1-11

"Oh! I almost forgot my two dollars for the Christmas missionary offering!" exclaimed Brad as he started out to the car one Sunday. "I'll go get it—be right back."

When he returned with the money, his mother questioned him about it. "You told me you had ten dollars for the offering," she said. "Where's the rest of your money?"

Brad blushed. "I . . . I needed it to help pay for my new Rollerblades," he replied. He hadn't meant to let it slip that he had only two dollars left. "I bought the best blades in the store as a special birthday present for myself, remember? I didn't have quite enough saved." He braced himself for a lecture, but his parents didn't say anything.

After church there was a special dinner and a cake with candles to honor Brad's birthday. Then Mom put two big gifts in front of him. He eagerly reached for them. "Hey, what is this?" he asked when he could see the tags. "These say, 'To Mom and Dad from Mom and Dad.' I don't get it. Why are you getting presents? It's my birthday!"

"We did buy them for you," said Mom, "but then we decided maybe we should keep them for ourselves instead."

Brad was puzzled, so Dad explained. "You saved money for a gift to Jesus in honor of the day we celebrate his birthday," he said, "but you kept most of it for yourself instead."

Mom nodded. "It's so easy to treat ourselves, our family, and our friends at Christmastime," she said, "and it's easy to forget Jesus."

Dad then removed the tags from the gifts on the table, "Here, Son," he said. "These are for you." *MRP*

HOW ABOUT YOU?

How would you feel if your family and friends gave gifts to themselves and each other on your birthday, but did very little for you? Remember how much Jesus has given you, and give a special Christmas gift to him. He can use your time, talents, and money.

GIVE TO JESUS
AT CHRISTMAS

MEMORIZE:
"Give as freely as you have received!"
Matthew 10:8

ALL FROM GOD

Read: 1 Corinthians 4:1-7

"Oh, Jered! You're always bragging about your good grades," complained Kyle. He stuck his nose in the air and mimicked his brother. "I got an A in this! I, and I alone, got 100 in that. I'm so smart!"

"Well, I am the smartest kid in my class. I heard my teacher say so," boasted Jered.

"Boys, that's enough!" said Dad sternly. Then, taking out his wallet, he removed some bills. "Look at this, Jered," he said.

Jered's eyes opened wide. "Wow! A fifty-dollar bill! And a hundred! Where'd you get them?"

"Remember the snowblower Uncle Joe asked us to sell for him when he moved to Florida?" asked Dad. "I sold it this morning, and the man paid me in cash. This is going to come in pretty handy for buying Christmas presents."

Jered looked at his father in surprise. "But, Dad, you can't spend this money."

"Why not?" asked Dad. "The man gave it to me."

"Yeah, but it's not yours," Jered insisted. "It belongs to Uncle Joe. If you keep the money, you'll be stealing!"

"You're right, Son." Dad smiled. "It would be stealing. Although the buyer handed the money to me, he was really paying Uncle Joe. I'm just the go-between. And there's something else you should know. All the abilities and talents you have, great or small, are from God who created you—they really belong to him. Sometimes people will hand you compliments regarding them, but you're just the go-between. God loaned you those abilities so you could use them to honor him, not yourself."

Jered looked embarrassed. "Oh . . . I see! I really shouldn't be bragging about being smart, should I?"

"No," answered Dad. "Instead, thank God for your talents and try to use them for him." *AU*

HOW ABOUT YOU?
Do you have a special talent? Are you better than someone else is at schoolwork or in sports? Are you especially attractive? You shouldn't try to deny your talents and abilities, but don't take the credit for them, either. Look at yourself realistically and thank God for making you just as you are. When you are given compliments, accept them graciously, then pass them along—to him!

MEMORIZE:
"What do you have that God hasn't given you?" 1 Corinthians 4:7

YOUR TALENTS ARE FROM GOD

RAGS TO RICHES

Read: Romans 8:14-18

Monty climbed onto his great-grandpa's lap. "Tell me about the wallet your daddy found when he was a boy," he begged. Monty never got tired of hearing the story.

Grandpa smiled. "My daddy was an orphan," he began, "and he sold newspapers at a bus stop. One day an old man bought a paper, and after he left, my daddy saw a wallet on the ground. He took it to the rooming house where he lived, and when he looked through it, he saw the name. . . ."

"Samuel Jeremiah!" shouted Monty.

"Yes, and there was a picture in the wallet of a pretty lady," continued Grandpa. "My daddy wished she were his mother."

"Was there money in the wallet?" asked Monty, already knowing the answer.

Grandpa nodded. "Yes, and about a week later, my daddy saw the old man again and gave it back to him."

"Then what happened?" asked Monty.

"Well, when Mr. Jeremiah saw my daddy, he was reminded of his own little grandson who had recently died. And when Mr. Jeremiah learned that my daddy was an orphan, he took him to live with him and his wife—the pretty lady—in their beautiful home," said Grandpa. "Mr. Jeremiah gave him everything he needed." Grandpa paused, then added, "One day my daddy was alone, cold, hungry, and poor. The next, he had all he could wish for, and more."

"And Mr. Jeremiah adopted him, and when he died, he left him his money, didn't he?" asked Monty eagerly.

"That's right," said Grandpa, "but that's not the best part. The best part is that he taught my daddy about Jesus."

"Yeah," agreed Monty "because that's the most important thing in the world." *AU*

HOW ABOUT YOU?

Do you realize how wonderful it is to be a Christian? Right now you can enjoy God's peace, joy, and contentment. Think also of all that's waiting in heaven for you as a child of God! Thank him each day for what he's given you.

GOD'S RICHES ARE YOURS

12

Jason's stomach told him it was lunchtime, so he headed for the kitchen. "Isn't lunch ready yet?" he asked. "I'm hungry!"

"I'll get it for you in just a minute," promised Mom as she finished decorating a cake.

"Whose birthday is it?" asked Jason.

"No one's," Mom replied. "This is for Angie's friend, Renae. She looked so longingly at the cake I had made for Angie's birthday party, that I told her I'd make one for her."

Jason leaned his elbows on the counter and watched his mother thoughtfully. "Why didn't you just surprise her instead of telling her about it ahead of time?" he asked.

"That would have been good," said Mom. "Sometimes that's the most 'fun' way to do something. On the other hand, being able to look forward to a gift might make it doubly good. We call that anticipation. Not only will Renae have the joy of receiving it, but she has the joy of anticipating it as well."

"I guess that's true," agreed Jason. "I really get excited when I know I'm going to get a present."

Mom smiled. "God promised a gift in advance, too," she said. "Hundreds of years before Jesus was born, God began telling people that someday he would send a Savior who would die for their sins."

Jason looked up. "Maybe he wanted people to enjoy looking forward to that."

"Maybe," said Mom, "and the Bible tells us about some other wonderful things God has in store for those who believe in Jesus."

"Like that Jesus is coming again and that we'll go to be with him in heaven someday?" asked Jason.

Mom nodded as she covered the cake. "I'll start your lunch now," she said.

"Thanks, Mom!" Jason grinned. "I'm looking forward to it already—and I'm sure it'll be worth waiting for!" *AU*

HOW ABOUT YOU?

Do you anticipate the future? If you know Christ as your personal Savior you can happily look forward to spending eternity in heaven with him. When things go wrong don't forget that God has much better things planned for you.

MEMORIZE:

"I will come and get you, so that you will always be with me where I am."
John 14:3

THE HAPPY HOME

Read: Matthew 5:13-16

It seems like Mom is always mad at me, thought Seth. *If I go away, it makes her mad, and if I stay home, that makes her mad, too. I'm always too early or too late, too busy or not busy enough, too noisy or too quiet.* He sighed. *After Bible club tomorrow, I'm going to ask Mrs. Davis about it.* Mrs. Davis, who lived next door to Seth, held a regular after-school Bible club in her home. Only a few weeks before, Seth had talked with her about becoming a Christian.

After the club meeting the next day, Seth asked, "How can I have a home like yours? My mom seems angry most of the time."

"Oh, I'm sorry," said Mrs. Davis. "Well . . . a few weeks ago, you asked Jesus to come into your life and change you, right?" Seth nodded. "Now that you're a Christian, you can pray for your mother," Mrs. Davis continued. "I'll pray, too, and ask God for an opportunity to talk with her. I think if your mother knew Jesus cared about her and her problems, it would help." Mrs. Davis gave Seth a hug. "Be sure to try hard to obey your mom, too."

Seth nodded. "I'll try," he said. And he did try. He made his bed without being told, and he often offered to do the dishes.

"What's come over you, Seth?" Mom asked one day. "You're so different lately." She looked thoughtful. "Is it that you've become a Christian?"

"Yes," answered Seth. "And that's what makes me different."

"Quite a while ago, Mrs. Davis told me about Jesus," said Mom after a moment. "Do you suppose she would come and talk with me again?"

"Absolutely," Seth answered eagerly. *AGL*

HOW ABOUT YOU?

Does Jesus make a difference in your life? When you do a task willingly and cheerfully—even without being told—your attitude and actions are a witness to your family and they help to make your home a better place.

WITNESS AT HOME

MEMORIZE:
"Therefore, if anyone is in Christ, he is a new creation; the old has gone, the new has come!" 2 Corinthians 5:17, NIV

14

Read: Psalm 34:1-9

"Quick!" whispered Larry. "Put this in your pocket." He held a shiny, new pocketknife toward Dane.

Dane looked at his big cousin in amazement. "But you have to pay for it first," he objected.

"Let me worry about that," hissed Larry. "Hurry up—nobody's watching."

"God is watching," replied Dane.

"Don't start preaching," growled Larry. "Now, put this in your pocket, or I'll beat you up."

Dane's eyes widened. He didn't know this older cousin very well, but he did believe Larry would beat him up. He took a deep breath. "No!" he said as he backed farther down the aisle. "Jesus, please help me," he murmured, unaware that Larry could hear him.

Larry was angry. He glared at Dane. "Are you going to put this in your pocket, or am I going to have to teach you a lesson?"

Larry grabbed for Dane's shirt. Dane dodged, and before they knew it, paper towels went rolling everywhere. "Look what you did," Larry gasped. "Let's get out of here."

A clerk came running. "I'll pick those up," he said. He looked at the pocketknife in Larry's hand. "Do you want to buy that?"

Larry's face turned red. "Oh, I was just looking."

As Larry put the knife in the clerk's outstretched hand, he heard the voice of Dane's father. "Hi, boys," he said. "Mom forgot to put bread on your list, so she sent me to get it. You can ride home with me."

When they were all in the car, Dane turned to his dad. "Jesus watches us all the time, and helps us when we need him, doesn't he?" he said confidently.

Dad looked puzzled. "Of course, Son. You know that."

Dane looked over his shoulder at his cousin's red face. "Yes, I do, and so does Larry . . . now," he said softly. *AU*

HOW ABOUT YOU?

Have you ever been in a situation where someone tried to force you to do wrong? Were you strong enough to say no? Remember—when others try to pressure you, Jesus is watching, and he is ready to help you. Ask him to give you the courage to do what is right.

MEMORIZE:

"The eyes of the Lord watch over those who do right; his ears are open to their cries for help." Psalm 34:15

GOD WANTS TO HELP YOU

ON TRACK

Read: Romans 13:1-5

Jayden was working on his electric train set when he heard his father come home. Soon Dad joined him in the basement. "How's the train project coming along?" asked Dad.

"Good!" exclaimed Jayden. "It's almost ready."

"And how was school today?" Dad wanted to know.

Jayden frowned. "Okay, I guess," he said, "but I'm getting tired of all the stupid rules we have. One rule says you have to stay in at recess if you're late more than three times. They just don't want kids to have any fun."

"I take it that you were late?" asked Dad.

"Only a couple minutes!" said Jayden. "I don't see why it matters if I was a little late. At least I was there!" He reached over to hook a section of track in place.

"Hmmm," murmured Dad. "Well, Jayden, let's see how your train runs." He reached over, pressed the start lever, and the train began moving.

"Dad!" exclaimed Jayden. "What are you doing? I don't have all the tracks down yet. It's gonna wreck!" As he spoke, the train rounded the turn and rolled off the track, falling on its side. "I told you," said Jayden.

"So the train needs the tracks. Would you agree that they're helpful and allow the train to run smoothly?" asked Dad.

Jayden nodded. "Sure," he agreed.

"Well, rules are like those tracks," said Dad. "When you follow the rules, they allow your life to run smoothly and even allow you to have fun. When you choose to disobey rules, you get off track, and everything seems a mess. God wants us to follow the rules of those he puts in charge of us—like parents and teachers."

"I get the point," admitted Jayden. "Tracks are good for trains, and rules are good for kids."

"Right," said Dad, "and for grown-ups, too." *MRC*

HOW ABOUT YOU?

Do you get tired of rules? Do you wish you had no rules? Rules are made to help you enjoy life, not to keep you from having fun. Be careful to obey your parents and teachers—and most of all, God.

MEMORIZE:

"Everyone must submit himself to the governing authorities."
Romans 13:1, NIV

OBEY RULES

THE GREATEST ENGINEER

Read: Isaiah 40:25-29

"Grandpa's going to like that birdhouse you're making for him, Ross," said Dad. "It looks great—but not quite like the one in your woodworking manual."

"I know," said Ross. "I left the perch off and made the hole smaller. This way, starlings won't move in before the songbirds get a chance."

"Reminds me of the model plane you made last summer," said Dad. "You know—the one that flew twice as far after you changed the design of the wings."

Ross grinned. "I like to make things work better. Maybe I'll be an engineer when I grow up."

"I thought you didn't like long trips," said Ross's little brother, David. "Wouldn't you get bored riding on a train all the time?"

Ross laughed. "I don't mean the kind of engineer who drives trains. I mean the kind of engineer who designs things," he explained. "Take bridges and dams, for example. Engineers carefully figure out how to build them so they'll be strong and safe and work the way they should. Engineers draw up the plans for skyscrapers and roads and . . . and all kinds of things."

"Wow! I bet you'll be the best engineer of all!" said David.

Ross grinned. "Thanks!" he said.

"Actually, the best engineer of all didn't just make buildings and machines," said Dad. "He designed the whole universe—the forests and the canyons and the mountains; all the plants and animals; the sun and the moon and the stars. Even us."

"I know who that is," piped up David. "It's God!"

"Right," said Dad. "I think he knew how much we would enjoy watching the birds and animals, climbing the mountain trails, and seeing so many stars at night. God made all that."

Ross nodded. "That's an engineering job no one could ever match," he said. *KES*

HOW ABOUT YOU?

Do big buildings, fast computers, or robots impress you? People can make amazing things, but only God could "engineer" the whole world and all that's in it. Enjoy and appreciate all the wonderful things in nature God has made.

GOD "ENGINEERED" THE WHOLE WORLD

MEMORIZE:

"In the beginning God created the heavens and the earth." Genesis 1:1

THE PRAYER CLOSET

Read: Matthew 6:5-8

Tony's father stopped at his son's bedroom to tell him goodnight, but no one was in the room! *Where's Tony, I wonder*, thought Dad. He turned to leave, but then a voice, which seemed to be praying, came from the clothes closet. The door was shut, and Dad was puzzled.

A few moment later, Tony came out of his closet. "I didn't mean to interrupt you, Tony," said Dad, "but I must admit I'm curious. Why did you pick a stuffy closet for a place to pray?"

"Well, I used to pray beside my bed," explained Tony, "but I just learned a verse for Bible club that says to go into your closet and shut the door when you pray, so tonight I prayed in the closet."

Dad smiled and nodded. "I think the closet in that verse means something a little different from your clothes closet," he said. "In fact, most Bible scholars agree that the word *closet* in your Bible could also be translated *room.*"

"Really?" asked Tony. "Oh, good! Then I can just pray beside my bed again, can't I?"

Dad nodded. "I'd say so," he replied. "The main thing Jesus is teaching in that verse is that we should not pray to show off before others. That's why it's good to get away by ourselves—perhaps in a separate room—and shut the door." Dad paused. "Remember, too, that you can pray privately anytime, anywhere, by shutting out other thoughts and praying in your mind."

Tony smiled. "It's like making a prayer closet out of my mind then," he said. "That's good, because I can't always run home when I need to pray!"

"Right," said Dad. "It's good to have a special time and place for prayer, but you can also pray at school, at church, when you're playing—anywhere at all." *HCT*

HOW ABOUT YOU?

Do you have a quiet time alone with God each day? He wants you to talk to him wherever you are, but also in quietness alone. Close your door, shut out the world, and think about God as you pray.

HAVE A QUIET TIME OF PRAYER DAILY

MEMORIZE:

"But when you pray, go away by yourself, shut the door behind you, and pray to your Father secretly."

Matthew 6:6

THE REAL JESUS

Read: Luke 2:15-20

Six-year-old Anton loved Christmas. He looked forward to homemade cookies and special breads. He also enjoyed helping decorate. And he especially liked to put the ceramic nativity set under the tree. Every year, as he carefully put the figures in place, his mother would tell him about the birth of Jesus. Sometimes when he went out to play with his friends, Anton would tell them the story, too.

"We've got Jesus at our house," Anton told Timothy one day. "He's there right now." Timothy didn't believe it. "He is!" Anton insisted. "You can come and see him." Together the boys marched into Anton's house. "See!" Anton pointed. "There he is, with Mary and Joseph and the shepherds and everything."

"That's not the real Jesus," scoffed Timothy. "The real Jesus is in heaven. He isn't a doll."

By this time Anton's mother had come into the room. "Timothy is right," she said. "Jesus, God's Son, is not a ceramic figure or a picture on the wall. He's a real person—the Savior of the world."

The boys listened as Anton's mother began once again to tell the story of the birth of Jesus. She explained that he came to earth to die for sinners. Then she looked at the two boys beside her. "Did Jesus die for you?" she asked, looking first at one and then the other. Slowly the boys nodded. Anton's mother nodded, too. "I'm glad you understand that," she said. "When we ask Jesus to forgive our sins, he does! Then the real Jesus lives not only in heaven, but also in your heart." She pointed to the figure under the tree. "This one is just a reminder of our real Savior." *RIJ*

HOW ABOUT YOU?

Do you know the real Jesus? Pictures and figurines are only reminders of our wonderful Savior. They are not real, so they cannot hear and answer prayer. Jesus is a real person. If you haven't already asked him to forgive your sins and save you, won't you do it today?

MEMORIZE:

"Christ Jesus came into the world to save sinners—and I was the worst of them all." 1 Timothy 1:15

IF I'D ONLY KNOWN

Read: Matthew 16:24-27

"That was some earthquake they had in Italy!" exclaimed Jake on the way home from church. "I wish I had a thousand dollars! I'd put it in the special offering for our missionaries next week. Then they could help those kids who were orphaned."

Dad smiled. "Well, just because you can't give a thousand dollars, don't let it keep you from giving what you can," he said.

"But I don't have much money right now," said Jake, "I'm saving to buy a snowboard." He paused. "If I gave to all the needy people in the world, I'd never have any money!"

"That's true," agreed Dad, "but I think this is a time when we should look at special needs compared to our own needs. Let's all pray about what we should give next week—you, too, Jake."

After church the next Sunday, Dad asked, "Jake, would you mind telling us how much you put in the missionary offering?" asked Dad. "We have a special reason for asking."

"I just gave a dollar," said Jake. "I know that's not much, but I still don't have enough for my snowboard." Dad pulled two dollar bills out of his pocket and handed them to Jake. "Wow! Thanks!" said Jake.

"God promises joy and rewards to those who give, and your mother and I decided we'd reward you, too," explained Dad. "We decided to give you twice the amount you gave in the offering."

"Oh, no!" Jake groaned. "If I'd only known, I'd have given more!"

"Jake, the Bible tells us that Christians will be rewarded according to what they have done for Christ," said Dad. "We can't begin to imagine the wonderful rewards God has prepared, but I'm afraid that in heaven some day, many people may say, 'If I had only known. . . .' " *HCT*

HOW ABOUT YOU?

Are you generous in giving to God? Do you give freely of your time, your money, and your service? Someday God will reward you for all you do for him. Be generous so that you won't be ashamed when Christ comes.

GIVING AND HELPING BRINGS REWARDS

MEMORIZE:

"See, I am coming soon, and my reward is with me, to repay all according to their deeds."

Revelation 22:12

THE BAR OF JUDGMENT

Read: Revelation 20:11-15

Brad trembled as he stood in court before a judge. He had been in trouble before—once for shoplifting and once for destroying public property. Because this was his third offense, he was afraid he would be placed in a correctional school for delinquent boys. He glanced at Mr. Gray, a social worker who was about to speak on his behalf.

"Judge," began Mr. Gray, "Brad's just 13—"

"Just 13," the judge interrupted, "and already he has a very bad record."

"That's true, but would you give me a chance to work with him?" asked Mr. Gray.

The judge frowned. "You've done fine work with some other boys," he admitted. He turned to Brad. "Are you willing to cooperate with Mr. Gray if I place you in his custody?" he asked.

Brad nodded. "Yes, Sir!"

After a long pause the judge spoke. "I've decided to grant your request," he said, "but I want you to know, young man, that the very first time you get out of line, you will be put in a correctional school."

Brad was very relieved as he left the courtroom with Mr. Gray. "I sure do thank you," he told Mr. Gray, "and I'll really try hard!"

Mr. Gray smiled. "Think about this, Brad," he said. "You were guilty and headed for punishment when I spoke for you and saved you from it. But do you realize you are headed for an eternal punishment that is far worse than any correctional school? One day you're going to stand before God to be judged. Who's going to help you then?"

"Uh . . . nobody, I guess," said Brad.

"There is only one Person who can save you from the eternal punishment for your sins. You need to turn to Jesus and receive his forgiveness. Then God, the Judge, will declare you to be 'not guilty.' " *HCT*

HOW ABOUT YOU?

Have you ever told a lie? Fought? Cheated? God says all have sinned. You are headed for punishment unless someone saves you, and the only One who can do that is Jesus Christ. Admit your guilt. Ask him to save you today.

MEMORIZE:

"For there is only one God and one Mediator who can reconcile God and people. He is the man Christ Jesus." 1 Timothy 2:5

ASK JESUS TO SAVE YOU

THE PRESCRIPTION

Read: John 14:27-31

"Why does God allow war?" Brent asked after hearing a news report on TV.

"That's a hard question," said Dad. "It's hard to . . ." He paused as the door opened and Mom came in carrying Trina. Dad took the whimpering little girl and laid her on the couch. "What did the doctor say?"

"She has strep throat," said Mom. "Dr. Tom gave her a shot and this prescription." She handed Dad a slip of paper. "Would you get this filled while I fix dinner?"

Brent reached for his sweater. "I'll go with you," he said.

When they returned, Dad smiled at Trina. "I'll give her a dose of this medicine," Dad told Mom.

"I don't want it!" Trina wailed. "My throat hurts!"

"This will make your throat feel better," Dad said gently. He held a spoonful of medicine toward her.

Trina hid her face. "It'll make my throat hurt worser."

"It will make it feel better," Dad again said patiently.

"I can't swallow," Trina wailed.

"If you can scream and cry like that, you can swallow," said Dad firmly. "Now take this."

The little girl recognized the "do-what-I-say-or-else" tone. She took the medicine and soon was sleeping soundly.

Later that evening, Brent returned to his question. "Why does God allow war?"

"I think I have an answer now," said Dad. "Think of war as a sickness caused by sin. When Jesus died, he gave this world the prescription for sin. The doctor's prescription wouldn't have done Trina any good if she hadn't taken it, and the prescription God offers doesn't help people when they don't take it by trusting in Jesus. I made Trina take her medicine, but the Lord Jesus does not force anyone to accept his prescription."

Brent nodded. "I get it," he said. "Because people refuse to follow Jesus' prescription, there is war." *BJW*

HOW ABOUT YOU?

Have you wondered why there is war in this world? You cannot stop war in the world, but you can follow Jesus' prescription and have peace in your heart. If everyone had the peace of God in his or her heart, there would be no war. Peace starts with you.

PEACE COMES FROM GOD

WHO SAID SO?

Read: John 14:13-14

"And I want a horse and saddle and cowboy boots. In Jesus' name. Amen," prayed Mitchell. "I hope Jesus answers my prayer tomorrow."

Dad smiled. "Sorry, Mitchell, but I hope he doesn't," he said. "We don't have a place to keep a horse."

"I could ask for a stable, too," said Mitchell.

"Sometimes God answers prayers by saying *wait* or *no*," Dad reminded him.

All the next day, Mitchell kept hoping to see a horse and stable. He was quite discouraged by dinnertime, when Mom asked him to tell his brother Jeff to come in. Mitchell found Jeff playing basketball with his friend Nate. "Jeff, come in now," called Mitchell.

"Who said so?" Jeff wanted to know.

"I did," said Mitchell. "Didn't you hear me?" Jeff tossed the ball through the hoop and ignored his little brother. Mitchell raised his voice, "Jeff, Mama said for you to come in right now!"

Jeff tossed the ball to his friend. "See you later, Nate," he said. "I gotta go."

At dinner, Mitchell said sadly, "I didn't think it would take Jesus this long to answer my prayer. I prayed in Jesus' name."

Mom passed the potatoes. "'In Jesus' name' isn't a magic phrase, Mitch," she said.

Dad nodded. "When your mother told you to call Jeff in, Jeff obeyed because you took the message 'in Mom's name.' When you ask for something in Jesus' name, it means you're asking for what he wants to be done. You can't ask for everything *you* want and get it."

"Why doesn't he want me to have a horse?" Mitchell asked.

"Maybe he does—we'll have to wait and see," said Dad. "Maybe he knows that only part of what you asked for would be good for you right now—like new cowboy boots for your birthday." *BJW*

HOW ABOUT YOU?
Jesus has given his children authority to pray in his name, but that doesn't mean just repeating the phrase. It's a privilege you must use carefully.

MEMORIZE:
"Yes, ask anything in my name, and I will do it!" John 14:14

PRAY IN JESUS' NAME

TWO KINDS OF TREASURE

Read: Luke 12:16-21

"There he goes," said Brent as he watched the plane take off. Mr. Bell, a friend of the family and a missionary to Africa, had been visiting Brent's family for the past week. "He sure works hard, doesn't he?" added Brent.

Dad nodded. "Yes, he does," agreed Dad, "but as he says, it's worth it all because many people are being won for Jesus."

As Brent and his family left the airport and headed back toward town, they came to a large, impressive home where many cars had pulled off the road and lots of people were milling around. "There's an estate auction going on here," said Mom. "I remember reading about it in the paper. A Mrs. White lived here—a very wealthy old lady who really clung to her possessions. She was always afraid people would steal them from her. She died recently, and they're selling every-thing and dividing the estate."

The family stopped to look around, and they saw some lovely and very expensive things. When they were once again on their way, Dad spoke thoughtfully. "We've seen quite a contrast today. Mrs. White was known for her earthly possessions. Mr. Bell is know for his service for Jesus. Two different lives—two different kinds of treasure."

"Was Mrs. White a Christian?" wondered Brent.

"Well, not as far as we know," replied Mom, "but we can't judge her heart, of course."

"She seemed interested only in hanging on to all her money and possessions," added Dad, "but all the riches and lovely things she had are of no use to her now. It's sad to see people more concerned about their earthly welfare than about their eternal destiny." *JLH*

HOW ABOUT YOU?

Is making money and having lots of "stuff" what you want out of life? That's of no eternal value. Begin to prepare for eternity now by accepting Jesus as your Savior.

MONEY AND
POSSESSIONS
DON'T LAST

MEMORIZE:
"How do you benefit if you gain the whole world but lose your own soul in the process?" Mark 8:36

December

24

Kenny and David knew they wouldn't get everything they wanted for Christmas, but they also knew their parents were generous. Many items would appear under the Christmas tree. But as Kenny looked forward to receiving lots of things, he began to worry about the boy who lived next door. "Matt will be lucky if he gets anything," he told David one day. "Don't you think we should do something for him this Christmas? His dad's been out of work for over six months."

"Well, that's their problem," David reasoned. "We can't help it. We can't give his dad a job!"

Kenny just couldn't give up that easily. "But he's our friend!" Kenny protested. "I still think we should do something for Matt."

As Christmas came closer, and the pile of presents under the tree grew, Kenny felt more concern for Matt. Finally he went to his parents and asked if he could give some of his presents to Matt. "Then he'll have some things to open Christmas morning, too," Kenny explained.

Mom and Dad were surprised—but pleased—at Kenny's request. Still, they were cautious. "Kenny, you know you won't get as much as David if you do this," Mom reminded him. "Will you feel bad when David has more presents to open than you do?"

"I don't know," replied Kenny honestly. "I might, but it's something I think Jesus wants me to do." So, with Mom's guidance, Kenny picked out a few presents and delivered them to the house next door.

On Christmas Eve, Kenny's best present came when Matt stopped in. He was wearing the new football jacket that could have been Kenny's. It had hurt Kenny a little to see David get more presents than he did, but now the smile on Matt's face made it worth it all. Deep inside Kenny felt good. *REP*

HOW ABOUT YOU?

Have you been more interested in getting gifts this Christmas than giving them? Have you ever noticed that the more you get, the more you want? Receiving gifts can never give as much true joy as giving gifts. Look for someone with whom you can share.

MEMORIZE:

"It is more blessed to give than to receive." Acts 20:35

SHARE WITH OTHERS

HOME AT LAST

25

Read: 2 Corinthians 4:6-9, 14; 5:1

"It's snowing!" exclaimed Terrence. He and his parents were traveling to spend Christmas Day with his grandparents. "I hope Grandpa takes us on a sleigh ride."

They arrived at their destination a few hours later. The day was bursting with good things, just like the Christmas stockings hanging on the fireplace mantle. There was delicious food, plenty of company, wonderful presents, a special time of devotions—and the sleigh ride Terrence had hoped for. They all had a great time, and at the end of the day, they hated to leave.

Several inches of snow blanketed the highway, and Dad wished that they had started home sooner. The snow swirled around, making visibility poor. Traffic crawled, and one time the car almost slid into the ditch before Dad got it under control. Tension mounted, and everyone was praying that they would get home safely.

"Let's sing to keep our minds on the Lord instead of the weather," Mom suggested. As they sang, they were surprised to find how much it helped. It was early the next morning before Dad wearily pulled into the driveway.

"Home at last!" yelled Terrence. "I never thought home would look so good."

"It sure is good to be here," agreed Dad.

Mom smiled. "As we traveled, we sang some songs about heaven," she said, "and I think this is how we'll feel when we get to heaven. There are many problems and stresses here on earth, but they will be behind us when we get to heaven. We'll never feel helpless or afraid again."

"Right," agreed Dad. "We'll really be 'home at last.' How good that will be!" *JLH*

HOW ABOUT YOU?

Do you ever have bad times that seem unending? Don't get discouraged by problems on earth. If you've accepted Jesus as your Savior, learn to keep your mind on him and your future in heaven instead of on the problems you're facing. Trust him, and take courage and look forward to the day you'll go "home" to heaven.

LOOK FORWARD TO BEING IN HEAVEN

MEMORIZE:

"For our present troubles are quite small and won't last very long. Yet they produce for us an immeasurably great glory that will last forever!"
2 Corinthians 4:17

Abe stared out the window, watching the icicles drip in the afternoon sun. "Christmas doesn't seem very real after the decorations and presents are gone, does it, Grandpa?" he said.

"Not real?" asked Grandpa, turning from the football game he'd been watching. He rubbed his head for a moment, then motioned toward the TV screen. "Is that football game real?" he asked. Puzzled, Abe nodded. "Is it as real for you as it is for the people in the stands?" asked Grandpa.

"Well . . . probably not quite," said Abe.

"Is it as real for you as it is for that player who just got hurt?" Grandpa asked next.

"Someone got hurt?" asked Abe in surprise. "I wasn't paying attention." He looked at the TV screen and saw that several people were crowded around a player lying on the grass. "Whew! I guess the game's real to him!"

"When you're involved, you get knocked around and feel some pain, but you also win victories—and you know the game is real," said Grandpa. He looked at Abe. "For Christmas to be real to you, you need to be involved. That goes for the Bible, too. Believing the Bible is true is like watching the game from home. Can you think of an event that might compare with watching a game with others and cheering for the team?"

"Ah . . . maybe going to church," said Abe. "I always go to church."

"Good," said Grandpa. "You're in the stands then." He leaned closer. "But do you actually practice the plays and run with the ball—not just on Sunday or on Christmas, but every day?"

"Well . . . " Abe hesitated.

Grandpa nodded. "Be a player, Abe," he said. "Be involved. Learn about God. Serve him. That's when the Bible and Christian living become real to you." *MMT*

HOW ABOUT YOU?

Do you believe the Bible is true? Good! Do you attend church? Great! Do you get involved in church activities? Do you talk about Jesus, pray, and obey and serve him? God's truth becomes real to you as you become involved in it.

MEMORIZE:

"Each one should use whatever gift he has received to serve others."
1 Peter 4:10, NIV

FAITHFUL IN THE LEAST

Read: Luke 16:10-13

"Where have you been, Son?" asked Jim's mother as he stomped into the room. "Dinner is ready, and several of your newspaper customers have called to ask why their papers weren't delivered on time."

"Aw, Mom," protested Jim, "the papers weren't delivered all that late. This lousy paper route is ruining my whole Christmas vacation. Can't I quit?"

Dad pulled out a chair and sat down. "Well . . . you made a commitment, didn't you?" he asked.

"Well . . . I said I'd keep my route till the new year," admitted Jim. "But that's only a week away. What would it hurt if I quit just a week early?"

"It would hurt the company because they don't have anyone to take your place until next week," answered Dad. "It would also hurt the customers because they would be missing their papers."

"But I just don't feel like doing it anymore," Jim grumbled.

"We all have times when we need to do things we don't feel like doing," Dad told him. "I daresay Mom doesn't always feel like cooking dinner or making lunches. And I don't always feel like going to work. But your commitment to the newspaper is much like my contract to work. It's important to be faithful." Dad reached for his Bible, turned the pages quickly, and continued, "Luke 16:10 says, 'Unless you are faithful in small matters, you won't be faithful in large ones.' If you aren't faithful in the small things you have to do, such as your newspaper route, you'll not be faithful in the big things of life later on."

Jim sighed, but nodded. "Okay, Dad." *AU*

HOW ABOUT YOU?

What is your "job" right now? Is it a paper route? Schoolwork? Helping Mom and Dad? Whatever it is, do it faithfully. God rewards faithfulness.

MEMORIZE:

"Now, a person who is put in charge as a manager must be faithful."
1 Corinthians 4:2

BE FAITHFUL

FOCUS TROUBLE

Read: James 4:7-8

Nathan loved football! He loved to play it, he loved to read stories about it, and he loved to watch it on television. At church he heard very little of the sermon because he was thinking football.

Recently Nathan's eyes had been bothering him, so Mom made an appointment with Dr. Jackson, an optometrist. Dr. Jackson chatted with Nathan as he slipped different lenses in front of his eyes. "Are you still crazy about football, Nathan?" he asked.

"Sure am, Doc," Nathan replied. "I love football more than anything."

"More than you love God?" asked Dr. Jackson.

"Naw," murmured Nathan, but he looked down at the floor because he knew he wasn't telling the truth.

"Hey, let's do an experiment," said the doctor. "I want you to focus your eyes intently on the big E on my chart while you read my diploma to me."

Nathan looked around. "Doc, I can't!" he said. "Your diploma is hanging on the back wall. You can't focus your eyes on two things at the same time. Even I know that!"

Dr. Jackson chuckled. "You're right, Nathan," he said. "It is impossible to focus your eyes on two things at once. It's also impossible for a person to please God if he tries to focus his heart on two things at the same time. God tells us to focus our hearts and minds on him, and not to be double-minded."

Nathan looked confused for a minute. Then he realized what Dr. Jackson meant. "I think I get the point, Doc," Nathan replied. "You're saying that I can love football as long as it does not interfere with my love for God—right?"

"Right," replied Dr. Jackson. "I'll be praying that God will help you keep your mind off football when it should be on him. Okay?" *REP*

HOW ABOUT YOU?

Are you double-minded? In other words, is it hard for you to concentrate on God because your mind wanders to something else? Obey the five commands given in today's Scripture reading, and God will help you to be single-minded for him.

MEMORIZE:

"A double minded man is unstable in all his ways." James 1:8, KJV

FOCUS ON GOD

FOR YOUR OWN GOOD (PART 1)

Read: Psalm 19:8-11

Billy just wouldn't listen to instructions. Several times he was warned about the danger of ignoring advice, but he went ahead anyway and did as he pleased.

At school, Billy was told that he had better study and do his homework, but he didn't listen. He goofed off and did poor work. "I'm sorry, Billy," his teacher said, "but you must stay in at recess and after school until all your homework is done correctly. I'm doing this for your own good. If you don't learn your lesson now, it will be much harder later on."

At home, Billy's parents warned him to stay off the lake because the ice was thawing. But one day Billy took a shortcut across the lake anyway. He fell in and got soaked. "Billy, you could have drowned," his mother said. "I'm glad you are okay, but because you disobeyed you are grounded for the next two weeks."

A few weeks later, Billy was riding his bike home from the playground. The red lights were flashing at the railroad crossing, but Billy figured he had plenty of time. As he raced across the track, his wheel hit the railroad tie and bent. Billy flew off the bike, and the next thing he knew, he was in the hospital with a broken leg.

"Thank God, you're alive, Billy. You could have been killed!" exclaimed Mom. "Didn't you see the train coming?"

"Yes, but I thought I could beat it," moaned Billy. "I should have stopped."

"The flashing red light was there for your own good. It was a warning to stop. Danger was ahead," Mom told him. "When we disobey warnings, we invite trouble into our lives." *JLH*

HOW ABOUT YOU?

Do you obey God's warnings? He wants to keep you from the dangers of sin, so the Bible gives warnings about disobeying, lying, cheating, hating, stealing, and following evil companions. God's warnings are for our own good.

HEED GOD'S
WARNINGS

FOR YOUR OWN GOOD (PART 2)

Read: Colossians 3:5-10

Billy was in the hospital for quite some time with a broken leg. He had to lie flat on his back, his leg up in the air with traction weights pulling on it. That was hard. Relatives and friends visited him, brought gifts, and played table games. Still, Billy was bored. "Please, Mom," he begged, "can't I get my leg out of this traction and go home?"

"It won't be much longer," encouraged Mom. "The traction is hard, but it's for your good. If the bone doesn't heal properly, it might have to be reset. Just be patient."

Finally, Billy was able to go home—but that didn't turn out to be like he expected, either. It wasn't easy getting a pair of jeans over a cast. Then he had to learn how to walk on crutches.

As Billy was watching his friends play baseball one day, he felt even more sorry for himself. "This cast is too heavy," he complained. "It's in my way. I hate having a broken leg. I don't know why God made it happen."

"God didn't make it happen, but he did allow it," his mother replied.

"But why?" Billy asked. "There's nothing good about it. I can't have any fun."

Mom searched for words. "Maybe God allowed it to get your attention—to let you know that if you kept ignoring warnings, you'd get into worse trouble. What do you think?"

"Well . . . maybe," Billy admitted.

"Your cast reminds me of sin in a Christian's life," continued Mom. "Wrongdoing weighs us down and keeps us from enjoying good things God planned for our lives."

"Wrongdoing?" asked Billy. "Like not listening to warnings?" he said slowly. *JLH*

HOW ABOUT YOU?

Do you let sin keep you from being all God wants you to be? Have you "put off" all the things listed in today's Scripture reading? Don't let them weigh you down. Instead, let God have complete control of your life.

MEMORIZE:

"Let us strip off every weight that slows us down, especially the sin that so easily hinders our progress."
Hebrews 12:1

TURN FROM SIN

FOLLOW THE SHEPHERD

Read: Psalm 23

"I think I'll be a preacher someday," said Roab.

"Speaking is easy for me, and good preachers are always in demand. I'd probably get a good job, make good money." He grinned at his brother Malin. "I'm entering the speech contest next month. How about you?"

Malin shrugged. "Not me!" he exclaimed. "You have to give a speech of your own, and then as part of the contest, you have to recite the 23rd Psalm. I don't like to memorize—or speak—all that well."

"It's a piece of cake!" Roab exclaimed. "I learned that Psalm in first grade." He recited it then looked to his parents for approval.

"This reminds me of a story I once heard," said Dad. "A well-known actor and an old minister were the guests at a banquet. After dinner, the actor was asked to recite the 23rd Psalm. He did, and when he was finished, all the people applauded. Then someone insisted that the old minister quote the Psalm, too. In a quiet voice that quavered once in a while with emotion, the minister quoted the Psalm. When he sat down, no one stirred, and no one clapped, but many people wiped tears from their eyes. The actor stood to his feet again, and with a catch in his beautiful, cultivated voice, he said, 'I know the Psalm, but this man knows the Shepherd.' "

After a short silence, Mom spoke up. "You talk about being a minister," she said, "but there's more to being a minister than public speaking. No matter how many contests you win, God will not call you to preach unless you know him personally."

Dad nodded. "Unless you know him yourself, how can you help others know him?" he asked. "You need to know the Shepherd and then follow him into whatever field he calls you." *HCT*

HOW ABOUT YOU?

As you read the 23rd Psalm today, did the words really mean something to you? Do you know the Shepherd? Jesus says he is the "Good Shepherd." Accept him as your shepherd—invite him to come into your life, and then allow him to lead you.

FOLLOW JESUS

MEMORIZE:
"The Lord is my shepherd."
Psalm 23:1

Index of Topics

God's knowledge
March 7, August 23

God's love
January 23, February 9, March 31,
July 29, October 5

God's names
March 4

God's power
January 5

God's presence
March 10

God's care and protection
April 16, June 23, July 4, August 24,
September 5

God's guidance
June 17, October 19

God's justice
January 19

God's love
June 27

God's wisdom
May 6

Good works
May 29, July 13, August 1,
December 1, 3

Gossip
January 22

Greed
May 18

Habits
October 1, November 24

Health
September 16, October 20

Heaven and hell
January 1, June 7, July 15, 28,
December 12, 25

Helping others
February 3, April 10, May 10,
August 5, 19, October 22

Holy Spirit
February 2

Honesty
April 7, May 17, 19, June 16,
September 14, November 6

Honor
January 4

Hospitality
October 26

Hymns
March 18

Jealousy
June 22

Jesus
January 17, 23, March 1, April 9,
17, 23, August 6, November 19,
December 18

Jesus' return
February 11, May 29, July 1,
November 17

Index of Scripture Readings

Index of Memory Verses

Proverbs 16:24 *September 26*
Proverbs 17:20 *November 6*
Proverbs 18:8 *January 22*
Proverbs 18:9 *September 12*
Proverbs 19:11 *September 29*
Proverbs 19:17 *February 3*
Proverbs 20:7 *January 14*
Proverbs 20:11 *July 19*
Proverbs 21:31 *October 29*
Proverbs 22:1 *January 10*
Proverbs 22:6 *February 17*
Proverbs 22:28 *February 18*
Proverbs 24:10 *October 17*
Proverbs 25:25 *May 9*
Proverbs 25:28 *August 16*
Proverbs 27:1 *May 14*
Proverbs 27:17 *November 13*
Proverbs 28:13 *May 27, September 19*
Ecclesiastes 4:9 *October 28*
Ecclesiastes 9:10 *April 29*
Isaiah 29:15 *March 7*
Isaiah 43:7 *January 31*
Isaiah 43:12 *April 12*
Isaiah 55:6 *June 14*
Isaiah 55:11 *April 13, May 20*
Isaiah 64:6 *August 1*
Jeremiah 1:7 *April 18*
Jeremiah 10:6 *March 4*
Jeremiah 13:23 *October 23*
Jeremiah 17:10 *February 28*
Jeremiah 31:34 *January 24*
Daniel 3:17-18 *October 3*
Matthew 4:19 *March 8*
Matthew 5:13 *July 17, August 20*
Matthew 5:16 *June 27, July 8*
Matthew 5:44 *July 25*
Matthew 6:6 *July 13, December 17*
Matthew 6:20 *August 10*
Matthew 6:21 *December 4*
Matthew 6:31 *April 19*
Matthew 6:33 *September 4, October 10*
Matthew 7:12 *October 22, November 20*

Matthew 7:14 *August 15*
Matthew 7:20 *September 14*
Matthew 7:24 *March 25*
Matthew 9:13 *October 14*
Matthew 10:8 *September 11,*
  December 9
Matthew 12:34 *March 28*
Matthew 13:23 *October 2*
Matthew 16:27 *June 19*
Matthew 24:44 *May 29, July 1*
Matthew 25:46 *June 7*
Matthew 28:6 *April 20*
Mark 8:36 *December 23*
Mark 9:24 *November 4*
Mark 9:50 *August 19*
Luke 2:52 *October 20*
Luke 9:24 *March 17*
Luke 10:27 *August 5*
Luke 12:15 *May 18*
Luke 12:40 *November 17*
Luke 15:10 *April 5, May 11*
Luke 15:18 *March 13*
Luke 16:10 *February 4, May 8*
Luke 16:11 *May 5*
Luke 18:13 *October 4*
Luke 19:8 *August 31*
Luke 19:10 *July 9*
John 1:12 *January 16*
John 3:15 *August 8*
John 6:35 *August 6*
John 6:37 *August 14*
John 10:9 *August 4*
John 10:11 *January 23, April 11*
John 11:25 *April 17*
John 13:35 *June 3*
John 14:2 *July 15*
John 14:3 *December 12*
John 14:14 *December 22*
John 14:27 *December 21*
John 15:5 *January 5*
John 15:13 *January 17*
John 16:13 *February 2*

Acts 4:12 *April 6, November 23*
Acts 4:20 *June 6*
Acts 16:31 *May 1, July 30*
Acts 20:35 *December 24*
Romans 1:16 *November 30*
Romans 5:8 *March 31*
Romans 6:12 *August 28*
Romans 8:28 *January 3, July 22*
Romans 8:38-39 *February 9*
Romans 10:12 *December 11*
Romans 10:14 *February 13, June 15*
Romans 12:3 *July 11*
Romans 12:5 *October 8, November 18*
Romans 12:6 *February 22*
Romans 12:13 *October 26*
Romans 12:15 *November 27*
Romans 12:20 *January 29*
Romans 13:1 *December 15*
Romans 14:7 *May 19*
Romans 15:4 *July 24*
1 Corinthians 3:7 *March 23*
1 Corinthians 3:9 *June 10,*
  November 10
1 Corinthians 3:11 *May 30*
1 Corinthians 3:13 *November 1*
1 Corinthians 4:2 *December 27*
1 Corinthians 4:7 *December 10*
1 Corinthians 4:10 *April 1*
1 Corinthians 4:14 *December 29*
1 Corinthians 9:22 *October 15*
1 Corinthians 10:12 *January 7*
1 Corinthians 10:13 *May 13, June 5*
1 Corinthians 10:31 *July 3, September 2*
1 Corinthians 11:26 *May 28*
1 Corinthians 12:22 *September 15*
1 Corinthians 13:12 *January 1*
1 Corinthians 15:57 *January 12*
1 Corinthians 15:58 *June 11,*
  September 25
1 Corinthians 16:13 *September 23*
2 Corinthians 2:15 *January 9*
2 Corinthians 3:3 *October 13*

2 Corinthians 4:16 *October 21*
2 Corinthians 4:17 *December 25*
2 Corinthians 5:7 *October 30*
2 Corinthians 5:8 *May 31*
2 Corinthians 5:17 *July 2,*
  December 13
2 Corinthians 6:2 *November 9*
2 Corinthians 6:16 *March 20*
2 Corinthians 8:21 *September 10*
2 Corinthians 9:7 *April 24*
2 Corinthians 9:8 *July 23*
2 Corinthians 10:5 *November 29*
2 Corinthians 10:12 *April 28*
Galatians 5:1 *November 24*
Galatians 5:13 *August 17*
Galatians 5:15 *June 30*
Galatians 5:22-23 *September 3*
Galatians 6:7 *February 23, May 3*
Ephesians 2:8-9 *April 22*
Ephesians 2:13 *May 16*
Ephesians 4:11-12 *February 7*
Ephesians 4:26 *February 10, June 9*
Ephesians 4:32 *March 3, April 3*
Ephesians 5:11 *November 8*
Ephesians 5:20 *May 15*
Ephesians 6:7 *November 12*
Ephesians 6:11 *August 2*
Philippians 1:3-4 *March 2*
Philippians 2:13 *January 26*
Philippians 2:14 *November 25*
Philippians 3:9 *December 7*
Philippians 3:10 *March 27*
Philippians 3:14 *February 5, May 23*
Philippians 4:6 *April 14*
Philippians 4:7 *September 17*
Philippians 4:13 *July 20*
Colossians 2:3 *June 26*
Colossians 3:2 *September 18*
Colossians 3:13 *March 12,*
  November 22
Colossians 3:17 *September 1,*
  November 7

Colossians 3:20 *August 13,*
November 28
Colossians 3:23 *June 1, June 25*
1 Thessalonians 4:11 *July 7*
1 Thessalonians 4:13 *July 28*
1 Thessalonians 5:17 *October 9*
1 Thessalonians 5:17-18 *February 26*
1 Thessalonians 5:22 *June 29*
2 Thessalonians 3:3 *April 16*
2 Thessalonians 3:10 *April 10,*
April 30
1 Timothy 1:15 *December 18*
1 Timothy 2:1-2 *April 8, November 2*
1 Timothy 2:5 *December 20*
1 Timothy 4:12 *March 16*
1 Timothy 4:14 *October 27*
1 Timothy 5:4 *January 4*
1 Timothy 6:8 *June 21*
1 Timothy 6:11 *June 13*
1 Timothy 6:18 *January 25*
2 Timothy 1:8 *September 6*
2 Timothy 2:19 *October 24*
2 Timothy 2:24 *February 14, July 18*
2 Timothy 2:26 *October 12*
2 Timothy 3:16 *March 26*
2 Timothy 4:2 *February 19*
2 Timothy 4:5 *September 30*
2 Timothy 4:7 *February 11, March 14*
Titus 2:12 *January 11, November 5*
Titus 3:5 *December 1*
Philemon 1:6 *October 25*
Hebrews 1:1-2 *January 21*
Hebrews 2:3 *October 7*
Hebrews 2:17 *March 1*
Hebrews 3:13 *August 27*
Hebrews 3:15 *May 22*
Hebrews 4:12 *January 13, August 26*
Hebrews 6:12 *February 25*
Hebrews 9:27 *September 7*

Hebrews 10:25 *January 20, May 7*
Hebrews 11:3 *June 12*
Hebrews 12:1 *July 26, December 30*
Hebrews 12:2 *March 21*
Hebrews 12:2 *April 23*
Hebrews 12:11 *August 25*
Hebrews 13:5 *January 6, March 10,*
December 6
Hebrews 13:17 *September 8*
James 1:3 *October 16, December 5*
James 1:8 *December 28*
James 1:22 *January 18*
James 2:10 *September 28*
James 2:18 *September 21*
James 4:7 *May 24, August 9*
James 5:16 *February 6, May 12*
1 Peter 1:7 *July 4*
1 Peter 1:13 *May 2*
1 Peter 2:9 *February 12*
1 Peter 2:21 *April 4, September 13*
1 Peter 2:23 *January 30*
1 Peter 3:15 *February 15*
1 Peter 4:8 *April 15*
1 Peter 4:10 *December 26*
1 Peter 5:7 *April 9, October 6*
2 Peter 1:4 *July 6*
2 Peter 3:18 *February 1, July 31*
1 John 1:3 *November 19*
1 John 1:7 *June 4*
1 John 1:9 *April 27, August 3,*
November 15
1 John 4:4 *March 24, October 31*
1 John 4:8 *October 5*
1 John 4:18 *June 18*
1 John 4:19 *April 25*
1 John 4:21 *February 20*
1 John 5:3 *January 27*
Jude 21 *July 29*
Revelation 22:12 *December 19*

Tim Carhardt is drifting through life with one goal—survival. Jamie Maxwell believes she can become—no, *will* become—the first female winner of the cup. But life isn't always as easy as it seems. What happens when dreams and faith hit the wall?

#1 *Blind Spot*
#2 *Over the Wall*
#3 *Overdrive*
#4 *Checkered Flag*

The four-book RPM series spans a year of the chase for the cup. Each story is filled with fast-paced races as well as fast-paced adventure off the track.

All four books available now!

CP0206